THE MAKING OF POETRY

The Making of Poetry

COLERIDGE, THE WORDSWORTHS, AND THEIR YEAR OF MARVELS

ADAM NICOLSON

With Woodcuts and Paintings by Tom Hammick

FARRAR, STRAUS AND GIROUX

NEW YORK

Farrar, Straus and Giroux
120 Broadway, New York 10271

Copyright © 2019 by Adam Nicolson
All rights reserved
Printed in the United States of America
Originally published in 2019 by William Collins,
an imprint of HarperCollins*Publishers*, Great Britain
Published in the United States by Farrar, Straus and Giroux
First American edition, 2020

Library of Congress Control Number: 2019951670
ISBN: 978-0-374-20021-3

www.fsgbooks.com
www.twitter.com/fsgbooks • www.facebook.com/fsgbooks

1 3 5 7 9 10 8 6 4 2

For Tom Hammick

The making of verses, the making of works, occurs in the edges of your life, of your time, in your late nights or early mornings ... And my words, the words for me, seem to have more nervous energy when they are touching territory that I know, that I live with ... I can lay my hand on [a place] and know it. And the words, the words come alive and get a kind of personality when they are involved with it for me. The landscape is image. It's almost an element to work with, as much as it is an object of admiration.

Seamus Heaney, speaking to Patrick Garland on *Poets on Poetry*, BBC 1, October 1973

CONTENTS

THE MAKING OF POETRY

1

Following

The year, or slightly more than a year, from June 1797 until the early autumn of 1798 has a claim to being the most famous moment in the history of English poetry. In the course of it, two young men of genius, living for a while on the edge of the Quantock Hills in Somerset, began to find their way towards a new understanding of the world, of nature and of themselves.

These months have always been portrayed – by Wordsworth and Coleridge and by Wordsworth's sister Dorothy as much as by anyone else – as a time of unbridled delight and wellbeing, of overabundant creativity, with a singularity of conviction and purpose from which extraordinary poetry emerged.

Certainly, what they wrote adds up to an astonishing catalogue: 'This Lime Tree Bower My Prison', 'Kubla Khan', *The Ancient Mariner*, 'Christabel', 'Frost at Midnight', 'The Nightingale', all Wordsworth's strange and troubling poems in *Lyrical Ballads*, 'The Idiot Boy', 'The Thorn', the grandeur and beauty of 'Tintern Abbey', and, in his notebooks, the first suggestions of what would become passages in *The Prelude*.

The grip of this poetry is undeniable, but its origins are not in comfort or delight, or, at least until Wordsworth's walk up the Wye valley in July 1798, any sense of arrival. The psychic motor of the year is something of the opposite: a time of adventure and perplexity, of Wordsworth and Coleridge both ricocheting away

1

from the revolutionary politics of the 1790s in which both had been involved and both to different degrees disappointed. Wordsworth was unheard of, and Coleridge was still under attack in the conservative press. Both were in retreat: from cities; from politics; from gentlemanliness and propriety; from the expected; towards nature; and – in a way that makes this year foundational for modernity – towards the self, its roots, its forms of self-understanding, its fantasies, longings, dreads and ideals. For both, the Quantocks were a refuge-cum-laboratory, one in which every suggestion of an arrival was to be seen merely as a stepping stone.

The path was far from certain. One of Wordsworth's criteria for pleasure in poetry was 'the sense of difficulty overcome', and that is a central theme of this year: their poetry was not a culmination or a summation, but had its life at the beginning of things, at a time of what Seamus Heaney called 'historical crisis and personal dismay', emergent, unsummoned, encountered in the midst of difficulty, arriving as unexpectedly as a figure on a night road, or a vision in mid-ocean, or the wisdom and understanding of a child.

It was not about powerful feelings recollected in tranquillity. Wordsworth's famous and oracular definition would not come to him until more than two years after he had left Somerset. This was different, a poetry of approaches, journeys out and journeys in, leading to the gates of understanding but not yet over the threshold. Even now, 250 years after Wordsworth's birth, it still carries a sense of discovery, drawing its vitality from awkwardness and discomfort, from a lack of definition and from the power that emanates from what is still only half-there.

This book explores the sources of this effusion. 'I wish to keep my Reader in the company of flesh and blood,' Wordsworth would write a couple of years later, and that has been my guiding principle too. The place in which these poets lived, the people they were, the people they were with, the lives they led, the conversations they had: how did all of that shape the words they wrote?

2

The received idea of these poets puts its focus on the immaterial, the floatingly high-minded. But here, in 1797, that is at least partly the opposite of the case. Thought for them, as the young Coleridge had written in excitement to his friend Robert Southey, was 'corporeal'. He would later coin both 'neuropathology' and 'psychosomatic' as terms to describe aspects of this new interpresence of body and mind. The full life was not the enjoyment of a view, nor any kind of elegant gazing at a landscape, let alone sitting reading, but a kind of embodiment, plunging in, a full absorption in the encompassing world, providing the verbal life and 'nervous energy' that came from what Heaney would call 'touching territory that I know'.

Here, then, was the invitation to which this book is an answer. If this was one of the great moments of poetic consciousness, it could best be understood as physical experience. By feeling it on the skin I could hope to know what had happened in the course of it. This was the subject that drew me: poetry-in-life, poetry-in-place, the body in the world as the instrument through which poetry comes into being.

The implication of that idea is that all currents must flow together. The way to approach this moment, its involutions and complexities, was to do, as far as possible, what the poets had done, to be in the Quantocks in all the moods and variations of the year at its different moments, to look for what happened and what emerged from what happened, to see how they were with each other, to feel the ebb and flow of their power relations and their affections. The timings and geography are closely known, often day by day, almost always week by week: what they were discussing, who they were meeting, how they were behaving, who their enemies and friends were, how poetry came from *life-in-place*.

Richard Holmes, the biographer of Shelley and Coleridge, has, unknown to him, long been my guide. When I was a young writer in the early 1980s he sent me a postcard out of the blue, encouraging me to keep going. So I have, and I think of this book as a tributary to the great Holmesian stream. Its method is his: to follow in the footsteps of the great, looking to gather the fragments they left on the path, much as Dorothy Wordsworth was seen by an old man as she was accompanying her brother on a walk in the Lake District, keeping 'close behint him, and she picked up the bits as he let 'em fall, and tak 'em down, and put 'em on paper for him'.

So I went to live in the Quantocks. I started to imagine the poets' lives. I bought the maps, I read what they had been reading, I immersed myself in their notebooks and the facsimiles of their rough drafts, starting to lower myself into the pool of their minds. Slowly I began to see these poets – and Dorothy Wordsworth should be included in that term – not as literary monuments but as living people, young, troubled, ambitious, dreaming of a vision of wholeness, knowing they had greatness in them but confronted again and again by the uncertain and contradictory nature of what they understood of the world, of each other and themselves.

It was a year focused on writing, on the search for forms of language that could, as Wordsworth later wrote of his own poetry, be 'enduring and creative', with 'A power like one of Nature's'. But it was not a sequence of solitudes. Coleridge's profoundly lonely need for others guaranteed that they were not alone. It was a busy, social, talkative time. The two great poets were almost constantly surrounded by friends, acolytes, followers, patrons and relations; Wordsworth's sister, Coleridge's wife Sara, and the children they had with them. All provided the frame in which they lived. It is striking how often the poetry appears at the edges of that sociability, when the others have just gone, or their arrival is just expected, another of the margins at which this margin-entranced sensibility dwelt.

What emerges is something more nuanced than a straightforward tale of miraculous productivity. Everywhere there are eddies in the stream: an interfolding of love and worry, ambition and doubt, a sense of possibility and of guilt, the patterns of human friendship oscillating between admiration and the recognition that the person you admire may not be entirely admirable, and may have the same hesitations about you.

The poets' differences pulled and rubbed against each other. Their friendship, with its intermingling of affection and doubt, was a mutual shaping. Each became a source for the other, and each moulded himself in opposition to the other. It was intriguingly gendered. Coleridge could detect in himself elements of the female, but 'Of all the men I ever knew,' he wrote, 'Wordsworth has the least femineity in his mind. He is all man. He is a man of whom it might have been said, – "It is good for him to be alone."'

The driving and revolutionary force of this year was the recognition that poetry was not an aspect of civilisation but a challenge to it; not decorative but subversive, a pleasure beyond politeness. This was not the stuff of drawing rooms. Its purpose was to give a voice to the voiceless, whatever form that voicelessness might have taken: sometimes speaking for the sufferings of the unacknowledged poor; sometimes enshrining the quiet murmuring of a man alone; sometimes reaching for the life of the child in his 'time of unrememberable being', beyond the grasp of adult consciousness; sometimes roaming in the magnificent and strange disturbedness of Coleridge's imagined worlds.

Wordsworth called poetry 'the first and last of all knowledge', using those words precisely: poetry comes both before and after everything that might be said. Its spirit and goal is to exfoliate consciousness, to rescue understanding from the noise and entropy of habit, to find richness and beauty in the hidden or neglected actualities. The strange, unlikely and unfashionable claim of this year stems from that recognition: poetry can remake assumptions, reconfigure the mind and change the world.

2

Meeting

June 1797

Early in June 1797, Coleridge was walking south through the lanes of Somerset and Dorset to visit Wordsworth and his sister Dorothy. I walked with him, the same lanes, the same air, absorbed in his frame of mind, my first embedding.

He was in the full flood of existence, bubbling and boiling with its possibilities and beauties, its conundrums and agonies, ensnared in 'the quick-set hedge of embarrassment' – money troubles always meant that 'whichever way I turn a thorn runs into me' – but ever alive to all that life could offer.

June in the west of England is frothing into colour and show: cow parsley and foxgloves, dark red campions mixed in with the alkanet and the nettles. The bees visiting each dangled foxglove hood in turn, as if turning in at a row of shops, pausing at each entrance, hesitating on the lip and then moving inside. The hawthorns are still clotted with blossom, the air double-creamy for yards around them. The elders are in bloom, their disk-like flower-heads held out into the roadway, dinner plates on the fingertips of an upturned hand. The first of the hay is being made in the paddocks and meadows, the swathes cut and laid across the buttercup hills. Bees in the brambles, honeysuckle in the hedges, the apple trees still just in blossom. Sprinkles of stitchwort. Every morning with a gloss on it, brushed and burnished.

The sociable time

FOLLOWING PAGE: His mind is full of starlings

A few years later Coleridge told a friend exactly how he felt when he found himself steaming along an inviting road like this, less a single man than a swarm of living things, animate nature itself, his mind as alive and mobile and endlessly self-reshaping as a concatenation of starlings oscillating and refiguring around his head. It was on the road like this, he told Tom Wedgwood, that

> my spirit courses, drives, and eddies, like a Leaf in Autumn; a wild activity, of thoughts, imaginations, feelings, and impulses of motion, rises up from within me; a sort of bottom-wind, that blows to no point of the compass, comes from I know not whence, but agitates the whole of me; my whole being is filled with waves that roll and stumble, one this way, and one that way, like things that have no common master ... Life seems to me then a universal spirit, that neither has, nor can have, an opposite. 'God is everywhere,' I have exclaimed, 'and works everywhere, and where is there room for death?'

Coleridge, aged twenty-four, slightly fat – his friends called him 'pursy' – but strong, quite capable of forty miles between a summer dawn and dusk, or more than seventy miles over two days, had been on the road for three days, feeling 'almost shillingless' and chewing over his desperate need for cash. He had just come from seeing Joseph Cottle, his publisher in Bristol. Coleridge needed him for his money, and Cottle had offered 'to buy an unlimited number of verses'. Cottle had ambitions as a poet himself: '*The scatter'd cots/Sprinkling the vallies round, most gaily look./The very trees wave concord ...*' It was an unequal relationship. Coleridge could flatter him when he needed to – 'My dear Cottle' – and just as easily dismiss him: 'It is not impossible,' he signed off one letter to this idealistic, helpful and generous bookseller-publisher, who did his best to promote the early careers of Coleridge, Southey and Wordsworth, 'that in the course of two or three months I may see you.'

Now, though, Coleridge had shaken him out of his hair and the dust of Bristol from his feet, and was hungrily en route to the man he wanted to meet. He had given a sermon at the Unitarian chapel in Bridgwater, which 'most of the better people in the town' had attended, and the following day breakfasted with a much-adored minister in Taunton – 'the more I see of that man, the more I love him'. The congregation in Bridgwater had admired his sermon, but was that right? Was admiration the reaction a sermon should evoke? He had 'endeavoured to awaken a Zeal for Christianity by shewing the contemptibleness & evil of lukewarmness', but even as those words came to him, he must have laughed. Lukewarmness was not a Coleridgean quality. He had a predilection for the extreme. Put him on a public platform and Coleridge would appear 'like a comet or a meteor in our horizon'. He usually wrote his lectures or sermons in advance, but more often than not

> against [my] better interests [I] was carried away with an ebullient Fancy, a flowing Utterance, a light and dancing Heart, & a disposition to catch fire by the very rapidity of my own motion, & to speak vehemently from mere verbal associations.

Now he was bowling down the summer lanes to meet Wordsworth. They had been corresponding for eighteen months, and Coleridge already admired him. He knew him as a poet, had met him in Bristol, and they had briefly stayed together in Somerset. He had quoted him in a poem of his own, and been quoted by Wordsworth in return. Coleridge already thought that Wordsworth was the greatest of men and 'the best poet of the age'.

South Somerset and Dorset looked then, as they do now in midsummer, like southern comfort, with big, gentle, ten-mile views, the hills coming to well-coiffed peaks, rolled and tufted, bobbled with woods. But there was an illusion at work. These southern counties in the late 1790s were a pit of desperation, one of the poorest places in England. Anyone alive to political or human realities would be enraged by what they saw. Harvests had been bad. Long-term malnutrition kept the average height of the poor under five foot. The diet was ruinously thin: broth made of flour and onions and water for breakfast, meat maybe twice a week, otherwise the relentless repetition of bread and cheese. Bullock's cheek was sometimes bought to flavour the broth. Potatoes were mashed with fat taken from that broth, and sometimes with salt alone.

In the evenings of early June, as the long days of the hay harvest made their demands on this underfed workforce, the labourers, watched by the diary-keeping gentry, were driven to the limits of exhaustion. William Holland, vicar of Over Stowey in Somerset, observed William Perrott, his aged parish clerk, always known as 'Mr Amen', struggling with the haymaking. He

> looked like a hunted hare towards the end of the day, very
> stiff, could hardly move along, with his neck stretched out
> and his eyes hollowed into his head.

Mr Amen and two others had mown three and a half acres in the day, scything five tons of grass. Holland gave them 'drink and some victuals, though the last not in the agreement'.

It was a world of brutal inequality. Your average high gentry family in the 1790s might be living off an income of £4,000 or more. There was scarcely any tax: Land Tax, Window Tax and Carriage Tax might add up to no more than £30 out of that £4,000. Local rates, to pay for the poorhouses in towns and villages, were levied, but came to only £10 extra per gentry family a year. Gifts were made to charity, to teach poor children or for the local infirmary, but the rich almost never gave away more than 1 per cent of their annual income.

Among the poor, general life expectancy was under forty. More than half of all babies born did not live beyond childhood. 'Bad teeth, skin diseases, sores, bronchitis and rheumatism were rampant. Diagnosis was more by the eye than the touch.' Most treatments were folk remedies in the form of leaves, roots, bark, spices and powders, and most were useless. There was no need for the poets to imagine or devise instances of human suffering. The wrongness of the social, economic and political system in England was apparent at every turn of every lane.

Coleridge, his person perhaps a little 'slovenly', as certain upright citizens had judged, with his stockings dirty and his hair uncombed, was walking through a country in crisis. New commercial capital coming into rural England meant that the landscape of small yeoman farms, which had been there for at least a thousand years, was being erased. What had been a class of independent farming families was now thrown back on work as servants, as piece workers in the woollen mills or as labourers on farms they had once called their own. By the late 1790s, Durweston near Blandford in Dorset, where there had been thirty or even forty smallholdings in 1775, was now concentrated into two large farms. The prevailing spirit among the dispossessed was unadulterated despair. Sir Frederic Morton Eden, the pioneering student of poverty in rural England, wrote of the Dorset poor in 1796 that the ex-yeoman families were 'regardless of futurity'. It is a resonant phrase, which would not have been out of place in one of Wordsworth's poems. Most of rural England was in a state of suspension, threatened by life without ambition or hope. The bonds of rural society had been broken, and this new class of the poor 'spend their little wages as they receive them, without reserving a provision for old age'.

You need to shed any sense of Arcadian wellbeing. Britain was at war with France, press gangs were roaming the country to find men for the navy, informers were everywhere, and the Home Office files were bulging with letters from all corners, reporting on possible and known suspects. Prices were rising, and the country was full of maimed soldiers and desperate widows. Fences were often stolen for firewood. If you owned a cow and kept it in a field, you could expect it to have been milked by the hungry overnight. Hayricks by the road were regularly 'plucked' by the poor wanting to feed their own animals. Anyone growing peas would find them 'swarming with the workhouse children' in the weeks when the pods ripened. The dark, sunburned faces of the people were creased into premature old age. For meat they occasionally ate badgers, or the 'Carrion Beef' of a cow that had died in calving. The Reverend Holland, recording his parish visits in his journal, described how he called on a woman 'in a most desperate way with a broken leg. She was glad to see me, and would crawl to the door.' Otherwise, he sent his wife on the necessary visits. She

> walked as far as the poor sick girl, who is indeed in a most
> deplorable state. I am advised not to go in to her as she is in
> a kind of putrid state – and indeed my wife I believe does
> not go in, but we send her something every day.

For all these and other outrages, for all his own anxieties, affected by toothache and neuralgia, by hideous dreams and pervasive worry, Coleridge was always able to dance and balloon into unbridled delight at the beauties of existence. Many years later, thinking of this wonderful summer, he wrote a short and Blake-like poem, a spontaneous aria celebrating the rich simplicity of friendship as 'a shelt'ring tree', and all the joys

> that came down shower-like,
> Of Beauty, Truth and Liberty,
> When I was young, ere I was old!

The ideal of friendship hovers over this whole story as its subtle and fickle if ministering angel, but it is not Coleridge's aria as much as his description of how it came to him that opens the door on to the form and habits of his mind in 1797. The poem was 'an air', he wrote, remembering the year of his youth in Somerset,

> that whizzed δία ένκέφαλου [*dhia enkephalou*] (right across the diameter of my Brain) exactly like a Hummel Bee ... close by my ear, at once sharp and burry, right over the summit of Quantock at earliest Dawn just between the Nightingale that I stopt to hear in the Copse at the foot of Quantock, and the first Sky-Lark that was a Song-Fountain, dashing up and sparkling to the Ear's eye, in full column, or ornamented shaft of sound in the order of Gothic Extravaganza, out of sight, over the Cornfields on the Descent of the Mountain on the other side – out of sight, tho twice I beheld its *mute* shoot downward in the sunshine like a falling star of silver.

It is a paragraph that describes quickness but must be read slowly, the trace of Coleridge's mind in the process of thinking: a bumblebee shooting past his ear half a lifetime before, holding the space between nightingale and skylark, whose song is now in his memory like a mountain stream in the eye of the ear (!), then becoming a high, rippling, barley-twist column of knobbled medieval beauty, but invisible, the bird itself disappearing into the wide lit spaces of the sky, but its *mute*, its droppings, gliding out of that ecstatic empyrean with the brilliance and glitter of a streaking meteor, a blob of mercury hurtling from the blue. Could there ever be inconsistency in a mind that thought like this? In which such potent synaesthesiac category-shifts dissolved all boundaries of time and space? In which inconsistency felt like the pulse of life?

I know this stretch of country well. I spent most of my twenties on foot, disenchanted with the world of cities. Paying for myself by writing about it in newspapers and magazines, I walked thousands of miles here in England, the same in France, and then in Europe, in Greece and Italy, not in pursuit of anything in particular except perhaps the reassurance of being able to engage with the physical world day after day, in fog and rain and snow, in the burnishing sunshine, usually alone, sleeping out in a small tent or in mountain bothies or in Greece inside the flea-ridden chapels. I was merely doing what Wordsworth and Coleridge, by some subterranean routes, flowing through the thousands of capillaries in Western culture, had taught me to do. All the years of education seemed less important than this. I once walked sixty miles in twenty hours across the Cotentin in northern France, most of the day and then all night, with a friend, an Anglo-Saxon scholar who had become a soldier, and who Coleridge-like for mile after mile didn't draw breath. We began at Cherbourg, had dinner in Briquebec, coq au vin and a bottle of wine. Had I read Alcuin's letters? Should he learn Farsi? What effect would living in a granite world like the Cotentin have on your mind, on your expectations of the solidity of things? Every hour or so we smoked a cigarette, leaning against one of those granite walls, sitting on the verge. The sun rose on the Normandy beaches and we swam in the golden, blue-eyed surf.

What is it about walking for days on end? Partly it is the love of self-reliance, of not needing to be dependent on anything or anyone. It is psychically naked, with the curious effect that this self-reliance seems to make your own skin more permeable. Alone on foot, not in any great heroic landscapes – these are not high mountain singular mist-visions – but in just such a place as the Somerset Levels, where the knitted ordinariness of everyday life forms the texture of the landscape through which you move – the small farms, the stalled animals, the life of the hedges – you become absorbent, inseparable from the world around you.

Walking in that way is a dissolution of the self, not a magnification of it, a release from burdens, in which all you have to do is walk and be, as plainly existent as grass growing, continuous with everything that is.

The great land-artist Richard Long was my hero, and I wrote to him, wanting to talk about his absorption in the walked line, but he replied courteously by letter to say that there was nothing much we could discuss that he or I didn't already know. And I wondered then if Romanticism, to which this habit of being was clearly the heir, alone out on the road, scarcely communicative with anyone except the self, was little but a form of loneliness, and of legitimising loneliness by being alone.

I spent one of those summers in the Levels, dropping into just the relationship with the country that Coleridge and Wordsworth had invented here two centuries before, at exactly their age, in my mid-twenties. One long afternoon remains in my memory when the water in the summer Levels, as always, was penned up in the rhynes that divide the low, damp fields, making wet fences between them.

Each rhyne shelters a particular world of butterbur or king-cup, water-mint or a flashy wedding show of flag-irises. If you sit on the bank, the high water in the field soaks up into the cloth of your trousers, so that the invitation to swim, to move over from watery peat to peaty water, is irresistible. Slowly that afternoon I lowered my body into the blood-warm cider-soup, crusty with frog-bit and duckweed, with seeds and reed shells. My feet were in the half-mud of the rhyne floor, a soft half-substance as if I were sinking into the folds of a brain. The arrowhead and bulrushes quivered in my wash and away down the rhyne – or so I always imagined – the eels released their bubbles as they shifted away from the disturbance.

This was embeddedness. The breadth of the water grows as you come near it to a generous private width, lobed into by the irises and the reeds. The air is warm and heady. Away down the rhyne a swan claps its wings. The meadows riffle in the wind. Heat and vapour wobble in the air above them. Everything hangs in suspension, and your skin turns a golden unnatural brown in the whisky water. Three hundred and fifty million years ago all life was water-life, and to float in a summer rhyne seemed then like a return to ancientness, to the deepest possible co-presence with the earth.

That idea – that the contented life was the earth-connected life, even that goodness was embeddedness – had its roots in the 1790s, perhaps drawing on what Wordsworth and Coleridge had read of Rousseau, or perhaps inheriting from him as I had inherited from them. Co-presence with the natural world, a closeness that was inaccessible in what Coleridge always described as the 'dim' light of the city – the persistent coal smog of eighteenth-century London – was somehow a release into a form of wellbeing which normal political, commercial, professional or even educational life would not only fail to approach but would actually disrupt and destroy. It is a powerful connection to make: love of nature as the route both to a love of truth and to a love of man.

No room in the world was closed to Coleridge. As he said to a friend, 'I hate the word *but*.' Every connection needed to be an *and*. Every corridor and every chamber branching off it was available to the roaming, skipping investigations of his mind, not ponderous but almost gravity-free, and in each store and warehouse to which he pushed open the door he found lying in wait for him caves of beauty and significance.

He walked as he talked, never pursuing a single line direct, but famously moving from one side of the lane or the path to another so that his companion would always have to shift to accommodate him. His mode was multiple but not anarchic. He could not put up with nonsense, and consistently searched for systematic connections across the whole width of what he had to know. That was the essence of his life: a never-ending appetite for all that was and had been, struggling with the need to bring it into a single frame of understanding.

Any talk of mere personality he detested: there was more to wisdom than the idiosyncrasies of the individual. Nor did he live in an unbroken morning of bland optimism. Excitement and despondency alternated within him. And he knew of his own failings. Forgive me, he would remark to his listeners, if sometimes you hear in what I say a verb orphaned of its subjective noun or a subjective noun widowed of its verb. He could get lost in his paragraphs like a man in a thicket. His relationship to knowledge was so hungry that knowledge itself came to live in his mind as an infinite sequence of overlapping and self-generating circles, in which no understanding of one circle could be complete without an understanding of its neighbour, an unending progression of unfolding spheres, like the universes that expand from the black holes each one contains, a multiverse strung out across space and time. It is little wonder that even his great and encompassing mind eventually faded under the strain of the challenge.

The energy, if undeniable, was fervid and troubled, drawing into itself at different times schemes for everything: a book on the modern Latin poets, an Epic Poem on the Origin of Evil, something on William Godwin, an Opera, a Liturgy, a Tragedy, editions of English eighteenth-century poets, a book on Milton, on the Greek tragedians, on the technicalities of scansion, on the laws upon wrecks, a poem in the style of Dante on Thor, on his hero the philosopher David Hartley, on the obscurities of Behmen, Helmont, Swedenborg, Philo Judaeus, Porphyry, Plotinus, Platypus, Mesmer, an address to Poverty, on the art of prolonging life – by getting up in the morning, an Ode to a Looking Glass, hymns to the Sun, the Moon and the Elements, an Ode to Southey, an Ode to a Moth, a history of night, or of privacy, or of silence, or the self.

For I am now busy on the subject, and shall in a very few weeks go to Press with a volume on the prose writings of Hall, Milton and Taylor; and shall immediately follow it up with an Essay on the writings of Dr. Johnson and Gibbon. And in these two volumes I flatter myself I shall present a fair History of English Prose ... I have since my twentieth year meditated an heroic poem on the Siege of Jerusalem by Titus. This is the Pride and the Stronghold of my Hope. But I never think of it except in my best moods.

It was a fountain of being, in which the pressure was always ready to flow, no urging needed. 'My heart seraglios a whole host of joys,' he wrote in his notebook, a new verb for the promiscuity of knowledge and happiness.

He knew too, in a way that was profoundly different from Wordsworth, that the endless liquidity of his self-conception, the flux and reflux of his mind, the stream of the organism called Coleridge, was the lens through which he perceived the world. He thought he had 'a smack of Hamlet myself', as a figure who partly observed and partly created the world around him. Hamlet's thoughts, Coleridge said in his lectures on Shakespeare, 'and the images of his fancy, are far more vivid than his actual perceptions, and his very perceptions, instantly passing through the medium of his contemplations, acquire, as they pass, a form and a colour not naturally their own'. What was within him imposed itself on what he saw. 'All actual objects are faint and dead to him.'

He was aware that his perceptions of the outward world were so shaped by what he already knew and remembered that when, for example, he saw the moon, he did not see a moon but instead experienced 'the dim awakening of a forgotten or hidden truth of my inner nature'. A nightingale's song, or the sound of a stream as it fell and slid over the rocks in its bed, or the frost creeping over the roofs of the village, or the swifts screech-screaming in the streets of Nether Stowey, or Stowey's own flowing gutter, or a cockerel in a farmyard holding its tattered tail aloft: all of these phenomena seemed to be aspects of himself. Anything his eye saw was 'supported by the images of memory flowing in on the impulses of immediate impression'. Nothing was uninflected by what he knew, trying to find a steady path through the jangling crowd of objects vibrating in his brain.

He could be teased. He knew he was 'a thought-bewilder'd man', and he knew he wasn't like the man who had once been his best friend, the poet Robert Southey. Southey, although undoubtedly capable of great and empathetic poetry, had an austerity and a self-preservative strictness about him. Coleridge had called him 'a man of *perpendicular Virtue* ... enlightened and unluxurious'. But those Roman virtues were accompanied by a deep self-regard. Southey was neat, clever, handsome, conceited, 'a coxcomb' in Wordsworth's eyes, well-mannered and well-ordered, a man who, Coleridge thought, had surrendered his idealism – they had planned to set up a Utopian community together in America – to a rational and rather mean self-interest. In their bruising and final argument in 1795, when Southey had decided to abandon any communitarian plans, Coleridge had told him, 'You are *lost* to *me*, because you are lost to Virtue.' Southey was someone, as Coleridge wrote later, who had 'the power of saying one thing at a time'. Can you imagine, one thing at a time! The sterility of it!

Coleridge knew he was not like that but instead 'a Surinam toad', a creature which has the habit of embedding her eggs in pouches set in the skin of her back. Up to a hundred of them can grow there, developing into little toadlets that, when the time comes, jump out of their nests, waving their tiny hands as they emerge and drop off their mother into the roadway, scattering around her like the pips from a pomegranate as she continues on her way through life.

That is the beautiful South American amphibian walking

down the road to the Wordsworths on the afternoon of 4 or 5 June 1797 – the exact date is unclear – a man who investigates everything and strews and sprinkles his own progeny around him, a king with guineas at his own coronation, a fountain of largesse, the volcano of ideas. He knew of course how he did not conform to the required ideal of manly self-containment, and that he spawned plans like a herring, but he recognised there was beauty in that. Orderliness is no more than a narrowing funnel through which to experience the world. *Every step an arrival* is the walker's credo; there can be no restrictive plot or narrative that remains true. That is the source of Coleridgean wonder. What happens happens, looseness is all and absorbency beauty. The good man blesses everything unawares.

'Southey once said to me,' Coleridge wrote to his son Hartley in 1820,

> You are nosing every nettle along the Hedge, while the
> Greyhound (meaning himself, I presume) wants only to get
> to sight of the Hare, & FLASH! – strait as a line! – he has it
> in his mouth! –

Coleridge thought that the kind of remark a cannibal would make to an anatomist as he watched him dissect a body, commenting on the time the doctor was taking to prepare his dinner. Must a man wait a whole day before he is allowed to eat? But it was the journey Coleridge valued as much as the arrival.

> The fact is – I do not care two-pence for the *Hare*; but I
> value most highly the excellencies of scent, patience,
> discrimination, free Activity; and find a Hare in every Nettle
> I make myself acquainted with.

That June afternoon, Coleridge, with a mind full of every hare in every nettle he had passed on the way, arrived at Racedown, the house in Dorset where the Wordsworths were living. Coleridge famously did not come down the path that led from the turn-pike, but across the field, diagonally, over a gate in the corner, and bounding through the corn to the garden where Wordsworth brother and sister were working.

It is rather a busy road now, with cars coming fast around blind corners, but Coleridge's gate is still there, if almost never used nowadays, sagging on its hinges and half-buried in the strands of a hawthorn hedge. Through its straggling opening, one can look down at the house the Wordsworths were living in. There is no access for modern pilgrims, but this is what I imagine: Coleridge bursting down the slope where the corncrakes had been croaking, as they had been all summer, across the green corn that the farmer Joseph Gill had yet to cut or get the men to cut for him. Each blue-green spear standing in that field blaz-ingly alive. The poet's long leaping footsteps, looping up and over and into the corn, his legs swathed in it and breaking through it, with his bag on his hip swinging up and out at each extended pace, leaving a dragged wake of stems behind him, breaking what had been the perfection of that field, so that after-wards, that evening, looking up at the way by which he had arrived, his mark was there on the country like the tail of a comet or the track of a meteor or the blunderings of a dog in the corn.

The house itself was the opposite of everything Coleridge brought to it. It was a gentleman's residence, a cliff of brick and grey stucco, sash windows, symmetry, multi-flue chimneys, outhouses, red stretchers with black headers laid in diaper-diamonds across its surface. 'An excellent house', Wordsworth called it to a friend; 'a very good house, and in a pleasant situation', his sister said. This was no poet's cottage, and Coleridge casually referred to it in a letter to Cottle as 'the mansion of our friend Wordsworth'. A tight parapeted formality confronted the visitor. There were two parlours, one with a fine Axminster carpet, one with an oil cloth on the floor, a kitchen and scullery, a pantry, a servants' hall and a butler's pantry. Above, four excellent bedchambers looked out over the willows and alders of the valley below the house, each chamber with a closet. There were four further bedchambers on the floor above.

Furnishings were not lacking: mahogany chairs and table, a tea chest and a reading stand, two bookcases filled with the classics and works of history and theology. There was a leather sofa, a pier glass in a gilded frame, a pianoforte, two blue and white Delft flower stands, a well-furnished hearth and a dinner service in Queen's Ware. Linen sheets were provided, and Betty Daly, at one and a half guineas a year, plus two shillings a week when the gentlemen were in residence, could come in to air and clean the house and do the laundry. Peggy Marsh worked as her maid. Wineglasses, tumblers and decanters could be provided, but these were all to be returned to Joseph Gill, the manager of house, farm and adjoining brickyard, when not required. A picture of Leda, naked with swan, in a gilt frame, belonging to the owners of the house, the Pinneys of Bristol, slave-owning plantation landlords and sugar-traders, was not required by the Wordsworths, and had been packed up and sent away.

It seems in retrospect the most unlikely situation for a man on the lip of revolution, but beneath the surface there is a more complex set of social and emotional conditions in play.

Wordsworth, aged twenty-seven, and his sister Dorothy, a year and a half younger, are borrowing, not renting, the house. They cannot afford the rent, and it has been lent to them by two young radical Bristol friends, the Pinneys, who have not told their far-from-radical father that they have lent out his house for nothing. The Wordsworths are camping here, happy to find a temporary perch in their peripatetic and impoverished life. They are living – or meant to be living – on the proceeds of a legacy which a young friend of Wordsworth had left to him when he died two years earlier. Wordsworth has in turn lent the money out to two other London friends who are meant to be paying him interest – at a handsome 10 per cent a year – but who regularly fail to come up with the payments or are late in doing so. For pin money Dorothy is now making shirts for her brother Richard, a London lawyer, cutting and sewing the linen from a huge bolt delivered to the house, for which she is also hemming sheets.

The Wordsworths in their gentleman's house have to borrow money from Joseph Gill, the farmer (himself a cousin of the Pinneys, but drunk and disintegrated after a life in the Caribbean), and are given coal during the winter by other neighbours. There is meant to be a gardener, but he is 'saucy' and won't do what either Wordsworth or Gill asks him, so Wordsworth does some of the gardening himself, uprooting hedges, planting potatoes and picking beans. He is, rather to his sister's surprise, 'dextrous with a spade'. She hires a boy to mow the lawns. Like the rural poor around them, they eat only vegetables and broth, and drink tea.

'I have lately been living upon air and the essence of carrots cabbages turnips and other esculent vegetables, not excluding parsley the product of my garden,' Wordsworth writes to a friend. They buy the worst of the meat at sixpence a pound from a butcher who comes with his cart from Crewkerne, and must depend for their clothes on the cast-offs from Richard in London. At times the whole household falls ill with coughs and colds. They walk everywhere, and the house has a 'perambulator', a measuring wheel which can clock off the distances along the road, although, as Wordsworth notes carefully in the inventory, its handle was already broken on their arrival. When the young Pinneys come from time to time, a moneyed interlude intervenes, during which Wordsworth goes shooting and hare-coursing with them and there is wine and meat and gravy, but when the Pinneys go back to Bristol, the austerity returns. Wordsworth must ask Gill to borrow household equipment, one tumbler or four sheets of paper at a time, and Gill carefully records each request in his diary.

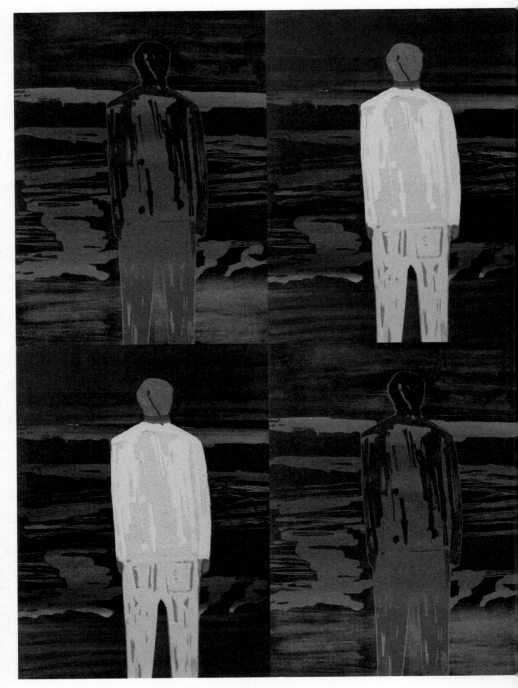

Wordsworth in Darkness

PREVIOUS PAGE: He comes like a comet to their door

Behind this there is a deeper personal history, hinged precisely to the gap between poverty and gentility. The Wordsworths' father had been law agent to Sir James Lowther, a great landowner in Westmorland. John Wordsworth was a power in the land himself, a coroner worth some £10,000 when he died, living with silver coffee pots and handsome watches, a life lubricated with good port and madeira. He had brought up his children in the most handsome of houses in Cockermouth, with a beautiful garden at the back along whose boundary the River Derwent ran, and the sound of whose water came in through the windows of the bedrooms. But both Wordsworth parents had died when the children were young, the mother of pneumonia in March 1778, when William was seven, their father of a dropsy after spending a night out, lost on the winter fells, five years later. With his father's death, their world collapsed. Sir James Lowther, soon to be the Earl of Lonsdale, owed John Wordsworth £4,625, but for years the Lonsdale estate refused to pay over the money. The key to the house the Wordsworths had lived in was surrendered to the Lonsdale agent, and the children were dispersed among their relatives, where they were treated as poor relations, humiliated and patronised by the servants and made to feel ashamed of who they were. 'How we are squandered abroad!' Dorothy had written of these years.

In 1787 Wordsworth was sent to Cambridge, and encouraged by those relations to think of a career in the Church. But at Cambridge, while ferociously aware of his own great gifts, he had refused to engage with the route required by a conventional career, and had been 'an idler among academic bowers'. The great emotional and intellectual experience of his time as an undergraduate was not at Cambridge itself, but on a heroic three-thousand-mile walk in the summer and autumn of 1790 through France in the first glow of its revolutionary fever, to Switzerland and the epic landscapes of the Alps. France then was 'standing on the top of golden hours/And human nature seeming born again'.

After he had left university, with no good degree, he went to London, directionless and unfocused, unable to commit to any life in the Church, the law, university, politics or commerce. He felt 'rotted':

> my life became
> A floating island, an amphibious thing
> Unsound, of spungy texture.

But the scent of liberty was coming across the Channel. A decade earlier, the Americans had cast themselves free. Now an ancient European monarchy was heading for a rational, liberated future. Richard Price, a suddenly famous dissenting minister-turned-lecturer, was drawing vast crowds to his London talks. 'A general amendment', he told his excited audience, was beginning in human affairs:

> the dominion of kings [is] changed for the dominion of
> laws, and the dominion of priests giving way to the
> dominion of reason and conscience. Be encouraged, all ye
> friends of freedom, and writers in its defence!

Once again, Wordsworth was drawn to France, not only to escape the urgings of his relatives, who had in mind a rural curacy, but to taste and know the sources of the future. This time he went to the Loire valley, where, even as the massacres were committed in Paris and the French Republic was being declared, he met two people who had a shaping influence on his life and thought. The first was an officer in the army, Armand-Michel Bacharetie de Beaupuy, known simply as Michel Beaupuy, an aristocrat from the Périgord, now in his mid-thirties, and a republican idealist, who in Wordsworth's loving remembering of him in *The Prelude* sounds like a vision of the perfect man. They

24

talked politics and the virtues of change, weighing the best of ancient republican systems against the extremes of revolutionary violence, sifting what seemed good from the horrors and strains of the moment.

Injuries

Made *him* more gracious, and his nature then
Did breathe its sweetness out most sensibly,
As aromatic flowers on Alpine turf,
When foot hath crushed them.
By birth he ranked
With the most noble, but unto the poor
Among mankind he was in service bound,
As by some tie invisible, oaths professed
To a religious order. Man he loved
As man, and, to the mean and the obscure,
And all the homely in their homely works,
Transferred a courtesy which had no air
Of condescension; but did rather seem
A passion and a gallantry, like that
Which he, a soldier, in his idler day
Had paid to woman: somewhat vain he was,
Or seemed so – yet it was not vanity,
But fondness, and a kind of radiant joy
That covered him about when he was intent
On works of love or freedom.

Beaupuy looked like an oasis in a bitter world, a source of hope and goodness in a violent time, a demonstration that human nature was capable of fineness and grace. With him, walking along the road in Touraine, Wordsworth had a sudden, formative encounter, one of those spots of time that make us what we are, remembered for the rest of his life:

And when we chanced
One day to meet a hunger-bitten girl,
Who crept along fitting her languid self
Unto a heifer's motion – by a cord
Tied to her arm, and picking thus from the lane
Its sustenance, while the girl with her two hands
Was busy knitting in a heartless mood
Of solitude – and at the sight my friend
In agitation said, ''Tis against that
That we are fighting,' I with him believed
Devoutly that a spirit was abroad
Which could not be withstood, that poverty,
At least like this, would in a little time
Be found no more, that we should see the earth
Unthwarted in her wish to recompense
The industrious, and the lowly child of toil,
All institutes for ever blotted out
That legalized exclusion, empty pomp
Abolished, sensual state and cruel power
Whether by edict of the one or few –
And finally, as sum and crown of all,
Should see the people having a strong hand
In making their own laws; whence better days
To all mankind.

It is difficult to judge how much *The Prelude* attributes later
thoughts and ideas to earlier events – Wordsworth was imperi-
ous in his relationship to time – but that moment with Beaupuy,
who in 1796 would be killed by a cannonball in battle against
the Austrians, and the simplicity and passion of the remembered words, ''Tis against *that*/That we are fighting,' seem now
to stand as one of the sources of Wordsworth's later life.
Beaupuy's name is among those cut into the stones of the Arc
de Triomphe, but these lines, in which he is described in the

beautiful, supple, easy blank verse of *The Prelude*, are a true memorial.

At the same time, Wordsworth fell in love with a young French woman. Annette Vallon was four years older than him. Their story, which was only ever known within the family circle in Wordsworth's lifetime, is exceptionally opaque. She was the daughter of a surgeon in Blois. Nearly nothing is known about her, except that during the years of the Revolutionary wars, in which her Catholic and Royalist family suffered at the hands of the Republic, she and her sisters behaved with extraordinary and resourceful courage, running messages for the Royalists, concealing enemies of the state, smuggling them to safety, evading the secret police, in turn, of the Terror, the Directoire and Napoleon, risking all. Wordsworth had fallen in love with a woman of mettle and fire. She had first encountered him late in 1791, at the house in Orléans of André-Augustin Dufour, a magistrate's clerk, and may have begun by teaching him French, but soon they moved together to Blois. In the spring of 1792 she became pregnant with their child.

Wordsworth scarcely communicated with anyone at home, only asking his brother Richard for some money, but saying nothing of Annette. In December 1792 their daughter, Anne-Caroline Vallon, was born and baptised in Orléans, the French clerk carefully recording the impossible name 'Anne Caroline Wordswodsth, daughter of Williams Wordswodsth, Anglois, and of Marie Anne Vallon'. Wordsworth had made arrangements for Dufour to represent him at the baptism, by which time he himself had gone, leaving Annette unmarried and unsupported. Astonishingly, he did not return immediately to England, but spent six weeks in Paris witnessing the drama of revolution.

It is, at the least, chaotic behaviour. Although their politics were directly opposed, Annette certainly expected him to marry her. She called herself Annette Williams, and her distraught letters long for his return, for him to be present in her life and the life of their daughter. Only obliquely did Wordsworth ever write of her, as an interlude in *The Prelude*, in which there is no suggestion that the love affair he describes was anything more than a story told to him by Beaupuy. But it is filled with memories of the 'delirious hour', the 'happy time of youthful lovers' he had known with her, the promise of that Loire valley beginning:

> his present mind
> was under fascination; he beheld
> A vision, and he lov'd the thing he saw.
> Arabian fiction never fill'd the world
> With half the wonders that were wrought for him.
> Earth liv'd in one great presence of the spring ...
> all paradise
> Could by the simple opening of a door
> Let itself in upon him, pathways, walks
> Swarm'd with enchantment, till his spirit sank
> Beneath the burthen, overbless'd for life.

It may be that, at the height of the reign of Terror late in 1793, with Britain at war with France, Wordsworth quickly and secretly returned to see her – there are suggestions of that in *The Prelude* – but he was soon gone, and her piteous letters resumed:

> Come, my friend, my husband, receive the tender kisses of your wife, of your daughter. She is so pretty, this poor little one, so pretty that the tenderness I feel for her would drive me mad if I didn't always hold her in my arms. She looks like you more and more each day. I believe that I hold you in my arms. Her little heart beats against mine and I feel as if it is your heart beating against me. 'Caroline, in a month, in a fortnight, in a week, you will see the most cherished of men, the tenderest of men' ... Always love your little daughter and

28

your Annette, who kisses you a thousand times on the
mouth, on the eyes … I will write to you on Sunday.
Goodbye, I love you for life. Speak to me of the war, what
you think of it, because it worries me so much.

Wordsworth never received that particular letter, as it was
impounded by the Committee of Surveillance, and was only
discovered in the 1920s, with one other, hidden in the files of a
sub-police station in the Loire valley. But others of the same
kind, all now destroyed, crossed the Channel, filled with appeals
to a desperate conscience.

On his return to London, Wordsworth sank into the deepest
depression of his life, besieged by guilt and 'dead to deeper hope',
his soul dropping to its 'last and lowest ebb'. He had lost all faith
in human endeavour. His abandonment of Annette and Caroline
was fused in his mind with the fate of the Revolution in France
and the turn to repression in England, with his own lack of any
future and the absence of much hope for the ideals Beaupuy had
embraced and the happiness Annette may have represented.

Wordsworth wandered lost through these years. After 1793
France was at war with England, and Wordsworth, in love with
liberty and in love with his own country, found himself torn in
two. He moved from place to place – Wales, Yorkshire, the Isle
of Wight, Salisbury Plain, London, Westmorland, Cambridge –
without employment, without prospects, without money, without love, almost without friends, living sometimes in London,
mixing in the circles around the rationalist republican William
Godwin, involved with radical politics, writing at least one
long attack on the Church and the establishment, sometimes
in the north of England, occasionally reunited with his adoring
sister Dorothy, just as often apart from her.

His depression was accompanied by radical, republican rage.
Compassion, he wrote, was to be done away with. Liberty was to
'borrow the very arms of despotism', and 'in order to reign in

peace must establish herself by violence'. The contempt with which the Wordsworth family had been treated by the Earl of Lonsdale fuelled his hatred:

> We are taught from infancy that we were born in a state of inferiority to our oppressors, that they were sent into the world to scourge and we to be scourged.

The British government was bent on suppressing the French contagion. In May 1794 Habeas Corpus was suspended and dozens of radicals were arrested. The following year seditious gatherings and pamphlets were banned. Free speech was gagged. Many writers, printers, publishers, booksellers and lecturers who had embraced the radical ideas of their generation were placed in the pillory, imprisoned for six months or more, harassed, interrogated, ruined or transported to Australia, from where few would ever return. Others were tried for treason or condemned to death in their absence. In these conditions, Wordsworth's tirades were too extreme for any printer to risk their publication, and he remained almost unknown.

Through connections of the Godwin circle he met the Pinneys, whose house at Racedown was offered to Wordsworth brother and sister as a place of refuge away from the stress and strain of the city, from the stress and strain of his own mind.

In September 1795, Dorothy and William retreated to Dorset, taking with them little Basil Montagu, the son of a young lawyer also called Basil Montagu, whose wife had died in childbirth and who was struggling to bring up his son in his chambers in Lincoln's Inn. The Wordsworths had the hope that other children might join them to make a little school at Racedown, whose fees they could add to the income from the investment of the legacy.

Darkness gathered around Wordsworth, although neither he nor his sister could admit as much in their letters. A disenchantment with political radicalism and its rationalist revolution had left him with a sense of having nowhere to go. He was afflicted with debilitating headaches. His nightmares of the Terror, as he would later tell Coleridge in *The Prelude*, had come with him:

> I scarcely had one night of quiet sleep,
> Such ghastly visions had I of despair
> And tyranny, and implements of death,
> And long orations which in dreams I pleaded
> Before unjust Tribunals, with a voice
> Labouring, a brain confounded, and a sense
> Of treachery and desertion in the place
> The holiest that I knew of, my own soul.

The sense of treachery and desertion was all-colonising: a betrayal of his own ideals, of the hope that had once glowed in France, of his youth, of his child, of her mother, of himself. It was an amalgam of fear and guilt. Wordsworth felt disconnected from the goings on of life and the world. He asked for newspapers to be sent to him, no matter if they were five days old by the time they arrived. He thought of himself as 'a man in the moon' who had no inkling of what was happening on earth. Coleridge would later describe Wordsworth's '*unseeking* manners', that drift towards isolation, the refusal to engage with anyone or anything beyond himself. A kind of sardonic humour seeped out of him. 'Our present life is utterly barren of such events as merit even the short-lived chronicle of an accidental letter,' Wordsworth wrote to his Cambridge friend William Mathews, now a bookseller in London.

> We plant cabbages, and if retirement, in its full perfection,
> be as powerful in working transformation on one of Ovid's
> Gods, you may perhaps suspect that into cabbages we shall
> be transformed.

He had heard that remarks of that sort were circulating in London. 'As to writing, it is out of the question.'

Cynicism and bitterness, a dark estimation of himself and others: these were the outlines of a Wordsworth lost. 'We are now at Racedown and both as happy as people can be who live in perfect solitude,' he wrote to Mathews.

> We do not see a soul. Now and then we meet a miserable peasant in the road or an accidental traveller. The country people here are wretchedly poor; ignorant and overwhelmed with every vice that usually attends ignorance in that class, viz – lying and picking and stealing &c &c

He had sunk inward, in a kind of paralysis, held in uncertainty and perplexity, not bounding down the flank of a wheatfield but stalled at the gate, balked and blocked. It was, he later wrote, 'a weary labyrinth'. He turned to bitter satire, imitating Juvenal, in which with 'knife in hand' his aim was to 'probe/The living body of society/Even to the heart'.

He made visits to London and Bristol, and on one of them, probably through the Pinneys, he met Coleridge and began to show him and send him the poetry he was writing. Coleridge's letters to him from that time have disappeared, but through the course of 1796 it seems as if, perhaps under Coleridge's habit of encouragement, Wordsworth began to emerge from the darkness, and to feel his powers returning as both a man and a poet.

Pieces survive in his notebooks from that year, never shown to anyone, in a form of almost undecorated poetry, never published, surviving only as fragments of rough manuscript on the back of sheets containing other lines. One describes an incident on the road outside Racedown, a transient scene reminiscent of the encounter with the poor girl with the heifer in the Loire valley five years before. A baker from Clapton, just outside Crewkerne, used to deliver to houses in the area, and regularly came past Racedown. The speaker begins by addressing a young woman he has met in the road:

> I have seen the Baker's horse
> As he had been accustomed at your door
> Stop with the loaded wain, when o'er his head
> Smack went the whip, and you were left, as if
> You were not born to live, or there had been
> No bread in all the land. Five little ones,
> They at the rumbling of the distant wheels
> Had all come forth, and, ere the grove of birch
> Concealed the wain, into their wretched hut
> They all return'd. While in the road I stood
> Pursuing with involuntary look
> The Wain now seen no longer, to my side
>   came, pitcher in her hand
> Filled from the spring; she saw what way my eyes
> Were turn'd, and in a low and fearful voice
> She said – that wagon does not care for us –

That wagon does not care for us. This is unfinished: he addresses the woman, but then describes to her the scene she would just have witnessed herself. She begins by standing next to her hut, but then arrives from the spring with her pitcher. Nor can he name her – Wordsworth left a blank at the beginning of the line. But in its under-qualities, its directness and the simplicity of its language, its rhymeless pentameters without an abstract noun or any large Miltonic reference to the important or the exotic, one part of what would happen this year is already underway. This is the first signpost towards Wordsworth's future as a poet. The truth of her statement – *that wagon does not care for us* – emerges from under the carapace of the brutalised-civilised. It seems as if poetry, allied to the language of the real, can do what politics and revolution can never manage: make vivid and present the reality of suffering, of human experience, for which no exaggerated language or theatrics are required.

No graph of a life pursues a single line, and the man Coleridge had come to see and be with, to admire and encourage, is a hazy compound of mentalities and influences. With his hair cut short in the republican manner, and a heavy stubble on his cheek, there was an intense, haunted and self-possessed air to him. The artist Benjamin Robert Haydon later said that there was something 'lecherous, animal & devouring' in Wordsworth's laugh, and there is no doubt of the almost predatory power that hung about him. He would always control anyone who came into his orbit. And his erotic life was real and vivid. When, later, after ten years of marriage, he was away from his wife for a few days, he wrote to her: 'I tremble with sensations that almost overpower me,' his mind filled with images and memories of 'thy limbs as they are stretched upon the soft earth' and 'thy own involuntary sighs and ejaculations'.

The writing of poetry could take hold of him in what he called 'the fit', the need to get it down before it left his mind. His sister Dorothy watched him one morning at breakfast:

he, with his Basin of Broth before him untouched & a little plate of Bread & butter.

He had not slept well, but the idea of a poem had come to him.

He ate not a morsel, nor put on his stockings but sate with his shirt neck unbuttoned, & his waistcoat open while he did it. The thought first came upon him as we were talking about the pleasure we both always feel at the sight of a Butterfly. I told him that I used to chase them a little, but I was afraid of brushing the dust off their wings, & did not catch them – He told me how they used to kill all the

white ones when he went to school because they were
Frenchmen ...

Uniforms in the armies of Bourbon France had been white,
decorated with golden fleur-de-lis, and any right-thinking
English boy in the 1770s would have pursued them with a
vengeance. Wordsworth was remembering that from the other
side of a revolution that had replaced the white with the tri-
colour, but in this tiny scene, away from public view or the need
to present himself as he might have wanted to be known, something of the undressed Wordsworth appears: quietly and gently
witty, preoccupied, getting up late, needing to catch the moment
of writing a poem before it fled, his memories and the present
moment interacting as two dimensions of one life, calmly there
in the room but, in the writing of that poem, entirely removed,
alone.

One further element reflects on Wordsworth in the late 1790s.
In the archive at Dove Cottage in Westmorland is the extraordinary and rare survival of some of his clothes. His waistcoats and
breeches from the last years of the eighteenth century open a
shutter on to this gentleman-poet, governor-radical, man of the
people who was also a man, in his own mind, set far above them.
Much of the poetry he would write this year was intended, as he
said, 'to shew that men who did not wear fine cloaths can feel
deeply', and one might imagine that a poet who wrote those
words might also wear the fustian and the grosgrain of the working man.

He did not. In Grasmere you can find his cream waistcoat
with linen back and silk front, with a kind of spreading collar
and decorated with embroidered flowers, its pockets edged with
red braid, its twelve fabric-covered metal buttons each decorated
with a flower. Beside it is a matching suit of waistcoat and
breeches also in cream silk, this waistcoat with a stand-up collar,
two small pockets with scallop-edged flaps, and eleven small

buttons covered in fabric. The breeches are knee-length, gathered into a band at the knee and secured by four fabric-covered buttons and a strap fastening. A third waistcoat is in ivory silk, decorated in careful pale-blue, red and white embroidery, scattering his chest and stomach with perfect, crystalline lilies of the valley.

Are these really the clothes of the man who would write *The Prelude*? Was Wordsworth a dandy? In Germany late in 1798, according to his sister, he went out 'walking by moonlight in his fur gown and a black fur cap in which he looks like any grand Signior'. The gown was green, 'lined throughout with Fox's skin'. At other moments he would appear in 'a blue spencer', a short double-breasted overcoat without tails, and a new pair of pantaloons. Perhaps one can see in this elegance and this air of distinction, this distance from mud and toil, a picture of the man who was living in Racedown and considering his position as an unacknowledged legislator of the world, preparing to convey to that world his vision of completeness and authority. 'The Poet binds together by passion and knowledge the vast empire of human society, as it is spread over the whole earth ...', he would write a year or two later. There is no retreat in those magnificent words to a cosy provincial irrelevance. The ambition is explicitly imperial. Here is a man who wanted to establish a form of poetry whose ligatures would bind up the whole of existence.

His sister Dorothy, part-hidden, is at the centre of this year. There is a surviving silhouette of her: small and bright, sharp, attentive, slight-bodied. Her hair is bound up, her whole being taut. A high lace collar, curly hair on her brow. Delicate, poised, a small bosom, half-open lips, drawn in this silhouette with all the expectations of femininity, her presence almost toylike, but nothing skittish or girlish: careful, exact, intelligent, enquiring.

Coleridge described her in a letter written a few weeks after he had arrived at Racedown:

Wordsworth & his exquisite Sister are with me – She is a
woman indeed! – in mind, I mean, & heart – for her person
is such, that if you expected to see a pretty woman, you
would think her ordinary – if you expected to find an
ordinary woman, you would think her pretty! – But her
manners are simple, ardent, impressive –

Above all they noticed each other's eyes. Hers were 'watchful in
minutest observation of nature – and her taste a perfect
electrometer – it bends, protrudes, and draws in, at subtlest
beauties & most recondite faults'. His were large and grey, lit and
sparkling when animated, sometimes half-absent, as if he had
sunk a quarter of an inch below the surface of the skin, but
otherwise rolling bright towards you, as if the sight within them
were not a receptive faculty but *active*, coming and reaching out
to grasp his hearers. The lower part of his face could look somehow unbuttoned. His mouth was always hanging half open – he
couldn't breathe through his nose. 'I have the brow of an angel,
and the mouth of a beast,' he used to say, the repeated binary
vision of himself, great and weak, good and bad, never ceasing
to oscillate between its poles.

She saw a poet in him. 'He is a *wonderful* man,' she wrote to
her great friend Mary Hutchinson, who had been staying with
them at Racedown and had left only a day or two earlier.

His conversation teems with soul, mind, and spirit. Then he
is so benevolent, so good tempered and cheerful, and, like
William, interests himself so much about every little trifle.
At first I thought him very plain, that is, for about three
minutes: he is pale and thin, has a wide mouth, thick lips,
and not very good teeth, longish loose-growing half-curling
rough black hair. But if you hear him speak for five minutes
you think no more of them. His eye is large and full, and
not dark but grey; such an eye as would receive from a heavy

soul the dullest expression; but it speaks every emotion of his animated mind: it has more of 'the poet's eye in a fine frenzy rolling' than I ever witnessed. He has fine dark eyebrows, and an overhanging forehead.

In return she sparkled with her own sharp-edged, discontinuous brilliance, a flashing light in her eyes, her mind not a grand instrument of connection like Coleridge's, nor vastly present to itself like Wordsworth's, but full of bright remembered visions, exactly recalled, seen in detail: the sky-blue hedge sparrows' eggs in a childhood nest, the bilberries in the bowl of a black porringer. She had the gift of what Keats would later call 'that trembling delicate and snail-horn perception of Beauty', precise and sensitive, alert to variation. The sensitivity meant, as Coleridge noticed, that her horns would draw in at the slightest touch, and she would easily weep at things seen or remembered. She often felt her heart was full. Her separation from her brothers in childhood meant that she had been 'put out of the way of many recollections in common', and that separation only served to heighten the value of closeness for her. She and Wordsworth now shared their everyday life, but they also shared the experience of a mutual absence when young, and then the denial by the Lonsdale estate of their inheritance, the compulsory impoverishment in which they were both now living.

So much had been denied to them, and so much had been broken, that it was her duty to tend to her brother. She was both stronger and weaker than him. He may have been, as he wrote, the mountain and she its flowers, yet he was broken and she was the mender of him. She loved him but she could admonish him, just as later she could tell Coleridge not to publish an unkind review, as it was beneath him and its value as criticism was not greater than its cruelty.

She saw her own and her brother's situation clearly enough: 'We have been endeared to each other by early misfortune,' she

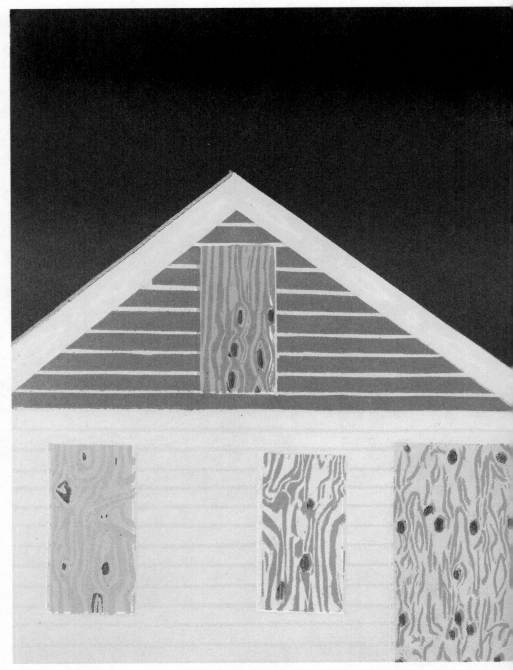

I crossed the dreary moor

PREVIOUS PAGE: Dorothy on the path of poetry

told a friend. Their love may or may not have sublimated the sexual – there is no evidence at all of anything approaching incest – but the form it took was admiration, protection and education, enabling him to leave behind the extremes of his broken self within her shelter and become the greater and more vulnerable poet she believed him to be. He had been addicted to a kind of exclusive masculinity, and only within her care, the shield of her above and around him, could he find the courage to melt and grow.

In *The Prelude* he said as much to her:

> I too exclusively esteemed that love,
> And sought that beauty, which as Milton sings,
> Hath terror in it. Thou didst soften down
> This over-sternness; but for thee, sweet friend,
> My soul, too reckless of mild grace, had been
> Far longer what by Nature it was framed –
> Longer retained its countenance severe –
> A rock with torrents roaring, with the clouds
> Familiar, and a favourite of the stars;
> But thou didst plant its crevices with flowers,
> Hang it with shrubs that twinkle in the breeze,
> And teach the little birds to build their nests
> And warble in its chambers.

Their intimacy was real. 'Neither absence nor Distance nor Time can ever break the Chain that binds me to my Brothers,' she wrote. They would wrap up together inside a single coat to stay warm. Her breath, he said, 'was a kind of gentler spring/That went before my steps'.

Dorothy, or Dolly as she had been called by her parents, loved robins, and there was something robin-like about her: the needle brilliance of their song, their alert restlessness, the tiny, flicker-instant acuity of body and being. She was not sweet in her person, more ardent than that, with a gypsy wildness in her, so that her eyes burned and flashed for almost anyone who met her, like the gold leaf in the electrometer that Coleridge saw.

It was this quality, her ability to respond to the instant, with an immediate attachment to what was in front of her eyes, that allowed her to teach the men around her how to see the world. Joseph Gill's diary shows that he bought her a notebook when they were at Racedown, but it has disappeared, and there is no written record of what she had been seeing there, as there is for part of the following year in Somerset. But when in March 1798 she wrote in her journal that 'A quiet shower of snow was in the air,' that is a moment, as Pamela Woof has written, that tells you who she was. The snow in Dorothy's perception is 'simultaneously both hovering and falling; the silent snow stays and does not stay in the air. Dorothy conveys at once the temporary and the timelessness.' Those moments of transient beauty were part of her daily experience. She saw 'the moonshine like herrings in the water', and the moonlight lying on the hills like snow. Categories blurred: the change of season became an active, animated process: 'The Fern of the mountain now spreads yellow veins among the trees'; the stars were 'almost like butterflies or skylarks in motion & lightness'. She heard the 'unseen birds singing in the mist' and saw the 'turf fading into mountain road'. She loved to look for nests in the privet and the roses; everything was part of a naked meeting with an exactly encountered and constantly shifting world.

There was nothing saccharine about this. She loved 'the strength with which nature has endowed me', and was indifferent to the demands and limits of femininity, loving solitary walks alone in the moonlight when in her early twenties, not submitting to the kind of ignorance thought suitable for many girls of her class and upbringing, socially engaged, giving money to beggars. She was busy, practical, organising a household around the poet who lived alongside her, broiling the gizzard of a hen with some mutton for his supper, baking bread and pies, sewing and laundering, writing letters, copying out his verses.

Over this entire relationship, of such intimacy and such mutual interpenetration – and with such undisputed dominance of male over female – hangs the question of Annette Vallon and her daughter Caroline. Racedown was a mirror-image of the situation Wordsworth had left behind in France. He and his sister were now living together in Dorset as he and the mother of his child were not in Blois. He was looking after and tending to a young child, Basil Montagu, as he was not his own daughter in France.

Guilt stalks these arrangements, and Dorothy's unqualified admiration of and service for her brother look like the necessary balm for a man besieged by it. Racedown was a parodic rerunning of the married life William had not begun in France. He had saved both Dorothy and Basil from the isolation and difficulty to which they might otherwise have been condemned, but to save them he had left Annette and Caroline to the same fate.

Did Wordsworth abandon one woman and child to attend to another woman and child? And for his own convenience? Or was it that only with Dorothy, and not with Annette, could he see his way to being the poet he knew he wanted to be? Writing in *The Prelude* of his years of despair at Racedown – and never admitting in that poem or anywhere else to the existence of Annette or her child – he very nearly said that. Dorothy was his saviour because she saw a poet in him and was prepared to fight for that poet. She was

> the belovèd woman in whose sight
> Those days were passed – now speaking in a voice
> Of sudden admonition like a brook
> That did but cross a lonely road; and now
> Seen, heard and felt, and caught at every turn,
> Companion never lost through many a league –

Maintained for me a saving intercourse
With my true self (for, though impaired, and changed
Much, as it seemed, I was no further changed
Than as a clouded, not waning moon);
She, in the midst of all, preserved me still
A Poet, made me seek beneath that name,
My office upon earth.

It is the most beautiful metaphor of love, of a woman as a mountain brook coming and going along the same valley as the road the poet is taking, bringing her irrigating, generous presence to the drought of his journey and his despair. In later revisions he added the beautiful suggestion that in the darkness of the waning moon, '*She whispered still that brightness would return*'. The moon would wax again. Love is in that line, love given and heard. There is a suggestion, as often in what he would write about her, of suppressed desire, in the physical intimacy of 'Seen, heard and felt, and caught at every turn', in the giving liquidity of her presence, in the brook's gentle washing of him and perhaps even in the atmosphere around 'intercourse', which by the late 1790s had already begun to carry the implications of 'sexual connection'. There is no suggestion of equality between them. She is the servant, he the walking hero; she quietly attends, he struggles with his greatness. He relies on her and dominates her; he uses her and she conforms to the idea that she is there to be used. One version of her usefulness is the strictness with which she can admonish him. Both master and servant are happy for one to be reproved by the other, and to understand that admonition as a form of love.

Here then, on this summer evening in early June 1797, assembled together in the small parlour of Racedown, with the oil cloth on the floor, and an air of warmth and mutual affection and value in the room – all his life Coleridge would remember the welcome they gave him this evening – the sun dropping outside, these three people, each in their varied, multi-layered conditions of longing and despair, genius and trouble, sit down together to talk, to discuss what they have written and seen, what they might write, what they have been and what they might yet be. It is the seeding moment of this year.

Coleridge came to love and revere them both, as one sensibility in two people. Much later, he wrote to Dorothy about their brother, who had come along with him and Wordsworth on a walking tour through the north of England:

> Your Br. John is one of you; a man who hath solitary usings
> of his own Intellect, deep in feeling, with a subtle Tact, a
> swift instinct of Truth & Beauty.

One of you: as if 'Wordsworth' is not the name of a person but a way of being, not entirely communicative to others, with a prompt tactility but unseen depths, both a flickering quickness and an immanence in all of them, as if their dwelling was some way far below the surface, profoundly attractive and curiously removed.

Sit in the valley of the little River Sydeford below the house, in the shadow of its willows and alders, with the evening hatch of olives speckling the yard of air above the water, the cattle grazing in the last sunlight on the sloping fields, their long-bodied shadows patched across the pasture, and an owl announcing itself in the wood across the valley, and it is not difficult to see the three of them there beyond the darkened panes of the parlour windows.

The owl is muted, like a trumpet with a cushion in its mouth. The robins are still singing in the hollies, one on each side of the river, bright as water. Next to them the owl is throaty-chesty. If a cough could sing, it would sound like this.

There is a sheet on the table, for want of a tablecloth. Coleridge is asleep upstairs. Wordsworth at the table looks across to Dorothy, where she is transcribing from his notebooks. Rough pages lie torn out between them, and she is copying in her neater more regular hand from his tragedy *The Borderers*.

He is looking at her, but there is a vacancy in his eye and he is looking across her, through her, his own pen poised over a notebook, as she is busy copying.

What is this word? she asks. *Sublimity?*

No, no. *Sterility.*

They sit there with a kind of contentment between them, no tension, a jointness, ease.

What does this say Will? I am the devil?

No, he half laughs with his outgoing breath. No, 'I am the *dark.*'

The dark? She laughs at him.

It runs on to the next line: 'I am the dark/Embracer of the superlunary world.'

As he speaks, the life-flame in him is barely visible. Only now and then, as some breeze blows over him, her breeze, a movement and change becomes apparent, a reanimation of the suspended life, a breath across coals. Wherever his vacant eye looks, he can see through to the bones and the soft inner parts. But that is because he is also transparent to himself, and in himself finds the boneyard of the past, a littered emptiness, the ashy remains of what he thought he might have been. Behind it, distant, is some other, larger and half-forgotten mountain world, his time in the Alps or in north Wales, his childhood in the Lakes. In certain lights he looks as gaunt as a new-dropped lamb.

3

Searching

June 1797

Coleridge stayed at Racedown for the next three weeks, and the talk began. For months Wordsworth's poetry had been fragmentary, fierce and strange, moving between the worlds of doubt and guilt, finding significance on the borders of madness. He read his poems to Coleridge. A set of sketches and revisions of one of them has survived on the reverse side of the same large folio sheet as his lines on the baker's cart, with further thoughts and rethoughts of it on a neighbouring sheet, both now in the Wordsworth archive at Dove Cottage.

Looking at these repetitive, hesitant drafts of something Wordsworth would come to call 'Incipient Madness' is like observing a man feeling for poetry with his fingertips in the dark.

There were at least twelve uncertain and twitchy stages. From the first moment are three words:

You see the

It is a tiny eruptive nodule of poetic substance focused on a ruined building, a small cottage or shed.

He pulls back a foot or two and starts again:

Though open to the sky yet stained with smoke
You see the swallows nest has dropp'd away
A wretched covert 'tis for man or beast
And when the poor mans horse that shelters there
Turns from the beating wind and open sky
The iron links with which his feet are clogg'd
Mix their dull clanking with the heavy sound
Of falling rain a melancholy

That has come easily, without correction, on this otherwise heavily corrected sheet, so materially realised that it seems likely to have been something seen by Wordsworth on his walks in Dorset. This poetry is already autobiographical, and its atmosphere describes the man Wordsworth was in his darkest hours. 'You' is 'you' the reader or the passer-by; it is also Wordsworth himself, and the 'you' also seems identified with the horse and his hobbling chains, both man and animal a prisoner, dulled by the conditions life has imposed, sheltering in a wreck of a building for which all hope is gone and which even the swallows have deserted. Coleridge accused Wordsworth of being a *'spectator ab extra'* – an observer from outside whatever conditions or predicament he was describing – but here the 'covert', the hiding place, is wretched for man or beast, no matter which, and all these creatures – Wordsworth, the horse, the poor man, the swallow, you – are inhabiting the same desolate landscape.

But the setting is not entirely true. There is a whiff of cliché in the air. The magazines of the 1790s were full of tragic scenes of rural poverty, and the word 'melancholy' seems to bring the movement to a halt. So Wordsworth stops and tries again:

And when the poor mans horse that hither comes
For shelter turns ab

That too, for whatever reason, is a dead end. And he takes
another run:

> And open sky the passenger may hear
> The iron links with which his feet ~~are~~ were clogged
> Mix their dull clanking with the heavy sound
> Of falling rain, a melancholy thing
> To any man who has a heart to feel. –

Those final words at last ring with an air of Wordsworth's own
truth. That is his subject: the grandeur in the beatings of the
heart.

But whatever this poem is, it won't come clean. He introduces
his own recent visit to the cottage:

> But two nights gone
> ~~I chanced to~~ I passed this cottage and within I heard
> The poor man's lonely horse ~~who~~ that hither comes
> For shelter, turning from the beating rain
> And open sky, and as he turned, I heard

At one level the horse was a 'who', but Wordsworth revises that
to the more conventionally impersonal 'that'. The various
elements and players need to be organised: himself, the horse,
the place, the stormy night, the connections between them. The
revisions now turn scratchy and directionless:

> I heard him turning from the beating wind –
> And open sky and as he turn'd I heard

But he cannot decide what the horse is doing there: 'to weather
the night storm' or 'to weather out the tempests'? 'Within these
walls', 'within these roofless walls', or 'these fractur'd walls'? Then,

47

at draft twelve of these few recalcitrant lines, another set of ingredients appears which suddenly mobilises this dark fragment of
experience:

> But two nights gone, I cross'd this dreary moor
> In the ~~still~~ clear moonlight, when reached the hut
> I looked within but all was still and dark

> Only within the ruin, I beheld
> At a small distance on the dusky ground
> A broken pain which glitter'd to the moon
> And seemed akin to life. – Another time
> The winds of autumn drove me oer the heath
> Heath in a dark night by the storm compelled
> > the hardships of that season

Those lines are still in thrall to an earlier way of doing poetry –
'dusky' is dead jargon; 'glitter'd to' is patently false language – but
that broken pain/pane of glass on the dark floor of the ruined
shed, a lifeless thing that seems to be full of life, grips and obsesses
him:

> I found my sickly heart had tied itself
> Even to this speck of glass – It could produce
> a feeling as of absence
> > on the moment when my sight
> Should feed on it again. ~~For~~ many a long month
> ~~I felt~~ Confirm'd this strange incontinence; my eye
> Did every evening measure the moon's height
> And forth I went before her yellow beams
> Could overtop the elm-trees oer the heath
> I sought the r   and I found
> That   speck more precious to my soul
> Than was the moon in heaven

Here now at last are the elements for a strange and lonely poem of experience on the edges of despair, an act of empathy. It is driven by an obsessive and disordered frame of mind, dissociated from the normalities of human love and community, in a world where, in its final form, a looming morbidity infects and pollutes all living things. It is a poem written by the desperate man Coleridge had come to cure.

Incipient Madness

~~I crossed the dreary~~ I crossed the dreary moor
In the clear moonlight when I reached the hut
I enter'd in, but all was still and dark
Only within the ruin I beheld
At a small distance, on the dusky ground
A broken pane which glitter'd ~~to~~ in the moon
And seemed akin to life. There is a mood
A settled temper of the heart, when grief,
Becomes an instinct, fastening on ~~the~~ all things
That promise food, doth like a sucking babe
Create it where it is not. From this ~~hour~~ time
I found my sickly heart had tied itself
Even to this speck of glass – It could produce
a feeling as of absence
                              on the moment when my sight
Should feed on it again. ~~For~~ many a long month
~~I felt~~ Confirm'd this strange incontinence; my eye
Did every evening measure the moon's height
And forth I went soon as her yellow beams
Could overtop the elm-trees. Oer the heath
I went, I reached the cottage, and I found
Still undisturbed and glittering in its place
That speck of glass more precious to my soul
Than was the moon in heaven. Another time

The winds of Autumn drove me o'er the heath
One gloomy evening: By the storm compell'd
The poor man's horse that feeds along the lanes
Had hither come ~~within~~ among these fractur'd walls
To weather out the night; and as I pass'd
While restlessly he turn'd from the fierce wind
And from the open sky, I heard, within,
The iron links with which his feet were clogg'd
Mix their dull clanking with the heavy ~~sound~~ noise
Of falling rain. I started from the spot
And heard the sound still following in the wind

These lines, firmly in a gothic tradition, nevertheless stand as a challenge to everything the eighteenth-century inheritance of elegant rural landscapes might have suggested or proposed. The heart of what Wordsworth sees is not the well-framed picture but the broken pane of glass, and the haunted sound of chains blown towards him on the vast and homeless winds of heaven. There is no connection yet to any larger significance – any movement beyond the gothic – that connection would have to wait until Coleridge had changed his relationship to the world.

There was one more poem, his most recent, that Wordsworth was keen to have Coleridge hear, and it marked an emergence from this darkness. He read him this first version of 'The Ruined Cottage', not giving it to him to read but making sure he heard it from his own lips. It is a descendant of the dark poetry which had poured out of him over the previous six or nine months, but this is different. In 'The Ruined Cottage', suffering and the disordered world are seen in tranquillity. The gothic furniture has been dispensed with, much of it hived off into 'Incipient Madness'. Instead, a calm and beneficent air emerges from a sad and simple story of suffering and failure, nothing over-heightened, no melodramatic lighting, but a rich simplicity in language and setting by which the place itself of the ruined cottage and its surroundings comes to portray the people whose lives it describes. His previous rhetorical habits have dropped away. Abstractions and pat responses are banished in favour of the tender, corporeal realities in the life of a poor woman and her family.

In Wordsworth's poem, the poet comes across a ruin and meets an old man, a pedlar, who had known the place many years before, when happiness had glowed from its windows. 'I see around me here,' the Pedlar says,

> Things which you cannot see. We die, my Friend,
> Nor we alone, but that which each man loved
> And prized in his peculiar nook of earth
> Dies with him, or is changed, and very soon
> Even of the good is no memorial left.

In the garden is a neglected spring, and the poet goes to drink there:

> A spider's web hung to the water's edge
> And on the wet and slimy foot-stone lay
> The useless fragment of a wooden bowl.
> It moved my very heart.

A young woman, Margaret, had lived in the remote cottage, and always welcomed passers-by. Her husband Robert had worked in the garden, often late,

> till the day-light
> Was gone, and every leaf and flower were lost
> In the dark hedges.

51

One or two other poets – Southey, Cowper – had managed to write of simplicity and suffering in this low, gentle, absorbent, un-self-proclaiming way, in which the reality underlying the poetry matters more than the surface of the poetry itself, but 'The Ruined Cottage' is something new in Wordsworth's life. Its facts, like those leaves and flowers sinking back into the darkness of the evening hedge, have become the modest elements of an unquiet landscape. The whole poem exists in a border state, 'without the application of gross and violent stimulus', as he would describe the qualities of valuable poetry the following year, but attentive to the sorrows of the story it tells.

It is tempting to think, given the permeability of the boundary in Wordsworth's mind between the remembered and the imagined, between some other reality and his own experience, that there is autobiography underlying this tale of distress. Margaret is one of the many women in Wordsworth's poetry who are left with their children to fend for themselves, and suffer as a result. He said himself that in 'several passages describing the employment & demeanour of Margaret during her affliction, I was indebted to observations made in Dorsetshire', but there was a more powerful stimulus than the poor he met on the paths and roads of Dorset: the knowledge and memory of the woman and child he had abandoned in France.

This sort of figure had haunted Wordsworth's imagination before he had met – or left – Annette Vallon, and they appear, usually in much more exaggerated form, in the poetry of many of his contemporaries. But here, in the simple, first version of 'The Ruined Cottage', there is a kind of conceptual democracy at work, by which Margaret's modest truth is allowed to be as valid as any other. There is no need to exaggerate, because exaggeration is a form of obscurity. And so the poem looks carefully at the quiet facts around her. The bad years had come – war and summers when 'the fields were left with half a harvest', a sickness everywhere and no work:

Searching: June 1797

> shoals of artizans
> Were from their daily labour turned away
> To hang for bread on parish charity,
> They and their wives and children, happier far
> Could they have lived as do the little birds
> That peck along the hedges or the kite
> That makes her dwelling in the mountain rocks.

Robert was driven to the army as the only source of employment, and before he went, left for Margaret and their children a bag holding ten guineas, eight months' pay for a labourer, given as a bounty to all who volunteered. She waited five years for him to return, a kind of vacuity in her:

> in that broken arbour she would sit
> The idle length of half a sabbath day;
> There, where you see the toadstool's lazy head;
> And when a dog passed by she still would quit
> The shade and look abroad.

Dorothy copied out for Coleridge the lines describing Margaret's paused and eviscerated life, in which, sitting in the ruin of her cottage,

> Her tattered clothes were ruffled by the wind
> Even at the side of her own fire

and he sent them in amazement in a letter to a Bristol friend, evidence that Wordsworth had broken through to a new level of poetic speech, in which the story was embodied in language that claimed no status greater than what it described. Wordsworth's language had itself become the medium for empathy and democracy, and for that Coleridge recognised greatness in him.

53

4

Settling

July 1797

Coleridge brought the Wordsworths over to Stowey from Racedown at the very beginning of July, at first for what they all thought was to be a short visit. He borrowed a one-horse chaise and drove them – 'always ... very cautious' – all day along the execrable Dorset and Somerset roads.

Even at first sight, arriving on a July evening, Nether Stowey is a place for entrancement. From the castle motte above the village, England is there in all its beauty. The low nose of the Quantocks pushes out dark blue and gold in the shadows towards the sea at Kilve. The sun is setting, at nine o'clock, well to the north of west over the Bristol Channel. The sheep grazing around the Norman mound are haloed by that last light. It falls on the power station at Hinckley, on the two purple, shadowed islands in the channel, Steep Holm and Flat Holm, with the line of Wales behind them, beyond the sky-blue band of sea.

Is this what people have always seen? Or am I seeing it because Coleridge has taught me to see it? It feels golden, honeyed, a sweetness poured over the country and into it, into the fescues and little vetches and vetchlings at my feet, all of which are glowing now as if they were part of the mended world.

Down the streets of the little town below the castle, the swifts are sweet-screaming, whistles blown through atom-wide mouths,

Honeyed world

Stowey swifts sweet-screaming

FOLLOWING PAGE: And what if all of animated nature be but organic Harps

with the martins above them, and midges alight in the sun-shafts between the buildings. Beyond the tile and slate of the roofs and the church tower are the blocks of woodland, the golden windows of the cornfields, the hedgerow oaks now nearly black, gone monumental in the dusk, the dabbed dark ink marks of summer trees.

Everything is still, but a dog barks and the young rooks chatter and caw between them. The swifts are making sudden power turns in among the buildings, weaving their paths down South Lane, back over the houses in Castle Street, over the road to Spaxton and then into the narrow canyon between the cottages in Lime Street before climbing up over the roofs, again and again. A stream from the hills runs down the streets in a wide stone gutter, almost soundless now in its reduced summer flow. Even on a beautiful sunlit evening, the little town closes by the time the sun sets. There are drinkers in the pubs, and the sound of televisions comes through open windows. If anywhere can seem well, this place does.

In reality, Nether Stowey in the 1790s was no dream world. It was still connected to its medieval past. Every winter, pairs of heavy oxen ploughed the red Quantocks soil. Old Somerset men talked in a way William Holland, the Oxford-educated vicar of Over Stowey, couldn't understand, shouting at their animals 'Jubb along, jubb along' – meaning, Holland guessed, that the vast oxen should somehow be skipping and jumping down their furrows. Every Tuesday, farm women brought their eggs and butter for sale to the market cross in the centre of Stowey. The poor climbed the hills to the commons, called the Stowey Customs, to cut the gorse or 'furze' for their bread ovens, bracken for animal bedding, picking up fallen wood for their own fires. The fields of the parish still bore their ancient names: Cockley Land, Strawberry Hill, Fuzz Ground, Great Warren, Castle Ground.

This rooted, intractable and impoverished life was dense with
pockets of isolation. Fevers broke out in individual villages, and
all hoped that the contagion would not spread across the fields.
On occasions a whole village forgot its connection to the rest of
the world, and when Holland arrived to conduct a service the
people asked him to remind them what time or date it was. In
some parts of the parish the poor still celebrated Christmas on
Twelfth Night, as the whole of England had a century or two
before.

In the winter, with lanes deep in mud, the vicar rode around
like a modern man in an ancient world, his servant Morris
following on foot. 'I had an umbrella and was obliged frequently
to shake off the snow and Morris every now and then shook the
skirts of my coats.' Arriving at one of the outlying hamlets in the
parish, wearing his clerical black and gaiters, he had the church
bell tolled, and the congregation walked slowly in from the fields,
a scene from the Brueghels. With sermons, weddings, baptisms,
funerals, he regulated the life of his flock. Forty days after the
birth of a child, according to the teachings of Leviticus, Holland
liked to 'church' the mother at a special ceremony in which a veil
was worn, reaccommodating women who were considered
defiled by the process of giving birth.

Returning from a summer walk, Holland called on an 'old sick
dropsical woman'. She was living in a kind of horror-slum which
he called 'the Indian village' – a few hovels gathered on the edge
of the Quantock woods. Her house

> was a shocking place. No chimney for the smoke – I could
> scarcely stand it, and was almost suffocated to death. The
> poor woman was brought downstairs, and her daughter and
> grand-daughters around her, and she gasping for breath.
> They told us that one part of the house was sold to Davies,
> who was to make a chimney for them.

The tiny hut had been subdivided on the condition that the man called Davies would take the smoke out of the rooms in which the family was trying to live. But Holland knew him. 'Davies is one of the greatest rascals that haunts the hills.' He happened that morning to be outside, in the field making hay. Holland went up to him, and asked why he had not done what he had promised. Davies lied calmly to his vicar.

> The man was civil to me, and assured me that he was by the agreement to do no such thing. At this the old woman's daughter rushed out of doors, and there was such a terrible set to that I and my family walked off; but the sound of their voices, shrill and deep, followed us most part of the way to Over Stowey. A sad set – the wretched inhabitants of three or four huts, like a nest in the bosom of Quantock, and living there without law or religion or the fear of God or man; for they never come to church, and what to do with them I scarce can tell.

These are the people of Wordsworth's poetry seen from the point of view of the hierarchy presiding over them. Holland may have felt resourceless in meeting them, but his answers were the stock ones: fear the law, submit to the disciplines of the Church of England, restore the picture because the picture is the frame of goodness. These were precisely the attitudes that the young men of the next generation were set on changing.

The Coleridges were embedded in this beautiful and troubled world. The three of them – Coleridge himself, his wife Sara and their son little Hartley – were living with a much-loved maid called Nanny in a small cottage up at the top end of Lime Street. They had a well and a garden at the back, in which Coleridge thought he could 'raise vegetables & corn enough for myself & Wife, and feed a couple of shouted & grunting Cousins from the refuse'. There were indeed two pigs, plus ducks and geese, and some apple trees whose trunks were 'crooked earth-ward' and whose boughs 'hang above us in an arborous roof'.

The house had three small dark rooms on each floor, in which the fires smoked and draughts found their way through windows and doors. The thatch was half-rotten. Anything left there would get damp. On wash days, the 'little Hovel is almost afloat – poor Sara tired off her legs'. On the street side, a cobbled pavement stood up out of the mud that caked the street itself. A small millstream ran down the side of the pavement, 'the dear gutter of Stowey' which Coleridge said he preferred to any purling Italian brook, but the road itself was dusty in summer and in winter 'an impassable Hog-stye ... a Slough of Despond'. The half-foetid smell of tan-pits at the back came wafting over everything. At night, the people living in the parish workhouse just down from the cottage fought and argued, so that as Coleridge joked to Sara, Lime Street more often than not was 'vocal with the Poorhouse Nightingales'.

Coleridge had been married to Sara for nearly two years. She was the sister of Robert Southey's wife Edith, and all of them had been planning to set out on a dream expedition to America, where, with eight others, they were going to establish a Utopian community called Pantisocracy, meaning 'the rule of all', to be set up on the cheap land along the banks of the Susquehanna River in Ohio. It was to be 'a *Social Colony*, in which there was to be a community of property and where all that was selfish was to be proscribed'. There were to be no formal laws, but 'by excluding all the little deteriorating passions – injustice, wrath, anger, clamour and evil-speaking, – an example would be set to the world of Human Perfectibility'.

Stephen Fricker, Sarah's father – only when she married Coleridge and at his insistence did she drop the 'h' from her name – had been a wine and coal merchant and publican in Bristol, with a good house in the country and another in Bath.

Her mother, who came from a rather more upmarket family, with moneyed connections, had overseen the family's life, and they had lived among the fashionable, in 'a smartish way'. Sarah and her sisters were well educated, learning mathematics and grammar, history and French as befitted young women of *bon ton*. Sarah all her life used to drop her h's in a distinguished, relaxed, upper-class way, and insert little French phrases into her conversation, discussing events *entre nous* and *en passant*, emphasising, *au fait* and *au fond*, how important it was to remain *au courant*. The seal she used to close up her letters, however despondent their contents might have become, year after year impressed the phrase '*Toujours gai*' into the wax.

Stephen Fricker had spent beyond his means, and had failed at every scheme he had tried. In 1786, when Sarah was sixteen, he was declared bankrupt. A few months later he died, broken, aged forty-eight. The Fricker family was destitute. Their mother opened a dame school in Bristol and the teenage girls were set to work as needlewomen. There was zest and spark in them. They retained their 'polished, calculated light style', and for all their poverty had moved happily in the modern, radical, open-minded Bristol circles to which Robert Southey had introduced Coleridge.

When Sarah first met him, at dinner one day, unexpectedly, he had been on a walking tour in Wales and had returned 'brown as a berry'. Her first evaluation was undeceived: 'Plain but eloquent and clever. His clothes were worn out; his hair wanted cutting. He was a dreadful figure.' Southey, who was 'very neat, gay and smart', agreed: 'He is a diamond set in lead.'

The diamond could talk, the heady prospects of 'the Scheme of Pantisocracy' were in the air, Sarah herself was a woman of courage and self-possession, both forthright and capable of discretion and delicacy, and within a fortnight of meeting they had agreed to marry. Things did not run smooth. Coleridge seems to have committed himself to her at first only philosophically and as a duty. He and Southey both thought she would make an excellent Pantisocratic bride, just as her sister Edith would for Southey and a third Fricker sister, Mary, already had for a third Bristol poet-Pantisocrat, Robert Lovell. The young idealists had plumped for brides *en bloc*. On top of that, Coleridge was still agonisingly and undecidedly in love with another girl, Mary Evans, and when he went back to London and Cambridge for a while, he failed – to Southey's and Lovell's consternation and disgust – to give a thought to Sarah or to write her a single line, despite writing to others in the same household.

Coleridge's chaos alienated Lovell and the other Frickers, who advised against the marriage and swirled superior offers in front of Sarah's eyes. Two rich young men proposed when Coleridge was away, but she would have neither. When Coleridge returned to Bristol early in 1795, something had changed, and he could begin to be amazed by this beautiful, competent, strong-minded woman, who was quite clearly and courageously in love with him, despite what all around her were saying to the contrary. By the summer of that year he had fallen in love with her in return.

For £5 a year, before their marriage, they rented a cottage in Clevedon, on the shores of the Bristol Channel, where the tallest of the roses in the garden looked in at the window of the first-floor bedroom, and there, away from the world, in August 1795, in anticipation of their happiness, Coleridge had written his first great poem.

As much as Wordsworth's twin entrancements with Annette Vallon and Michel Beaupuy, and his lines on the baker's cart, this poem, called 'Effusion 35' in 1795, later 'The Eolian Harp', stands at the headwaters of the Quantocks year. Coleridge and Sara – no 'h' was an attempt to classicise her – are together on a warm and quiet August evening, within earshot of the sea. They sit beside their cottage, 'o'ergrown/With white-flower'd Jasmin, and the broad-leav'd Myrtle', and while Venus appears in the evening sky they watch the light fading from the clouds. Quietness envelops them, and the revolutionary world is a universe away.

> How exquisite the scents
> Snatch'd from yon bean-field! and the world *so* hush'd!
> The stilly murmur of the distant Sea
> Tells us of Silence.

Detailed, located, precise, simple, receptive. In the window of the cottage they have placed an Aeolian harp, a ten-stringed musical instrument, a yard long and about five inches square, part of the domestic equipment for all aesthetic middle-class families in the late eighteenth century, by which the wind passing over the strings plays strange and ethereal music, seeming at times like audible moonlight, quiveringly present and absent as the breeze shifts across it and the vibrations in one string summon the harmonics in the others.

For Coleridge, writing as if talking gently and conversationally, almost whispering, abandoning the public and stentorian address of so much eighteenth-century verse, including his own, this floating coming and going of the wind-music becomes, first, a gently erotic replaying of the feeling between the two of them:

> And that simplest Lute,
> Plac'd length-ways in the clasping casement, hark!
> How by the desultory breeze caress'd,
> Like some coy Maid half yielding to her Lover,
> It pours such sweet upbraidings, as must needs
> Tempt to repeat the wrong!

Then, as the gusts strengthen over it, the music seems to create a world of delicious fantasy, a soft and suggestive prefiguring of the dreams of Kubla Khan:

And now, its strings
Boldlier swept, the long sequacious notes
Over delicious surges sink and rise,
Such a soft floating witchery of sound
As twilight Elfins make, when they at eve
Voyage on gentle gales from Faery-Land,
Where *Melodies* round honey-dropping flowers,
Footless and wild, like birds of Paradise,
Nor pause nor perch, hov'ring on untam'd wing!

Coleridge's mind knew no divisions. He may have been imagining these sounds as audible hummingbirds, but he was thinking, too. 'I feel strongly and I think strongly,' he wrote to a friend the following year, 'but I seldom feel without thinking or think without feeling. Hence, though my poetry has in general a hue of tenderness or passion over it, yet it seldom exhibits unmixed and simple tenderness or passion. My philosophical opinions are blended with or deduced from my feelings.'

And so the drifting half-sounds of the wind-harp, as if summoned from nowhere by nothing, become in his mind not merely the charged atmosphere between him and his wife-to-be, or a dream of sugared otherness, but the manifestation of everything that essentially *is*, in a universe full of significance. The Aeolian harp, it occurs to him, may be the mute world speaking, a legible or audible version of what could, if you were properly aware, be heard everywhere and all the time as the music of existence.

And what if all of animated nature
Be but organic Harps diversely framed,
That tremble into thought, as o'er them sweeps
Plastic and vast, one intellectual breeze,
At once the Soul of each, and God of all?

That trembling into thought, that vast 'plastic' breeze – the adjective means what it does in Greek, the moulding wind of a divine and universal spirit – blows through the Quantocks year. It is the shaping wind, standing opposed to the winds that often threaten in Wordsworth's poetry, where they are the unsettling agents of otherness, bordering on the meaningless and the broken.

The idea of the world as a harp to be played on by the winds of intelligibility and significance is rarely absent from Coleridge's mind, although this poem eventually withdraws from such a suggestion. Sara could not agree with him that the harp in the window might be speaking with the voice of God, and she reproved him for his heresy. But the suggestion remained – in the poem, in Coleridge's mind, and soon, under Coleridge's influence, colonising the mind of the Wordsworths – of a beautiful connectedness in all living things, by which all were part of one life, a coherence to which human society should be tuned and in which poetry, if it was to be valuable, needed to find its language.

At the end of 1796 the Coleridges moved to Nether Stowey, and into the frankly unsatisfactory house in Lime Street. An old woman called Mrs Rich came in to help Sara with the housework. She lived next door with a poor Stowey man called Daddy Rich. They had a son for whom they had scrimped and saved to set up in a currying business, cleaning the flesh from hides before they were tanned. The son knew no gratitude, had abandoned the business to go into the Marines and left his parents grieving for his absence. As Coleridge wrote to Southey, Daddy and Mrs Rich spent their lives

> wishing & praying only to see him once more/and about a fortnight ago he returned, discharged as an ideot. – The day after I came back to Stowey, I heard a cry of Murder, & rushed into the House, where I found the poor Wretch,

whose physiognomy is truly hellish, beating his Father most
unmercifully with a great stick –/I seized him & pinioned
him to the wall, till the peace-officer came –/– He vows
vengeance on me; but what is really shocking he never sees
little Hartley but he grins with hideous distortions of rage,
& hints that he'll do him a mischief. –And the poor old
People, who just get enough to feed themselves, are now
absolutely pinched/& never fall to sleep without fear &
trembling, lest the Son should rise in a fit of insanity, &
murder them.

In the Lime Street poorhouse, men in a fit would be given gin –
a whole bottle if need be – to calm them. A man living there
had twice made his sister-in-law pregnant. His brother, her
husband, had been transported to Australia. The man told
William Holland, the vicar, that he wished to know whether it
was 'more sinful in the eye of God' to live with her as his mistress
or his wife. Holland had no answer. Conventional morality could
not accommodate a living husband imprisoned on the far side of
the world. The troubles of the 1790s had found their way into
every nook and cranny, and this combination of war, despair,
hunger, a global perspective and the fracturing of lives lay as the
background to much of what the poets would write in their year
together.

The Coleridges had dreamed of a perfect rural retreat in which
the consolations of nature, a bit of ground to cultivate and vegetables to grow, would provide the life in which Hartley could
blossom and his parents could be happy. They had been promised for a moment a beautiful little smallholding in the valley at
Adscombe, the far side of Over Stowey and just under the
Quantocks, but that had fallen through, and Lime Street was all
that was on offer. It was scarcely the place for bliss, but as one of
their visitors wrote to his sister, 'Here you can be happy without

superfluities. Coleridge has a fine little boy about nine or ten months old. This child is a noble, healthy-looking fellow, has strong eyebrows and beautiful eyes. It is a treat, a luxury, to see Coleridge hanging over his infant and talking to it, and fancying what he will be in future days.'

Without doubt, gaiety rollicked around the house, for all their poverty and discomfort, toothache and neuralgia, and for all Coleridge's habit of walking up and down, 'composing poetry, instead of coming to bed at proper hours'. Among their friends this was a time of real delight, of games and laughter, of cups of flip and jugs of cider. Anna and John Cruikshank, the son of the Earl of Egmont's steward and an admirer of Coleridge, had a child the same age as Hartley and often had them to supper at Ivy Cottage in Castle Street. Sara was friends with Mrs Roskilly, whose husband, the curate, 'a most amiable liberal-minded man', ran the boarding school. James Cole the watchmaker and his wife, John Brice the vicar of Aisholt, a beautiful green hamlet on the edge of the hills, and his daughters, and a whole family of Chesters, John and his sisters, all welcomed them in.

These were the more democratically-minded of Stowey's inhabitants, the free thinkers, those for whom events in France and on the Continent had not been mere catastrophe. The conservative elements of the town continued to dislike and suspect the Coleridges. One Stowey woman thought Coleridge 'an absent-minded, opinionated man, talking everybody down, fatiguing to listen to', while William Holland, the diary-keeping rector of Over Stowey, despised anyone who associated with them.

The worlds of the Georgian vicar and the Romantic poets collide on the very first page of the earliest surviving volume of Holland's diary, from October 1799. He and his wife Mary have gone shopping for a gown at Frank Poole's 'every-thing shop' in St Mary's Street, where, as usual, the unctuous Mr Poole 'smiled and bowed graciously'. Then:

> Saw that Democratic hoyden Mrs. Coleridge, who looked so
> like a frisky girl or something worse that I was not surprised
> that a Democratic libertine should choose her for a wife.
> The husband gone to London suddenly – no one here can
> tell why.

Here, from nowhere, a glimpse of the hostile world in which the poets were living. *Hoyden* – rude, rough, dirty, saucy, immodest, whorish, sexual, self-sufficient, not submitting to the require-ments of social deference or feminine modesty. *Frisky* – only ever used elsewhere by Holland of horses that had not been adequately exercised. *Something worse* – salacious talk of the Fricker girls' sexual *mores* in Bristol and in London, where, in another euphe-mism, they had been described as 'haberdashers', had reached Stowey. *Democratic* – suspect, Francophile, eroding all that Holland valued most. *Libertine* – the fusion of the worst sexual and political freedoms. *No one here can tell why* – the hostile, supervisory talk in the street. The reality was that the Coleridge marriage was in crisis and 'the husband' had gone north to see the Wordsworths.

What in the end emerges from this cascade of disapproval? The alluring freedom, directness and attractiveness of Sara Coleridge in 1799, a liberty woman in a closed and controlling world. Coleridge when he loved her called her 'Sally Pally', and it is Sally Pally Coleridge one should think of walking the streets of Nether Stowey, indifferent to the sneers of its inhabitants. When Southey, in the midst of a ferocious row with her husband, pouring 'heart-chilling sentiments' into the room, had claimed that he liked Coleridge more than ever, Sara 'affronted [him] into angry Silence by exclaiming What a Story!' It is one of the ironies of this year, so carefully and agonisingly dedicated to the finding and telling of truths, that one of its principal truth-tellers was excluded from its inner circle.

* * *

Coleridge loved the Quantocks, but the centre of Nether Stowey for him, and the reason he was there, was neither a landscape nor a building but a man. Tom Poole was a tanner, in his mid-thirties, the son of a tanner and entirely self-educated, bright-eyed, 'not of a yielding disposition', and with a rough and abrupt manner that he never attempted to refine or conceal.

In the early 1790s he had read *The Rights of Man* by Tom Paine and had been radicalised by the news from France. A network of Pooles – lawyers, landowners, men of the cloth, 'the very top of the yeomanry', the Reverend Holland called them – was spread across Stowey, Bridgwater and the neighbouring villages. Except for Tom's brother Richard, most of them disapproved of him. His cousin Charlotte bristled with resentment: 'Tom Poole,' she told her journal, 'has imbibed some of the wild notions of liberty and equality that at present prevail so much.' He had set up a book society in Stowey, and when Richard Symes, a Bridgwater lawyer, found a young man with a copy of *The Rights of Man* given to him by Poole, he tore it from his hand and stamped it to shreds on the pavement of Castle Street. Effigies of Tom Paine had been burned in Bridgwater and Taunton, and after Poole prevented the same being done in Stowey, stories ran around the rumour-networks of his town that he was now distributing seditious pamphlets. There is no doubting his radicalism. It went much further than a simple concern for the poor of Somerset. When war broke out against France he was unequivocal:

Many thousands of human beings will be sacrificed in the ensuing contest; and for what? To support three or four individuals, called arbitrary kings, in the situation which they or their ancestors have usurped. I consider every Briton who loses his life in the war as much murdered as the King of France, and every one who approves the war, as signing the death warrant of each soldier or sailor that falls.

He tormented Stowey with his democratic sentiments. He talked politics when out shooting woodcock. He thought England 'a declining country, too guiltily leagued with despots'. He told whoever would listen that if he ever had a son he would call him John Hampden, after the great seventeenth-century revolutionary, and was always ready to have some good radical talk in his parlour, providing a comfortable and well-stocked book room in his own house for Coleridge and others to read and write in, helping with his mother – another committed radical – to make the new radical hotbed of the cottage in Lime Street as comfortable as he could. To his cousin Charlotte, he was a propagandist. She thought he always wanted 'to load the higher class of people indiscriminately with opprobrium, and magnifies the virtues, miseries, and oppressed state of the poor in proportion'.

Not surprisingly, Poole started to come to the attention of the government's spy networks. His letters were secretly opened and their contents reported to Whitehall. A Bridgwater friend told him that he was

> considered by Government as the most dangerous person in
> the county of Somerset, and, as it was well known that this
> part of the country was disaffected, the whole mischief was,
> by Government, attributed to me.

Poole laughed at the idea, but his tone was bitter. 'Now an absolute controul exists,' he wrote. The souls of Englishmen were 'as much enslaved as the body in the cell of a Bastile'. That is not far short of revolutionary talk, and William Holland knew him as the enemy:

> Met the patron of democrats, Mr Thomas Poole, who smiled
> and chatted a little. He was on his gray mare, Satan himself
> cannot be more false and hypocritical … very grand and
> important, took out his French gold watch and affected

much the travelled man, coxcomby and with all the
appearance of greatness and liberality he is the most shabby
dodging man to deal with I ever met ... a selfish vain artful
man.

There was undoubtedly a touch of self-importance about Poole.
'For these opinions I would willingly go to the Tower,' he once
said at a meeting in Nether Stowey. 'The Tower indeed!' came
from the corner of the room. 'I should think Ilchester Gaol
would do for you.' And not unlike Joseph Cottle, the Bristol
bookseller, Poole was entranced when the brilliant young radical
poets turned up in Somerset. He had met Coleridge and Southey
in 1794 when they were on a walking tour, scandalising the good
people of Stowey by the violence of their principles, claiming
that Robespierre was a ministering angel of mercy, sent to slay
thousands so that he could save millions. Southey had laid his
head on the table in one Poole house and declared that he would
rather hear of the death of his own father than the death of
Robespierre, a gesture which would have been less effective if his
audience had known that Southey's father was already dead.

The Somerset tanner, concerned for the wellbeing of his
people, on the good side of the increasingly polarised political
divide, full of admiration and reverence for the genius of the
young, also appealed to the poets. They saw in him, with a
certain gentlemanly condescension, a version of the ideal man
who would later appear in Wordsworth's lyrics, above all as the
good shepherd Michael, 'stout of heart, and strong of limb'.

It was an idealisation of Poole in which Poole himself was
prepared to play his part, arranging for six or seven of his friends
to subscribe £40 a year for seven years to save Coleridge from
hackwork and encourage him to write the great works that were
surely in him.

Poole was the equivalent, as a man, of what the Quantocks
could offer as a place. He was an amalgam of the safe and the

free, reliable, practical, enfolding but enlarging, no intellectual rival, but radically minded and providing a bower of friendship, a kind of organic rootedness in which liberty and poetry could blossom. 'Where am I to find rest!' Coleridge had written to him before coming to live in Stowey, when for a few days it looked as if Poole would be unable to find him a house nearby. The answer Coleridge arrived at was: only when I am with you. 'I adhere to Stowey,' he wrote imploringly. Without it, and without him, Coleridge thought he would be 'afloat on the wide sea unpiloted & unprovisioned'. Poole was the home and harbour Coleridge needed and longed for.

The year in the Quantocks was not a question of a few gentle strolls in a charming corner of England, but setting up a colony of radical hope, 'a small company of chosen individuals', in Coleridge's phrase, embracing more than politics could ever embrace, thinking that with the writing of a poetry that was true to the beatings of the heart, with working in the garden, days spent out on the high tops and evenings in the lush richness of the midsummer combes, some kind of change could be wrought in the soul of England.

This was the cluster of ideas-in-a-place to which Coleridge brought Wordsworth and Dorothy in early July 1797. Their arrival was only one part of his more general gathering of friends and allies. It was not to be a lonely year. He had Poole there already. Soon to come was Charles Lamb, his great and brilliant boyhood friend from his school days at Christ's Hospital in London. Also walking down from London was a man he knew only by correspondence, John Thelwall, famous across England for his radical lectures, his still more famous treason trial of 1794, at which he had been acquitted, and his continuing harassment and persecution by the spy system of the Home Office and its attendant bullies. There was a chance that Robert Southey, Sara Coleridge's brother-in-law, would also come, with her sister

Sally Pally

FOLLOWING PAGE: Broken Park

Edith. Coleridge had broken with Southey, but it was to him that he was continuing to write his most intellectualised of letters. The Wedgwood brothers, the Pinneys, his Bristol publisher John Cottle, his unstable pupil and protégé Charles Lloyd – all were to be swept into the Coleridgean embrace. Nether Stowey in his mind was to be a nest of nightingales, singing for the future.

Just how the Wordsworths, the Coleridges, Lamb, Hartley, Nanny and Mrs Rich were crowded into the tiny house, with the prospect of all these others in the offing, is difficult to imagine. At least there was the outside, the vegetable patch and orchard with the leaning tree, the gate and lane at the back leading to Tom Poole's house and garden. There Poole had built a rustic summer house made of slabs of oak bark, with a jasmine trained over them, all under the shade of a lime tree – nothing more richly or thickly honey-scented in early summer – and with four big elms ballooning above them. Beyond that were the hills and the combes. The Quantocks beckoned them that July. It scarcely rained, just over an inch in the whole month, with one dry day succeeding another. The thermometer stood above seventy degrees Fahrenheit on more than twenty of those July afternoons, occasionally climbing into the eighties, and with hot nights to follow.

It was a recipe for English summer freedom. Sometimes the walks were solitary, Wordsworth and Dorothy exploring the world Coleridge had brought them to, Coleridge going out on his own, but often all of them went, six or seven of them heading out into the hills. There was nothing inherently odd about this kind of walking. As William Holland repeatedly described, everybody walked, and not only the poor who had no choice. Errand boys did indeed 'walk from place to place on messages', and one man walked all the way from London to Over Stowey to get a marriage licence, but gentry neighbours also walked to visit each other, or to have tea, to give people news or to deliver the newspaper whose subscription they shared, up the hill to look at the ships in the Bristol Channel with the spying glass, for picnics, with children to look for birds' nests, in the dusk or the early morning, or 'after supper by a fine moonlight'. Husbands and wives, children and young women all went walking on the lanes and paths of the parish.

Walking could be preferable 'to the jogging of the cart', or a pleasure in itself: 'After dinner the young nymphs took a walk ... I walked home by the light of the good moon.' A 'trudge' in the snow, or at night with a lantern, or in the rain with an umbrella, were all part of everyday life. In bad weather the women wore pattens, high-soled wooden overshoes to keep the ordinary shoes dry and above the mud, and men heavy boots.

And so, soon after their arrival, the Wordsworths sauntered off on their own. Coleridge had judged them right. Dorothy suddenly expanded into all-enveloping enthusiasm for a country that felt like a mild version of their childhood mountains, even with woods that seemed to match those that had belonged to the Earl of Lonsdale, who had cheated them of their inheritance for so long:

> ... There is everything here; sea, woods wild as fancy ever painted, brooks clear and pebbly as in Cumberland, villages so romantic; and William and I, in a wander by ourselves, found out a sequestered waterfall in a dell formed by steep hills covered with full-grown timber trees. The woods are as fine as those at Lowther, and the country more romantic; it has the character of the less grand parts of the neighbourhood of the Lakes ...

They had rambled as far as a large seventeenth- and eighteenth-century house, Alfoxden, hipped roof, wide cornice, far-gazing windows, in a large park, with seventy head of deer grazing and browsing around it. The sequestered waterfall was in the dell or combe or glen that formed the eastern boundary of the park, with the village of Holford on the far side. It turned out that the house was for rent – its owner, a St Albyn, was a minor, away as an undergraduate at Balliol College, Oxford, and the Wordsworths could have it for £23 a year, taxes included. Tom Poole made the arrangements, and the lease was signed.

'The house is a large mansion, with furniture enough for a dozen families like ours,' Dorothy told her childhood friend Mary Hutchinson.

There is a very excellent garden, well stocked with vegetables and fruit. The garden is at the end of the house, and our favourite parlour, as at Racedown, looks that way. In front is a little court, with grass plot, gravel walk, and shrubs; the moss roses were in full beauty a month ago. The front of the house is to the south, but it is screened from the sun by a high hill which rises immediately from it. This hill is beautiful, scattered irregularly and abundantly with trees, and topped with fern, which spreads a considerable way down it. The deer dwell here, and sheep, so that we have a living prospect. From the end of the house we have a view of the sea, over a woody meadow-country; and exactly opposite the window where I now sit is an immense wood, whose round top from this point has exactly the appearance of a mighty dome. In some parts of this wood there is an under grove of hollies which are now very beautiful. In a glen at the bottom of the wood is the waterfall of which I spoke, a quarter of a mile from the house. We are three miles from Stowey, and not two miles from the sea. Wherever we turn we have woods, smooth downs, and valleys with small brooks running down them through green meadows, hardly ever intersected with hedgerows, but scattered over with trees. The hills that cradle these valleys are either covered with fern and bilberries, or oak woods, which are cut for charcoal ... Walks extend for miles over the hill tops, the great beauty of which is their wild simplicity: they are perfectly smooth, without rocks. The Tor of Glastonbury is before our eyes during more than half of our walk to Stowey; and in the park wherever we go ... it makes a part of our prospect ...

Somehow the Wordsworths had brought their gentlemanliness with them, and had stumbled on a handsome pedimented house, filled with old hangings and 'covered with the round-faced family portraits of the age of George I and II', not unlike and actually larger than Racedown, with hints of Lonsdale grandeur. The way in which Dorothy described it to her friend feels nearly like an heiress coming into her own. Her language is virtually without the stock Romantic or even pre-Romantic phrases that would have displayed the fashionable attitudes to place. The only hint in these letters that she is not a straightforward member of the landowning classes is her love of the 'wild simplicity' of the hill tops. Otherwise it is a land surveyor's account, allied to a calm and proprietorial description of an elegant landscape seen as the declaration of a well-ordered life and a contented household. The much-admired, sparkle-eyed observer of the slivers and specks of the natural world, the empathiser with the poor and troubled, the poet of the unnoticed and the everyday, seems to have slipped away here under the manners and modes of the gentleman and the squire.

Perhaps one can see in this the Dorothy who was the source of strength and connection in their lives, who sustained her broken brother, the irrigating woman-brook, 'seen, heard, felt, and caught at every turn'. Audible in that account is 'the voice of sudden admonition' with which she recalled Wordsworth to his 'office upon earth', his destiny as a poet. Its authority is unmistakable. None of this was coming from Wordsworth himself, and in the months that followed, that ownership of settled beauty was the very opposite of what Wordsworth himself would find here.

Alfoxden – called by Coleridge 'All the Foxes Den' and by most people, dully, Alfoxton – remains a beautiful and haunting place. The house is now decrepit, and the park broken and ragged. It is scarcely visited. Unlike Coleridge's spruced-up cottage in Nether Stowey, no National Trust care is applied to the flaking and rotting surfaces of these buildings. Little wrens play on the cornices and pied wagtails pick through the gravel where the moss roses used to flower. The roof in places is breaking through, and the paint on the doors looks as if it has been peppered with gunshot. The walled garden is abandoned, and the trees lie collapsed and broken where they have fallen, vast twisted and spiralled chestnuts lying riven on the hillside, as if a war had been fought through them.

That very condition, on a thick summer evening, with the leaves darkening in the dusk, the bats flicking and scouting over-head, and the deer rustling their anxious, hidden bodies some-where up in the bracken, has over the centuries absorbed, ironically enough, a Wordsworthian atmosphere. Now Alfoxden seems more than ever like his place, with an ancient grandeur, poised and beautifully placed between hill and sea, with its own apron of hedge and field spread out in front of it towards the grey waters of the Bristol Channel to the north. Everywhere the atmosphere is of decay and breakage, as if forgotten, a fraying cloth, a place shut up and shuttered, ragwort on the lawns and marsh thistles in ranks in front of the house like ushers at its death. On the upper edges of the park the rim of beech trees stands waiting for the old beast to lie down.

Allow night to fall here, and memory and hauntedness come easing out of the ground, a dusk in which Alfoxden's half-ruin summons the sense of marginal understanding, of something growing in significance because only half-seen, which is one of

Wordsworth's lasting gifts to the world. It is easy to imagine that he was like this himself in these years, a man glimpsed but never quite grasped, always a suggestion of a resolution in him, making half-gestures, a raised eyebrow, an almost-smile, so that his whole being appeared more latent than present.

His repeated habit in poetry, and perhaps in speech, was to use the double negative. Pleasures were not unwelcome, sounds not unheard, understandings not ungrasped. Even when he feels, for instance, the 'mild creative breeze' lifting within him, the very centre of his being as a poet, he calls it 'a power/that does not come unrecognised'.

Everything hangs there as a suggestion. The wind of poetry is no more than a breath of stirring air, and Wordsworth only half-knows it for what it is. That half-state, a not-unreality, is the condition of his inner life, his duskiness, and now, through neglect, is the very state that Alfoxden has come to. There are no mathematics here; the two negatives do not cancel each other out, or at least in their mutual cancelling leave the ghost of a third term, something which might have been or might yet be. The mild creative breeze is itself an aspect of the tentative, a half-feeling, a stirring of the inner atmosphere that might or might not be the making of poetry. There is no certainty that it is; nor any that it is not. That very hanging in a qualified neutrality, which smells of something and suggests something but isn't quite the thing itself, is the revelatory thing. It is the simmering of a presence, not the memory of a presence but the promise of a presence which bears the same relationship to the future as a memory does to the past.

Over the smooth, curved carriage drive leading back to the village, buzzards turn in the wind off the sea. A dog barks in Holford Glen, and in response the buzzards catcall over the dying ashwoods. Looking down from the footbridge, the rocks and all the ferns beside them are invisible under the roof of summer leaves. As Alfoxden drops into its felt-lined dark, I stay up and walk along the easy way through the edge of the park. Miles off to the north, the surge of a westerly swell breaks and draws on the stones at East Quantoxhead.

There is the slightest undulation in the surface of the carriage-way, an easy coming and going beneath the trunks of the ancient chestnuts. There is no need for light here. This was the way loved by Wordsworth for its continuousness, a zero space whose fluency of form allowed the steady, uninterrupted and murmured composition of his verses as he walked, a place in which his music could hold sway, the body-rhythm of a man who, in one half of his own self-conception, belonged in the park of a fine house, suited to a naturally Miltonic and magisterial frame of mind. Wordsworth had a powerful sense of his own promise, and, in 1797, of his failure to fulfil it. Alfoxden now is a picture of Wordsworth then. What could be more fitted to this great man in trouble than a house in ruins and a park in greater ruins, along whose lightless paths he must make his way to find the greatness he knows is in him?

5

Walking

July and August 1797

Coleridge would not have taken long to urge his friends on their first walk out and up into the hills. This was to be the frame of their time here, an emblematic topography which came to play a central part in shaping the poetry they wrote in the course of the year. The whole pattern of life and work swings around the alternations of out and in, up and back, engaged and removed, obscure and revealed that the Quantocks provide.

That drama and setting was a function of geology. The Quantocks are at least twice as old as the comfortable and rather soft Jurassic and Cretaceous rocks around Racedown in north Dorset. The ridge of the Quantocks, or the Quantock as it is called in Somerset, not plural but a single long hard object, stands out above the wet moors of the Levels to the east of them. That single line is a block on the horizon to the west as you approach from the lowlands, a black bulk in the light of the evening, its ridge-line rising and falling, with the trees of its woods standing out against the last of the light. Most of it is no more than 1,200 feet high, and the whole ridge is only about twelve miles long and four or five miles wide, but it looks and feels more than that, a distinct world, an upland province away from the willow and dairy country below it.

These hills are made almost entirely of Devonian rocks, more than 350 million years old, often dark red or in places copper blue from the mineral dust of the ancient deserts, which have been twisted and uplifted in more than one mountain-building episode since. The result is a hardness and strength that mean they now stand proud of the cowy vales that surround them. This hill is built out of dense, dark and intractable slates and grits, with metals and minerals embedded in them, precisely the rocks the Wordsworths would have known as children in Westmorland.

Far more than Dorset, the Quantocks create the kind of highly figured topography to which the aesthetic needs of these people at this moment could respond. The geological structure of England is such that, almost without exception, the further south and east you go, the newer the rocks and the softer the landscapes. In many of the places Wordsworth had been living, in Cambridge and around London, you will find low-lying meadows and rivers brown with silt. Hardness and antiquity, higher hills and hard running water, high outcrops and the stony beds of streams, are all to be found only to the west and north. This was the shift Coleridge had urged on the Wordsworths late in June 1797, and from then, the year acquired its formative geological structure: friends coming to stay nearly always came from the soft east; whenever any of them wanted or needed to engage with the world of business or work, politics or the theatre, they would also travel east, to Bristol or on to London. But whenever they needed stimulus or adventure, beyond what the Quantocks themselves could provide, they walked west, to hardness, over the high tops and on into the wild woods and rocky valleys of Exmoor and Devon. Again and again in the poetry of this year, the implications of this hard but riven landform make themselves apparent: a clear and distinct difference between empty hill and occupied valley, high tops and buried combes, with the brilliant streams acting as the veins and arteries of the whole body of country.

The lane at the southern end of Stowey, just along from Tom Poole's house, soon leaves behind the clustered domesticity of the village. The road itself in summer is dry and stony, rimmed with the grey-pink dust of the Quantocks, while a stream, which even in July does not fail, runs down the ditches, the first of the bubbling watercourses that give the Quantocks, for all their southern Englishness, a sense of mountain life. They were what Dorothy loved when she first came here: the ever-present sound of water over stones. And so here, physically and immediately, is the first pair of qualities which make this a stimulating place: orderliness and vitality, a mutually enriching and fertile meeting of the natural and the cultural, Welsh poppies growing in the gravel next to a cottage door.

In the height of summer there is a thickness and a richness here too, no northern austerity. Leaves shadow the world. Bindweed is in the hedges and the brambles are in flower. Lady's bedstraw and mallows grow in the shady damp places under the hedges. The roses overtop the garden walls, up and over them,

dropping in long tendrils into the lane. Wood-pigeons hoot and strum in the garden trees, and the meadowsweet bubbles beside the road.

The boundary between the cultivated lowland and the hill is quite sharp, no suburban blurring. A stream runs along the floor of the lane itself. Hazels and field maples arch it over into a green tunnel 'so overshadow'd, it might seem one bower', and the sun pushes in there in narrow rods, so that the watery floor is spattered and mapped in leopardskin light.

This is the first slight lift of the hills away from Nether Stowey, but the sensation is not of climbing on to the hill but into it, following the wet shaded path as if into a vein. Even on a hot summer day the damp hangs and clings in there. Big lolling hart's-tongue ferns, feathery polypody ferns and others more like giant shuttlecocks, with the luxuriant undergrowth of dog's mercury around them, make a jungled Amazonian lushness beside the stream. A broad-bladed frondy apron of fern spreads over the water. This is an English rainforest, coomby with buttercups and little cranesbills, water dropwort and fat, snaking ivies on the trunks of the trees, the whole place womblike, interior. Beyond the hedges, the sunlit meadows beside the lane are spangled with daisies as if they belonged to another and more obvious world.

Whichever way you climb, whether through the damp combes made by the streams or on the old charcoal burners' tracks that net the hills on all sides, you soon come to the next element: the Quantock oakwoods, one of the great, scarcely regarded beauties of England. They coat the flanks and thighs of each hill, coppiced every sixteen years or so in the 1780s and 90s, so that each new oak, as it grew, curled towards the light, competing with its neighbour. The result is a wriggling snakepit of a wood, in which the trees weave and twist upwards, blotched with lichen, the dancing stems springing from mossy and ferny groins, sometimes four or five to each stool. Their canopy, thirty or forty feet above the bilberries or whortleberries, creates a mosque-like room in which the green carpet of the berries glimmers for thousands of acres beneath them, lined out in avenues of sun-spotted green, an arcaded temple and shrine to growth and light.

In the early morning, when the leaves are grey with dew, the air in these oakwoods is as cool as a glass of cider. Cloud floats in the tops of the woods like another element, another sphere between you and the blue of the sky. Occasionally a big old pollard oak hangs its branches over the path. This is not wild country, not impressive in the way of grand or famous landscapes – far more intimate than that, and thick with the sensation that Wordsworth came to embrace in the course of this year. In some unused manuscript lines from 1798 he described how, after he had been walking for a long time in a remote and lonely place, away from people,

> If, looking round, I have perchance perceived
> Some vestiges of human hands, some stir
> Of human passion, they to me are sweet
> As light at day break or the sudden sound
> Of music to a blind man's ear who sits
> Alone & silent in the summer shade.
> They are as a creation in my heart …

Those words record the education of a mind, the sudden seeing of what had not been seen before. Man and nature fuse in those places. Human presence is no pollution in these woods, but the means by which a communal, multi-generational beauty has evolved, the co-production of man and the world of which he is a part. This is also part of the great gospel of interfusion of all in all and each in each to which this year is dedicated. When the wind is right, the bells of Holford church reach deep into the air between the trees.

Beyond the woods the world changes again, and the path emerges on to the tops, just above the treeline, or at least into one of the wind-sheltered nooks still surrounded by the wood but open at its upper edge. All above you, hill country: an occasional thorn, abused by storms or grazing mouths, and hung in the sunlight with gossamer threads, standing among the heather and gorse, the scrambled feathers of a young pigeon, a peregrine kill, a pair of buzzards mew-crying over the trees, tormentil in the acid turf.

Ahead, the lit outlines of the open-headed hills, a sun-drenched roof for the world. Over to the north, the Bristol Channel, with its two little islands, and the hazed Welsh mountains beyond them, to the east the milky distance of the low moors of the Somerset Levels, and on the far side the steady line of the Mendips.

It is a place, in that sunshine, to lie down and look: the woods on the lower slopes of these hills, the scatter of big farms and fields beyond them, multicoloured, green and tan, the shadowed hollows and dips in the farmland, the grey-blue plume of a distant bonfire smoking in the sun. Pies and doughnuts of woods dropped across the chequered fields.

Wordsworth loved to remember precisely how 'in many a walk', as he wrote later in his notebook, when they had reached this top and

> reclined
> At midday upon beds of forest moss
> Have we to Nature and her impulses
> Of our whole being made free gift, – and when
> Our trance had left us, oft have we by aid
> Of the impressions which it left behind
> Looked inward on ourselves, and learn'd, perhaps,
> Something of what we are.

The mind and the world were – 'perhaps' – part of one substance. To look outward was to look inward. The perceiving self was only the finest of strata buried in that doubly enveloping universe. The inner world was as vast as the outer. All the old impressions were ringing in his heart. Here was a place where the very movement of coming up and out allowed a movement down and in, the geography of the self becoming an inverse mirror of the material and external world.

It was true for Coleridge too. He described in his notebook how, when he forgot a name, only by not thinking of it could he remember it:

> Consciousness is given up and all is quiet – when the nerves are asleep, or off their guard – and then the name pops up, makes its way and there it is! Not assisted by any association, but the very contrary – the suspension and *sedation* of all associations.

Sedation was one of the roots of understanding. Too much noise interfered with the mind's engagement in the world. Only when you reduced the vibrations coming into your mind, and into your self, could things begin to seem as they were.

Many years later, on a return visit to the Quantocks, but filled with regret for the passing of time, Coleridge lay in reverie in just one such nook on the margins of wood and heath, easing himself back on to the perfect elastic mattress of the heather, but dreaming of love lost and love never to be had.

> How warm this woodland wild Recess!
> > Love surely hath been breathing here;
> > And this sweet bed of heath, my dear!
> Swells up, then sinks with faint caress,
> > As if to have you yet more near.

Walking: July and August 1797

Eight springs have flown, since last I lay
    On sea-ward Quantock's heathy hills,
    Where quiet sounds from hidden rills
Float here and there, like things astray
    And high o'er head the sky-lark shrills.

This is where the wavering wind-songs of the Aeolian harp could soothe and seduce the mind. When the wind was right, a long, continuous and minimal music eased out of it. The sound belonged on empty heights like these – not the buffeting white noise of wind in the ear or in a chimney but something more hidden, tapered, as if the harp were releasing an element that was buried in it, or in the air. Deeper tones come from the heavier strings, along with witchery notes from the others, as if this were dream music or, as Coleridge says, the sound of the world singing.

Again and again, the year was filled with walks that followed this movement, the two poets up ahead, always a few dozen yards ahead, Dorothy following at their heels, always slightly behind. It is the deep psychic structure of the year, repeatedly drawing from these landforms, up from the settlements of the valley, through the combes and the oakwoods, on to the sunlit widths of the wide-ranging tops and then down again, back into the rowan and oakwood, as if into a bath of shade.

Nothing in the walk together would ever have been silent. Talk was the medium in which Coleridge swam. 'He runs up and down the scale of language,' Virginia Woolf wrote of him in her notebook,

stretching and suppling prose until it becomes pliable enough and plastic enough to take the most subtle creases of the human mind and heart. But while he disports himself like a great sea monster in his element of words, spouting, snorting, he uses them most often to express the crepitations of his apprehensive susceptibility.

You only have to read Coleridge's own notebooks to feel that these hill-paths are still crackling with the crepitations of his apprehensive susceptibility. There is one place on the way down, in the little sub-hamlet of Over Stowey, or Upper Stowey as Coleridge called it, where an old well near the church had entranced him. Years later, from a time when he was abroad in Malta and in distress, he remembered gazing into its waters:

> The images of the weeds which hung down from its sides, appeared as plants growing up, straight and upright, among the water weeds that really grew from the bottom/& so vivid was the Image, that for some moments & not until after I had disturbed the waters, did I perceive that their roots were not neighbours, & they side-by-side companions. So – even then I said – so are the happy man's *Thoughts* and *Things* –

There, preserved in his memory, is a tiny fragment of Coleridge's ebullient, ever-referential talk, perhaps to Wordsworth as they were coming down one day off the high tops.

It is his governing vision of the intimate co-existence of everything the mind shapes – the *Thoughts* – with everything that comes to him through his senses, the *Things* that seem so solidly present around us. The two are side-by-side companions. Thoughts and things are *friends*, and this for Coleridge is not a description of any sort of delusion but of happiness.

Intriguingly, Wordsworth had a parallel but different experience, which appears in *The Prelude*. He too is looking down into weedy water, not at a well but hanging over the side of a slow-moving boat, floating on stillness. The Wordsworth figure,

> solacing himself
> With such discoveries as his eye can make
> Beneath him in the bottom of the deeps,

Quantocks moon

FOLLOWING PAGE: Fallen ash

Sees many beauteous sights – weeds, fishes, flowers,
Grots, pebbles, roots of trees – and fancies more,
Yet often is perplexed and cannot part
The shadow from the substance, rocks and sky,
Mountains and clouds, reflected in the depth
Of the clear flood, from things which there abide
In their true dwelling;

Upper and lower surfaces are interlaced here too, but there is a difference between them. For Coleridge, this twinned condition of the seen and the imagined was an aspect of how things were, the intertwining of sense impressions and the constructions of the mind. For Wordsworth, it was part of how *he* was, a description of himself, an entangled muddle of what he had been and what he was now. The figure in the boat is Wordsworth's own self hanging

Incumbent o'er the surface of past time,

his own invigilator, the priest of his own being, wrapped up in the ever-entrancing story of his own evolving self.

As Mary Warnock has said, it was Coleridge's belief 'that *in understanding one's feelings* one can understand the riddle of the world'. Because 'the mind is not a mere spectator', but a shaper of existence, only by knowing the forces at work in the self could any understanding be had of the world beyond it. For Wordsworth, something of the opposite was true. He naturally had a sense of the world, Warnock wrote, 'as *his* world, in some deep way lying behind his eyes, in his own mind. The framed pictures were pictures for which he was, in a sense, responsible.'

These are cousin ideas. Both men thought there was no boundary at the skin, and for both of them self and world were in a close, mutual and fluid relationship. Only with time would it become clear that their positions were opposed. A power difference lay between them: Coleridge thought of himself as belonging to and infused by the world at large; Wordsworth, at some depth, and with some justification given the scale of his being, saw the world as belonging to and infused by himself. Coleridge had long thought 'we should remove the *selfish* Principle from ourselves'; Wordsworth's great recognition was coming to think that the selfish principle, deeply cultivated, was the central means of understanding how things were.

On 7 July 1797, Charles Lamb arrived from London. He was three years younger than Coleridge, and had probably hero-worshipped him when they were schoolboys together at Christ's Hospital. But Lamb, for all his brilliance and charm, was afflicted with a stammer which meant he could never give a sermon, and so, in the 1790s, could not think of a scholarly career, of university or the Church, the intended route for both Coleridge and Wordsworth, as it was for their brothers. Lamb had met up again with Coleridge in London in the winter of 1794–95, sitting together for evening after evening in the Cat and Salutation in Newgate Market, between Bart's Hospital and St Paul's, Lamb nineteen, Coleridge twenty-two, talking and talking 'in that nice little smoky room – with all its associated train of pipes, tobacco, Egghot' – a kind of posset, not unlike flip, made of eggs, sugar and brandy – 'welch Rabbits, metaphysics and Poetry'. Along with the Egghot, Lamb drank up the genius that Coleridge poured all over him. He was already employed, as he would be all his working life, as a clerk at the East India Company, but it was those evenings he lived for. 'You first kindled in me, if not the power, yet the love of poetry, and beauty, and kindliness,' he wrote to the great man, in the open, modest, adoring and gentle way for which Coleridge loved – and patronised – him.

Lamb was tiny, a small, spare man with 'almost immaterial legs', always dressed in black, as fine-boned as Charles I with, according to one of his contemporaries, 'a light frame so fragile that it seemed as if a breath would overthrow it'. And his habit of mind, stammering and punning, never quite arriving at the solidly stated but always tentative and provisional, seemed to be a part of that physical existence. He shunned stolidity, loved London, was never much in love with the country, and insisted that to be happy he 'must have books, pictures, theatres, chit-chat, scandal, jokes, ambiguities, and a thousand whim-whams'. His thoughts, he wrote, were 'rather suggestive than comprehensive', and made 'no pretences to much clearness and or precision in their ideas, or in their manner of expressing them'. Instead, his favourite practice was to take his mind for a walk, finding interesting whatever he came across, 'content with fragments and scattered pieces of Truth, [with] hints and glimpses, germs and crude essays at a system'.

This was a version of the ideals animating the group Coleridge was gathering around him in the Quantocks summer. Contingency was a form of humanity. Openness was civilisation. Half-thoughts, or at least thoughts in the making, were the best thoughts. All the rigidities of Enlightenment rationality were sloughed off with a kind of gaiety and liberty that feels like sunshine on a spring morning. In Lamb's illuminated and irradiated mind, the half-conditions do not have to be dark to be revelatory. Wordsworth's turn towards the sombre was only part of what this revolution meant.

Even Wordsworth was susceptible. A few years later, he remembered these weeks wandering in company, when little deskwork seems to have been done. *The Prelude* solemnly announces that sometimes it is 'better far than this to stray about/Voluptuously through fields and rural walks/And ask no record of the hours given up' than to struggle with the dead and boring contents of one's own mind. Voluptuous wandering was precisely the purpose of these Quantock mornings. Openness was the fuel for the memories all of them nurtured for the rest of their lives, for those mornings and evenings when walking was like thinking and thinking like walking, when mind and body, self and others, person and place all joined in one encountering and liberating whole, where the fullness of life and its possibilities for once seemed present in the air around them.

'The bird a nest, the spider a web, man friendship', William Blake had written, and for Coleridge there is no doubt that friendship, and the love that animated it, was the only way of making life whole. To walk with friends was to be alive. 'FRIEND,' he had written, 'is a sacred appellation,' and a life without love would be a life in pieces. In a letter to a grieving friend, he described the

> friable, incohesive sort of existence that characterizes the mere man of the World, a fractional Life made up of successive moments, that neither blend nor modify each other – a life that is strictly symbolized in the thread of Sand thro' the orifice of the Hour-glass, in which the sequence of Grains only counterfeits a continuity, and appears a line only because the interspaces between the Points are too small to be sensible …

This spotty and grainy quality of life was for Coleridge the problem to be solved – and love was the solution. Love was a completion of the self, the matrix of existence, a remaking of the self. Friendship was more loving than filial or conjugal or parental love: 'Friendship is sympathy, but in [other forms of] love there is a sort of antipathy, or opposing passion. Each strives to be the other, and both together make up one whole.' The fusing of individuality in romantic love required a 'feeling-against', an antipathy, a hostility in which the new unity of lover and lover was forged; friendship stayed short of that, preserved identities, and so the feeling in friendship was a 'feeling-with', a sympathy, a more loving kind of love that gave room to the other and did not possess him. Friendship loved in a way love itself could not equal. 'The Heart, thoroughly penetrated with the flame of virtuous Friendship,' he thought, 'is in a state of glory.' And friendship could go further, becoming the source of what he called 'Philanthropy', the Greek word for a general, universal love of all mankind. As he wrote to Robert Southey, his fellow poet and co-visionary, his greatest friend before Wordsworth,

> Philanthropy (and indeed every other Virtue) is a thing of *Concretion* – Some home-born Feeling is the *center* of the Ball, that rolling on thro' Life collects and assimilates every congenial Affection.

That metaphor is at the heart of Coleridge's life-vision: friendship as the great gathering of love, the snowball of being-with, turning through the world, rolling up humanity in its ever-enlarging globe of affection.

These weren't watertight categories in Coleridge's mind. He could neglect, patronise and ignore those who loved him, but all were part of the bond of humanity, the element in this life which partook of the divine beauty of the universe. He often complained of loneliness, and of the bigoted ignorance of his own family, who had rejected him and made him lonely. Because his life was bound up with a need for the existence of others, he had what he called an 'instinctive Sense of Self-insufficingness'. Without friendship he knew he would shrivel and fade. Love was animation:

> I cannot love without esteem, neither can I esteem without loving. Hence I love but few, but those I love as my own Soul; for I feel that without them I should not indeed cease to be kind and effluent, but by little and little become a soul-less fixed Star, receiving no rays nor influences into my being, *a Solitude which I so tremble at, that I cannot attribute it even to the Divine Nature.*

Even God, to be truly God-like, in this perfectly Coleridgean view of the universe, must be surrounded by his friends. How could God possibly tolerate an evening on his own? What could Heaven be but a room full of conversation?

And so, all his life, Coleridge had been constantly embroiled with friendship, with friends clustering around him at Christ's Hospital, where he had been sent by his family as a charity boy; at Cambridge, where evenings were filled with his effortlessly memorised passages from the latest news sheets or his latest verses; in the Cat and Salutation, where the publican was so pleased with his endlessly diverting talk that he offered to pay him to stay there, as his presence was bound to attract more custom. Coleridge was always talking and spouting – the Greek dramatists, Shakespeare and Milton, philosophy, his hero David Hartley – living an entirely surrounded existence, always among a hubbub of humanity, both dead and alive, drawing from them everything and anything that might revolve in the extraordinary whirl-brain of his mind.

Intensely sociable walking was a way of dramatising these truths. It is scarcely the received idea of the Romantic poet out on the hills, but it was central to this year. As part of my own embedding experiment, I also asked down to the Quantocks for a day or so some people I thought might stand in for Coleridge's flock of nightingales: a painter, a professor, a man in love with nature, a novelist, a critic and a political journalist – wanting to see how much or how little a party of friends might notice or absorb through the fog of their unending chat.

They talked and talked: politics, memory, the government, justice, privacy, beauty, art dealers, friends, rivals, loss, death, parents, children, upbringing, publishers, films, morphic resonance, network theory, the best of wines, what if anything you could say about 'the time of unrememberable being', gender, class, poverty, money, and on and on as we followed the Quantock paths on which, until then, I had been alone and thinking of what was there and what I might feel was there.

What did this voluble crew receive from the world around them? I thought at first: nothing much. Everyone talked away half the evening and on into the night, as the moon rose and the snipe drummed unnoticed above us and we strolled across the moors.

As time went on and the world darkened, this lovely, easy co-being started to evolve. The group clustered and declustered at changes in the path. The talk drifted in and out of *joco* and *serious*, sometimes leaving one or other person alone, or alone with one other, dropping down off the high moory tops into the shadows of the combe woods. The big track up on the hill had looked like a pale river of stone, as wide as that, in the first of the moonlight. Now the moon was swelling with each passing hour and its light fell on the bilberry floor of the wood, half reflected and half absorbed by it, a silvery sea-surface as if in a masque. The oaks cast their forms over a theatrical world, puck-filled, a midsummer's night in a wood near Stowey, blue on blue, the surface of the earth as soft and mottled as the moon's. It quietened the talk. The man who loves birds said he felt no fear and how the wood's stillness was its comfort. The professor held my hand in the dark as we stepped over fallen branches and the deer moved in the shadows. The painter looked at the oaks in the moonlight, the net of branches against the smear of cloud.

I realised then the pleasure of being with friends in a place like this. It depended on my previously having been there alone. A solitary place now occupied by people who are your friends, with their alternating babble and silence, the shared looking between them, the questions and the jokes, the teasing and the sense of joint presence in the feeling that friendship allows a dissolving of the boundaries of the self, a flooding out of who you are into them and of them into you – these are all constituents of a heightened form of life, in which the acts of friendship – the helping hand across a stream or a steep place, the stumbling into one another, the half brush, half hug when a foot sinks into the bog mud – all come to seem more valuable than in a place where sociability is the norm. Remembered solitariness elevates present friendliness, and that surely is what Coleridge also loved here, a confirmation of his connectedness in the world. And afterwards, once they had gone, the places we had walked together continued to hold the memory of them, so that each condition, as I moved between them, improved the other: friendship seemed wonderful in a lonely place; solitude was enriched wherever I had been with friends before.

In July 1797, it was to be high-summer perfection. But Lamb was not well. There was madness in his family, and the year before, perhaps disappointed in love, he had spent some weeks in an asylum himself. The previous September, his much-loved sister Mary had also been showing signs of instability. On the morning of Thursday, 22 September, Lamb had gone looking for a doctor for her but failed to find one, and in the afternoon, while the family was preparing for dinner in their rooms in Holborn, Mary grabbed a knife lying on the table and 'in a menacing manner pursued a little girl, her apprentice, round the room'.

Her mother, who was old and infirm, called on her to stop, at which Mary turned and stabbed her in the heart as she sat in front of her in a chair. She then wounded her father in the head by throwing forks at him. Charles grabbed the knife out of her hand as the landlord, alerted by the screaming child, arrived up the stairs. Mary was acquitted of the charge of murder on the grounds of lunacy, and was sent for a few weeks to Hoxton Asylum, until Charles released her by undertaking to look after her for the rest of her life, living together with their father in a pool of distress at their lodgings in 'Pentonville, near London'.

For Lamb, the reports he had of life at Nether Stowey made it sound like a general Elysium. After the catastrophe, Sara

Coleridge had written to invite him down, but his work and his need to stay with father and sister had held him in London. Still, he wrote to Coleridge,

> May I, can I, shall I come so soon? ... I long, I yearn, with all the longings of a child do I desire to see you, to come among you, to see the young philosopher [Hartley] to thank Sara for her last year's invitation in person, to read your tragedy, to read over together our little book [they were to publish a new edition of their poems together], to breathe fresh air, to revive in me vivid images of 'Salutation scenery.'

In his depression, Lamb felt 'a calm not unlike content. I fear it is sometimes more akin to physical stupidity than to a heaven-flowing serenity and peace ... If I come to Stowey, what conversation can I furnish to compensate my friend for those stores of knowledge and of fancy, those delightful treasures of wisdom, which I know he will open to me?'

He arrived by coach from London in non-communicative gloom, but the Coleridges treated him with a kindness he felt he could repay 'only by the silence of a grateful heart'.

> I could not talk much, while I was with you, but my silence was not sullenness, nor I hope from any bad motive; but, in truth, disuse has made me awkward at it. I know I behaved myself, particularly at Tom Poole's, and at Cruikshank's, most like a sulky child; but company and converse are strange to me. It was kind in you all to endure me as you did.

Wordsworth had read to them all one of the poems he had written a few weeks earlier at Racedown, which in its restrained and mage-like tones appealed to Lamb. Coleridge had been lamed in a domestic accident in the crowded house when Sara had spilled a skillet of hot milk over him and scalded his leg and foot. For the week Lamb was there, his host couldn't go walking out on the hills, or more than two hundred yards or so, and so this reading was down in Stowey itself, probably in Coleridge's Lime Street garden or in Poole's just along the back lane. After Lamb had returned to London, he asked Coleridge to copy the poem out for him and send it, along with the greatcoat which he hadn't needed on the walks over the summer hills but which in his distractedness he had left behind.

Wordsworth's 'Lines Left upon a Seat in a Yew-tree' might have been designed to appeal to Lamb in his semi-absent state, reaching out across the silences to a person who felt submerged, no more than half-present to himself. What Wordsworth had read to him was full of empathy for a man in a broken condition. The sad central figure of the poem – he is both Wordsworth and Lamb – sits under the dark boughs of a yew tree and feels his hopelessness and loss:

> here he loved to sit,
> His only visitants a straggling sheep,
> The stone-chat, or the glancing sand-piper;
> And on these barren rocks, with juniper,
> And heath, and thistle, thinly sprinkled o'er,
> Fixing his downward eye, he many an hour
> A morbid pleasure nourish'd, tracing here
> An emblem of his own unfruitful life.

Resonances of Wordsworth's own failures and of Lamb's despair echo quietly through the solitary birds and the sprinkling of the moorland plants. That downward look appears in one Wordsworth poem after another from these months. It may be a reflection of his own physical habit, head down as he walked. It is the physical attitude of a spirit for whom any view to the wide horizon was, apparently, impossible.

Lamb had loved and remembered Wordsworth's lines describing a man mired in hopelessness. Already, though, perhaps under Coleridge's influence, Wordsworth was moving beyond that bleakness, and now added to the poem. The man sitting under the yew tree was made to lift his head from the ground, and 'would gaze/On the more distant scene'. There, first, he saw that it was beautiful, but also recognised something more: that only because he had been dwelling on his own failings did the world around him seem so bereft.

It didn't need to be like that. To others, whose minds were

Warm from the labours of benevolence,
The world, and man himself, appeared a scene
Of kindred loveliness.

This poem is scarcely remembered now, cast in shadow by Wordsworth's later poetry, but it marks a moment of transforming importance. The date of composition is uncertain, but it may be that here, for the first time, Wordsworth was speaking with the benefit of Coleridge's understanding of a beneficent world. The underlying meaning of 'Lines Left upon a Seat in a Yew-tree' is Coleridge's belief that the living world, properly heard and seen and connected with, speaks with a voice of goodness far beyond human understanding. Only through the connections established by benevolence can that voice be heard. Lovelessness and self-regard will block the channels, so that, as Wordsworth says, lecturing himself as much as any other, we need to recognise that

                    pride,
Howe'er disguised in its own majesty,
Is littleness; that he, who feels contempt
For any living thing, hath faculties
Which he has never used.

These half-tortured lines, in which Wordsworth was reaching for a sort of humility, are the graph and record of the Coleridgean spirit spreading through him. Coleridge, the *wonderful* man, was teaching his friend how to find goodness in himself, how to see the world as good and how to find goodness in the connection between them.

Left behind with his scalded leg and foot one evening that week in the arbour Thomas Poole had made in his garden, just through a gate from his own, Coleridge wrote the first great poem of the great year. Sara and Hartley were at home. The others had all gone for a long walk of a few hours: up and over the Quantocks; on to the heights, filled with the prospects west into Devon and over the sea channel to Wales; coming down into the thick and woody combes through which the streams ran over ancient rocks to the sea; before making their way back through the patterned farmland in which Stowey sat, to where Coleridge was waiting for them in his arbour, with the trees and the birds and the dropping sun around him.

His poem borrows this form of the Quantocks: out-and-up-and-back-and-in, enlargement and containment, extent and privacy, solitariness and connectedness, other people and the world at large, this world and a world beyond. It is the master template of the year, the double quality of this particular place in England; Coleridge's poem, which is also a response to 'Lines Left upon a Seat in a Yew-tree', re-enacts it.

The poem is in part addressed to Lamb, in part to himself, and in that way is about friendship, a voice gently wavering between companionship and solitude, inner thoughts and murmured talk. His friends are not there, but he knows they soon will be, and that what he is now writing will be heard by them. For a man who longs for companionship, this is a populated solitude. His language is warmth itself. 'Well,' he begins, as if continuing a conversation when others have just left the room, 'they are gone, and here must I remain,/This lime-tree bower my prison!'

Of course it is no prison. All sorts of prison had hung over their lives for years: in Paris; in London and Edinburgh where other radical writers and lecturers had been confined for months before their trials; for the members of the radical London Corresponding Society who had met in a fug of beer, tobacco and rhetoric in rooms next to the Cat and Salutation in Newgate Market, whose spokesman, orator, firebrand and organiser John Thelwall was even now making his way down the roads of southern England towards them. Beyond that, there had been the other prisons, the endless money anxieties, the maltreatment by relations and connections, or most devastatingly, the terrifying crisis in the Lambs' rooms in Holborn. But not here and not now for Coleridge, for all his present scalded incapacity. This lime-tree bower, in full flower in early July, with its incarcerating sweetness and enveloping honey-dews, was an intoxicating, immersive hammam of a prison.

Reaching out through its bars, Coleridge could travel in his mind with his friends along the hilltop edge and down into

The roaring dell, o'erwooded, narrow, deep,
And only speckled by the mid-day sun;
Where its slim trunk the ash from rock to rock
Flings arching like a bridge; – that branchless ash,
Unsunned and damp, whose few poor yellow leaves
Ne'er tremble in the gale, yet tremble still,
Fann'd by the water-fall!

The ash in its shadowed dell is a version of Coleridge in his lime-tree bower. He too is away from the world and its winds, and he too is trembling still, alert with the vibrancy of life. He wanted above all to give this beauty to his friend Lamb, as a kind of balm, using the very word Milton had used of a troubled and dark-minded Satan as he arrived from Hell and luxuriated in the beauties of Paradise:

> for thou hast pined
> And hunger'd after Nature, many a year,
> In the great City pent, winning thy way
> With sad yet patient soul, through evil and pain
> And strange calamity!

The gift of the Quantocks was also the gift of this poem, a landscape co-opted by Coleridge as his own, producing a vision of wholeness from this hill-ridge in the evening sun, when the colours of the heather and the woods and the ocean glowed into an unworldly richness.

> So my Friend
> Struck with deep joy may stand, as I have stood,
> Silent with swimming sense; yea, gazing round
> On the wide landscape, gaze till all doth seem
> Less gross than bodily; and of such hues
> As veil the Almighty Spirit, when yet he makes
> Spirits perceive his presence.

The enveloping and melting wholeness of Coleridge's perceptions – or of his remembered and imagined perceptions of an evening on the heights of the ridge – spreads down the hillslope and begins to enfold him too as he sits in Tom Poole's arbour:

> A delight
> Comes sudden on my heart, and I am glad
> As I myself were there!

All around him he begins to appreciate the scenes of kindred loveliness. The dropping sun lights up the leaves above him; the higher leaves cast their shadows on those below; the darkening ivy makes the branches of the elms 'gleam a lighter hue/Through the late twilight'. He is taking notes on anything the world might offer: the swallows have gone for the day, but the bats are in flight, and

> still the solitary humble bee
> Sings in the bean-flower! Henceforth I shall know
> That Nature ne'er deserts the wise and pure;
> No plot so narrow, be but Nature there.

The birds that cross his sight will also cross Lamb's, wherever he is. And now, addressing his friend, he realises that

> when the last rook
> Beat its straight path along the dusky air

the same rook

> Flew creeking o'er thy head, and had a charm
> For thee, my gentle-hearted Charles, to whom
> No sound is dissonant which tells of Life.

Everything connects, and the imagining mind plays its part in creating this ecstatic vision. The language of nature, the creaking rook, the realities of friendship and the essence of life are all one with the possibilities of beauty and love.

No sooner had Lamb gone back to work in London than their publisher Joseph Cottle arrived from Bristol, to the best of parties.

Mr. Coleridge welcomed me with the warmest cordiality. He talked with affection of his old school-fellow, Lamb, who had so recently left him; regretted he had not an opportunity of introducing me to one whom he so highly valued. Mr. C. took peculiar delight in assuring me (at least, at that time) how happy he was; exhibiting successively, his house, his garden, his orchard, laden with fruit; and also the contrivances he had made to unite his two neighbours' domains with his own.

Lunch was ready:

After the grand circuit had been accomplished, by hospitable contrivance, we approached the 'Jasmine harbour,' when to our gratifying surprise, we found the tripod table laden with delicious bread and cheese, surmounted by a brown mug of true Taunton ale. We instinctively took our seats; and there must have been some downright witchery in the provisions which surpassed all of its kind; nothing like it on the wide terrene, and one glass of the Taunton, settled it to an axiom.

Cottle couldn't help his pretentiousness, but through the fog of wrong language one can at least glimpse a moment of unalloyed wellbeing:

While the dappled sun-beams played on our table, through the umbrageous canopy, the very birds seemed to participate in our felicities, and poured forth their select anthems. As we sat in our sylvan hall of splendour, a company of the happiest mortals, (T. Poole, C. Lloyd, S. T. Coleridge, and J. C.) the bright-blue heavens; the sporting insects; the balmy zephyrs; the feathered choristers; the sympathy of friends, all augmented the pleasurable to the highest point this side the celestial!

Creaking rook

FOLLOWING PAGE: A road beyond the limits of knowing

While thus elevated in the universal current of our feelings, Mrs. Coleridge approached, with her fine Hartley; we all smiled, but the father's eye beamed transcendental joy!

* * *

That summer I rented two or three rooms in a farmhouse just up from Over Stowey at Adscombe, across the lane from the cottage in which Coleridge had first wanted to live. Whenever the late afternoon seemed right and all the reading and writing that could be done had been done, I climbed up Quantock, up through the wood, along the banks and then above the running stream that poured night and day past my bedroom windows, into a distant bracken nook of warmth away from the wind, with long, ranging prospects over the head of the hills, the valley to the west and the sea to the north. There I could find a place in which to lie down and watch the red deer grazing between the gorse and the heather and listen to the larks making their manifestos above me.

The Quantocks are still now as cushiony-receptive as the poets remembered them, whether on Wordsworth's moss (genuinely comfortable) or Coleridge's spongy, elastic, giving heather (less so). Where the sun has been shining all day on the earth, both give back their warmth to your skin. Mould yourself to that evening hillside and it welcomes you. Often, as calm, deep, high-pressure summer air settled over England, the glowing distances of the Quantocks' long curved heights drifted off into a thickened particulate atmosphere, so that the sea and Wales beyond it became invisible. And when an evening mist gathered in the combes below me, filling the gaps between the trees, so that nothing remained coloured and substantial except the place I had chosen to lie, the hill-ridges haunched into the combes as if they were the limbs and thighs of a vast recumbent animal on whose flanks I was lying.

These are the rare and precious moments of absorption. It is difficult to know if they were ever experienced before the 1790s. Dorothy's word for the repeated sensation that she and the others loved on the heights in the evening was '*melting*', when the boundaries between the certainties of the material world loosened and drifted around them. Things are not elegantly disposed up here as they would be, say, in a Repton park or a carefully tended and orcharded valley. These Quantock heights are not Arcadian places, nor are they shapely in the way of Alpine or Cumbrian landscapes. They are more blank than that, more abstract, and so able to allow a more total and encompassing dissolution of the distinctions between things. The pigeons strum their guitars below you. A buzzard drifts and flickers on the wind. A little leatherjacket comes up out of the bracken and begins to explore the folds of your sleeve as if they were the ridges and hollows of a strange new hillside. The old pollards on Lady's Edge reach their arms out across the combe as carelessly as courtiers greeting their sovereign. And the streams continue to play their distant music, only heard if you pause for a while and suppress the sound of your own body moving on the heather or the bracken, allowing that whispered dropping of the water to come up towards you from the depths of the oakwood. But this is the difference made by the poets' having been here, having heard all this and having felt the significance of it: in those melting moments, the material world matters less than your own presence in it. Being here and being involved with this world, recognising that others have been here in that same way, is what seems good. The legacy of these poets is a universal human inheritance, one of the bonds between us, so that to be alone in the world is not to be alone at all.

6

Informing

July and August 1797

In July 1797, with his blue democrat's coat off in the heat, wearing glasses and a broad-brimmed white hat against the sun, the most famous radical in England was walking down from London, heading for the shores of the Bristol Channel. John Thelwall was stout and small, with something a little fox-like and even furtive about him, and he had announced to his followers that there on the Somerset coast he had 'an invaluable friend, well known in the literary world'. They had yet to meet in the flesh, but had already engaged in a 'familiar and confidential correspondence'. The 'young man' he was heading down to see was 'one of the most extraordinary Geniuses & finest scholars of the age', and, needless to say, had issued the invitation to come to the Quantocks. Somerset was some kind of refuge where, under the branches of the sheltering tree, Thelwall, his wife and children, among a 'fraternal band' of 'minds congenial', could find the means 'In philosophic amity to dwell'.

Thelwall represents a new element in Coleridge's great gathering, one that stems from the violence and trouble of the times, coming from the opposite pole to the mind-melting, bracken-lined nooks of the Quantock heights above Butterfly Combe or Holford Glen. He was a household name, known to anyone in England who read a newspaper, one of the veteran targets of Pitt's regime, its caricaturists and the reactionary mobs which did its bidding. The great radical orator, nicknamed 'Tellwell', who could address London crowds tens of thousands strong, was thirty-two that summer, narrow-chested but firm-bodied, with a large nose and a ragged, rat-chewed republican haircut.

His was another version of the Romantic self generated by the conditions of the 1790s: not the darkness of Wordsworth's post-revolutionary despair, nor the religious expectations of Coleridge (Thelwall was an atheist), nor the parochial meliorism of Poole, or Lamb's feeling that the inconsequential was the best to be hoped for, but a fiercely engaged activism, charting a highly emotional and personal zigzag between his own quasi-revolutionary demands – fiercer in their language than in their politics – and the threats of oppression.

He is a demonstration of what Coleridge and Wordsworth were not. He had begun life as the son of a silk mercer from Chandos Street in Covent Garden, but he had been drawn to the theatre, to poetry, to painting, to midnight rambles, and then to the law. He had been born asthmatic and with a stammer – one of the hostile epithets was 'the lisping orator' – but he developed into a powerful speaker, knowing how to milk a room for its energy and applause, and the language he habitually turned to was explosive. Coleridge admired him, but didn't like his atheism nor his volume: 'You talk loudly and rapidly,' he wrote, 'but powers of vociferation do not constitute a PATRIOT.'

Thelwall was in trouble in 1797. For five years he had been proclaiming the wickedness of society in the booming world of late-eighteenth-century Britain, where new industries and a growing empire were spinning the economic wheel into ever more polarised forms of injustice. The government had doggedly spied on him, consistently and secretly reporting his conversation, which was peppered with regicide jokes. He had been spotted cutting the frothy head off a pot of porter while saying to his friends, 'So should all tyrants be served!' and toasting '*The Lamp-irons in Parliament street*', from which a tyrant could happily be hanged, as they had been in Paris. Spring-loaded knives had been seen in his lodgings. Inevitably the attention of the Home Department turned towards him.

The government spy-centre was still a tiny organisation, with fewer than two dozen men working there under the Secretary of State, Henry Dundas, and the Under-Secretary John King. Its small secret-service section was run by a man called James Walsh, based in Bow Street, just across from the Opera House in Covent Garden, where the Home Department funded a small body of policemen.

Walsh is, of course, a shadowy figure, but judging from his notes and letters to Dundas, to his successor the Duke of Portland and the other functionaries in Whitehall, which are all now gathered in the Home Office files in Kew, he was a man of efficiency, courtesy, sceptical intelligence, skill and some brio. Almost the only physical facts recorded about him are that he too had a big nose, and that the buttons of his coat were embossed with the words 'King and Constitution'.

He had done all kinds of work for his masters, creating disturbances at radical meetings, investigating suspicious plumbers who were sending consignments of musketballs to would-be revolutionaries in Dublin, making secret trips to Peterborough, Dover and Maidstone, occasionally attending the King when visiting Weymouth, perhaps as a protection officer. The printers and sellers of seditious pamphlets, those with a surprisingly regular connection to Paris, the odd sorts in the provinces, when reported to London all came under his purview.

The Home Office files containing the reports of Walsh and others like him portray a country and its government gripped by anxiety. There had been talk of invasion, and even a bungled landing of some French troops – mostly convicts in uniform – in Pembrokeshire, and the whole of Britain was on the alert. The port-reeve of Swansea had heard from the master of a Swedish vessel that sixteen French ships of the line, with frigates and troopships, had been spotted seven leagues west of Scilly, steering to the north. The postmaster at Dover had intercepted a letter written in cyphers, and, 'apprehending the contents may be of a political or improper tendency', had sent it to Mr King. Certain strange men had been seen exercising in the night at Wolverhampton: 'There can I fear be no doubt of their purpose,' the Home Office was told. Sir Cecil Wray, the sixty-five-year-old baronet at Summer Castle in Lincolnshire, wanted to set up a mounted militia of forty local farmers. He appointed himself their captain and arranged for them to 'assemble on Horse Back every Sunday evening at four o'clock in my Park to be trained and exercised'.

Someone suggested that every parish should be given two or three howitzers to keep the enemy at bay. Farm carts could be turned into 'extempore *Tumbrills*' and be stored full of ammunition inside parish churches. Each parish band might be put under the instruction of a Chelsea Pensioner, and 'the peasantry and yeomanry, well accustomed to *the Plough* and *the Spade*, would form an excellent Rustic Artillery'.

In response to this enthusiasm came the smooth and consistent authority of Portland and King, conveyed in the seamless copperplate of the government clerks. The Lord Lieutenants of the counties where trouble was brewing were instructed to 'represent to the people the impropriety of the conduct they are pursuing and the consequences which must follow if it is persisted in'. The Earl of Lonsdale, the peer who was still refusing to pay his debt to the Wordsworths, was told that the counties of Westmorland and Cumberland, for which he was responsible, were 'of riotous disposition, secretly directed and encouraged by designing individuals', and that he was to do something about it sooner rather than later.

Dundas himself signed a memorandum to Pitt and the Cabinet, discussing the 'Coastes and Bays of Great Britain and Ireland and the general Defence': 'Our general outline and frontier is so immense, that it is impossible to guard or strengthen every available place.' Choices had to be made. All defensive effort should be concentrated on the great anchorages of the Downs, Dover, Portsmouth, Plymouth and Falmouth, plus the Humber and the Firth of Forth. As for 'the coasts of the Bristol Channel', they 'demand such peculiar and great arrangements to attack them, that they probably do not enter into the Contemplation of an Enemy who has greater objects to aim at nearer at hand'. The Quantocks were in no one's front line.

Thelwall, with his lecturing and his printed journal, *The Tribune*, was, needless to say, firmly in view. Through the early 1790s James Walsh had been involved with arranging *agents provocateurs*, paid for from secret Home Department funds, to disrupt Thelwall's meetings, which could then be shut down. He attended Thelwall's lectures so regularly that his face became known. One evening in May 1794, Thelwall was met at the door of his lodgings in Beaufort Buildings, on The Strand, 'by Walsh, an itinerant spy, and five or six other persons, several of whom were wrapped up in great coats, &c.' Two King's Messengers, as well as John King, the Permanent Under-Secretary, and a Bow Street Runner surrounded him, and Thelwall was arrested 'for treasonable practices'. They rummaged through his clothes, confiscating his pocketbook and his penknife, before moving on to the drawers in the house, from which they removed all his papers. He was then taken in a carriage to the Secretary of State's office in Downing Street.

Along with some forty other radicals, who were picked up in a series of raids that same week, often at dawn, Thelwall was questioned by the Privy Council. Habeas Corpus was soon suspended, and Thelwall was kept in the Tower and then in the charnel-house in Newgate, for seven long months before he was finally brought to court on a charge of high treason. Life in prison was no joke, but when it came to the famous Treason Trials of the autumn of 1794, at which Thelwall and his co-defendants were threatened with death by hanging, drawing and quartering, the Crown was unable to make its case stick. The government had no evidence that the suspects offered any threat to the life of the King, and in English law, no threat to the King meant no treason. Thelwall and the others were carried high through the streets of London as champions of Liberty.

But that is where Thelwall's travails began. He was now a 'Jacobin fox' on the run from government repression. Lecturing on English politics was no longer allowed, and so the talks he gave around the country were on the inadequacies of the Roman constitution. No one failed to see through that, and gangs of thugs, encouraged and directed by Walsh's network of government spies and informers, stalked him from one meeting to the next.

Others gave up their public lives in the face of this oppression, but Thelwall continued, and his audiences continued to love him. He understood what he was about, maintaining that change could not be achieved 'by writing quarto volumes, and conversing with a few speculative philosophers by the fireside'; and so, in the service of humanity, he could still turn on the rhetorical fire:

He was possessed, infuriated with the patriotic mania; he seemed to rend and tear the rotten carcase of corruption ...
The lightning of national indignation flashed from his eye; the workings of the popular mind were seen labouring in his bosom.

This chosen mission came at a sometimes terrifying cost. At one meeting, in Yarmouth, 'about ninety sailors armed with bludgeons burst in upon the audience and laid about them on all sides'. Thelwall tried to escape the 'banditti', but the sailors and their officers with cutlasses grabbed him, at which he drew his pistol. He made a run for it, while the sailors attacked members of the audience and stole their shawls, bonnets, wigs, shoes, hats, coats – and Thelwall's rather serious books on Roman constitutional law. They had been planning to take him aboard a naval vessel bound for Kamchatka, on Russia's far north-eastern coast. Other radicals, condemned to transportation to Australia, had never returned, and that may also have been Thelwall's intended fate, a sentence to the far end of the world, not of death, but of death-in-life.

All around England, as he was pursued by informers, local zealots were drummed up against him, and he was 'driven like a wild beast, and banished, like a contagion, from society'. The War Secretary William Windham had said in the Commons that ministers 'were prepared to exert a vigour more than the laws', and Thelwall was on the receiving end of their efforts. At King's Lynn, Wisbech, Derby, on the borders of Leicestershire, at Stockport and in Norwich, mobs attacked him, windows were broken, and again and again he escaped by drawing his pistol and threatening to shoot those who molested him.

This whole story was public knowledge. It lies behind the word 'prison' in Coleridge's beautiful paean to love and contentment in Tom Poole's arbour. Thelwall was not some ranter from the lunatic fringe. After the attack on him by the naval ratings in Yarmouth, twenty-two people from the audience (of about two hundred) subscribed the enormous sum of £50 each – three years of a labourer's pay – to prosecute the offenders. Among the subscribers were merchants, a gentleman, a carpenter, a single woman, a fiddler (and his son), a carter, a shipwright, a coachman, a book-keeper and a brewer. These were professional, middle-class and clearly moneyed people for whom Thelwall spoke with the voice of mainstream legitimacy, in which his and their shared principles were threatened by an oppressive regime. The question these events posed to the

Stowey group was stark enough: how could retirement to the country and the writing of poetry, however elegant or consoling, be an adequate response to the English government's denial of liberty?

Even Thelwall was in two minds: where did the answer lie? In the Rousseauesque vision of a contented family in nature? Or out in public, advocating political change, his life in danger and his wellbeing threatened? In the late spring of 1797, in a parallel move to Coleridge's and Wordsworth's, Thelwall decided that the time had come to withdraw to the country, away from the violence and strain of political life, to look after his children, his wife and himself, and to write poetry.

He decided to walk to Somerset, partly because walking felt like a democratic way of travelling, partly because on a walk 'the volume of nature is ever open at some page of instruction and delight … These fields, these hedgerows, this simple turf, Shall form my Academus.' The walker was no landowner, and in that way democracy and nature, walking and liberty were the same thing.

For all these good intentions, and for all his brilliance on the platform, it is obvious that Thelwall had no idea how to talk to anyone unlike himself. He had been on previous excursions when he had attempted it.

I have been rambling, according to my wonted practice, in the true democratic way, on foot, from village to village … I have dropped, occasionally, into the little hedge ale-houses to refresh myself. I have sat down among the rough clowns, whose tattered garments were soiled with their rustic labours; for I have not forgot that all mankind are equally my brethren; and I love to see the labourer in his ragged coat – that is love the labourer: I am sorry his coat is obliged to be so ragged. I love the labourer then, in his ragged coat, as well as I love the Peer in his ermine; perhaps better …

Thelwall was giving lectures on his way, in Salisbury, Frome, Bath and Bristol, to the usual admiring nest of Jacobins among the mercantile classes, but when he tried to get information on 'the condition of the labouring poor' from those who might know about it first-hand, things did not go so well. He spoke to an old thresher at work in a barn.

> Every question was repelled by some *sly rub*, or *sagacious* hint; and his arch gestures, and emphatic half-syllables, displayed the self-congratulating cunning of suspicion.

This 'jealous reluctance of communication' met him everywhere he turned. Eventually a rare labourer turned out to be 'inquisitive, shrewd, and communicative', a man who read the papers, but who, to Thelwall's disappointment, could not talk in general terms but only of the mutiny in the Royal Navy ships at Portsmouth, 'of war and of parties. In short, he was too full of liquor and *temporary politics*.'

These failed encounters between the champion of the poor and the poor themselves suddenly make something clear – the extent to which Wordsworth and Coleridge were moving faster and further than the most famous radical in England. Thelwall was still seeing the poor as a political problem, while the Somerset poets were wanting to understand them as people. The culture gap between Thelwall and the labourer in his ragged coat is precisely the chasm that both Coleridge and Wordsworth had been wanting and struggling – and would go on wanting and struggling all year – to bridge in their poetry. Thelwall was still thinking of life in the country as an escape from the problems of politics; the poets in Somerset had begun to see that being in the Quantocks was a form of engagement with politics at a deeper level, reaching for the understanding that poetry, because of its basis in imagination, could do more than politics or political theory ever could to change the presuppositions and expectations on which injustice was founded. If you assumed clownishness in the poor, their degradation was inevitable. But enter their imaginative world, and the old barriers to comprehension and humanity had a chance of dissolving.

If the world was to be remade, only the imagination could remake it. Coleridge would tell the young William Hazlitt the following winter that there was an inevitable 'ascendency which people of imagination exercised over those of mere intellect'. That, essentially, was the task of this year, and the beginnings of any answer they might give to the burning questions: How could life in the Quantocks engage with the need for social change? What could poetry do for justice? The reply: the imagination which lies at the core of poetry could transform the basis on which the world was to be understood.

It is always dangerous to use Wordsworth's own account of his development in *The Prelude* as any kind of evidence, but, set against Thelwall's anxious and alienated difficulties on the road, Wordsworth's love of the road is both the greatest hymn to walking ever made and a testament to his own deep-reaching humanity. The road was, for him, not an escape from reality but a plunging into it, an engagement with people and with the depths of time beyond anything a drawing room, a public platform or a library could offer:

> I love a public road: few sights there are
> That please me more: such object hath had power
> O'er my imagination since the dawn
> Of childhood, when its disappearing line,
> Seen daily afar off, on one bare steep
> Beyond the limits that my feet had trod,
> Was like a guide into eternity,
> At least to things unknown and without bound.

That unhemmed edge, the disappearing of the road beyond the limits of knowing, and the people he met on it always seemed to him, he said, to be invested with the grandeur of the great mariners, sudden vast prophetic figures, 'the Wanderers of the Earth'. There was a time when that scale was disturbing for him, and meeting a madman out of Bedlam or a simple vagrant would alarm him, and he would walk past more quickly than before. But at some moment – he does not say when – he changed:

> When I began to inquire,
> To watch and question those I met, and held
> Familiar talk with them, the lonely roads
> Were schools to me in which I daily read
> With most delight the passions of mankind,
> There saw into the depth of human souls,
> Souls that appear to have no depth at all
> To vulgar eyes.
> I prized such walks still more; for there I found
> Hope to my hope, and to my pleasure peace
> And steadiness; and healing and repose
> To every angry passion. There I heard,
> From mouths of lowly men and of obscure
> A tale of honour.

It is the deepest of transformations, written six or seven years after he had left Somerset, addressed to Coleridge, then in despair and away in Malta, but perhaps remembering their Quantocks year, when Wordsworth, under Coleridge's tutelage, began to shed both his own anguish and the skin of gentlemanliness and, out on the road, started to encounter the human and cosmic truths he had always shunned before.

Thelwall arrived in Stowey late on the evening of 17 July,

walking up the lanes from the ferry over the Parrett at Combwich. He found Sara in the Lime Street house doing the laundry, and helped her with it. The previous day, she and Coleridge had been with the Wordsworths as they moved into Alfoxden. Coleridge was still over there with them, and early the next morning, which was beautiful, fair and already warm by seven o'clock, Sara and Thelwall walked over to join them, along the turnpike between Stowey and Holford, skirting the lower edges of the hills, under the branches of the oakwood reaching out over them, coming through the park to the house before breakfast.

For Thelwall, it was an arrival in a dream world. Here was a living, thinking, working, writing, walking version of a revolution that had already happened, a sort of Pantisocracy in miniature. He wrote home to his wife about his first outings with the two poets:

> Everything but my Stella and my babes are now banished
> from my mind by the enchanting retreat (the Academus of
> Stowey) from which I write this … We have been having a
> delightful ramble to-day among the plantations, and along
> a wild, romantic dell in these grounds through which a
> foaming, murmuring, rushing torrent of water winds its long
> artless course. There have we some times sitting on a tree –
> sometimes wading boottop deep thro the stream & again
> stretched on some mossy stone, a literary & political
> triumvirate passed sentence on the productions and
> characters of the age, burst forth in poetical flights of
> enthusiasm and philosophised our minds into a state of
> tranquillity which the leaders of nations might envy and the
> residents of Cities can never know.

The hosts may have loved his presence rather less than he loved them. Coleridge told Cottle in Bristol that Thelwall was deficient in that patience of mind which can look intensely and frequently at the same subject. He believes and disbelieves with impassioned confidence. I want to see him doubting.

He lacked, in other words, precisely those qualities Coleridge loved in Lamb, who had left only a day or two before. But Thelwall was settling in. He told his wife that he could not yet say 'how many days I may loose the world in this scene of enchantment'. Perhaps he and Stella and the children might move in to the Wordsworths' far too enormous house? 'During the whole of this ramble I have had serious thoughts of a cottage. Do not be surprised,' he told her, 'if my next should inform you that I have taken one.'

They talked poetry and politics, discussions in which, by his own account, Thelwall was the constitutional moderate in a nest of revolutionary extremists. A couple of decades later, in his autobiography, Coleridge would deny any radical thoughts he might have had in the 1790s, but Thelwall's copy of *Biographia Literaria* survives, and he wrote indignantly in the margins. Coleridge had said of the Stowey years 'how opposite even then my principles were to those of Jacobinism or even of democracy'. Not as far as Thelwall could recall:

Mr C. was indeed far from Democracy, because he was far beyond it, I well remember – for he was a down right zealous leveller & indeed in one of the worst senses of the word he was a Jacobin, a man of blood.

I visitted him [at Stowey] & found him a decided Leveller – abusing the democrats for their hypocritical moderatism, in pretending to be willing to give the people equallity of privileges & rank, while, at the same time, they would refuse them all that the others could be valuable for – equality of property – or rather abolition of all property.

Perhaps this was just another case of Coleridge, against his better interests, 'being carried away with an ebullient Fancy, a flowing Utterance, a light and dancing Heart … to speak vehemently from mere verbal associations'? But Thelwall's account sounds coherent enough. Coleridge would claim the following spring (admittedly to his conventional brother) to have snapped his 'squeaking baby-trumpet of Sedition', the fragments of which were now lying 'scattered in the lumber-room of Penitence'; but that was still months away, and it is more than likely that the conversations under the trees of Alfoxden park and in the dell by the waterfall in Holford Glen drifted into revolutionary talk.

Wordsworth, Coleridge and Thelwall all remembered years later a moment between them. Thelwall himself, as 'Edmunds', put the memory into an 1801 novel, *The Daughter of Adoption*. The sun has set, and in the glowing dark of the evening Coleridge, as 'the pensive Henry', sits on a 'fragment of mossy stone' beside the burbling stream and starts to talk.

> Thought followed thought, and subject succeeded subject without apparent connection, until he too fell silent.
> 'What a scene, and what an hour, Edmunds,' said he, bantering, 'to hatch treason in!'
> 'What a scene, and what an hour', replied Edmunds, with the most undisturbed composure, 'to make one forget that treason was ever necessary in the world!'

As Thelwall remembered it, Wordsworth was silent. Coleridge himself said something over-excited, or at least something bantering, sliding between the all-important and the absurd, playing with Thelwall's sensibilities. Thelwall, the 'acquitted felon' who had been tried for his life and threatened with assassination, who had taken to wearing a hardened, cudgel-proof hat, could only be the most serious of the three, looking for a

Night comes

FOLLOWING PAGE: And the moon sails on

refuge away from the realities with which, in their Somerset insulation and their lack of violent experience, Coleridge and Wordsworth could still afford to be engaged. The famous steep-sided dell they all loved could be both a place to forget revolution and a place, in another more oblique form, to hatch it.

Their habit was to set off for a walk – at any season – after dinner, in the early evening as the day was fading and the enveloping and enlarging beauties of the Quantocks started to reveal themselves. They took with them their notebooks and pens, their spyglasses and folding camp stools, with portfolios of paper in which to record what they saw. 'What an hour,' the Coleridge figure in Thelwall's novel had said of the evening, and this violet hour, spreading on into the night, whether moonlit or not, was again and again the time they encountered their new-found world.

The moon had been full on 8 July, and so the ten nights Thelwall was with them, from 17 to 27 July, although warm and fair, were only half-moony. They walked, at least at first, in the evening light, through the heavy shadows of Hodder's or Holford Combe, with the glitter beside them of the pebbled streams that run along the feet of those wooded valleys. Of all their experiences it is the most recoverable.

In these summer nights, even when a wind is blowing across the high tops of the hills, down in the shadowy combes all can be still and warm. This is the moment to recognise that the Romantic sensibility is especially attuned to dusk. The last of the light seems to give significance to everything on which it falls. Nothing looks ugly or tawdry. It is the moment, to use Coleridge's terms in *Biographia Literaria*, when 'the truth of nature' and 'the modifying colours of imagination' coalesce. Honeysuckle climbs up into a thorn tree and flowers as its roof. Ivy hangs as a judge's wig in the branches of an ancient oak pollard. All colours are dense, all forms enriched. Everything acquires a depth, a third dimension not revealed in the light of day.

Then up out of the combes, through the fraying edges of the trees and on to the heather and gorse tops. The fleeces of the sheep above the moor grasses, and the moor grasses themselves, glow in the luminosity of dusk. Venus, the evening star, appears, staring-bright in the sky, 'washed', as Coleridge said, so unadorned a white that even in the light of the evening it is as brilliant as a spaceship, sprinkling and flickering its light across the dusk, casting its own shadow if you hold one hand up against the other, and only yellowing as it sets. Around it, the whole of the western horizon glows with the afterlight of the sun. The sea looks bruised, thick with evening purple. Beyond it, the lights in Wales.

As the half-moon rises, its light spreads in lobes and ponds across the path. At first, the moonlight and the last of the sunlight merge. Only then, with the dropping of the sun, does the world turn lead-silver. A cloud that drifts near that moon brightens on its leading edge, as if a door from a corridor had been pushed open. And when that cloud moves on and masks the moon, it sails across the blue-black sky with a vast white fire alight behind it. Over the Levels, ten thousand acres of mist rise from the moors. An oceanic feeling spreads through the world, in which the silver-rimmed clouds become the archipelagos of a map-maker's heaven.

Time drifts on. The shadows fall on the cart-rutted path. The red deer hinds cluster on the horizon, as much the possessors of this dark as you could ever be. They stand as still as a grove of trees. Beneath the beeches, the little shrews dance in and out of the leaf litter. The owls begin on either side of the hill ridge, their solemn songs unfolding like flowers in the night.

From that high and beautiful battlement walk, on which the skyline is marked with the dark outlines of Bronze Age barrows, the old road to Bridgwater drops back down towards Alfoxden and Holford. Its pale surface gleams in the night, reflecting a sky that is lighter than the surrounding earth and into which the dark itself seems to sink. As you come down from the tops, led by that lit path, and as the chattering of the streams slowly gathers around you, the world of humanity begins to smell delicious, as the smoke of apple and cherry wood fires curls up from the houses in Holford and the moon sails on.

They walked every day, sometimes over to Stowey, meeting people on the road, including the man who William Holland called 'a rascally faced fellow as ever I met with', the huntsman Christopher Trickie, or Tricky, who lived on the common at the entrance to the park at Alfoxden, and Rabbin Woodhouse, a gossip and eccentric who, according to Holland, 'lived in a little house entirely by himself – a kind of snarling life, giving and taking offence'.

They would arrive and have supper parties in Coleridge's garden. By high summer, what was meant to be the vegetable patch was rough and neglected. Thelwall remarked on the weeds, but Coleridge explained that they were only an example of the liberty he gave to all living things. There were to be no mouse-traps in the house and no weeding in the garden. 'I thought it unfair in me to prejudice the soil towards roses and strawberries,' he told Thelwall, as an elitist or authoritarian might have done.

Or they walked the whole length of the little brook that rises in the uncertainty and undefinition of the wet ground by Wilmot's Pool on the Quantock ridge, there beginning its course to the sea. The first rivulets emerge from the moor grasses, then gather down Frog Combe and into Hodder's Combe, past and through the bark-grinding mill, where its waters drive a giant wheel, and then on through Holford, running at the foot of the cottage gardens before making its way to the roadside village at Kilve, along a lane past a medieval chantry to the beach at Kilve Pill. It is a journey that can be done in half a day, twice five miles or so of part-fertile ground, easily followed under the oaks and hollies, and all of it carefully examined by Coleridge, always asking those he met what it was like further down. He felt that the progress of a brook through its life might be the organic frame for a great work on man, society and nature:

> a stream, traced from its source in the hills among the yellow-red moss and conical glass-shaped tufts of bent, to the first break or fall, where its drops become audible, and it begins to form a channel; thence to the peat and turf barn, itself built of the same dark squares as it sheltered; to the sheepfold; to the first cultivated plot of ground; to the lonely cottage and its bleak garden won from the heath; to the hamlet, the villages, the market-town, the manufactories, and the seaport.

'Almost daily on the top of Quantock, and among its sloping coombes', Coleridge was busy. 'With my pencil and memorandum-book in my hand, I was making studies, as the artists call them, and often moulding my thoughts into verse, with the objects and imagery immediately before my senses.' His notebook, now in the British Library, preserves these jottings. In among the murmurings of Hartley in his cot – 'Discontent mild as an infant low-plaining in its sleep' – and hopeful statements of a blessed world – 'Love transforms the souls into conformity with the object loved' – are the summer sights of what he saw on these walks: on the high tops 'the neighing wild-colt races with the wind'; and at night alone or in reverie 'the prophetic soul/of the wide world dreaming on things to come'; further down, 'a long deep Lane/So overshadow'd, it might seem one bower'; then the harsh methods with which the Somerset shepherds drove their sheep before them 'and affright them with dogs & noises', the practice of a fallen world compared with those in the Gospels, where the sheep always followed the voice of their master; the mill in Holford Combe, where on a Sunday, when no work was done in Sabbatarian Somerset, even the brook was at rest, and 'from the/Miller's mossy wheel/the waterdrops dripp'd leisurely';

on the banks of the stream as it made its way seaward, 'Broad-breasted Pollards with broad-branching-head'; beneath and around them, the midges on a summer evening 'Dim specks of Entity – applied to invisible Insects'; and as the brook came to the sea and ran over the seaweed beside the surly brown waters of the Bristol Channel, 'The swallows interweaving there mid the paired/Sea-mews, at distance wildly wailing. –'

Everything seen in these accumulating pages is a vehicle and carrier for a meaning beyond itself. 'Never to see or describe any interesting appearance in nature,' Coleridge wrote to his friend the poet and translator William Sotheby,

> without connecting it by dim analogies with the moral world, proves faintness of impression. Nature has her proper interest; & he will know what it is, who believes & feels, that every Thing has a Life of it's own, & that we are all *one Life*. A Poet's *Heart & Intellect* should be combined, *intimately* combined & *unified*, with the great appearances in Nature ...

Connection between divergent realms of life and mind is the governing principle of everything Coleridge was and wanted to be, and for one reason. His mind can only be understood by recognising that a sense of an all-pervasive, all-powerful and all-loving divinity was its grand underlying fact. He knew that all aspects of existence were connected, through God, in that One Life, and that any description which did not attend to the membership of the whole was by definition partial and inadequate. It was not always easy to hold to that vision of completeness, but it was both destiny and duty. 'The needle trembles, indeed,' he wrote to a friend, 'and has its dips and declinations, but it is pointing to the right pole, or struggling to do so: and as long as God does not withdraw his polar influence, nor the soul its polar susceptibility, I must not dare withdraw my love.'

All beings were aspects of that loving unity. When the neighing wild colt races in the wind, he is the wind. When the swallows weave between the wild wailing of the sea mews, their weaving is part of the fabric that embraces the whole of life. Before it was ever made explicit in the intellectual and critical part of his mind, this was the heart of his practice as a poet. The great marshalling and boundary-crossing power of the imagination was at work

> incorporating the Reason in Images of the Sense and organizing (as it were) the flux of the Senses by the permanence and self-circling energies of the reason, [giving] birth to a system of symbols, harmonious in themselves, and consubstantial with the truths, of which they are the conductors.

Consubstantiality – the interfusion of flesh and spirit, symbol and fact – is at the heart of what this year gave to posterity. The imagination is not the inventing power, but the great gathering power, doing for all ideas and all sensations exactly what Coleridge was doing for his friends and co-writers in assembling them in Somerset. His life's work in 1797 seemed to be this: the bringing together of all and everyone that mattered in one sanctified whole, 'his darling hobby-horse', as the atheist Thelwall rather gripingly described it, 'the republic of God's own making'.

The Wordsworths were settling. William went over to Racedown and brought their maid Peggy Marsh and little Basil Montagu back to Alfoxden with him. On 18 July, as the first climax of this gathering, a celebratory dinner was held for the Stoweyists in the handsome panelled dining room at Alfoxden. Old Mrs Poole provided a forequarter of lamb, and the party was invited to assemble first at eleven in the morning to hear Wordsworth reading his tragedy *The Borderers* under the trees of the park. About thirteen people were there: the two Wordsworths, the two Coleridges, Thelwall, Thomas Poole and his apprentice secretary Thomas Ward, his neighbours John and Anna Cruikshank, Mr and Mrs Willmott from Woodlands, a house half a mile from Alfoxden – he was the son of a silk manufacturer in Sherborne, and may have had some radical leanings – and perhaps the curate schoolmaster Mr Roskilly and his wife, who was Sara Coleridge's friend in Stowey.

It was the democrat version of a gentry party of the sort William Holland regularly attended. A serving man called Thomas Jones, who lived in a farm dwelling next to Alfoxden, waited on them. Alfoxden had no shortage of fine silver and porcelain. After dinner, Thelwall stood and addressed the whole company as alarmingly, passionately and loudly as if he were speaking to a crowded meeting on Hampstead Heath. Thomas Jones didn't like the rabid political talk, and was anyway at odds with these unlikely, half-gentry people, not least because he had watched them mending and washing their clothes on a Sunday, which was both déclassé and anti-Sabbatarian.

Thelwall left in late July. He wanted to stay near Stowey, but he was, as Coleridge told John Chubb, the radical mayor of Bridgwater, 'particularly unpopular, thro' every part of the kingdom'. Thomas Poole was reluctant to find him a cottage, as any association with the name of Thelwall would be too much for his own reputation. Besides, as Coleridge wrote to Chubb, had Poole 'not already taken his share of odium –? has he not already almost alienated, certainly very much cooled, the affections of some of his relations, by his exertions on my account?' Could Chubb not find Thelwall a house?

There was no good outcome to these requests. No one in Somerset was prepared to accommodate Thelwall. Coleridge wrote to him, laying the blame on Poole's need to keep his life in order. If Thelwall came to live in Stowey, Coleridge apologised, the whole Malignity of the Aristocrats will converge to him, as to the one point – his tranquillity will be perpetually interrupted – his business, & his credit, hampered & distressed by vexatious calumnies – the ties of relationship weakened – perhaps broken.

Poole's bringing of Coleridge and Wordsworth to Somerset had already played havoc with his life.

You cannot conceive the tumult, calumnies, & apparatus of threatened persecutions which this event has occasioned round about us. If *you* too should come, I am afraid, that even riots & dangerous riots might be the consequence –/ either of us separately would perhaps be tolerated – but *all three* together – what can it be less than plot & damned conspiracy – a school for the propagation of demagurgy & atheism?

He wasn't exaggerating. The Stowey rumour mill was working hard. On 23 July, Charlotte Poole, Tom's cousin, had written in her journal:

We are shocked to hear that Mr Thelwall has spent some time at Stowey this week with Mr Coleridge and consequently with Tom Poole. Alfoxton House is taken by one of the fraternity, and Woodlands by another. To what are we coming.

The outcome was inevitable: a stream of gossip from observations of the Stowey radicals found its way to the Home Office in Whitehall. The Duke of Portland was alerted by a patriotic antiquary from Bath called Daniel Lysons. Lysons had heard from his cook, who was a friend of a man in Hungerford called Charles Mogg, a friend of Thomas Jones, who had been waiting at the

Wordsworths' table at Alfoxden, that things were amiss there, as an 'emigrant family' had

> contrived to get possession of a Mansion House at Alfoxton,
> late belonging to the Revd. Mr. St. Albyn, under Quantock
> Hills – I am since informed, that the Master of the House
> has no wife with him, but only a woman who passes for his
> Sister – The man has Camp Stools, which he & his visitors
> carry with them when they go about the country upon their
> nocturnal or diurnal expeditions, & have also a Portfolio in
> which they enter their observations, which they have been
> heard to say were almost finished – They have been heard to
> say they should be rewarded for them, & were very attentive
> to the River near them – probably the River coming within a
> mile or two ~~from~~ of Alfoxton from Bridgewater – These
> people may *possibly* be under Agents to some principal at
> Bristol –

It was the sort of letter that came in to the Home Department most days of most weeks. Portland, if he ever saw it, passed it on to his Permanent Under-Secretary John King – one of the men who had arrested Thelwall – and King immediately despatched his itinerant spy James Walsh – Thelwall's old enemy – to investigate. Walsh, taking the road west from London, found Charles Mogg in Hungerford. Mogg told him that Thomas Jones had told him that

> some French people had got possession of the Mansion
> House and that they were washing and Mending their
> cloaths all Sunday, that He Jones would not continue there
> as he did not like It. That Christopher Trickie and his Wife
> who live at the Dog pound at Alfoxton, told Mogg that the
> French people had taken the plan of Their House, and that
> They had also taken the plan of all the places round that part

127

of the Country, that a Brook runs in the Front of Trickie's House and the French people inquired of Trickie wether the Brook was Navigable to the Sea, and upon being informd by Trickie that It was not They were afterwards seen examining the Brook quite down to the Sea That Mrs. Trickie confirmd every thing her Husband had said. Mogg spoke to several other persons inhabitants of that Neighbourhood, who all told him, They thought these French people very suspicious persons, and that They were doing no good there ... They were Visited by a number of persons, and were frequently out upon the heights most part of the night.

But Walsh was his usual sceptical self:

As Mr. Mogg is by no means the most intelligent Man in the World, I thought It my Duty to send You the whole of his Storry as he related It.

> I shall wait here Your further Orders and am
> Sir
> Your most obedient
> Humble Servt.
> J. Walsh.

John King sent Walsh £20 and gave him further instructions: 'You will narrowly watch their proceedings ... Should they however move you must follow their track, & give me notice thereof, & of the place to which they have betaken themselves.'

Walsh then headed west and got himself a room at the Globe inn, next to the market cross in Nether Stowey.

I had not been many minutes in this House before I had an opportunity of entering upon my Business, By a Mr. Woodhouse asking the Landlord [Mr Tucker] If he had seen any of those Rascalls from Alfoxton. To which the Landlord reply'd, He had seen Two of them Yesterday. Upon which Woodhouse asked the Landlord, If *Thelwall* was gone. I then asked if they meant the famous Thelwall. They said yes. That he had been down some time, and that there were a Nest of them at Alfoxton House who were protected by a Mr. Poole a Tanner of this Town, and that he supposed Thelwall was there (Alfoxton House) at this time. I told Woodhouse, that I had heard some-body say at Bridgwater that They were French people at the Manor House. The Landlord & Mr. Woodhouse answered No. No. They are not French, But they are people that will do as much harm as All the French can do.

I think this will turn out no French Affair but a mischiefuous gang of disaffected Englishmen. I have just procured the Name of the person who took the House. His Name is *Wordsworth* a Name I think known to Mr. Ford.

Rabbin Woodhouse was clearly in his element. But why the name Wordsworth might be known to Mr Ford, one of the Under-Secretaries of State at the Home Department, was for a long time something of mystery. Only in 1994 did the personal paybook of the Duke of Portland, Home Secretary in the late 1790s, reach the hands of Wordsworth scholars in Grasmere. Among the secret payments listed in its pages was one of 92 pounds 12 shillings, 'to paid Mr. Wordsworth's draft', on 13 June 1799. Was this the poet? Was Wordsworth in the paid employ-ment of the Pitt regime, which had sent its agent to spy on them in Somerset? For a year or so, evidence was gathered to suggest that he was intimately connected to the world of Ford, Walsh and the Home Office spy network. None of it was conclusive, and by 2000 it had become clear that the Wordsworth known to Mr Ford was William's slightly younger contemporary and cousin, Robinson Wordsworth, a collector of customs at Harwich in Essex. As such, this Wordsworth had helped arrest two men accused of treason, a business in which he incurred the expenses for which the Home Secretary had reimbursed him. The poet had nothing to do with it, and Walsh had confused the two cousins.

The spy went about his task assiduously, and the next day wrote to King again from the Globe:

Sir

The inhabitants of Alfoxton House are a Sett of violent Democrats ... The Rent of the House is secured to the Landlord by a Mr. Thomas Poole of this Town. Mr. Poole is a Tanner and a Man of some property. He is a most Violent Member of the Corresponding Society and a strenuous supporter of Its Friends. He has with him at this time a Mr. Coldridge and his wife both of whom he has supported since Christmas last. This Coldridge came last from Bristol and is reckoned a Man of Superior Ability. He is frequently publishing, and I am told is soon to produce a new work. He has a Press in the House and I am informed He prints as well as publishes his own productions ... By the direction on a letter that was going to the Post Yesterday, It appears that Thelwall is now at Bristol.

Walsh reported that Poole had established a gang of supporters under the name of 'the Poor Mans Club', and 'has the entire command of every one of them'. Letters were being opened, gossip being listened to, misinformation disseminated. Walsh also interviewed Thomas Jones:

He exactly confirms Mogg of Hungerford, with this addition that the Sunday after Wordsworth came, he Jones was desired to wait at Table, that there were 14 persons at Dinner, Poole & Coldridge were there, And there was a little

Stout Man with dark cropt Hair and wore a White Hat and
Glasses (Thelwall) who after Dinner got up and talk'd so
loud and was in such a Passion that Jones was frightned and
did not like to go near them since. That Wordsworth has
lately bean to his former House and brought back with him
a Woman Servant, that Jones has seen this Woman who is
very Chatty, and that she told him that Her Master was a
Phylosopher …

Peggy Marsh had also reported two men coming to Alfoxden,
one of them 'a Great Counsellor from London and the other a
Gentleman from Bristol'. This was Basil Montagu and one of the
Pinneys, yet further members of the Wordsworth–Coleridge
team assembling here.

Walsh then persuaded Jones, with a few shillings, to take a
job weeding the garden at Alfoxden so that he could keep an eye
on the people there and find out who the Great Counsellor
might be. Walsh had also heard that Thelwall was coming back
to share Alfoxden with the Wordsworths. But there Home
Office file 42/41 at Kew falls silent. Walsh must have understood that, despite the country's war footing and the threat of
invasion, political or military conspiracy was not the poets'
business.

Much later, in *Biographia Literaria*, when laying down smoke-
screens across his radical past and joking over the way the Stowey
people had summoned a spy *'pour surveillance'* over him and his
friend, Coleridge claimed that Walsh had once joined him on the
road between Alfoxden and Stowey, 'and, passing himself off as
a traveller, he had entered into conversation with me, and talked
of purpose in a democrat way in order to draw me out'. Coleridge
said he had seen Walsh off with his own sparkle, and then –
drawn to the dramatic as much as Thelwall – gave his own
version of an interrogation of Mr Tucker, hay and straw merchant
and the landlord of the Globe, by a local magistrate.

Coleridge calls the grandee Sir Dogberry, after the bumbling and self-important constable in *Much Ado About Nothing*, but he was actually the legendarily rich John Acland of Stogursey, 'large and tall and very personable', according to William Holland, if 'rather fat, with amazing fat legs … and proud – there is an insolence in his civilities'. The subject of the interview was Coleridge's behaviour in Stowey and surroundings.

> ACLAND: Answer the question, Sir! does he ever harangue the people?
>
> TUCKER: I hope your Honour an't angry with me. I can say no more than I know. I never saw him talking with any one, but my landlord [Tom Poole, who owned the Globe], and our curate [Roskilly], and the strange gentleman [Wordsworth].
>
> ACLAND: Has he not been seen wandering on the hills towards the Channel, and along the shore, with books and papers in his hand, taking charts and maps of the country?
>
> TUCKER: Why, as to that, your Honour! I own, I have heard; I am sure, I would not wish to say ill of any body; but it is certain, that I have heard –
>
> ACLAND: Speak out, man! don't be afraid, you are doing your duty to your King and Government. What have you heard?
>
> TUCKER: Why, folks do say, your Honour! as how that he is a Poet, and that he is going to put Quantock and all about here in print; and as they be so much together, I suppose that the strange gentleman has some consarn in the business.

Walsh's huge nose had allowed Coleridge to make his most famous joke, an entirely invented scene on the shore at Kilve:

[Walsh] had repeatedly hid himself for hours together behind a bank at the sea-side, (our favourite seat,) and overheard our conversation. At first he fancied, that we were aware of our danger; for he often heard me talk of one Spy Nozy, which he was inclined to interpret of himself, and of a remarkable feature belonging to him; but he was speedily convinced that it was the name of a man who had made a book and lived long ago.

Any talk of Spinoza, whose vision of a God-infused nature had inspired Coleridge, was scarcely the point. Hidden within these exchanges is something else. Thelwall was of course notorious, but no one in the Home Office seems even to have heard of a man called Coleridge or Coldridge. He was a figure, apparently, only in Bristol. Nor had his presence in Somerset raised suspicions. The Stowey antennae had only been set on edge by 'the strange gentleman', the 'Phylosopher', 'the emigrant family', the woman passing herself off as a sister, 'the French people', the 'very suspicious persons', so gentry-like but so unlike, who had taken Alfoxden and stalked about their country. Coleridge regaled Joseph Cottle with stories of what the Quantocks had been saying about Wordsworth. He was known to roam over the hills 'like a partridge'. A man 'had heard him mutter, as he walked, in some outlandish brogue, that nobody could understand'. He was a 'wise man', a conjuror, a smuggler. Another thought he was 'surely a desperd French jacobin, for he is so silent and dark, that nobody ever heard him say one word about politics'. In those phrases, and the sense of power in Wordsworth's unaccommodated presence, the people of Stowey, with their 'dark guesses' (Coleridge's own expression), had somehow grasped the otherness latent in him.

Thelwall, leaving them all, felt bereft. On 27 July, his thirty-third birthday, he wrote a verse letter to his wife. His soul was

sick of public turmoil – ah, most sick
Of the vain effort to redeem a Race.

He thought, at Stowey, he had been given a glimpse of how
things might be, how

> it would be sweet,
> With kindly interchange of mutual aid,
> To delve our little garden plots, the while
> Sweet converse flow'd, suspending oft the arm
> And half-driven spade ...

Lime Street, even close up, had looked like heaven on earth.
Their children would play together. They would eat together
and talk and write. To Coleridge, he hoped that they would be
joined by

> Thy Sara, and my Susan, and, perchance,
> Allfoxden's musing tenant, and the maid
> Of ardent eye, who, with fraternal love,
> Sweetens his solitude.

In a Coleridgean way, all the others were also to be gathered:
Tom Poole, described by Thelwall as 'Arcadian Pool, swain of a
happier age,/When Wisdom and Refinement lov'd to dwell/
With Rustic Plainness', and the various Chesters – known to
Thelwall as 'Sylvanus [and] the sister nymphs', one with 'radiant
eye', the other 'The Fairy of the brooks'.

Few things are less forgivable than bad poetry, but Coleridge
stands behind Thelwall's lines as their encouraging and enabling
spirit. Beside him, or perhaps slightly apart from him, scarcely
present, is the great and sceptical silence of the tenant of
Alfoxden, mysterious and disengaged, surely doubting the validity of Thelwall's degraded language and the thoughts it gave rise

Talking of Spy Nosy

FOLLOWING PAGE: Fruiting time

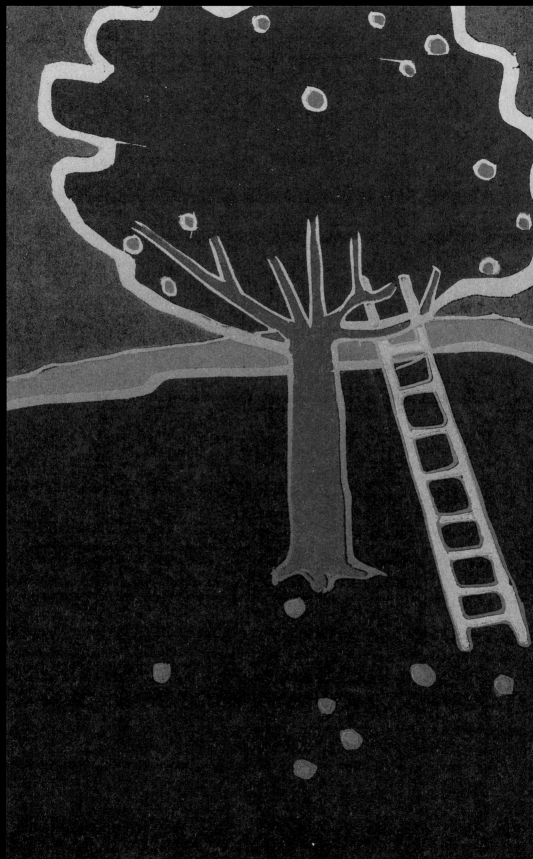

to. It is at least likely that Wordsworth would have had no truck with the idea of Thelwall, and all his accompanying noise and histrionics, ever coming to live with him and his sister. They were acting to different imperatives. As the coming winter would reveal, only a truer frame of mind, and a truer language, could allow anything resembling these ideas to become a reality.

7

Dreaming

September and October 1797

Any evidence of what Wordsworth was doing this summer is thin on the ground. Next to nothing survives of what he wrote or said, and in that mysterious silence and virtual wordlessness, he stands apart from the psycho-mayhem encircling Coleridge. The 'tenant of Alfoxden' seems to have been sufficient in himself. But the notebook he had used at Racedown also contains drafts and sketches for poems, perhaps from these weeks. A solitariness comes out of them. Again and again, scratching at the verses, Wordsworth tries to find a form that can embody the life of a lonely man, sometimes in his own anxious hand, sometimes in Dorothy's transcription, which he then crosses out and interlines with other suggestions, in none of which the punctuation is ever perfect or even present.

'The Description of a Beggar' is one of Wordsworth's versions of himself, the gaze fixed downwards:

> He travels on a solitary man
> His age has no companion. On the ground
> His eyes are turned and as he moves along
> They move along the ground ...

No flight of the mind. Animation appears around him, but the spirit does not rise to meet it:

the little birds
Flit over him and if their shadows strike
Across his path does not lift his head
Like one whose thoughts have been unsettled

Nothing can penetrate the almost static disengagement of this mind. One beautiful image returns, surely seen by Wordsworth head-down on his walks. The words are written again and again and erased again and again, so that the sequence becomes virtually unreadable on the notebook page, but stands as an emblem of frustration:

he sees some straw
Some scattered leaf or marks which in the track
~~Of Cart or Chariot wheel the nails have left~~
~~The nails of cart or chariot wheel have left impressed~~
~~Impress'd Impressed on the white road in the same line~~
In the same never-ending line impress'd
~~One never ending Line the~~   ~~nails~~
~~at distance still the same~~
~~Of cart or chariot wheel have left impress'd~~
~~On the white road — at distance still the same~~
~~One never ending Line the nails of cart~~
~~Or chariot wheel have left on the white road~~
~~Impress'd at distance still the same.~~

Here is a man reaching over and over again for that turning wheel, with its nailed rim, marking out the road with its sequence of impressions, the same unending line for miles however far it goes, and as he writes and rewrites the same line, unchanged or scarcely changed in one turn of the wheel after another, near-absence and near-nothingness fill the pages, the repeating marks merely recording the passing hours and days, in a silence by which even the dogs are bored:

his slow footsteps scarce
Disturb the summer dust. He is so still
In look and motion that the miller's dog
Is tired of barking at him

For Coleridge, everything this autumn was in flux: emotional instability in himself and almost everyone else; a sense, in the aftermath of Thelwall's visit, of being hunted, spied on and caballed against; money worries; an awareness of great inner poetic power that had yet to find its proper outlet; a friendship with Wordsworth whose workings, in the face of his overwhelming silence, seem throughout this summer to be almost subterranean. These were the conditions of Coleridge's mind in the autumn of 1797. It is not surprising that he too might have longed for escape.

September and October was the time for collecting the fruits of the summer. Plums were on the trees, and the poor boys were up there stealing them. The wheat and barley had been clamped in the barns, and cattle were grazing on the regrowth of grass after the hay had been taken and stacked. Autumn shooting brought partridges to the tables of the rich. Horse dung was now to be spread on the growing grounds. Houses were stocked with wood for the winter. Wordsworth, this autumn, was met coming out of a Quantock wood 'with a vast quantity of nuts in a bag or apron before him'. They were for the purpose, he said, 'of helping out the scanty meal to which the family had to sit-down on that day'. This was also the time for honey to be taken from the hives, and brought as a present, still in the comb, by anyone visiting for tea. Nectarines were picked in glasshouses and fallen apples collected from the orchard floors. Hedges were 'shorn', asparagus haulms cut, their beds dunged, the strawberries tidied and the cabbages hoed. On the fine days, the poor were out planting winter wheat by hand. Women were given a little stick tipped with iron, and so made a hole with one hand, and dropped the seed in with the other. The men had two short poles tipped with iron, and so made holes two at a time with both hands, and children followed with the corn.

The barley for malting was delivered to Poole's works in Stowey. The frosts came in mid-September, and greatcoats were brought out for the first time since the spring. Women and children went mushrooming. Even in the rain, as William Holland recorded, the gentry took autumn outings:

The Pooles and their company passed by on a walk up the Quantock. Charles in the garden and I have been somewhat busy in earthing the celery. Saw the Pooles under a bank on the ascent to the Quantock, and the rain most tremendous. I could not find Charles, and so ran myself towards them with three umbrellas, but they were gone. [Later] the heroes and heroines passed by like drowned rats. I ran out and gave them two umbrellas.

At some time that autumn, perhaps early in October, Coleridge also set off on an expedition of his own. It was for a few days, heading west, out past Williton and down into Watchet, into the thick, dropping, wooded, coastal hills on the borders of Devon.

He was feeling ill, perhaps with a hint of dysentery, but also with some more pervasive uncertainty in his mind. He wrote to Thelwall in October, desperate about money and his prospects as a writer. But more fundamental than either was an overwhelming sense of *anomie*, of lacking that unifying frame of love and understanding which he so often promulgated to his followers. There was too much too fragmentary in his life, so that frequently *all things* appear little – all the knowlege, that can be acquired, child's play – the universe itself – what but an immense heap of *little* things? – I can contemplate nothing but parts, & parts are all *little* – ! – My mind feels as if it ached to behold & know something *great* – something *one &* *indivisible* – and it is only in the faith of this that rocks or waterfalls, mountains or caverns give me the sense of sublimity or majesty!

Only then, when the frame was whole, when away from the noise and trouble of the people he insisted on gathering about him, could the details signify. Only then, in that moment of solitary, suspended and comprehensive bliss, could '*all things* counterfeit infinity!'

His longing was for a place of ease:

It is better to sit than to stand, it is better to lie than to sit, it is better to sleep than to wake – but Death is the best of all! – I should much wish, like the Indian Vishna, to float about along an infinite ocean cradled in the flower of the Lotos, & wake once in a million years for a few minutes – just to know that I was going to sleep a million years more.

The softness of death, the enveloping folds of an opium dream, where the petals could close about him in an exquisite, eternal and comfort-bedded refuge. He quoted from his play *Osorio*, describing the very landscape through which he had walked westwards for a night and a day to Porlock and on towards Lynton in Devon:

The hanging Woods, that touch'd by Autumn seem'd
As they were blossoming hues of fire & gold,
The hanging Woods, most lovely in decay,
The many clouds, the Sea, the Rock, the Sands,
Lay in the silent moonshine.

In those bronzed and gilded, silvered, dream-lit woods, beautiful
as they died, there was a kind of contentment to be found, somewhere both safe and floating, an untethered bliss, where 'in some
small skiff/Along some Ocean's boundless solitude', he could

> float for ever with a careless course,
> And think myself the only Being alive!

There he would find peace, where all stimulus was suspended
and the wholeness of being could make itself apparent to him
again, as it had been that blessed summer evening in Tom Poole's
arbour, when delight had come sudden on his heart.

In this mood,

> At a Farm House between Porlock & Linton, a quarter of a
> mile from Culbone Church, in the fall of the year, 1797, in a
> sort of Reverie brought on by two grains of Opium, taken to
> check a dysentery,

Coleridge wrote 'Kubla Khan'.

Walking westwards is a walk towards wildness. As you move
into the woods and up on to the rough brown open-weave spaces
of Exmoor, the Quantocks start to seem smaller and more ordinary by comparison, a gentler younger brother of this big moory
expanse on the fringes of Devon. On this path now, high on the
broken cliffs, the scale changes. Islands of shadow breeze across
the brown and turgid sea. The Bristol Channel looks as earthy as
a ploughed field. The path plunges on, up over the rounded
thighs of each valley, slipping into the declivities, down into the
ferny damp of the streams running off Exmoor, up again to the
sound of the sea that rises from the surf breaking miles away in
a constant single outbreath from below.

There can be few places in England where human habitation
seems so embedded in the land. Where the streams run off

Exmoor, they cut deep combes in the half-hard rocks. There are no sharp angles; every form is rounded, down off the moor, down into the combes, down towards the sea. Every combe shelters a wood, and at the top of every wood a farm is tucked into its hollow, the silver-grey slates of its roofs just lifted above the land from which they have come.

These half-animal forms of thigh-pasture and combe-hollow are as old a landscape as anywhere in England. Lanes are creased into the land below the surface of the fields. In the damp of the autumn woods, the blackbirds sing the last of their summer songs. Between the blankets of moss and wood spurge, the deer have kicked and stomped their way down into the earth.

Embedded in one of these combes is the little church at Culbone. It is a tiny grey lichened box, fringed with fern and cranesbills, with a needle-nest of birdsong around it and a big dark yew shadowing the gravestones. Orange and grey lichens blotch them. All the sensuous signals are here: the broken music of the stream, the deer half-present in the wood, the antiquity of a hollow where a dark-age hermit, St Beuno, lived in a place whose even older name *Kitnor* means 'cave by the sea'. It is all poor and simple, holy and forgotten. I pulled on the bell-ropes and rang the two bells of the church, one brighter, one heavier, one Victorian, one fourteenth-century, the oldest bell in Somerset. Where there is a knot in the timber, the green oak pews twisted as they cured six centuries ago, and since then have been polished dark on the upper edges where the hands of shepherds and charcoal burners have held them as they stood or knelt.

Upstream from the church, three or four farms claim to be the place in which Coleridge rested to take his opium and recover from his dysentery. Most think it might have been Ash Farm, perhaps only because it seems to look as such a place might look. Some think Parsonage Farm – but would the parson have taken him in? Few claim Silcombe Farm. Mr R.J. Richards, who is the fourth generation of Richardses to farm there, and all of whose ancestors are buried in Culbone's tiny streamside churchyard, thinks Coleridge wouldn't have come so far. 'If he was ill he would have gone to the nearest and the most likely spot, to my mind,' he told me over the farm wall. 'That's a place that is no longer there. Withycombe. There is a pond there. Every house had a pond.'

Half a mile along the lane from Silcombe, the little valley of Withycombe itself is a steep cut into the shore-facing hill, with a sharp drop into it, so that as you arrive on the lane your eye is level with the tops of the oaks. Just down from the gate off the lane is a flattened spot which is, I guess, where the house once stood. Ground ivy now covers the grass there. What Wordsworth called 'the calm oblivious tendencies of nature ... the silent over-growings' have made Withycombe their own. It had always been a cold spot. 'It was always going to be the first to be left behind,' Mr Richards had said.

The water of the Withycombe stream still bubbles through the abandoned place. The stone dam across the stream, built to make the pond, is still there, but broken, so that the stream now runs over the flat and nettly bed of what was once the pond. On its edge, an enormous oak, undoubtedly growing when Coleridge was here, is now encrusted and burdened with ivy. A confluence of old tracks, connecting this place to its land, to the church and shore, now lead off only into blackthorn thickets. Limbs of fallen ashes block the paths, so that Withycombe now is buried in space as much as in time, occupied on this late autumn morning only by two old ewes. Bumblebees drift down on the wind. Some ponies arrive, coming down through a half-open gate, four or five mares and their foals, the mothers moving easily and elegantly, long, glossy tails and sun-reflecting, careless flanks. The legs of the foals beside them are as long as their mothers', all knee and bone, the pale young bodies carried above them as lightly as baskets. This is where Coleridge in his illness had written the great fragment.

Opium would have been the oasis within this oasis. The drug was available in all sorts of forms – and was to be found in almost every household as an 'anodyne', a painkiller. Nelson used to take it when his wounds hurt; Dorothy Wordsworth took it for tooth-ache. It was prescribed for asthma and rheumatism. Women with menstrual pains or in labour were given it, although the child when born was often found to be under the influence of the opium, with a slow pulse and breathing.

When the Reverend Holland of Over Stowey had a face that hurt, he summoned Mr Lyng, the apothecary from Stogumber on the far side of the Quantocks, who applied leeches to his cheeks and then gave him Dover's Powders, a mixture of opium and ipecacuanha, a South American root which cleared the chest and was an emetic. Holland stuck with daily doses of what he called 'Dr Dover' for several days until his face went down.

As Victoria Berridge has described, you could buy opium in all kinds of preparations: mixed with honey, as an electuary, meaning 'something to be licked up'; powdered with chalk; sugared as an opiate confection; mixed with soap; in a liquorice lozenge or troche; in vinegar or wine; as a suppository or enema; as a plaster or embrocation; or, most popularly of all, dissolved in alcohol, as laudanum, a name given it in the sixteenth century and meaning 'the thing to be praised' because it was so effective at relieving pain and distress. Infants were often given Godfrey's Cordial (also called The Mother's Friend), a mixture of opium, water and treacle, to keep them quiet. In some places, opium was added to the beer. In corner shops it could be had from jugs that stood on the counter. Customers could buy 'Children's Draughts, a penny each'. Those customers were often the children themselves.

The opium sensation – to different degrees with different doses – is of liquefaction, a suspension of the anxieties, a sort of death before death, another kind of death-in-life, a delicious and

suicidal other-state, the temporary ceasing of life and its struggles. Opium makes existence beautiful, creating an oasis in which
love seems to be the natural and normal relationship between all
beings. It is the ideal Coleridgean state of mind in a medicine,
the warm druggy dusk of no pain, a dissolver, a slow loosening
of the bonds. Opium does not make you high or elevated, but
the opposite, beautifully lowered, with a sense in the drug of
going down and in, away from pain, to an inner hidden distant
place which is a kind of lower heaven, of the sort that bees in
summer warmth or fish in the sweetest part of a pool might feel,
a fittedness between organism and world, where existence feels
like a glove for the self. The duvet did not yet exist in England –
Coleridge when he went to Hamburg the following year could
not understand why the Germans seemed to sleep between two
feather mattresses, one above and one below – but he already
knew in the laudanum he took, for tooth pain and gut pain, for
dysentery and neuralgia, exactly what a duvet could do for a
troubled soul.

At home, Coleridge had been reading a large 1626 folio of
travel stories called *Purchas His Pilgrimage*, in which one paragraph described the glittering summer palace and perfect estate
of a Mongol prince called Cublai Can, grandson of the great
Cingis Can, with its 'sumptuous house of pleasure' with 'all sorts
of beasts of chase and game', its beautiful parkland and its air of
elegant magic. That was the seed in his mind:

In Xannadù did Cubla Khan
A stately Pleasure-Dome decree;
Where Alph, the sacred River, ran
Thro' Caverns measureless to Man
Down to a sunless Sea.
So twice six miles of fertile ground
With Walls and Towers were compass'd round:

And here were Gardens bright with sinuous Rills
Where blossom'd many an incense-bearing Tree,
And here were Forests ancient as the Hills
Enfolding sunny spots of Greenery.

It is written like a song, with the simplest of rhymes. Khan is pronounced Can, and once his Stowey friends knew the poem, the word they always used for a water container was a 'Kubla'. It is also a Quantocks journey, or at least a Quantocks journey interfolded with everything Coleridge had come to know of exotic otherness. What the great American critic John Livingston Lowes would call 'the hooks and eyes of memory' had gathered all possible material from everything Coleridge had read on Asia, Tartary, Cathay and Hindustan, on the sources of the Nile and travels in North America. And so, drawing on that enormous memory bank, this was an account of medieval Shangdu fused with a description of Alfoxden: a beautiful house in a beautiful park with beautiful woods on beautiful hills, and a river laced through it running down to the sea.

The rhythms of the poem are lulling and soporific, so that Xanadu seems to float in a melding of the dreamlike and the real whose elements cannot and never could be disentangled. The place is the hero. Its geography is rich and certain, but within it the people are unreal. Kubla Khan himself has no third dimension. He is merely the ordaining, decreeing, defining, lordly presence at the heart of the beauty he has summoned. In that way he is the great artist, a lord of the imaginative world, and, inescapably, given the conditions of this moment in Somerset, he carries echoes of William Wordsworth. However obliquely, this poem is a depiction of Wordsworth Khan, private, powerful, excluding, presiding in Alfoxden over the deer-filled landscapes of the pleasure ground around him, and a man who for Coleridge seemed at least pregnant with greatness.

The poem, in the first of its slewing turns, then cuts into that vision of wholeness. Everything in the second movement suddenly disrupts the gentlemanly view of the perfect world, and does so hurriedly, diagonally and slashingly, athwart and slantedly.

> But o! that deep romantic Chasm, that slanted
> Down a green Hill athwart a cedarn Cover,
> A savage Place, as holy and inchanted
> As e'er beneath a waning Moon was haunted
> By Woman wailing for her Dæmon Lover:

The wild and the erotic carve a ravine into the settled world, indifferent to any stately or mundane power, or its contentment with picnics beside the burbling stream. What was Kubla Khan to that wailing woman? What was everyday life to her Daemon Lover?

The Quantocks are now left behind as Coleridge moves out into a broken and operatic landscape of vast tectonic drama, the substance of the earth itself subject to the same anxious and horrifying turmoil as Coleridge had experienced, and for which he had in the past dosed himself with laudanum. His description of the great seething, panting river pumping out its life in spasms of energy and creativity is the sexuality of the world itself, a planetary orgasm, followed beautifully and dreamily by post-coital lassitude, a slumping and sinking away from the tumult into the ease and quiet of a forgotten sea.

> ~~And from~~ From forth this Chasm with hideous Turmoil
>   seething,
> As if this Earth in fast thick Pants were breathing,
> A mighty Fountain momently was forc'd,
> Amid whose swift half-intermitted Burst
> Huge Fragments vaulted like rebounding Hail,
> Or chaffy Grain beneath the Thresher's Flail.

And mid these dancing Rocks at once & ever
It flung up momently the sacred River:
Five miles meandring with a mazy Motion
Thro' Wood and Dale the sacred River ran,
Then reach'd the Caverns measureless to Man
And sank in Tumult to a Lifeless Ocean;

Southey had described the events in France to Coleridge as 'the orgasm of the Revolution'. These lines are a translation of that experience, but also of the very place in Holford Glen where Coleridge, Wordsworth and Thelwall had talked treason, turning the world upside down and transforming the relationships between people to make a world in which giant rock layers, like the big blue slabs over which the Quantock rivers poured, could dance and vault like rebounding hail. This too, in its uncertain and mazy way, is an account of revolution, a place in which Ancestral Voices might prophesy war.

Again Coleridge pauses and turns. The vision was given him in a reverie – not asleep but in the opium-induced condition, where the doors and barriers were down between different parts of the mind, between memory and imagination, the verbal and visual, the musical and sensual. Of any poem ever written, this is most like the music of the Aeolian harp, full of half-suggestions and inner echoes, with the sounds of individual words reverberating in a kind of reflective embrace with their neighbours, so that the sound of 'Kubla Khan' half-mirrors into 'Xanadu', and a damsel becomes a version of the Aeolian harp whose name sounds like her, a dulcimer, and whose strings are played by her fingers, as if they were the breezes of the air.

A damsel with a Dulcimer
In a Vision once I saw.
It was an Abyssinian Maid,

And on her Dulcimer she play'd
Singing of Mount Amara.

Already now, as the poem moves towards its close, loss and regret and the fading of powers start to colour the lines. It is a curiously Wordsworthian moment: a vision of poetry and beauty which evaporates with time and the facts of existence. Had the two of them already spoken of Wordsworth's great and future subject, the loss of vision, the withdrawal of beauty? Here in Xanadu, what was once richly apparent and present now starts to move into the past, so that the poet longs to make the world of Xanadu for himself, a vision of beauty dependent on hearing and finding again the music of the dulcimer. Everything now, at this tapering away of the beauty, becomes conditional.

Could I revive within me
Her Symphony & Song,
To such a deep Delight 'twould win me,
That with Music loud and long
I would build that Dome in Air,
That sunny Dome! those Caves of Ice!

The dome is no longer real, but a shadow floating midway on the waves, a thing made only of words and music. But then finally, fiercely and triumphantly, removed from worldly sanction, the poet, along with the damsel and her echoing harp, becomes the hero of his own vision. Kubla Khan is forgotten, and in his place appears a strange and unruly giant, alive with subversion and magic, enormous with the potency that the milky Eastern drug had given him, his hair not part of the well-dressed world, his eyes flashing with their own internal fire, the poet as prophet, cut off from ordinariness, enlightened and miraculously free. The great poet of connectedness dreams of a world without connections.

And all, who heard, should see them there,
And all should cry, Beware! Beware!
His flashing Eyes! his floating Hair!
Weave a circle round him thrice,
And close your Eyes in holy Dread:
For He on Honey-dew hath fed
And drunk the Milk of Paradise.

The whole performance is a spell and an incantation. It is almost a liturgy, a service held in glimmering candlelight, surrounded by the chanting devotees. Later, Coleridge would claim that 'Kubla Khan' is no more than a fragment. The person from Porlock had disturbed him before he could write down all that he had composed. Who knows if that was true? What business could the visitor from Porlock have with Coleridge in the remoteness of Withycombe where he had holed up with his dysentery for a day or two? Besides, for all its slantwise moves, the poem seems complete: a vision of worldly perfection and dominance, undercut by something larger and more anarchic, which then fades with the witchery sounds of the dulcimer and leaves the visionary poet alone in his magic realm, set apart from the fears and desires of existence.

Rousseau had thought that early man would always 'be a light sleeper like animals which, thinking little, sleep all the time they do not think'. The reverie, the half-sleep, the waking dream was a return to that simplicity, to a place in which hierarchy was unimportant. The world of reverie enfolds the revolutionary: not in a programme for political change, but in a change of consciousness by which the beautifully imagined supplants the impositions of human existence. 'Kubla Khan' is both an act of dissolution and an invitation to dissolve those fixities. Every boundary blurs there, every structure breaks and ferments, every authority is denied and undermined, every strangeness welcomed in. The poem's bodiliness, its seething, breathing, panting,

Beneath a waning moon

PREVIOUS PAGE: Withycombe Dream

wailing, dancing, flinging, sinking motions, its memories of the swallows and the sea mews at Kilve, is one of its guarantees of truth, since in bodies there is no social hierarchy; all is shared. It draws on the Quantock geometries, the wide extents, the hills and forests, the inner combes, the all-presence of fast and falling water, and it contains, scarcely acknowledged, a sense of the danger of the Wordsworthian insistence on the normal and the ordinary as the subject of poetry, from which it must proclaim a fierce and anxious independence. But it is also a search for a refuge, a hidden place: caverns and chasms inside a dream world, inside a poem, inside an opium reverie, in a remote farmhouse, out away to the west from the Quantocks, which themselves are away from cities and their struggle and control. Shell after shell protects Coleridge here. He is in his own lair, buried in Withycombe, where all the demands of the world cannot reach him and yet there is no sense of claustrophobia; if anything, this is a poem about the opposite, claustrophilia, amniosis, a world that is freed because it is safe, a return to the egg, where the poet is given access to the inner miracles and where he becomes himself through a descent into the beautiful strangeness that lies within him.

8

Voyaging

November 1797

Late in the autumn, the trunks of the windtorn beeches above Alfoxden turn black with the wet in draped patches of sodden bark. Some of the trees are painfully twisted, strange at night, separating and rejoining like submarine creatures. Others have hollow, ragged, Francis Bacon mouths where old limbs have been prised out in storms. One of them has had its top wrenched away, leaving a fibrous stump full of rot and savagery.

November means withdrawal. The ocean of leaves in the combes acquires a kind of sombre enclosing seriousness. The world drips and your hood is up. The rain tap-drums on to the continuous carpet of wet oak leaves. The bracken starts to break. When it was green, the peaks of the fronds bent over in gothic curves, but now that the first frosts have done their work, there is no strength in them and the stems hang limp or trashed, all their steeples broken, by age or deer or wind, the fibres splintered like the bones of unmended limbs. A woodcock comes up out of the orange, jagging and skidding above the darkening bracken-mat but with no slur in its path; a sharp, angular, italic cut to the line as it drives for the woods and their shadows.

The winter is colonising the days, first accelerating to the equinox and then slowing, coming to the darkest weeks much as a tide sinks from springs to neaps, quietly, a few inches or minutes a day, seeping to its end.

It is the year's dusk, the softest and most hidden of seasons, magical, acquiring latency, its purposes and products unseen and beautiful not because of their fullness or their extent but for their discretion and inwardness. It is the grand annual evening of existence, one character after another carefully slipping out through the closing doors, the latches shutting on an empty stage.

Coleridge himself felt that the coming of winter was no dying. 'Trees in winter neither dead nor inactive,' he wrote in his notebook.

> Nor, tho' the sap may not flow, are they sapless – but they are forming new radicals underground, for an additional supply for Spring & Summer – not merely to supply the same as last year but more – to be more progressive.

The Quantocks year is usually described in terms of its glowing summers, the picnic era of the poets' lives, but for Wordsworth and Coleridge it was this winter, edging into the next spring, which became the most productive moment they would ever know, deeply dependent on dark and strangeness, on all the conditions of a world that is putting itself away. The summer out on the tops or in the 'still, roaring dell' had been a time in which a passionate friendship had surged between them, powered by Coleridge's vital life-spirit pouring into Wordsworth, allowing some kind of interflood, as though Coleridge were the multiple streams running down through the combes and valleys that Wordsworth was offering up to him.

That living summer intimacy was changing now, and in this winter each poet, on his own and differently, began to write some of the great poetry of the year. Much of what was happening is unrecorded in surviving letters or journals. It is as if the winter was the under-time, the seedbed of creation, connected to the life of the well-lit months before and after as the pages of a notebook might be to a completed or published poem. As the surface noise drops away, that cellar-existence comes into focus. Fires and candles are alight in the recesses of life and mind. Darkness is the suggestive condition, of good and bad, of the remembered and the imagined. Phrases occur, connections grow, poetry happens.

They did not know or recognise the isolating winter power at first, and Coleridge planned – twice – for them to write something together. Twice in early November they set out on a walk to the west, heading with Dorothy for the rocky valleys at Lynton, sometimes taking an inland path, sometimes by the coast. The departure, continuing their summer habit, was at dusk, with the sun dropping over Exmoor and the Bredons, and the light in the valley between the western horizon and the Quantocks turning violet, or at least violet-grey, the colour that seems to drain all other colours from the woods and fields.

The day withdraws as the year withdraws. It is then, as Dorothy, ever-quiveringly alert to the signals, would write in her journal, that you hear the robins singing in the distant hollies and faintly, in the stripped winter condition of the world, the beating of the surf on the shore at Kilve or at West Quantoxhead. It is impossible now to know if the faint murmuring in one's ears is that distant sea or the sound of the wind in the moor grasses. The movement of air through ten thousand stems at your feet or the stirring of waves on a hundred thousand pebbles, stone on stone, three miles away, become indistinguishable.

Leaving Alfoxden at 4.30 in the afternoon, they walked up and over the ridge on the old stony road. At night, or not quite at night, as the night comes on, the air in the combes quickly darkens, but the sky above them can sometimes glow a backlit radiant blue, the blue of Himalayan poppies, with the last tatters of sunlit cloud blown across them. And so, as you make your way west in the evening on the old road to Devon, you have that light by which to see the darkness. It is both a dark and a luminous place, a kind of lit dusk.

They talked as they walked on the half-lit road past the thorns and hollies out on the gorsy moors. All the books that Coleridge had ever read, as the great American critic John Livingston Lowes showed in the 1920s, were afloat and mingling in his mind, ready to power the great poem on which he was about to embark, but just as potent and just as present were these physical conditions through which they were walking.

I do not know that they discussed Milton on this walk, but there is no doubt that Milton presided over their joint consciousness. At every turn, echoes of Milton's poetry appear in theirs, and Milton is the master-poet of the half-visible, the light in which the terrifying and revelatory truth of things can be glimpsed. These are the conditions of the sublime – a state in which the majestic seems to lurk in ill-defined vastness – to which both Wordsworth and Coleridge were drawn this winter and to which their winter poetry would turn again and again. The atmosphere of the summer's lime-tree bower was long gone.

What they had read of Edmund Burke was with them too. 'To make anything very terrible,' Burke had written in his great essay on the sublime,

> obscurity seems in general to be necessary. When we know the full extent of any danger, when we can accustom our eyes to it, a great deal of the apprehension vanishes. Every one will be sensible of this, who considers how greatly night adds to our dread … For this purpose too the Druids performed all their ceremonies in the bosom of the darkest woods, and in the shade of the oldest and most spreading oaks.

155

More than any other poet, Burke thought, Milton 'seems better to have understood the secret of heightening, or of setting terrible things, if I may use the expression, in their strongest light, by the force of a judicious obscurity'. When Satan first encounters Death himself in *Paradise Lost*, Death has no form but is merely a 'shape,/If shape it might be called that shape had none/Distinguishable, in member, joint, or limb;/Or substance might be called that shadow seemed'. 'Shape' says nothing of what the shape is, when shadow seems to be its only substance, but, as Burke says, Milton portrays Death with such 'a significant and expressive uncertainty of strokes and colouring' that 'all is dark, uncertain, confused, terrible, and sublime to the last degree'.

> Like one, that on a lonely road
> Doth walk in fear and dread,
> And having once turn'd round, walks on
> And turns no more his head:
> Because he knows, a frightful fiend
> Doth close behind him tread.

Uncertain light, Miltonic grandeur, threat, strangeness, the unaccommodated wild, a haunted world in which beings seem to be present even when they are not, the ghost over the shoulder, the ghost that is not there when you turn to find it, the churning sea and the scale of its shore, the interpenetration of inner and outer worlds: all this is joined in a winter night walk across the Quantock tops by the sea-roar of wind in the woods below you.

Wordsworth often quoted in later life the lines from *Paradise Lost* that begin

> Millions of spiritual creatures walk the earth
> Unseen, both when we wake, and when we sleep

and some of them were surely walking with him on this night-time road. If a storm comes in, the Quantock heights are a haunted place on such an evening. There is a barrage of wind in the woods, a bawling and baying in the gusts as they make their way through the trees, a repeated swaggering, growling, browbeating irruption of wind under which the woods give and sway as if in pain.

It was Coleridge's idea, that night when they stayed in Watchet on the coast the far side of the hills, that he and Wordsworth should write a prose epic together on the subject of Cain in exile, driven away by God from the rest of humanity after he had murdered his brother Abel. It is, in the circumstances, the most vivid and pointed of choices. Adam and Eve had two sons, Cain a tiller of the earth, his brother Abel a shepherd. God liked what Abel could bring him as an offering but rejected everything Cain offered, and so out of jealousy Cain killed Abel and was condemned by God to wander the world 'as a fugitive and a vagabond ... in the earth'.

Cain and Abel are brother poets, each embarking on what seems to be a new life, wanting to bring new and precious gifts to the approving powers of the world, each somehow allied to the other as brothers but each sensing that a destructive jealousy lies beneath the surface of their friendship, and that companionship has darkness in its heart. One of them is accepted and taken up by the governing powers, but one is exiled and dishonoured, made to feel less adequate than his brother, told that what he brings as an offering is wrong or lesser than the gifts brought by the brother now basking in divine approval. Many of the bitter and tortured ingredients of *The Rime of the Ancyent Marinere* are already in play here: Coleridge is already suggesting – intuitively or not – that one of them will thrive in the world, its happy guest, and one will fail and be excluded, and that the rage and despair of the broken, excluded and tortured man will forever want to hold his happy brother in his grasp and wreak a kind of vengeance on him.

They agreed – or more likely Coleridge suggested – that Wordsworth should write the first part or canto of the *Wanderings of Cain*, about the murder itself, Coleridge the second, and whoever finished first should write the third.

Coleridge hurried through his lines. It is among the worst pieces he wrote, but full of the circumstances of their night journey over the Quantock top, walking in the moonlight, feeling their way in the dark through woods and the moonlit shadows, looking for the path under the trees 'as dark as a cavern'. After the murder, Cain finds that God 'pursueth my soul like the wind, like the sand-blast he passeth through me; he is around me even as the air!'

They walk to a giant rock, and there Cain encounters the ghost, or 'Shape', of his murdered brother.

> Thus as he stood in silence and darkness of Soul, the SHAPE fell at his feet, and embraced his knees.

That embracing of knees is a sign of supplication taken at root from Homer, where all victims clasp the knees of their murderers, but it is a cousin gesture to the Ancient Mariner's bony hand, grasping the wedding guest in all his happiness and finery, refusing for all eternity to let his listener go.

Once he was done, Coleridge hurried back to the other room in the inn at Watchet, where he hoped Wordsworth would have written just as much on the first canto. Thirty years later, Coleridge remembered the scene:

> Me-thinks I see his grand and noble countenance as at the
> moment when having dispatched my own portion of the
> task at full finger-speed, I hastened to him with my
> manuscript – that look of humourous despondency fixed on
> his almost blank sheet of paper, and then its silent mock-
> piteous admission of failure struggling with the sense of the

exceeding ridiculousness of the whole scheme – which broke up in a laugh: and the Ancient Mariner was written instead.

It is the most intimate memory of Wordsworth in this year. That downturned smile of the mock shame-face, the lifting, apologetic eyebrows, the empty paper, the laugh hesitating at the corner of his lips, his relaxed openness with Coleridge, the communication beyond words between friends who have come to know each other, and then the laughter breaking out, dissolving the tension, burying the hidden meanings of this tale in a sense of its ridiculousness. The deeper question remains hanging in the air: how, essentially, could Wordsworth ever have collaborated in a work that aimed to describe his own murder by his friend and brother, for whom the first inklings of failure, pain and exclusion were already blowing through him?

Nevertheless, the urge in Coleridge to co-opt that friend and rival would not be denied. A few days later he would try again, pressing Wordsworth to collaborate with him on a poem. On 13 November, just as the light was going, they had set out again. 'The evening was dark and cloudy,' Dorothy wrote to her friend Mary Hutchinson. 'We went eight miles, William and Coleridge employing themselves in laying the plan of a ballad, to be published with some pieces of William's.'

Almost five decades later, Wordsworth told Isabella Fenwick how

in the autumn of 1797, [Coleridge], my sister, and myself, started from Alfoxden pretty late in the afternoon, with a view to visit Linton, and the Valley of Stones near to it; and as our united funds were very small, we agreed to defray the expense of the tour by writing a poem ... Accordingly we set off, and proceeded, along the Quantock Hills, towards Watchet; and in the course of this walk was planned the poem of the 'Ancient Mariner,' founded on a dream, as Mr. Coleridge said, of his friend Mr. Cruikshank. Much the greatest part of the story was Mr. Coleridge's invention; but certain parts I suggested; for example, some crime was to be committed which should bring upon the Old Navigator, as Coleridge afterwards delighted to call him, the spectral persecution, as a consequence of that crime and his own wanderings. I had been reading in Shelvocke's Voyages, a day or two before, that, while doubling Cape Horn, they frequently saw albatrosses in that latitude, the largest sort of sea-fowl, some extending their wings twelve or thirteen feet. 'Suppose,' said I, 'you represent him as having killed one of these birds on entering the South Sea, and that the tutelary spirits of these regions take upon them to avenge the crime.' The incident was thought fit for the purpose, and adopted accordingly. I also suggested the navigation of the ship by the dead men, but do not recollect that I had anything more to do with the scheme of the poem. We began the composition together, on that to me memorable evening.

Again Wordsworth withdrew, holding himself apart from the joint enterprise on which Coleridge was set. There were limits to friendship, limits to his readiness to pour himself into a Coleridge-shaped mould. 'As we endeavoured to proceed conjointly,' Wordsworth told Isabella Fenwick, '(I speak of the same evening), our respective manners proved so widely differ-ent, that it would have been quite presumptuous in me to do anything but separate from an undertaking upon which I could only have been a clog ... The style of Coleridge and myself would not assimilate.' Those are modest and graceful words, but the truth of Wordsworth's reaction to the poem, its manner, its language and its form, was more hostile. These courteous remarks conceal a reluctance to waste his spirit on an enterprise devised by Coleridge for his own fulfilment.

Coleridge was more honest about the gap that had opened between them. There was an obstacle in Wordsworth himself, he wrote later, the difficulty 'for a mind so eminently original to compose another man's thoughts and fancies'. Wordsworth was unaddressably himself, non-cooperative to his roots; he could not fit himself to Coleridge's scheme; and besides, as the poetry finding its way into his notebooks would soon reveal, he was already embarked on a different path.

Coleridge wrote a poem-in-disguise, a Miltonic and Burkean exercise in the sublime dressed up as an ancient ballad. Its structure is simple, and the form of *The Rime of the Ancyent Marinere* is another of Coleridge's out-and-back journeys, in which a man travels away from safety, out into the strangeness of existence, and back finally to harbour and home, returned but transformed. A sailor drops away from all he knows, with no great stated aim, commits the crime for which he must pay long and desperate penance, finds some kind of redemption in his acceptance of the beauty of things, and then returns, but with his being altered by what he has seen and so needing, above all, to repeat his tale, this tale, over and over, ten thousand times as Coleridge once said, to anyone he can persuade to listen.

The voyage is heir to the great epics of journeying in our cultural memory, an Odysseyan plunge into a dark and lonely place, where it seems more like torture than an adventure, both irrational and revelatory, encountering beings and powers which usually lurk in the subconscious but are here brought out into vivid and oppressively physical reality, so that the soul of the mariner must suffer almost overwhelming grief and pain, before returning a changed man, both wiser and diminished. Its subject is, essentially, the inequality of the struggle between the self-possession of a man, his will, and the enormous and destructive powers at loose in the world and in his own heart.

En route to that destination, the atmospherics are many and entrancing: the ship driven 'like Chaff' before the wind; the 'wond'rous cauld' where 'Ice mast-high came floating by/As green as Emerauld'; the nights when 'thro' fog-smoke white/ Glimmer'd the white moon-shine'; its opposite, the 'hot and copper sky' where 'The bloody sun at noon/Right up above the mast did stand,/No bigger than the moon'; and then the most beautiful of Quantock transmutations, as the singing spirits that Coleridge had absorbed in Somerset enter the bodies of the dead sailors:

> The day-light dawn'd – they dropp'd their arms,
>   And cluster'd round the mast:
> Sweet sounds rose slowly thro' their mouths
>   And from their bodies pass'd.
>
> Around, around, flew each sweet sound,
>   Then darted to the sun:
> Slowly the sounds came back again
>   Now mix'd, now one by one.
>
> Sometimes a dropping from the sky
>   I heard the Lavrock sing;
> Sometimes all little birds that are
> How they seem'd to fill the sea and air
>   With their sweet jargoning,
>
> And now 'twas like all instruments,
>   Now like a lonely flute;
> And now it is an angel's song
>   That makes the heavens be mute.

For all that account of a spirit-filled world, the poem's central understanding is as a picture of the human predicament. Every moment of the external landscape – the ice seas, the fogs, the calms, the burning sun, the tutelary spirits, the presence of death in life, the irruption of strangeness into the ordinary – is grand metaphor. Every raising of a sail, every anxiety in a storm, every moment of despair and stillness, every suggestion of being lost, every longing for home, every sense of wind and windlessness, every doom-filled look from a dead man's eye, is more than just an aspect of the journey. These are parts of the inner geography of the mariner who tells the tale, and, as the unrolling of the poem reveals, of us who hear it. He is not – and we are not – sailing on the world ocean, but through the fears and desires of life itself. That is why his eye glitters, why this poem's strangeness never lessens, and why we are children in its grip.

Wordsworth would, soon enough and quite openly, disparage *The Rime of the Ancyent Marinere* as poorly made, poorly written in its cod-medieval vocabulary and faux-simplicity, and in its failure to attribute to the mariner any role in his own destiny. The mariner is merely the passenger on a voyage into hellishness. His one act, the shooting of the albatross, has no source or motivation, and seems an arbitrary destruction of the beautiful, bringing in its wake levels of cosmic vengeance that seem barely connected to the crime.

The ferocity of Wordsworth's rejection of the poem addresses something more significant than a matter of style. *The Rime of the Ancyent Marinere* is a poem filled with threat, a threat from which Wordsworth needed to insulate himself, not only because he was feeling his own way towards something very different, a naked and unadorned simplicity of language with a rhetoric that could transcribe his own encounters with the world and its people, but because the *Rime* is a tale of self-destruction, of a man ruining his own life with a terrible act, summoning not the consolations of beauty and connectedness but the forces of death in the world.

One way of understanding the ballad is to recognise it, however concealed, as Coleridge's account of his own tendency to self-destruction, a sucking whirlpool of damage from which Wordsworth knew at some level he needed to keep away.

Before leaving *The Rime of the Ancyent Marinere* to his friend, Wordsworth made one or two wonderful suggestions, contributing first the grip of the mariner's 'glittering eye' and the image of the wedding guest listening to him 'like a three year's child'. Those two pairs of eyes, one narrowly watching, the other widely open, are each other's opposite: experience as desperation and obsession watching innocence that has retained its vulnerability.

Coleridge had written the first two lines of an anxious stanza, spoken by the wedding guest:

> I fear thee ancyent Marinere,
> I fear thy skinny hand!

to which Wordsworth added:

> And thou art long, and lank, and brown,
> As is the ribbed sea-sand.

In those few words, Wordsworth saw the mariner for what he was: a shape indistinguishable from the sterilities of the shore, browned and worn by a shelterless life under the sun, rubbed and rerubbed by the passing of sea and time, a kind of life-in-death. The mariner is a version of Cain in exile, the archetypal murderer, whether of brother or seabird, savaged by fate, not initially responsible for who he was but murdered by the murder he has committed, banished, now a fugitive and vagabond on the earth, a vision of a man who has been unable to find home, harbour or happiness in the world.

It is possible to think that Wordsworth, intuitively or not, saw the mariner as Coleridge himself. And if that is a viable identification – Coleridge as mariner as Cain – then it is not unreasonable to think that at this emblematic level, the friendship and brotherhood between Coleridge and Wordsworth finds its reflection in the friendship and brotherhood of mariner and albatross. The Wordsworth-bird had come and brought the good south wind to the Coleridge-mariner:

> The breezes blew, the white foam flew,
> > The furrow follow'd free:
> We were the first that ever burst
> > Into that silent Sea.

They had sailed all summer together, pioneer navigators, with that shining wake brilliant behind them through seas, they felt, no one had sailed before. Only then did a kind of inadvertent, murderous and uncontrolled rivalry in Coleridge, which in his life would result in repeated damage being done to those he loved and to the breaking of many friendships, begin to make itself present in his mind. He would shoot the albatross just as Cain had murdered Abel.

Coleridge was supremely aware of the disaster that would follow from behaving according to the dictates of these most primitive levels in the mind. He was no uncritical worshipper of the unconscious, that part of ourselves which may contain revelatory truths but which in Thomas Mann's words 'knows no values, no good or evil, no morality'. For Coleridge, speaking to himself and about himself, the action of the conscious will was critical to the healthy workings of an integrated self:

If the will, which is the law of our nature, were withdrawn from our memory, fancy, understanding, and reason, no other hell could equal, for a spiritual being, what we should then feel, from the anarchy of our powers. It would be conscious madness.

'Conscious madness' is a succinct description both of the mariner's obsessed and repetitive state of mind as he tells his tale of sin and suffering, and of Coleridge's own agonised fits of despair and self-loathing. He would, in time, write how he could not experience the pleasure that came from hearing Wordsworth read *The Prelude* without feeling that his delight in it 'roused a throng of Pains', which reminded him of his own 'Manhood come in vain,/And Genius given, and knowledge won in vain'. Love, rivalry, admiration, profound self-knowledge and self-destruction circle about each other in those lines, much as the wandering albatrosses of the southern ocean swing around the mastheads of any ships that enter those seas.

The Rime of the Ancyent Marinere was written over many weeks and months, three hundred lines in November and December, but not completed until March the following year. Although one sketch of a few lines from a letter survives in the British Library, no drafts survive of this first making moment, and so it is impossible to trace the stages by which the poem was written. Only the psychological structure suggests a possible evolution, with the descent into the depths of a hell-vision in the winter months, perhaps some kind of movement to an ambivalent redemption with the turning of the year.

The life of the ocean itself, and the sailor's attitude to it, track the change. In the pit of his horror and disconnection, once the albatross is dead and hung about his neck:

In the bosom of the darkest woods

FOLLOWING PAGE: He sails through the fears and desires of life itself

The very deeps did rot: O Christ!
      That ever this should be!
Yea, slimy things did crawl with legs
      Upon the slimy Sea.

About, about, in reel and rout
      The Death-fires danc'd at night;
The water, like a witch's oils,
      Burnt green and blue and white.

Beyond the shadow of the ship
      I watch'd the water-snakes:
They mov'd in tracks of shining white;
And when they rear'd, the elfish light
      Fell off in hoary flakes.

Only when the mariner can look at these creatures with another eye, which does not envy or destroy the thing it loves, does the frame of the world shift.

Within the shadow of the ship
      I watch'd their rich attire:
Blue, glossy green, and velvet black
They coil'd and swam; and every track
      Was a flash of golden fire.

O happy living things! no tongue
      Their beauty might declare:
A spring of love gusht from my heart,
      And I bless'd them unaware!
Sure my kind saint took pity on me,
      And I bless'd them unaware.

The self-same moment I could pray;
      And from my neck so free
The Albatross fell off, and sank
      Like lead into the sea.

That seems to be an alleviation of pain, but there is no easy consolation here. The poem does contain a pat and inadequate moral, perhaps a failure of nerve on Coleridge's part and a reluctance to accommodate the implications of what he had written:

He prayeth best who loveth best,
      All things both great and small:
For the dear God, who loveth us,
      He made and loveth all.

That scarcely embraces the truths the poem had dared to encounter. And, as a response to the inadequacy of those words, the poem moves beyond them, concluding with a troubling bleakness, the image of the mariner himself still in the grip of the suffering he has summoned. The great neoPlatonic spirits, rising up from Coleridge's reading in the arcane and esoteric philosophy of the medieval Mediterranean, discuss the significance of what they have witnessed:

The spirit who 'bideth by himself
      In the land of mist and snow,
He lov'd the bird that lov'd the man
      Who shot him with his bow.

The other was a softer voice
      As soft as honey-dew:
Quoth he the man hath penance done,
      And penance more will do.

That penance is not confined to the mariner himself. Everyone who hears the tale will be transformed by it. Every hypocrite reader, consoling himself with the idea that he is neither similar to nor a brother of this crime-committing mariner, will have learned something different:

> The Marinere, whose eye is bright,
> Whose beard with age is hoar,
> Is gone; and now the wedding-guest
> Turn'd from the bridegroom's door.

> He went, like one that hath been stunn'd
> And is of sense forlorn:
> A sadder and a wiser man
> He rose the morrow morn.

9

Diverging

December 1797 and January 1798

Both poets had worked all summer and autumn writing tragedies for the London stage. The theatre held out the same prospect of cash in the eighteenth century as Hollywood did in the
twentieth. It would not have been unreasonable to hope for as
much as £600 from a successful production in London, the
equivalent of the annual rent for Alfoxden over twenty years. A
play by 'Monk' Lewis was said to have taken £18,000 at the box
office in a single London run. Coleridge's play had been commis-
sioned by Richard Sheridan, the playwright-manager at Drury
Lane, but Wordsworth's had been written on spec for Thomas
Harris, the co-owner and manager of the theatre in Covent
Garden, one of Coleridge's connections. Both plays turned out
to be failures, essentially undramatic, cul-de-sacs for their talents,
and although William and Dorothy went to London in
December to promote his work, and revise it in the light of some
advice from an actor, both were rejected and would bring nothing to their authors.

The two poets reacted to this failure in opposite ways.
Coleridge was in a state of uncertainty. The need for money was
pressing, and his life-course itself was in doubt. His rich friends
the Wedgwoods had offered him £100 to keep him going, but he
was uncertain whether to take it. Sara, having had a miscarriage
during the summer, was pregnant again. He had written some

joke sonnets mimicking the styles of his friends Charles Lamb, Charles Lloyd and either Southey or himself, carelessly publishing them without thought of the consequences. Posing as Nehemiah Higginbottom, Coleridge had mocked their fashionable 'affectation of unaffectedness' and 'puny pathos'. The friends took umbrage. Lloyd, perhaps egged on by Southey, began to write a novel in which an absurd Coleridge figure is held up to ridicule. Southey remained cold and distant. Lamb, who was fed up with being patronised by Coleridge, raged in letters heavy with contempt. Coleridge's Stowey nest of nightingales happily singing together was collapsing as he watched. As Wordsworth would also soon be embarking on his own experiment in the 'affectation of unaffectedness', you have to ask what he might have thought of Coleridge's sonnets, but no hint remains.

No one has ever been more aware than Coleridge of his own failings. He knew he had what he later called

an inward feeling of weakness ... above all, a faulty delight in the being beloved, without having examined my heart, whether, if beloved, I had any thing to give in return beyond general kindness & general Sympathy.

In that letter written to Southey in 1803, he turned inside out the analogy of organic wholeness he had repeatedly used as the image of a happy and integrated life. In him there was, he repeated,

A sense of weakness – a haunting sense, that I was an herbaceous Plant, as large as a large Tree, with a Trunk of the same Girth, & Branches as large & shadowing – but with pith within the Trunk, not heart of Wood/– that I had power not strength – an involuntary Imposter – that I had no real Genius, no real Depth/–/This on my honor is as fair a statement of my habitual Haunting, as I could give before the Tribunal of Heaven.

All were connected: the sense of inner weakness, the show of outer brilliance, the longing for love and friendship, the actual inability to return love for love. This was the shape of Coleridge's psyche: a desire for togetherness, an inability to be together, and overlying that gap between intention and performance, an involuntary deceit, an unacknowledged chasm within the folds of friendship.

Looking for solid ground, Coleridge in early January went to Shropshire, where he had been offered a post as a Unitarian minister, well paid, well housed, a role that seemed to hold out for him a financial and functional certainty in which he, Sara and their children might be content and happy. Here, in one of the great meetings of the Romantic era, the young William Hazlitt encountered him for the first time.

Hazlitt – the name pronounced with a long 'a' and written 'Haseloed' by Coleridge – was a nineteen-year-old boy, brilliant, shy, ambitious, whose father was a dissenting minister at Wem in Shropshire. He already knew of Coleridge, and worshipped him from afar. One of these frozen January mornings, before daylight, Hazlitt woke in Wem and set out to walk ten miles to Shrewsbury in the mud, to hear Coleridge preach.

When I got there, the organ was playing the 100th Psalm, and when it was done, Mr. Coleridge rose and gave out his text, 'And he went up into the mountain to pray, HIMSELF, ALONE.' As he gave out this text, his voice 'rose like a steam of rich distilled perfumes,' and when he came to the two last words, which he pronounced loud, deep, and distinct, it seemed to me, who was then young, as if the sounds had echoed from the bottom of the human heart, and as if that prayer might have floated in solemn silence through the universe.

Coleridge, for all his denials of radicalism, then launched into a ferocious denunciation of Church and state, their wicked collusion in a wicked campaign against the French, where bishops and ministers had 'inscribed the cross of Christ on banners dripping with human gore', transforming England's young shepherds into wretched drummer-boys, 'tricked out in the loathsome finery of the profession of blood'.

Hazlitt's mind and heart leapt with excitement at this fusion of eloquence, radicalism, poetry and God. When, two days later, this phenomenon of a man came to visit his father in Wem, Hazlitt was, not unsurprisingly, bashfulness itself, a quality that would remain with him for much of his life.

> I was called down into the room where he was, and went half-hoping, half-afraid. He received me very graciously, and I listened for a long time without uttering a word.
>
> His appearance was different from what I had anticipated from seeing him before. At a distance, and in the dim light of the chapel, there was to me a strange wildness in his aspect, a dusky obscurity, and I thought him pitted with the small-pox. His complexion was at that time clear, and even bright – His forehead was broad and high, light as if built of ivory, with large projecting eyebrows, and his eyes rolling beneath them, like a sea with darkened lustre. 'A certain tender bloom his face o'erspread,' a purple tinge as we see it in the pale, thoughtful complexions of the Spanish portrait-painters, Murillo and Velasquez. His mouth was gross, voluptuous, open, eloquent; his chin good-humoured and round; but his nose, the rudder of the face, the index of the will, was small, feeble, nothing-like ... Coleridge, in his person, was rather above the common size, inclining to the corpulent, or like Lord Hamlet, 'somewhat fat and pursy'. His hair ... was then black and glossy as the raven's, and fell in smooth masses over his forehead.

For Hazlitt, as for Sara Fricker, the physical person mattered less than the talk, and the young man drank in the miraculous stream open-mouthed.

> I was stunned, startled with it, as from deep sleep; but I had no notion then that I should ever be able to express my admiration to others in motley imagery or quaint allusion, till the light of his genius shone into my soul, like the sun's rays glittering in the puddles of the road. I was at that time dumb, inarticulate, helpless, like a worm by the way-side, crushed, bleeding, lifeless; but now ... my ideas float on winged words, and as they expand their plumes, catch the golden light of other years.

Coleridge had provided his soul, Hazlitt wrote much later, with 'a language to express itself', a phrase that embodies a central understanding of his hero. Coleridge had the supreme gift of giving, an all-embracing ability to meld his own consciousness with everything and everyone around him. That gift gave language to everything that might not otherwise speak. It was his greatest quality and he knew it. 'To have a genius,' he wrote in his *Philosophical Lectures* twenty years later,

> is to live in the universal, to know no self but that which is reflected not only from the faces of all around us, our fellow creatures, but reflected from the flowers, the trees, the beasts, yea from the very surface of the [waters and the] sands of the desert. A man of genius finds a reflex to himself, were it only in the mystery of being.

He is everything, however limited his understanding of that everything might be.

They dined on a leg of Welsh mutton and turnips and talked of many things, of writers and contemporaries, with Coleridge in unstoppable flow. 'His thoughts had wings: and as the silken sounds rustled round our little wainscoted parlour, my father threw back his spectacles over his forehead, his white hairs mixing with its sanguine hue: and a smile of delight beamed across his rugged, cordial face, to think that Truth had found a new ally in Fancy!'

In the midst of it, Coleridge added that some of his circle 'had expressed a very indifferent opinion of his friend Mr. Wordsworth, on which he remarked to them – "He strides on so far before you, that he dwindles in the distance!"' Those words, remembered by Hazlitt a quarter of a century later, provide a glimpse of the figure Wordsworth struck in the first days of 1798: on the road or distant path, far ahead, alone, walking fast and purposefully, unaccommodated, the singular man, headed for a destination that no one else had yet discerned. Two years later, Wordsworth would describe himself in just those terms. 'Possessions have I wholly, solely, mine,' he wrote in 1800,

> Something within, which yet is shared by none,
> Not even the nearest to me and most dear,
> Something which power and effort may impart.
> I would impart it; I would spread it wide,
> Immortal in the world which is to come

Here are the two poets, powered by opposite visions, opposite virtues, opposite failings, opposite modes of being: world as self for one, self as world for the other. Coleridge felt that he was dispersed into everything that was; Wordsworth detected within himself a presence and power so vast that it could outreach and outlast anything in the material universe.

The following morning, Hazlitt found Coleridge at breakfast. The poet had just received a letter from his friend Tom Wedgwood, making him an offer of £150 a year if he chose not to become a minister and instead devote himself entirely to the study of poetry and philosophy. 'Coleridge seemed to make up his mind to close with this proposal in the act of tying on one of his shoes.' The Wedgwood money was liberty itself, and in his enthusiasm and relief

> Coleridge, asking for a pen and ink, and going to a table to write something on a bit of card, advanced towards me with undulating step, and giving me the precious document, said that that was his address, *Mr. Coleridge, Nether Stowey Somersetshire*, and that he should be glad to see me there in a few weeks' time, and, if I chose, would come half-way to meet me.

Hazlitt walked with him that morning for six miles, reluctant to allow the oracle to leave his sight.

> In digressing, in dilating, in passing from subject to subject, he appeared to me to float in air, to slide on ice. I observed that he continually crossed me on the way by shifting from one side of the footpath to the other. This struck me as an odd movement; but I did not at that time connect it with any instability of purpose or involuntary change of principle, as I have done since. He seemed unable to keep on in a straight line. We parted at the six-mile stone; and I returned homeward, pensive, but much pleased.

Meanwhile, as Coleridge was putting on the inimitable Coleridge show in Shropshire – Hazlitt said that he never stopped talking for three weeks – the Wordsworths returned from their unsuccessful attempt to sell William's play in London. They stopped at Bristol for a few days before arriving at Alfoxden on 6 January. The failure of Wordsworth's play seems to have had the opposite effect to the anxious search it brought on in his friend, releasing him from the expectations of an orthodox audience, from what he came to think of as the depraved taste of a sensation-hungry public, and quite suddenly opening the floodgates on a kind of winter poetry that was different from anything he had written before, drawing on many of the ideas that Coleridge had been giving him for the last few months and which would lead towards his future as a great poet.

In the first months of 1798, Wordsworth began to find his way. In three different notebooks, all pocket-sized, the pages no more than 4 x 6 ¼ inches, written quickly, hurriedly, sometimes on consecutive pages, often not, sometimes working backwards through a notebook, or turning the book over so that what had been the last page became the first, he began his first investigations of his own life and mind, finding in the landscape a reflection of himself.

In the preface he would write to the second edition of *Lyrical Ballads* in 1800, Wordsworth described the goal of his poetry as 'excitement without the application of gross and violent stimulants'. These first spring-like surges of poetry are thick with that sense of excitement. Nothing gothic, but life revealed in nature. 'Visionary power/Attends upon the motions of the winds,' he would write in *The Prelude*, famously and all-importantly qualifying that with 'Embodied in the mystery of words'. The emergence of vision in words, without looking for the words, but finding them appearing at the very moment of vision, *as* the moment of vision, was the core understanding that came to Wordsworth this winter. Here were 'objects recognised/In flashes, and with a glory scarce their own'. Things are glimpsed by the senses, but the thinking mind gives them glory. Anything approaching an intellectual system was impotent, however good its purposes. Only poetry that could 'proceed from the depth of untaught things' could 'become a power like one of Nature's', both 'enduring and creative'.

Now, in the early months of 1798, came the first deep retrospections into his youth, retrospection as introspection, and his experiences there with the power of nature. No distinction was maintained between what had happened then and what was happening now. Different moments in time lay before him, to be picked up and used in response to the poetic moment, and not to any sense of sequence or history. All boundaries seemed to melt in him: landscape into mind and the past into the present, child into adult consciousness, each flowing into the other, each a companion for the other, every fragment written as if Wordsworth were allowing the words to lead him on. These are not thoughts that were made and whole before the writing began, but poetry which unfurled and rolled out across the notebook pages as they came into being at the point of his nib.

The frame for all of it was his walking alone or with Dorothy, in frost or moonlight, in the combes or on the stony roads over the heights. Just as much as the months of summer pleasure had fed into this moment, these wet, dark, damp-gripped or frost-held weeks lie at the beginning of what Wordsworth would become.

Winter arrives in the Quantocks as a wind – rain-laden, snow-laden, a darkness at its heart. Water streams off the hills and down through the streets of Stowey, the gutters there running so full that if you shut your eyes they sound like the wake of a boat under way, as if the whole town were moving through a sea. In the dusk, fleets of icing-pink clouds, 100,000 acres wide, drive across the blue and darkened evening of the Levels. Up on the tops, wind-coiffed ponies, wind-pruned hollies, wind-torn sky. In a little cluster of pines on the ridge above Holford, a memorial plantation to the men of Holford and Kilve who fought in the wars of the twentieth century, each new gust sounds at first like a cataract driving through rocks, rolling up and through the branches of the trees, but then sighing away, as if an engine were slowing. A pause, and then the next.

I spent much of the winter living in the small farmhouse in Adscombe that I had taken during the summer, much of it alone, talking to the farmer Ben Bartlett about his cows and his health, the hunt and the tiny fish that rise in summer to the still surface of the pool in the stream beside his house, and living as much as I could out in the world that the Wordsworths had known and absorbed. Adscombe is a beautiful settled place, nested in its valley, pantiled, pink-plastered, but even so, at home there in the old farmhouse kitchen, reading with a light down over a book in the dark, each gust on a storm-driven evening felt like a different being, an animal presence. The dogs I had with me came and sat close as the wind rolled over the ridge and beat down into the woods. The gusts used to burst at the door of the farmhouse, pushing its heavy, studded timber against the frame and lock, requiring entry, impatient, clamouring for admission from the cold. And not with any kind of gentle tapping, but the thumping demand of a wind not to be denied.

If anything in you is attuned to the idea that there are spirits abroad in the world, as there was in both Wordsworth and Coleridge, this was the time for the emergence and eruption of them. The cold at night bit the ends of my fingers. When I came back in the dark, the lane down towards Adscombe always shone pale between its banks, the surface reflecting the last of the day's sky. The slight dark ridge between the tyre tracks on each side loomed up as a strange and separate thing. It could look without effort like a shrouded figure, humped against the cold, just as the crows sat with their feathers shuffled up around their shoulders in the winter trees.

Arctic air descended on the Quantocks. Puddles froze and froze again, the flakes from the old and broken ice-surface standing as angled fins in the new. The snow lay for days, half-melting in any sun, renewed at night as if it were an ever-filling cup.

When the air on the tops was pregnant with that snow, ice blades of light dropped from between the clouds on to the plate of the sea. Looking north to Wales, there was often a glow in the upper reaches of the snow clouds, while their shadows beneath them sailed up the zinc-lined channel to the east. Sheep out on the fields to the north had herring gulls standing between them like thieves. At dusk, the moonlight on a cloudy night found the scattered snow and took it up as a cousin substance. On the northern fringes of the woods, the old snow glowed in that moonlit dusk, lying there in shadow disks, the whites in a thumbnail, or the ghosts of snow from the night before.

When it fell, even in a wind above the trees, the snow fell between the branches in the wood, dark and weightless, and then passed over, out across the Levels, as a greyness, a glaucoma in the air, blurring the boundaries of fields and rhynes. After the gusts had gone, the oak trees, newly laden with snow, sometimes went on stirring slightly in their fingertips, at least in their upper parts, a little tremor in the hand, while all below was still, and then the snow-dust fell on my shoulders and face, into my eyes, like fall-out drifting into the world.

I am not quite sure how this happened, but at some time during the winter, when living in Adscombe and walking the combes and sensing the reality of moonlight and cold, trying to feel my way back into the lives of these poets, I began to suffer bodily pains much as they did. Both were subject to frightening and sometimes disabling aches and spasms, often brought on by the stress of their lives, or more particularly by the struggle to write, never more than when revising what they had written, or for Wordsworth, when trying to fulfil the dreams of greatness Coleridge had for him. As he wrote to Coleridge later this year, 'I should have written five times as much as I have done but that I am prevented by an uneasiness at my stomach and side, with a dull pain about my heart.' What he called

> the obstinate pains
> Of an uneasy spirit, with a force
> Inexorable would from hour to hour
> For ever summon my exhausted mind.

Coleridge could also feel that he was all too easily 'a prey to anxiety, and Anxiety, with me, always induces Sickliness'. Both he and Wordsworth regularly suffered from what he called 'seas of pain', for which he would turn ever more to laudanum as a bath of calm and relief, but from which withdrawal would then bring on its own even more deleterious symptoms.

As I read of their lives, which were often agonised in this way, and picked my way through the drafts of poems and fragments of poems in Wordsworth's notebooks, and through the fugitive thoughts, moments of vision and impossible schemes in Coleridge's, my own body, to my surprise, also started to fill with those pains, in my back and legs, tightening across my chest, numbing one arm or another, sometimes so severe that after an hour or so I could not stand up from the chair and desk at which I had been sitting. The pains were intense muscular spasms, a low-level tightness and then sharper stabs of tension followed by a kind of paralysis, alarmed into rigidity at the thought of whatever pain might strike next. They would come in the morning, enter my dreams and wake me at night, spiking as a kind of fear in the dark.

It was psychosomatic. Once I had stood up and left the house in Adscombe, it could be cured by walking, into the pool of the night, leaving behind the knotted tangle of ambition and desire, rivalry and love recorded in the poets' notebooks, all the difficult mental world that had clumped up around these two young men, both of them looking into the entrails of uncertainty for a kind of understanding which was not immediately apparent but which lurked just within the borders of vision, tauntingly within and then out of reach. 'The hiding places of my power,'

Wordsworth would write in *The Prelude*, 'Seem open, I approach, and then they close.' It came to seem as if pain was the inevitable accompaniment of this poetry, as if painfulness somehow lay behind the surface of the words, the matrix out of which those words came, even if the poetry itself would appear steady and resolved.

Perhaps there was an answer in just that relationship. The beautiful relaxedness of much of what Coleridge wrote this winter, and the calm authority of the verses Wordsworth was reaching for at the same time, so easily unwinding line after line in the way a ribbon streams off its spool, may have been the distillate of the process, leaving behind in the body the trouble, tension and anxiety which were the necessary preconditions for it.

In the notebooks, Wordsworth takes repeated runs at a recalcitrant idea, teasing and tugging at the words until they come clear, untangling what he needed to say. Pleasure, Wordsworth was adamant, was the purpose of poetry, and it may be that distilling pleasure from this tangle of words required a kind of psychic polarisation, in which pleasure in the verse would only come if some kind of pain was left behind. The goal of the notebook may have been pure liquidity; if so, the body would be its sump.

Wordsworth was quite explicit about the role of pleasure. It was not to 'be considered as a degradation of the Poet's art'.

It is far otherwise. It is an acknowledgment of the beauty of the universe, an acknowledgment the more sincere because not formal, but indirect; it is a task light and easy to him who looks at the world in the spirit of love; further, it is a homage paid to the native and naked dignity of man, to the grand elementary principle of pleasure, by which he knows and feels and lives and moves.

The Arctic air descends

FOLLOWING PAGE: On winter paths

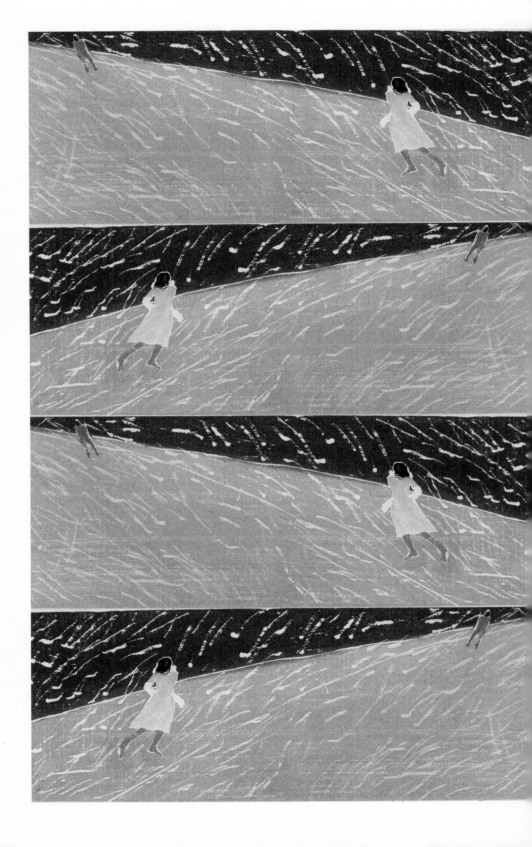

Only after a long time did I realise that this was as it should be, that I could not expect to receive all the blessings and beauties from them without incurring some version of the costs, especially when I spent time with those notebooks, where the struggle to register and respond to the realities swaying and surging between mind and world are evident on every page. This was, in fact, the price of poetry, a price that is rarely allowed to surface in any published text but surely lies below much of it, the cost of beauty, the fee exacted by the need for resolution. 'Do you not see,' Keats would write in a letter to his siblings, 'how necessary a World of Pains and troubles is to school an Intelligence and make it a soul? A Place where the heart must feel and suffer in a thousand diverse ways!'

In Wordsworth's notebooks, the scattered lines read as if gobbets of music and language are pushing out through his pen on to the surface of the visible world. The atmosphere is of retrieval, of quite literally the re-collection of ideas and associations, the memory of sights and sounds he had gathered when out in the woods and on the high tops of the Quantocks. It is tempting sometimes, from these ragged, scratched-at, fragmentary pages, to think that they must have been written on site, notations from the living world, from his presence in that world; but that was not his method. He was clear, when asked about this late in life, that for poetry to surface it had first to pass through the great digestive organ of his mind. Poetry did not lie out in the fields and woods like mushrooms or autumn leaves. Poetry existed only in the meeting of mind and world. Poetry was that act of becoming, feeding on what had been ingested long before.

He told Aubrey de Vere, the Irish Victorian poet and his life-long admirer, that he 'had hardly known anyone but [himself] who had a true eye for Nature', and talked about another poet, but did not name him, who went out with his pencil and notebook, and jotted down whatever struck him most – a river rippling over the sand, a ruined tower on a rock above it, a promontory, and a mountain-ash waving its berries. He went home, and wove the whole together into a poetical description.

Is this, darkly, a description of Coleridge, for whom no friend was more loyal or trustworthy than his notebooks, and without which he never went out of the door? Or even Southey, who as Hazlitt noticed, was never without his notebook in hand?

De Vere described how Wordsworth paused at this point, for effect, and went on with a 'flashing eye and impassioned voice', saying that

> Nature does not permit an inventory to be made of her charms! He should have left his pencil and notebook at home; fixed his eye, as he walked, with a reverent attention on all that surrounded him, and taken all into a heart that could understand and enjoy. Then, after several days had passed by, he should have interrogated his memory as to the scene. He would have discovered that while much of what he had admired was preserved to him, much was also wisely obliterated. That which remained – the picture surviving in his mind – would have presented the ideal and essential truth of the scene, and done so, in a large part, by discarding much which, though in itself striking, was not characteristic.

That may have been the Victorian mage speaking. Certainly the notes from the winter of 1798 do not read as calmly and monumentally resolved as those words suggest. They arrive fragmentary and immediate on the page, the traces left by moments of expansion and recognition, in which Wordsworth seems surprised at their emergence into the world, as if he were not the source but merely the conduit for them.

He tussles with the Coleridgean idea that love between human beings is somehow dependent on love of everything that is. At first, it is expressed in the negative:

> Why is it we feel
> So little for each other but for this
> That we with nature have no sympathy
> Or with such ~~idle objects~~ things as have no power to hold
> Articulate language

But then he draws a strong horizontal line across the page

---

and starts again in a positive register:

> And never for each other shall we feel
> As we may feel till we ~~have~~ find sympathy
> With nature in her forms inanimate
> With objects such as have no power to hold
> Articulate language. In all forms of things
> There is a mind.

This is one of his great transitional moments, leaving behind that negative figure who walked the roads with his eyes turned down into the dust and becoming instead the disciple of his friend. 'In all forms of things/There is a mind', he writes, as if sitting at Coleridge's knee, a moment of recognition that what his friend had been telling him all year was true. Then, written in between two drawn horizontal lines:

The echoes beat the rocks as if with wings.

Self and world are melting into each other at their boundaries. On another page, something longer, rolling out under its own unsummoned impetus:

> Transfigured by his feelings he appeared
> Even as a prophet – one whose purposes
> Were round him like a light – sublimed he seem'd
> One to whom solitary thought had given
> The power miraculous by which the soul
> Walks through the world that lives in future things

He writes that as it comes, no revision, no punctuation apart from the two dashes, eased perhaps by using the third person, not daring quite to enunciate a naked recognition of himself as a prophet, which this surely is, but disguising it as the description of another. Nevertheless, this can be seen as what it is: the proclamation by a poet, to himself, about himself, that his subject is the greatness of his own human spirit, and that the realm across which he now intends to stride is nothing less than eternity.

No record exists of Wordsworth writing these lines. The notebooks are their own and only record, written in the dark of that winter, supremely solitary, and enabled by that solitude. To hope for more would be contradictory. By definition, these lines and this turn in Wordsworth's poetry could only have occurred in private and in secret, these pages a precious trace of that transformation. There is nothing public in them. They can often flirt, in their vagueness and their striving to express something which seems no more than half-known to Wordsworth himself, with the borders of the meaningless. And they can only be read with a conscious attempt at empathy, listening for what they are and what he wanted them to be: a poet reaching for a form of poetry, both epic and personal, both confessional and declaratory, for which he had no model.

It is all far from programmatic. Quite suddenly two lines appear in the notebook, written in the dark ink of a newly charged pen, that sound as if they are a memory of Annette Vallon:

> And thought of that poor woman
> Whom I had known & loved.

That was its naked first form, later – perhaps immediately – amended and obscured to:

> And thought of that poor woman as of one
> Whom I had known and loved.

He then turns again to Coleridge's sense of a universal connectedness in all things that are living now or have ever lived:

> Of unknown modes of being which on earth
> Or in the heavens or in the heavens and earth
> Exist by mighty combinations, bound
> Together by a link, & with a soul
> Which makes all one

After one false start, crossed out with rapid, authoritative vertical lines, he writes this:

> ~~There would he~~ wander ~~in the~~ storm and there
> Would feel
> ~~He felt~~ whateer there is of power in sounds
> To breathe an elevated mood – by form
> Or image unprofaned of sounds that are
> The ghostly language of the antient earth
> Or make their dim abode in distant winds

187

These are the earliest of lines that would find their way into *The Prelude*, almost a transcription of a winter's night on the Quantock ridge. The winds watched over Ulysses like dogs, Wallace Stevens suggested in 'The World as Meditation', and no phrase could be truer of Wordsworth this winter. All is uncertainty, distant in time and space. The scale of what he is describing is enlarged by its unembraceability, by the strange substanceless substance of the winds, which can nevertheless transmute into the bodily intimacy of a breath. The feeling man stands at the centre of an ancient cosmos that speaks to him through its winds.

> He lov'd to contemplate
> The mountains and the ~~antient~~ aged hills
> To ~~feed~~ stand
> ~~His spirit in their solitudes~~
> And feed his spirit in their solitudes

The poetry is in the communication of those opposites, in the connection between the most inward, private aspects of the mind with the most unimaginably vast extent of what has been or could ever be.

Then:

> Oh listen listen how ~~sounds~~ that wind away
> While the last touch they le[?eva] upon the sense
> Tells they [?have]
> the [?firs]
> ~~Hush they are coming — they have passed~~
> ~~And run~~ There would he stand
> ~~Beneath~~ In the ~~warm~~ still covert of some [?lonesome] rock
> Or
> would gaze upon the moon untill its light
> Fell like a strain of music on his soul
> And seem'd to sink into his very heart

Any sense of sociability has gone. The life of the household, his friendship with Coleridge, the children, Dorothy – all are banished from his mind. Wordsworth himself seems to occupy the universe, as a stream that runs through time, or more than that, a tide that ebbs and flows, a tidal self that floods out into all the far and shrouded corners of the world and then withdraws, seeping out into everything he might feel around him, only then for the surge to come again, his enormous boundaryless self fluxing and flexing into the hidden provinces of being.

> I lived without the knowledge that I lived
> Then by those beauteous forms brought back to life again
> To lose myself again as if my life
> Did ebb and flow with a strange mystery

Coleridge's sense of one life embracing all is never far from these winter pages. Wordsworth here and there simply repeats what Coleridge had been saying to him.

> ~~In~~ To every natural form, rock, fruit, & flower
> Even the loose stones that cover the high-way
> He gave a moral life; he saw them feel
> Or linked them to some feeling. In all shapes
> He found a secret & mysterious soul
> A fragrance & a spirit of strange meaning

Both Wordsworth and Dorothy were able to enter trance-like states, and there are snatches here of Blake-like questioning of the universe:

> Are there no groans in breeze or wind
> Does misery leave no track behind
> Why is the earth without a shape & why
> Thus silent is the sky

Is every glimmering of the sky
Is every lamp hole [?] in the world an eye
Has every star a tongue?

The night at times remains infused with guilt and pain, a haunted
universe of strangeness, bodily suffering and high visions, human
life invigilated by unknowable and higher powers:

Away away it is the air
That stirs among the wither'd leaves
Away away it is not there,
Go hunt among the harvest sheaves
There is a bed in shape as plain
As form of hare or lion's lare
It is the bed where we have lain
In anguish and despair

Away and take the eagle's eyes
The tygers smell
Ears that can hear the agonies
And murmurings of hell
And when you there have stood
By that same bed of pain,
The groans are gone the tears remain.
Then tell me if the thing be clear
The difference betwixt a tear
Of water & of blood.

Night walks up the steep and stony road on the winter hill above
Alfoxden fed straight into the lines, where ecstatic transcendence
was never without an awareness of the body that was experienc-
ing it:

>   and beneath the star
>   of evening let the steep and lonely path
>   The steep path of the rocky mountain side
>   Among the stillness of the mountains hear
>   The panting of thy breath

This connection of the human and the more-than-human is the organ at the heart of the poetry, and the night buffeting of the storm winds became for him a central emblem of that connectedness of mind and world:

>   Many a time he wish'ed the winds might rage
>   When they were silent, far more fondly now
>   Than in his earlier season did he love
>   their voices & hear
>   Tempestuous nights the uproar and the sounds
>   That live in darkness

>   I love upon a stormy night
>   To hear those fits of slender song
>   Which through the woods and open plains
>   Among the clouds or in the rains
>   The loud winds bear along

All is fragmentary and disconnected, a kind of impassioned roaming through these new-found elements of scale, self, uncertainty, listening to the under-music of the wind, disquiet playing its role as a path that drops into the sublime, the body as the frame of being in the physical world, a portal to worlds both beyond and within the physical:

>   Sensation, soul and form
>   All melted into him.

Repeatedly in these pages you catch Wordsworth in the making of poetry, the sudden translation into words of the moment of being, running over whatever he found in his hand, shifting it, testing and retesting what feels like the way to say it, stating and restating, refining his meaning in consecutive phrases like a man moulding and reshaping the nature of what it is he needs and wants to say, trying always and repeatedly to catch the animated greatness of the wind in these trees and on these heights.

The forms that emerge in the notebooks are the shape of a mind thinking, a process more than a conclusion, so that it becomes clear that a poem is not an idea. It does not exist outside itself. It only is as it is, as it develops, through the turning of its lines and the breathing of its metre, so that the real poems in these notebooks are not the lines in their final form but the sequence by which Wordsworth felt his way towards them. The finding of the way is the poem itself, a walk through the pages of the notebook. And so a poem that tries repeatedly to encapsulate the breath of a moment on the hill or the fluttering of the flames on a fire is more of a poem, more whole, than one which addresses an objective fixity, or anything that existed before the poem made it what it was.

I often wondered if it could only be coincidence that Dorothy's journal begins – or at least the first surviving and partial transcript of her journal begins – from just the moment when Wordsworth was embarking on the poetry he was born to write. If it was a moment of liberation and fecundity for him, was it also for her? Or more subtly than that, a suggestion which the journal itself and its relationship to his poetry seems to bear out: was this a joint emergence into the light?

Jointness is there at the beginning. There is some obscurity about this, because except for the very first lines, which are written in Wordsworth's and not in Dorothy's hand, no manuscript survives of her Alfoxden journal. There was a manuscript a hundred years ago, partially transcribed in 1889 and perhaps again in 1913 by Professor William Knight, the Scottish moral philosopher and Wordsworthian editor, but it has disappeared. Much of what appears in the journals she would write in the Lake District – her own feelings, accounts of her neighbours and friends, the beggars that walked past the door, all the business of everyday life at home, their illnesses, her own thoughts on poetry – all of that is absent from her Alfoxden journal. There is no telling if it is absent because Knight left it out, or if Dorothy did not yet feel it was right to include it.

Nevertheless, reading her entries that begin on 20 January 1798 is like a glass of spring water after the concentrated drafts in Wordsworth's own notebooks. Her clarity of vision is a window opened on to their lives and minds, the mufflers removed. 'The green paths down the hill-sides are channels for streams,' the first words say: visual, exact, as true now in a wet winter as it was then. 'The young wheat is streaked by silver lines of water running between the ridges.' Painterly, but without the conventional vocabulary of the picturesque, attendant to the real and dispensing with the aesthetic stage-machinery of the century they were leaving.

These words are clean of any presupposition. A few years later, Wordsworth would write to an admirer that the purpose of a great poet was 'to rectify men's feelings, to give them new compositions of feeling' – all part of his vision of himself as a governor of the world. A poet would make his readers' 'feelings more sane pure and permanent, in short, more consonant to nature, that is, to eternal nature and the great moving spirit of things'. That sanity, purity and permanence is the frame of Dorothy's journal. 'Those oaks fanned by the sea-breeze thick with feathery sea-green moss, as a grove not stripped of its leaves ... The ivy twisting round the oaks like bristled serpents ... The sound of the sea distinctly heard on the tops of the hills, which we could never hear in summer ...' These are the observant eyes and attentive ears for which her brother remained grateful all his life.

Scattered through the surface of these entries, very occasionally, is a line which breaks the careful and grounded habit of her observations. Why can they hear the sea in winter but not in the summer months? she asks. 'We attribute this' – the analytical conversation going on between them –

to the bareness of the trees, but chiefly to the absence of the singing of birds, the hum of insects, the noiseless noise which lives in the summer air. The villages marked out by beautiful beds of smoke. The turf fading into the mountain road. The scarlet flowers of the moss.

Most of that is note-taking, the assembling of the ingredients of the true, but in the midst of it is a line of poetry:

The noiseless noise which lives in the summer air

as though her brother's voice is suddenly present on the page, perhaps a glimpse of the talk between them as they walked, the twist towards the rhythmic utterance, an inescapable habit of his mind, but perhaps not of hers. Later in life, Dorothy told a friend that she had experimented with copying her brother's mode of composition: 'I have often tried when I have been walking alone (muttering to myself as is my Brother's custom) to express my feelings in verse,' but 'nothing ever came of it'.

This unannounced arrival of the metrical often occurs in the journal. The owner of a small silk mill on the Holford stream had a dog.

The manufacturer's dog makes a strange, uncouth howl, which it continues many minutes after there is no noise near it but that of the brook.

And then she enters the rhythmic line:

It howls at the murmur of the village stream.

They are walking in the wind-stirred woods back from Stowey:

The trees almost *roared*, and the ground seemed in motion with the multitudes of dancing leaves, which made a rustling sound, distinct from that of the trees. Still the asses pastured in quietness under the hollies, undisturbed by these forerunners of the storm. The wind beat furiously against us as we returned. Full moon.

And then again, what sounds like her brother's words, coming to his lips as they walked, never making it in his own hand into a notebook, but recorded by Dorothy after reaching home, William's description of the moon they had both seen lifting from the waters of the channel.

She rose in uncommon majesty over the sea.

There are questions of status and power that attach to this repeated pattern in the journal. Wordsworth was clear that the mere transcription of sense impressions into words, poetry as transcribed vibrations, was not enough. Poetry for him was grander and more architectural than that. Dorothy plays the role in this journal of feeder to that poetry, as if she were a primary resource, a quarry, giving access to a sensuous normality in which nothing is moralised or generalised, but seen for itself, but which nevertheless has the air of a maidservant's provision, of her being the under-partner in an unequal relationship, one in which she waters and facilitates, supports and sustains, but in which the role is consistently secondary.

That indifference to any sense of fulfilment needed by the women in the Quantocks world, beyond service to their heroes, is an inescapable part of the psychic shape of this year. They were to be treated considerately, and Southey for one spoke up for them, but their life goals, their discoveries and their self-realisation always came after those of the men they served. They were subservient in a way modern social consciousness finds difficult to accept. Why did the radical challenge of so many dimensions of these men's lives not extend to a sense of fairness towards or equivalence in the women who were helping them to become who they wanted to be?

At least Dorothy was out on the walks and talking with both Coleridge and Wordsworth. For Sara Coleridge, the diminution was immeasurably worse. She said herself that she had a 'more literal Fricker temperament' than her husband or his friends. The most high-minded talk would have left her cold. The house to which Coleridge had committed them was miserable, more miserable than ever in the winter, when the chimneys smoked and the damp was ineradicable. Her biographer Molly Lefebure has said that Sara, despised by the local gentry, besieged by the demands of wifehood and motherhood, having had a miscarriage in the summer and now pregnant again, serving Coleridge in 'his privileged role of exclusive man of letters', only truly belonged to 'the sisterhood of domestic slavery'.

Nor, it seems, was there much solidarity as sisters between Dorothy and Sara. Thomas De Quincey, later and scurrilously, suggested that Dorothy and Coleridge had some kind of love affair in Somerset, not physical but intellectual, sensuous maybe but not sensual, an affair of the mind which had at its heart a diminishing of Sara. De Quincey is the most unreliable of witnesses, but his description of Dorothy does give her a life that moves far beyond the beautiful observations of the journal:

She was all fire, and, as this ardour looked out in the very gleam of her wild eyes ... I may sum up in one brief abstract the amount of Miss Wordsworth's character, as a companion, by saying that she was the very wildest (in the sense of the most natural) person I have ever known; and also the truest, most inevitable, and at the same time the quickest and readiest in her sympathy with either joy or sorrow, with laughter or with tears, with the realities of life or the larger realities of the poets!

If there was wildness buried within Wordsworth's solemn demeanour, that shared wildness found something of an outlet to the world in his sister. But this was a manner that had no appeal for Sara Coleridge. Her daughter, also called Sara Coleridge, wrote much later that Dorothy had 'greater enthusiasm than my mother possessed. *She* never admires anything she doesn't understand,' adding that her mother's 'very honesty stood in the way'.

Day after day Sara would suffer the trial of seeing Coleridge off into the hills with the two Wordsworths, or, as Dorothy's journal occasionally shows, with Dorothy alone. One small incident between Sara and Dorothy, which De Quincey claimed was told him by Dorothy herself, hints at the nature of the relationship.

Often it would happen that the walking party returned drenched with rain; in which case [Dorothy], with a laughing gaiety, and evidently unconscious of any liberty that she was taking, or any wound that she was inflicting, would run up to Mrs. Coleridge's wardrobe, array herself, without leave asked, in Mrs. Coleridge's dresses, and make herself merry with her own unceremoniousness and Mrs. Coleridge's gravity. In all this she took no liberty that she would not most readily have granted in return; she confided too unthinkingly in what she regarded as the natural privileges of friendship.

According to De Quincey,

> Mrs. Coleridge viewed her freedoms with a far different eye: she felt herself no longer the entire mistress of her own house; she held a divided empire; and it barbed the arrow to her womanly feelings that Coleridge treated any sallies of resentment which might sometimes escape her as narrow-mindedness; whilst, on the other hand, her own female servant, and others in the same rank of life, began to drop expressions which alternately implied pity for her as an injured woman, or contempt for her as a very tame one.

De Quincey's relish at Sara's distress depends on an understanding that Sara, like the other Frickers, had always been well-dressed, an expert needlewoman, who took infinite pains with her wardrobe. The power structures are complex and interlaced here: Coleridge looking up to Wordsworth; Dorothy feeling she was the keeper of the Wordsworth flame; Sara feeling only her exclusion from the magic triumvirate; Wordsworth probably indifferent to Sara's fate or feeling; Coleridge, for all his celebration of the idea of home, and for all the love he still felt for her, keener to affirm the value of his attachment to Wordsworth than to his own wife; Wordsworth perhaps unthinkingly allied to the sister who laboured in his shadow; and Dorothy confirming the grounds for Sara's exclusion. That 'laughing gaiety' has cruelty in it.

Dorothy was certainly closely involved with the making of the poetry, in a way Sara never was and never could be. Poetic ideas and phrases migrate between Coleridge's notebooks, Dorothy's journal and Wordsworth's notebooks – fragmentary in one, evocative in the other, aiming for a certain largeness in the third. As

She follows on the moonlit path

PREVIOUS PAGE: Companion moon

Coleridge returns from Shropshire, newly funded with the guarantee of the Wedgwood money, with Wordsworth embarked on a new vein of poetry, and Dorothy writing every day in her journal, often at some length, the three of them had entered the dark and glowing moment of the year.

In her journal for 25 January (for which the manuscript does not survive) she tells how they went to see Thomas Poole in Stowey 'after tea'.

> The sky spread over with one continuous cloud, whitened by the light of the moon, which, though her dim shape was seen, did not throw forth so strong a light as to chequer the earth with shadows. At once the clouds seemed to cleave asunder, and left her in the centre of a black-blue vault. She sailed along, followed by multitudes of stars, small, and bright, and sharp. Their brightness seemed concentrated, (half-moon).

This was a careful transcription of the world and its subtleties. But there was more than this to the evening of 25 January 1798 on the half-dark road between Alfoxden and Stowey. From that moment, some tentative notes appear inside the front cover of Wordsworth's Alfoxden notebook, drafts of lines that are partly, as usual, in Wordsworth's handwriting, but also, intriguingly, partly in Dorothy's, as follows:

> spread out
>   a broad & undetermined orb ~~spread out~~
>   ~~an undetermined~~
> Dimly discovered chequering not the ground

This is as close as one can get to the co-presence of brother and sister in the act of writing. She is not writing out a fair copy but taking down their first thoughts, changing them as he or she changes them, co-actor with him in the moment of writing, or more precisely of speaking-and-writing. He speaks, she writes, she writes, he speaks again, she writes again. He then takes the little leather-bound book back from her, and the pen, and on the same inside cover adds one or two ideas for later lines of his own. Over the page, now entirely in her neatest script, Dorothy then copies out the poem her brother had composed from the raw materials that had been jointly and indistinguishably theirs:

A Fragment

The sky is overspread
With a close veil of one continuous cloud,
All whitened by the moon, that just appears
A dim-seen orb. Yet chequers not the ground
With any shadow – plant, or tower, or tree.
At last a pleasant, instantaneous light
Startles the musing man whose eyes are bent
To earth. He looks around, the clouds are split
Asunder and above his head he views
The clear moon and the glory of the heavens
There in a black-blue vault she sails along
Followed by multitudes of stars, that small
And bright, and sharp, along the gloomy vault
Drive as she drives. How fast they wheel away!
Yet vanish not. The wind is in the trees
But they are silent, still they roll along
Immeasurably distant, and the vault
Built round by those white clouds, enormous clouds,
Still deepens its interminable depth.
At length the vision closes, & the mind
Not undisturbed by the deep joy it feels,
Which slowly settles into peaceful calm
Is left to muse upon the solemn scene.

Wordsworth claimed much later to have composed this as he walked that evening. And so, had she been taking notes for him? Had she been jotting down what he had been seeing and saying? Or had she composed her journal entry before he had written the poem? Or contemporaneously with it? So many of the words are shared – the sky overspread, the continuous cloud, the whitening by the moon, the non-chequering shadows, the cloud split asunder, the black-blue vault (a double adjective that was already part of their lingua franca, used by Coleridge weeks before in his notebook), the way the moon sails along, the multitudes of stars, all so small and sharp and bright – that this goes beyond their simply having witnessed the same events. It is a joint presence in the world, a joint consciousness and a joint being.

The difference between them is not in the noticing; both have receptive and absorbent faculties at full stretch. It is a conversation shared even before the phrases are articulated: every word says 'look' to every other. The only difference between them is in the sense of assumed authority. Wordsworth's premise is that what he feels, the inner landscape of his mind, has a legitimate place alongside the cosmic phenomena of the night sky. He feels himself as infinite as what he sees. She remains locked into second place, the absorber, the taker-in; he begins from the idea that his inner landscape is an equivalent to the outer, as good, as great and as worthy as anything the universe might provide. His vision, his calm, his delight, his not-undisturbedness: that constitutes his claim on grandeur. She, apparently, does not feel qualified to make it for herself.

The occluded or the ebbing moon will be a repeated metaphor for them, and this sudden lit emergence of its light is a signal, private and to themselves, that his genius, the thing that makes him who he is, and to whose service she is dedicated, is also now emerging from the dark days. She stands alongside him, bathed like him in that moonlight, his amanuensis, his enabler, his sister, his other self, his love-ground, his designated inferior.

10

Mooning

January and February 1798

The originals of Wordsworth's notebooks are carefully preserved in the Dove Cottage archive in Grasmere, but the great Cornell editions of them, published between the 1970s and the 1990s, in which every dot and blur of the fragile pages is photographed, transcribed, analysed and compared with the final text, were my companions in Somerset. They are miracles of modern scholarship, often rescuing meaning and suggestion from pages that stall on the very edge of the legible, the ink or rubbed pencil rushed in its writing, hurried when what Wordsworth is describing hurries on itself, fugitive, more self-communing than communicating, sometimes faint, ink-splashed or scribbled over, heavily corrected and rewritten, feeling for what he might mean, for the meaning that might be waiting for him in the act of writing itself, from all of which the Cornell editors have managed to find the words themselves, or at least guess at them, all the half-meanings with which the thinking mind flirts and struggles.

> When shape was [?not ?no] figure to be seen
> Low [?breathing] and steps
> and sounds
> Of undistinguishable motion, steps

Reading these pages, in this weather and in this place, was like watching a wild creature that does not know it is being watched: a blackbird, a kestrel – its busyness and then its stillness, its sudden alert halts, suspecting some presence in the shadows around or below it, then the moments of preoccupation, blind to everything but what it is about, absorbed in the momentary, doing what it must do, as if its life depended on it, and then, just as sudden, its disappearance, absent from the page as though it had never been.

They are mindmaps, inadvertent and revelatory fragments of autobiography, preserving moments, recording first gestures, little private reliquaries of suggestion and hesitation, the pause in which the pen is reloaded with ink, and then the continuation, or sometimes the tailing off in uncertainty and lack of conviction, the recognition that a thought or a line is going nowhere, or somewhere unexpected.

Poems can take on a surrealist, Eliotic form. To try out a new nib, both Wordsworths were in the habit of writing the word 'amen' in a scatter across drafts that had already filled the page, with results that read like lines from some early-twentieth-century imagiste sketch:

Without a touch of melancholy thought
        amen   *amen*   *amen*
        a clear grey light
Felt in the mind
        amen amen
        a dead shade
        amen
Falls on the very heart
        amen   a sober dead grey light
        ascend
That covers field and forest   *amen*
        Amen

The notebooks have as much of an inner landscape as the Quantocks themselves. At each new visit they are filled with different weathers and qualities, different corners, different lights thrown on the Wordsworths' lives. Only on a dark winter evening in the Adscombe farmhouse, having read it many times before, did I realise that one small note, probably from January 1798, seemed to contain the germ of almost everything Wordsworth would write in the months to come. The idea that there might be a vacuum at the heart of any grand statement – a lifelong trap for a poet whose natural torque was to the eternal and cosmic reach of his words – is quite suddenly addressed in some incomplete additions to 'Lines Left upon a Seat in a Yew-tree', the poem that had so moved Charles Lamb in the summer. At the bottom of a page in the notebook he had also used at Racedown, Wordsworth wrote:

Howeer disguised in its own majesty
Is ho~~llow~~ness worthless

Those lines never appeared in print during his lifetime, at least in that form. They are a recognition that his natural bent was somehow caught between grandeur and its opposite, with the buried implication that the only place to look for majesty lay in ultimate simplicity, and that without simplicity majesty was inevitably a cloak for emptiness, hollow and worthless. Only integrated substance, continuous from heart to heaven, could be of any value. That need for solidity, and for a language that reflected it, became the spur for the poems that would soon pour from him and appear in *Lyrical Ballads* in the summer. Worthless hollowness was the charge he would lay on his contemporaries, 'the gaudiness and inane phraseology' of their writing, compared with his own poetry, seen as 'a natural delineation of human passions', the thing itself, 'the language of conversation', close to the lived reality of life. Is hollowness worthless? The question provides its answer before it is even asked.

Night after night in January and February 1798, the two Wordsworths would be up and out in the moonlight on the hills and in the wooded combes. It became a nightly habit for me, leaving Adscombe in the late-afternoon dusk, the damp above the stream a gauze in the air, the golden glow of evening soaked into the beech trees, crows chasing one another out to the west across the band of last light, often, in the cold of the winter evening, stained the yellow of a sheep's eye.

Walking on in the growing dark. All the arbitrary ingredients of the post-romantic world. Dusk a smoke so fine you cannot see its substance. Pheasants squawk-clucking far below. The self becoming spongy, the boundaries porous. On the tops, the breathy champing of a horse grazing in the near-dark, its muzzle brushing against the moor grasses, its hoofs knocking on the stones. In the quiet of the night you can hear the different notes of the streams, the undernotes beneath the brilliance, that bath-like gurgle where water flops into a filling basin, then a chuckle, a runnel-chuckle running over stones to a lower pool.

Everything is noticeable. In the slightest of winds, oaks are silent but beeches sigh. Lie on the moss in the wood of Frogscombe and look up at the trees. The heads of the oaks do not fill the air around them. Between each tree there is a kind of *cordon sanitaire*, a third of the diameter of each tree, their sway room, or at least the zone in which they rub and knock in a wind, so that each oak trims and maintains its neighbours and is trimmed and maintained in return. They do not intergrow. Each stands clear in its space of air, companionate, a co-presence, no intimacy. Crown shyness, mutual pruning. They do not need sway room to survive, but the winter gusts, bulling down into the combes, create it. Each little path of blue night air between the dark oaks above you is a memory, the trees' own recording of their winter trouble.

Once you know it, a night seems wasted unless you are out on the moon-gleaming roads, or can catch that moment the Wordsworths loved on their 25 January, when the moon suddenly appears from behind its diffused and cloud-obscured state and brings a sense of revelation, a plunge into the depths, not in the lighting of whatever there is on earth, or in the darkening shadows of tree and rock, the chequered ground, but in the curtain pulling back on the black-blue infinities around and behind the moon and stars.

These were the times to visit all the parts I had come to know of these hills and woods, the shadowed privacies of Ramscombe and Lady's Edge, Slaughterhouse Combe and Rectory Wood, Seven Wells, Five Lords, Great Bear and Butterfly Combe. Up on to Longstone and Hare Knap, where the hollies grow like wind-torn flags, to the iron-age camp at Danesborough, where the pelt of twisty, snaky coppice oaks rolls up and over the ancient banks. Then looking out from below those woods to Glastonbury, the Mendips, the sea channel and the mountains of Wales all blue in moonlight like provinces of a metal world.

Ships look stilled in the channel, their nav lights the only points of colour, their hulls fixed to the surface as if pinned to a board. Sometimes there is an island of moonlight in the sea, driven by the clouds, ghosting with the tide. As that tide drops, and as Dorothy noticed, seas break on sandbanks in the middle, appearing and disappearing in the silent comings and goings of the surf. Eastwards, the water-intake at Hinckley looks like a stranded galleon; to the west the headlands step away, each one silver-gilded in the dark.

In an old cupped lane, sunk and grooved into the wood going down to West Bagborough, the moon lights up the wheel ruts of the track, each puddle brightening into glitter as I pass. Elsewhere, the netted light coming through the coppice stems drops on to the fallen leaves of the wood in a set of dull constellations, but on the slick-wet rocks of the lane and in those puddles, the specks and splinters of moon become momentary flakes of light, animated by my own movement past them, each one rising from the ground like an eye suddenly brightened in torchlight. Only the apricot-yellow lamps of the houses in the village below seem like part of the human world.

The alien nature of a moonlit walk served the Romantics' purposes. They were here to disown the ordinary, to penetrate the depths of psyche and universe, to abandon the middle ground, and to find in the reductions of the night and the simplicities of human ordinariness the secrets and the wisdom which the civilised must necessarily ignore. Moonlight is a distillation of the Burkean and the Rousseauist condition, defamiliarising the known world, as available now as then, not as any aspect of historical experience, but a gateway into a form of being that most of us most of the time can never find our way towards.

The moon drifts through the months of Dorothy's journal, her accompaniment when it was clear as she went for eggs or sticks or to the baker's. In its light, 'the hawthorn hedges black and pointed, [were] glittering with millions of diamond drops'. She would sit for an hour with the window open at Alfoxden, watching the moon slowly ascend through the clouds. In the frost, it was 'a silvery line and thready bow'. Jupiter and Venus were her companions. She walked on the hills, with 'the moon, a many-coloured sea and sky'. Sometimes in the evening, day and night became entrancingly interfused:

While the twilight still overpowered the light of the moon, we were reminded that she was shining bright above our heads, by our faint shadows going before us. We had seen her on the tops of the hills, melting into the blue sky.

We are so much the heir of these people, that on these winter, cold-gripped nights, the full moon remains a blessing, search-light-bright in the open, pastures glazed with it as if with a frost, the streams in the combes moon-bright inside the shadows of their banks, the winter trees lattice-nets against the sky, some clumped and clustered, dense with ivy, but every last hazel catkin a silhouette, every holly leaf a mirror.

Everywhere the earth smells woody, leafy, earthy. A haze of moonlit damp hangs over the Levels to the east. Crusty, riven, python ivies clasp the trunks, coeval with the trees on which they suck. The lane gleams silver beside its gleaming river and Ben Bartlett's cattle clump and shuffle in their byre as they have done these last few thousand years.

They were far from alone on these walks. The repeated encounters in Coleridge's and Wordsworth's poetry with people at the door or on the road, in which the poets suddenly find themselves in close and urgent conversation with strangers who are quickly and insistently present, is no literary trick. The paths and roads of the Quantocks were full of men and women for whom there was no barrier to instant talk. Dorothy met woodmen with their ponies carrying charcoal or bark down to Stowey. Even in February, she saw 'young lasses on the hill-tops, in the villages and roads, in their summer holiday clothes – pink petticoats and blue. Mothers with their children in arms, and the little ones that could just walk, tottering by their sides.' The whole of the south of England was filled with retired or wounded or returning soldiers, walking from the ports at which they had been discharged to wherever they still called home. The patriotic and conservative Reverend William Holland of Over Stowey found himself in conversation one day on the road over Quantock:

Met a soldier; my horse started. He moved his hat low and marched aside from the road. 'My horse is no soldier' said I. 'No your honour' answered he smiling. Certainly the army polishes and civilises men very much, and it is pleasant for a Briton to reflect that these men, so civil and so polished, are the very men who in the day of battle make the nations of the world to tremble.

On 23 February 1798, Dorothy writes in her journal of a meeting the night before:

Wm. and I walked after dinner to Woodlands; the moon and two planets; sharp and frosty. Met a razor-grinder with a soldier's jacket on, a knapsack upon his back, and a boy to drag his wheel. The sea very black, and making a loud noise as we came through the wood, loud as if disturbed, and the wind was silent.

The razor-grinder in a soldier's jacket was the occasion for the most psychically powerful poem Wordsworth would write in Somerset, never given a title by him, but now known as 'The Discharged Soldier'.

Everything about it is different from Holland's meeting. The Wordsworths are on foot. It is dark, and the silk miller's dog is howling at the stream. Wordsworth himself is exhausted, drained by his work. He would later transfer this episode to his own boyhood in the Lake District, where it appears in Book IV of *The Prelude*, set on his holidays from Cambridge in the summer of 1789, but that is only symptomatic of Wordsworth's loose way with time and place. The situation of 'The Discharged Soldier', its geography and atmospherics are inseparable from Alfoxden, the Quantocks, its hill and stony road, all interfolded with a knowledge of *The Rime of the Ancyent Marinere*, which Coleridge was completing at the same time, and to which this is a reply.

For the first time, Wordsworth makes a drama out of his presence here. All the Quantock ingredients are in play: his own wearisome existence; his new familiarity with night and its universal scale; the sense that climbing the hills is to move out from the ordinariness of life, but that the valley also continues to offer shelter and peace; the fear that lurks in the dark; his concern for the mind-landscapes of others; his growing feeling that those he might meet on the road can give him understandings he cannot reach on his own, the recognition that there is wisdom in strangers and a redemptive power in sympathy between men; and all this under the umbrella of his old idea of himself as a gentleman whose task it is to redeem the lives of the poor and weak, an idea which this poem blows away.

Milton and the sublime, and even the shadow and ghost of Lear on the heath, haunt this poem, and the Quantocks provide all the turnings, hollows and openings, the darkness, enclosure and exposure that the landscape of guilt, loss and resolution could require. The tops of the hills are the shelterless moor, but they also reveal a high and open sky, where some kind of answer can be found. The shut-in village is both the closed and wearying mundane world and a place of rest, even of love.

The first version that survives is a fair copy made by Dorothy in a small red leather notebook, its cover stamped 'D.W.' in gold, which they used in Germany late in 1798, copying out roughs from Alfoxden pages that had been torn out, leaving only the stubs on which one or two initial letters survive, and that have now disappeared. Wordsworth remembers at first his summer walks up on the hills, away from all the others, not the sociable walking of Coleridge's vision in the lime-tree bower, but alone at night in the dark.

> I love to walk
> Along the public way when for the night,

> Deserted in its silence, it assumes
> A character of deeper quietness
> Than pathless solitudes.

The very absence of others is the night roads' beauty. But this isn't the summer. Dorothy had remarked a day or two before in her journal that the sheer wet of the Quantock winter made the winter roads look like streams.

> At such a time
> I slowly mounted up a steep ascent
> Where the road's watry surface to the ridge
> Of that sharp rising glittered in the moon ...

> Thus did I steal along that silent road
> My body from the stillness drinking in
> A restoration like the calm of sleep
> But sweeter far.

It is an animate world, filled with undersounds and murmurings, a bed of brackeny, aural life into which Wordsworth feels his body sinking with relief, with

> A consciousness of animal delight
> A self-possession felt in every pause
> And every gentle movement of my frame

This is not the destination of the poem. Quite suddenly, Milton's sublime 'shape' appears to trouble the peace in Wordsworth's mind. The meeting is his version of the drama in *The Ancyent Marinere*, but with Wordsworth himself playing the part of the reluctant, withdrawing wedding guest:

                    a sudden turning of the road
Presented to my view an uncouth shape
So near that stepping back into the shade
Of a thick hawthorn, I could mark him well
Myself unseen. He was of stature tall
A foot above mans common measure tall
Stiff in his form & upright lank & lean
A man more meagre it seemd to me
Was never seen abroad by night
His arms were long & bare his hands …
                    and his mouth
Shewed ghastly in the moonlight

Wordsworth as a boy had read the old books of romances and
chronicles, in which the 'strange and uncouth wooden cuts' had
shown

                    dire faces, figures dire
Sharp kneed, sharp-elbowed & lean-ankled too
With long and ghostly shanks forms which once seen
Could never be forgotten.

This horror-figure is their descendant. He is weak and strange,
unable to hold himself upright in the world, defeated by life, out
alone on the hill road with no apparent purpose, his moorings
cast off, any journey uncertain:

                    from behind
A mile-stone propp'd him and his figure seemed
Half-sitting, & half-standing. I could mark
That he was clad in military garb
Though faded yet entire.
                    he appeared
Forlorn and desolate, a man cut off

From all his kind, and more than half detached
From his own nature.

He is a mirror-version of Wordsworth himself, not ecstatic at the
night-time peace he has found, but eviscerated and evacuated
by it:

> He was alone
> Had no attendant neither dog nor staff
> Nor knapsack, in his very dress appear'd
> A desolation, a simplicity
> That seem'd akin to solitude. Long time
> I scannd him resting there, with a mingld sense
> Of fear and sorrow. From his lips meanwhile
> There issued murmuring sounds as if of pain
> Or of uneasy thought
>
> at his feet
> His shadow lay and moved not.
> he remained
> Fixed to his place, & still from time to time
> Sent forth a murmuring voice of dead complaint
> A groan scarce audible.
> ~~Yet all the while~~
> ~~The chained mastiff in his wooden house~~
> ~~was vexed, & from among the village trees~~
> ~~Howled never ceasing.~~

And then the poem shifts its ground. Wordsworth, ashamed of his
own fearfulness, approaches and addresses the soldier, who replies
by raising 'his lean & wasted arm/In measured gesture', a salute,
the night-time version of the salute the soldier had given William
Holland on his horse. 'With a quiet uncomplaining voice/A
stately air of mild indifference', he tells his story, how in 'the

Tropic islands he had served', then, on arriving back in England, ten days before, had been cast aside by an indifferent state that no longer had any need of him, and so was now walking home.

> He all the while was in demeanor calm
> Concise in answer: solemn & sublime
> He might have seemed, but that in all he said
> There was a strange half-absence & a tone
> Of weakness & indifference as of one
> Remembering the importance of his theme
> But feeling it no longer.

Wordsworth's own complacency begins to unravel on the page. His own authority and command seems trivial, wrong, and perhaps even part of the indifferent establishment that had cast this man aside. Listen instead, the lines insist, to the unworldly, disconnected, semi-present wisdom in the soldier's words. They turned back towards the combe.

> As we advanced I asked him for what cause
> He tarrid there nor had demanded rest
> At any inn or cottage, he replied in truth
> My weakness made me loth to move and here
> I felt myself at ease, & much relieved
> But that the village mastiff fretted me
> And every second moment rang a peal
> Felt at my very heart

Wordsworth takes him to a labourer's cottage down in the combe, where he will find shelter for the night, and then reproves him, telling him that he should look to his needs more carefully and should not 'linger in the public ways', but 'demand the succour which his state required'. He was 'feeble', Wordsworth told him, in need of alms. In reply,

Grow like good boys!

PREVIOUS PAGE: The discharged soldier

With the same ghastly mildness in his face
He said 'my trust is in the God of heaven
And in the eye of him that passes me.'

This comes at a high cost for Wordsworth. It is an open humili-
ation of his own patronising tendencies. What in the end does
Wordsworth know that this soldier does not know? What is the
difference between the ease and peace Wordsworth had found on
the starlit road and the calm the soldier had known there, troubled only by the barking of the miller's hound, which is the voice
of the insistent, anxious, busy world? How deep is the soldier's
trust in the universe and in the humanity of those who pass him?

It is a moment of revelation for Wordsworth, a key turning
point of this year, in which the words of a discharged soldier
show him the road to an understanding which until now he has
glimpsed only darkly and in part. This is an instruction from
beyond the normal bounds of life, in which the hill road, the
night sky, the murmuring streams, the troubled mastiff, the
cottage in the waiting combe, and above all the dark shape, who
becomes as he speaks a source of wisdom, all play their part in
leading Wordsworth towards a deeper connection with world
and self than he had yet known.

11

Remembering

February 1798

Children were everywhere in their lives. Hartley Coleridge, who was one and a half years old, and Basil Montagu, who was five, played the part of messengers from the childish world. Coleridge, Wordsworth and Dorothy all watched and listened to them. 'Basil is a charming boy,' Dorothy Wordsworth wrote to her old friend Jane Marshall. 'He affords us perpetual entertainment. I do not think there is any Pleasure more delightful than that of marking the development of a child's faculties, and observing his little occupations.'

It went deeper than that. The baby and the boy led the poets to rekindle their own memories of childhood, the everlasting hurts suffered when they had been wronged, the moments of fear or trouble, their glimpses of freedom and ecstasy. These months are when Coleridge started to develop his theory of imaginative education, of a mind shaped by the image-filled worlds into which a child can disappear; and Wordsworth began to discover the opposite, of childhood as the realm not of creative freedom but of unadulterated experience, of moments and spots of time that burned themselves into a child's being, so that memory became the sculptor of the person.

Children were a source of suddenness, of revelatory frankness, of understanding the world in a way that did not depend on the

understanding of others. Little Hartley was a fountain of
unedited brilliance: 'When I told him, you had sent your love to
him in the Letter,' Coleridge told Southey, 'he sat, & thought, &
thought, and at last burst into a fit of Laughter –/.'

Hartley, who was 'a very Seraph in clouts', 'a spirit that dances
on an aspin leaf', also had a way of saying the right thing to the
wrong people. At the end of Coleridge's life, the doting father
remembered how little Hartley had once astonished 'a party of
very grave persons, his aunt's connections' – the proper Frickers,
one of them a bishop – who asked him if he had learnt any
hymns. Hartley said 'that Papa had taught him a pretty Resur-
rection Hymn' – which he repeated with great glee as follows:

Splother! splother! splother!
Father and mother!
Wings on our shoulders –
And UP we go!

It was a version of the great Coleridgean gospel of ascent, leaving
behind the nonsense of the world, all the politesse, its valued
connections, and instead strapping on the wings and leaping
lark-like into the blue!

For Coleridge, the youngest children were living in a super-
sensory world, where all stimuli were connected. 'Babies touch
by taste at first – then about 5 months old they go from the Palate
to the hand – & are fond of feeling what they have to taste ...'
Immediacy was and should be everything to them, even in
calamity:

Hartley fell down & hurt himself – I caught him up crying
& screaming – & ran out of doors with him. – The Moon
caught his eye – he ceased crying immediately – & his eyes
& the tears in them, how they glittered in the Moonlight!

Both nature and culture were to be part of the happy child's world. Hartley could learn, but he should also be taught. He should be shown the riches of the world's knowledge, but there should be no assumption that his own mind was not already brimming with life. The little boy's imagination was in play long before he had language or grammar to express what he knew. The very search for wisdom and simplicity on which the poets had been embarked this year was effortlessly alive in him:

> Hartley, just able to speak a few words, making a fire-place
> of stones, with stones for fire – four stone= fire-place – two
> stone= fire –/ arbitrary symbols in Imagination.

The idea of the one life inhabiting everything, to which Coleridge had been urging and persuading Wordsworth all year, was an unsummoned part of the little boy's mental universe:

> Hartley's intense wish to have Ant-heaps near our house/his
> *Brahman* love & awe of Life/N.B. to commence his
> Education with natural History –
>   I hear his voice at this moment distinctly; he is below in
> the garden, shouting to some foxgloves and fern, which he
> has transplanted, and telling them what he will do for them
> if they grow like good boys!

This habit of close attention to the reality and dignity of a child's mind stayed with Coleridge all his life. His third son, Derwent, named after Wordsworth's native river in Westmorland, once came back into the house from playing outside, to find

> all the *Cake* was eat up, & he by no means willing to accept
> dry Toast & butter as a Substitute. 'Don't eat all the Cake!' –
> Well, we will not tomorrow! – 'O but don't eat the Cake!
> You have eat the Cake! O but don't eat up all the cakes!' –

His Passion had compleatly confounded his Sense of Time,
& its Consequences – He saw that it was done; & yet he
passionately entreated you not to do it – & not for the time
to come/but for the present & the Past. 'O but you have! O
but don't now!'

Empathy comes pouring out of these notebook entries, with an
understanding of the interfoldings of past, present and future
that Derwent was feeling. Coleridge knew and heard from his
baby son that the crime of the parents having eaten all the cake
existed not only in the past but had present force. All times are
fluid in the light of all others. Here were the themes of *The
Ancyent Marinere*: guilt, understanding and damage all cohabit
in the present moment as the multiple existence of a crime after
the fact.

The previous September, Tom Wedgwood, one of the enormously rich sons of the great pottery entrepreneur Josiah
Wedgwood, had arrived in Somerset. He was twenty-six, high-
minded, radical, philosophical, brilliant and febrile, and had
been sick since he was boy, with recurrent and debilitating fits of
depression that left him in paralysed gloom for weeks at a time.
Along with the rest of this generation, he too was now turning
to thoughts of childhood. He had been part of the circle in
London around William Godwin, and had known the Pinneys
and Tom Poole. Here, probably at Alfoxden, he met Wordsworth
and Coleridge for the first time. Wordsworth remained shut
away, but with Coleridge, Wedgwood immediately embarked on
wide-ranging conversations. The two of them were born
companions: walkers, fascinated by chemistry and electricity,
and by the relationship of the self to the world, by education and
by theories of perception. Wedgwood had been taught chemistry
as a boy and he was already a great experimenter, trying out a
wide variety of light-sensitive silver compounds in laboratories

paid for and provided by his father at the Etruria works in Birmingham.

It is not difficult to see how the behaviour of light-sensitive chemicals would take a turn, in a chronically metaphorical mind, towards thoughts of an image-imposing world, above all in childhood, and it is likely, in their philosophical conversations that September, that Wedgwood and Coleridge talked about a science-cum-art that had been a part of Wedgwood's life for almost a decade but had yet to acquire its name: photography.

Experimenting with different chemical solutions and different substrates, Wedgwood had discovered that when white paper, or soft white leather, was moistened with nitrate of silver, it became sensitive to light. If the treated surface was kept in the dark, no change could be seen. 'But on being exposed to the daylight, it speedily changes colour, and after passing through different shades of grey and brown, becomes at length nearly black.' The brighter the light, the more quickly the paper darkened. 'In the direct beams of the sun, two or three minutes are sufficient to produce the full effect. In the shade, several hours are required, and light transmitted through different coloured glasses acts upon it with different degrees of intensity.'

By exposing figures painted on glass, so that their image fell 'upon a flat surface of shamoy leather wetted with nitrate of silver, and fixed in a case made for a stuffed bird', Wedgwood was consistently able 'to obtain and fix the shadows of objects'. But there was a problem. 'We obtained a temporary image or copy of the figure on the surface of the leather, which, however, was soon obscured by the effects of light.'

> The copy of a painting, or the profile, immediately after
> being taken, must be kept in some obscure place. It may
> indeed be examined in the shade, but in this case the
> exposure should be only for a few minutes; by the light of

candles and lamps, as commonly employed, it is not sensibly affected. Nothing but a method of preventing the unshaded parts of the delineation from being coloured by exposure to the day is wanting, to render the process as useful as it is elegant.

Wedgwood had discovered the chemical change at the heart of photography, but had yet to find a way of preventing the whole surface of the paper from darkening in the light. The eighteenth century could make photographs, but had yet to find a fixative.

Here was a self-recording world, a self-making mirror, in which existence was not an inert condition but a process in everlasting action. *Natura*, Coleridge would write, thinking of its etymology, is 'that which is about to be born, that which is always *becoming*'. The poignancy – and perhaps the underlying truth – lay in Wedgwood's inability to fix the image, to make it material. The very same process that had created the picture – the darkening of the silver nitrate salts – then went on to destroy it. Each of his photograms was remembering and forgetting combined in one physical fact. Nothing simply was; everything was either becoming or decaying, so that Nature, in Coleridge's words, was 'an ever industrious Penelope for ever unravelling what she had woven, for ever weaving what she had unravelled'.

What were the metaphorical implications of these experiments? Was the mind a mere recipient of its surrounding circumstances? Or was the mind, and the body of which it was a part, somehow a silver-coated organism like that leather or paper? A coating to which we give the name of consciousness? Did the very material of our consciousness-sheath create the forms we think of as the realities of the world?

And what did that say about the nature of the child's mind? And how should children be brought up if they were indeed as photo-receptive as the silver nitrates of the photography experiment?

Nothing is more striking than the intellectual and spiritual troubles of these young men. Their very explorations led them to places where it was difficult to find coherence, so that mental distress seems bound up with the revolutionary changes of this year. In one form or another it seems to have been almost universally present: Charles Lamb, his sister Mary, Charles Lloyd, Basil Montagu, Tom Wedgwood, John Thelwall, William Wordsworth and Samuel Taylor Coleridge were all touched or teetering around the fringes of madness. Sara Coleridge, Dorothy Wordsworth, Robert Southey and Tom Poole look like the sheet anchors in this cross-cut sea. And Wedgwood, his mind perhaps sensitised by his photographic experiments, was to come up with an educational scheme that seems like a desperate response to that feeling of dissolution and uncertainty.

He had been struck, perhaps from his own experience, by the unencompassable volume and variety of sense-impressions which any child was exposed to. Life was an anarchy of information. You could not hope to bring up a person of balanced mind if all they experienced was 'a host of half-formed impressions and abortive conceptions blended into a mass of confusion'. The photograms were of single leaves or radically simplified images. That, surely, might be the basis for a carefully and reasonably controlled programme of education?

To bring about the scheme, as he had written to William Godwin in the previous July, there would be various philosophers in charge, but they would also need

one, or two, superintendents of the practical part. The only persons that I know of as at all likely for this purpose, are Wordsworth and Coleridge. I never saw or had any communication with either of them. Wordsworth, I understand to have many of the requisite qualities and from what I hear of him, he has only to be convinced that this is

the most promising mode of benefiting society, to engage
him to come forward with alacrity. The talents of Coleridge,
I suppose are considerable &, like Wordsworth's, quite
disengaged. I am only afraid that the former (viz. Coleridge)
may be too much a poet and religionist to suit our views.

This was before Wedgwood had met either of them or formed
any coherent picture of who they were or what they believed. His
own conception of the future for children could scarcely have
been further from the nature-engaged ideas of the two poets.
'My aim is high,' he wrote to Godwin. 'Should not the nursery,
then, have plain, grey walls with one or two vivid objects for
sight and touch? ... Let hard bodies be hung about them so as
continually to irritate their palms.' The 'child must never go out
of doors or leave his own apartment'. And there should be no
'romping, tickling and fooling'.

This idea, fuelled by an exceptionally strong recognition of
how the world impinges on consciousness, was not a thousand
miles from how Coleridge was thinking. He too had become
powerfully aware of the mind as a sensation-sensitive organ,
which recorded every impression made on it, however slight
or transient. The difference between him and Wedgwood was
only in their reaction to this understanding: Coleridge's
was to embrace the multiplicity, Wedgwood's to limit and steri-
lise it.

Any sense of reverie or the spontaneous, the border conditions, had no part in Wedgwood's vision, but were critical to
Coleridge's. Super-absorbency was the core of poetic consciousness. In July 1802, Coleridge would write to William Sotheby, a
fellow poet, that poetry has nothing to do with hallucination, or
any false vision of how things might be, but was entirely dependent on close attention to the realities and subtleties of how things
are. 'A great poet,' Coleridge told his friend,

must have the ear of a wild Arab listening in the silent desert, the eye of a North American Indian tracing the footsteps of an enemy upon the leaves that strew the forest and the touch of a blind man feeling the face of a darling child.

It is as if his ideal were a mind and a being, a body, entirely coated in Wedgwood's world-recording minerals.

Here was the foundation of one of the core Romantic values, what Wordsworth would call 'wise passiveness', and what Keats would describe to his friend John Hamilton Reynolds in 1818:

Let us not therefore go hurrying about and collecting honey-bee like, buzzing here and there impatiently from a knowledge of what is to be arrived at: but let us open our leaves like a flower and be passive and receptive – budding patiently under the eye of Apollo and taking hints from every noble insect that favors us with a visit – sap will be given us for Meat and dew for drink – I was led into these thoughts, my dear Reynolds, by the beauty of the morning operating on a sense of Idleness – I have not read any books – the Morning said I was right …

Both Coleridge and the Wordsworths practised this gospel. Dorothy Wordsworth described her own and her brother's ideal for little Basil.

Till a child is four years old he needs no other companions, than the flowers, the grass, the cattle, the sheep that scamper away from him when he makes a vain unexpecting chase after them, the pebbles on the road, &c. &c.

That is what would make him 'a stout fellow' with 'a most excellent temper ... quite free from selfishness ... extremely active, and never fretful or discontented'.

This breezy recognition of the value of a child's presence in nature, open to the shaping power of the light, began to lead both Coleridge and Wordsworth towards an exploration of what they knew of themselves as children. How had the world made them who they were? Tom Poole asked Coleridge for a description of himself, perhaps thinking he might write the life of his friend and hero. Coleridge responded with a series of autobiographical letters written at intervals all through these months, a surge of vivid recollections, which focused not on nature but on culture, on what the imagination embedded in the written word had given him. His aunt had a shop in Crediton, where as a boy he had begun to devour all the stories he could find in the chapbooks she had for sale, 'Tom Hickathrift, Jack the Giant-Killer &c. & &c. &c. &c.' After reading these stories, he would run up and down in the churchyard acting out everything he had read, loving the stories precisely because they made him forget himself, and allowed him to roam through all the realms his mind might dream of. When he was six, he discovered *The Arabian Nights*,

one tale of which (the tale of a man who was compelled to seek a pure virgin) made so deep an impression on me (I had read it in the evening while my mother was mending stockings) that I was haunted by spectres, whenever I was in the dark – and I distinctly remember the anxious & fearful eagerness, with which I used to watch the window, in which the books lay – & whenever the Sun lay upon them, I would seize it, carry it by the wall, & bask, & read –. My Father found out the effect, which these books had produced – and burnt them.

The world of the father, of paternal, rationalist definition and restriction, could act as a limit on what a boy might be, but the visions in stories were themselves a form of liberty. Nevertheless, Coleridge's father could also appear as the kindest and most encouraging of guides in the enlargement of his son's mind.

> I read every book that came in my way without distinction – and my father was fond of me, & used to take me on his knee, and hold long conversations with me. I remember, that at eight years old I walked with him one winter evening from a farmer's house, a mile from Ottery – & he told me the names of the stars – and how Jupiter was a thousand times larger than our world – and that the other twinkling stars were Suns that had worlds rolling round them – & when I came home, he shewed me how they rolled round –/. I heard him with a profound delight & admiration; but without the least mixture of wonder or incredulity.

Those first experiences of the enlarging story, as he told Poole, shaped him as a person.

> For from my early reading of Faery Tales, & Genii &c &c – my mind had been habituated *to the Vast* – & I never regarded *my senses* in any way as the criteria of my belief. I regulated all my creeds by my conceptions not by my *sight* – even at that age. Should children be permitted to read Romances, & Relations of Giants & Magicians, & Genii? – I know all that has been said against it; but I have formed my faith in the affirmative. – I know no other way of giving the mind a love of 'the Great', & 'the Whole'. – Those who have been led to the same truths step by step thro' the constant testimony of their senses, seem to me to want a sense I possess – They contemplate nothing but *parts* – and

all *parts* are necessarily little – and the Universe to them is but a mass of *little things*.

I have known some who have been *rationally* educated, as it is styled. They were marked by a microscopic acuteness; but when they looked at great things, all became a blank & they saw nothing.

Those words are spoken by the poet of *The Rime of the Ancyent Marinere* and 'Kubla Khan', and implicit in them is a criticism of Wordsworth's increasing addiction to the reality of the real thing, to the flat-soled closeness of his needing the real to be the ground and substance of poetry. It is a sign of a small chasm opening between them, an early inkling of the distrust and even disdain that would come in time to colour their friendship.

Coleridge had abandoned his tragedy *Osorio* when it was rejected for the London stage, but it remained active in his mind, as another way of dramatising his own idea of himself as a great soul outside the normal bounds of existence. He would rescue one fragment of the play for inclusion in *Lyrical Ballads* this summer. It told yet another version of this repeated story: of a person whose destiny was to know things the rest of the world around him did not know, giving him access to understandings that world did not have, but also consigning him to everlasting exile.

The story of the fragment describes an orphan, discovered as an infant in the wilds of Spain and brought up by a nobleman.

And so the babe grew up a pretty boy –
A pretty boy, but most unteachable –
And never learnt a prayer, nor told a bead;
But knew the names of birds, and mocked their notes,
And whistled, as he were a bird himself!

The boy learned to read, and could not stop himself from reading:

> Till his brain turned – and ere his twentieth year,
> He had unlawful thoughts of many things.

His unorthodoxy meant he was imprisoned by the authorities, but he escaped and ran back out into the wilds of the world:

> He went on shipboard
> With those bold voyagers, who made discovery
> Of golden lands ...
> 　　　　　　the poor mad youth,
> Soon after they arriv'd in that new world,
> 　　　　... seized a boat,
> And, all alone, set sail by silent moonlight
> Up a great river, great as any sea,
> And ne'er was heard of more: but 'tis supposed
> He lived and died among the savage men.

Not the Ancient Mariner, but the Boy Mariner, the visionary Coleridge-Hartley-Kubla-Mariner, his river a prefiguring of Conrad's great river in *Heart of Darkness*, a journey into a heartland that was wild, threatening and revelatory. All this was there, perhaps in embryo, in the elfin sprite who lived alongside them in their crowded Lime Street cottage and the little boy who played at Alfoxden with the farm labourers' children, climbing the giant trees and exploring the dropping stream.

Wordsworth also now embarked on a journey into his own past. He had left 'The Ruined Cottage' in the previous summer as a simple tale of sorrow and loss, but now he took it up again and began to evolve a far richer character for the Pedlar who was telling the tale to the poet. What was his life, what his origins, what the source of his calm and rich understanding of the fate of Margaret and her family? How could a simple travelling sales-man have such wisdom?

Wordsworth began to explore this growing element of the poem in a new notebook. It had been handmade, probably by Dorothy, out of large sheets of laid paper, torn to size and sewn together by her. In its pages, Wordsworth added to and changed a fair copy of 'The Ruined Cottage' that she had made for him. As he worked, he found the descriptions of the Pedlar transform-ing under his hands. Soon it became clear enough: the boyhood of the Pedlar was Wordsworth's first description of the growth of his own mind.

Coming back home in the evening, the Pedlar

> saw the hills
> Grow larger in the darkness and beheld
> alone the stars come out above his head.

That physical and sensuous memory, the dark enlarging of the lightless hills, the sudden presence of the night sky above his loneliness, begins the summoning of what he had been in his 'time of unrememberable being'. As Wordsworth feels his way into that boyhood sensibility, the verse turns towards a grand, organic music. As he walks, there is no one alongside him 'to whom he might confess the things he saw'. In the darkness, that giant world fuses with his solitude.

> So the foundations of his mind were laid,
> In such communion, not from terror free
> While yet a child and long before his time
> He had perceived the presence and the power
> Of Greatness, and deep feelings had impress'd
> Great objects on his mind with portraiture
> And colour so distinct that on his thought

229

They lay like substances and almost seem'd
To haunt the bodily sense. –

In these lines, Wordsworth starts to discover the great themes of *The Prelude*: the beginnings and growth of his own mind, of his making as a poet. Here his story acquires its lifelong architecture. He is the great and lonely soul embedded in the grandeur of nature, in a relationship of such tangible and physical intimacy that, in his closeness to it, those giant forms feel as present as a parent or a lover.

Nothing in the daily world could ever match the sense of grandeur sinking into his mind which this night walking in the darkened hills conveyed to him with such solemnity. In the wake of it, the pages of this manuscript notebook quickly filled with a sense of the marvellousness of things. The Wordsworth who looked down at the toes of his boots in the road-dust – that figure has gone. Instead, the ecstatic boy, filled with everything Coleridge had been saying for months:

>   ... he had felt the power
> Of nature, & already was prepared
> By his intense conceptions to receive
> Deeply, the lesson deep of love, which he
> Whom Nature, by whatever means, has taught
> To feel intensely cannot but receive.

The boy whom Wordsworth was imagining-remembering was not yet nine years old. But his being was on a scale with the world.

> Oh! then what soul was his! when on the tops
> In the high mountains he beheld the sun
> Rise up and bathe the world in light.
>   He looked,

In the high mountains the boy beheld the sun

PREVIOUS PAGE: And, all alone, set sail by silent moonlight

The Ocean and the earth beneath him lay
In gladness and deep joy. The clouds were touched
And in their silent faces did he read
Unutterable love.

Here again are lines that had first appeared in the Alfoxden note-book: 'Sensation, soul and form/All melted into him', using the verb that always occurred to Dorothy in moments of visionary wholeness on the heights of the Quantocks. This was a vision of godliness. Wordsworth was quite explicit about that, even if the expression he used was strange. 'He did not feel the God: he felt his works./Thought was not. In enjoyment it expired.'

These are very nearly notes for the poetry Wordsworth would write for the rest of his life. There is nothing about ordinary religion. 'He neither prayed, nor offered thanks or praise.' The experience was both more and less than that. It was his own existence which was itself the miracle of creation.

His mind was a thanksgiving to the power
That made him. It was blessedness & love.

It was the most astonishing claim: not the mountains, nor the night sky, nor the vastness of the cosmos, but the mind of Wordsworth itself was evidence of the blessed nature of the universe. He had of course read the books of the Bible, but they were only printed words, to be read not felt:

But in the mountains did he <u>feel</u> his faith
There did he see the writing – All things there
Looked immortality, revolving life
And greatness still revolving, infinite;
There littleness was not, the least of things
Seemed infinite, and there his spirit shaped
Her prospects nor did he <u>believe</u> – he saw.

Wordsworth struggled for years to fit this large addition about the Pedlar and his visionary power to the story of Margaret in her cottage. He never resolved the problem, because the two parts of the poem come from different parts of his own mind: Margaret is essentially pre-Coleridgean, with no vision of wholeness; the Pedlar is from after the time Coleridge had led him to a vision of universal coherence, the source of which Wordsworth found in his own boyhood. In the Pedlar are the seeds of Wordsworth's lines to be written above Tintern Abbey in the summer, and after that, of *The Prelude*. The force that drives the poetry is an interfusion of Wordsworth's own egotistical turn of mind, his recognition of himself as his great subject, with Coleridge's gospel of one life, which could bind together a love of nature and love of humanity, and which suggests that in the repeated habit of loving nature, a mind will inevitably acquire the habit of loving man.

In February and on into March, this poetry of the rediscovered self rolled out of Wordsworth. Coleridge had been dwelling for years on the idea of a huge, epic, philosophic poem. He long thought he was the poet to write it. 'I should not think of devoting less than 20 years to an Epic Poem,' he wrote to Cottle.

Ten to collect materials and warm my mind with universal science. I would be a tolerable Mathematician. I would thoroughly understand Mechanics, Hydrostatics, Optics and Astronomy, Botany, Metallurgy, Fossilism, Chemistry, Geology, Anatomy, Medicine – then the *mind of man* – then the *minds of men* – in all Travels, Voyages and Histories. So I would spend ten years – the next five to the composition of the poem – and the last five to the correction of it.

That is, as ever, half-serious; but once Coleridge had encountered the depth and scale of Wordsworth's mind and ambition, he transferred this huge project to the poet he admired more than any other. Wordsworth believed him, and these hundreds of lines in early 1798 are all making their way towards that epic, to be called 'The Recluse', on which he would work for decades to come.

Wordsworth's first mention of it was in two letters sent from Alfoxden in early March. To one old friend, the excitement buried in understatement:

I have written 1300 lines of a poem in which I contrive to convey most of the knowledge of which I am possessed. My object is to give pictures of Nature, Man, and Society.

And to another, the faux-modesty breaking up:

[I have been] tolerably industrious within the last few weeks. I have written 1300 lines of a poem which I hope to make of considerable utility; its title will be The Recluse or views of Nature, Man, and Society ... I know not anything which will not come within the scope of my plan.

It was to be the great poem of the modern world, the successor to Milton, the one figure who for these poets played the part of another moon or sun, 'that mighty Orb of Song', in Wordsworth's ungainly phrase. As part of that idea, Wordsworth had the Pedlar make a long and powerful statement of his beliefs. It is, at its core, Wordsworth's expression of gratitude to Coleridge for all that he had given him, all the new sun-and-sky-absorbing view of the world which allowed him to leave his previous sterilised, downward-looking self behind. 'Not useless do I deem,' he began this epoch-making statement, hovering as usual in the uncertainty of a double negative, always the sign in Wordsworth of an intention he recognised as too large to be encompassed in words:

> Not useless do I deem
> These shadowy sympathies with things that hold
> An inarticulate language; for the man
> Once taught to love such objects as excite
> No morbid passions no disquietude,
> No vengeance & no hatred needs must feel
> The joy of that pure principle of love
> So deeply that unsatisfied with aught
> Less pure & exquisite he cannot choose
> But seek for objects of a kindred love
> In fellow-natures & a kindred joy.

More perfectly expressed than in anything Coleridge ever wrote, this is what the year in the Quantocks meant to say. Coleridge quoted these lines in a letter to his brother, written this March, embodying everything he also now believed. An ecstatic unity with life awaited the enlightened man:

> All things shall live in us & we shall live
> In all things that surround us.

The moment of inspired understanding, spoken through the mouth of the Pedlar, comes to an end.

> The old man ceased
> The words he uttered shall not pass away
> They had sunk into me, but not as sounds
> To be expressed by visible characters
> For while he spake my spirit had obeyed
> The presence of his eye, my ear had drunk
> The meanings of his voice.

Unlike so much of what Wordsworth had written in his notebooks this winter, this reads not as a tentative approach to understanding, a stepping towards the sense with each newly apparent
word, but the unrolling of a certain truth, 'his thoughts now
flowing clear – from a clear fountain flowing'. All the fluency of
the Quantocks streams, their waters running over their stony
beds, all the sensations of confluence and influence which the
poets' co-existence here had generated over the year, seem to be
alive in this sense of meaning itself being beyond the meaning of
words, but embodied instead in the very breathing and sensing
of embodied souls alive in the world. We are neither merely
receivers of the world through our senses, nor are our minds the
shapers of it. We are both more and less than that, mindbodies,
embedded because embodied, mentally alive because physically
alive, with no boundary at the skin, perhaps even no skin, no
difference between thought and being. The world pours into us
and we into it in an ever-turning mutual tide, ebbing and flooding with love and acceptance:

> with bliss ineffable
> He felt the sentiment of being, spread
> O'er all that moves, and all that seemeth still.

As Wordsworth was writing this in one of Alfoxden's many
panelled rooms, four miles away in his damp and smoky cottage
in Lime Street, Coleridge was also writing in the depths of the
winter night. 'The frost performs its secret ministry,' Coleridge
begins the most famous of his Conversation Poems, written on
one of the four or five frosty and snowy nights in the middle of
February that Dorothy recorded in her journal. The air temper-
ature sank to six or seven degrees below freezing all over southern
England on several of those nights. It may have been the evening
of the 17th, after a day in which Coleridge had first walked over

through deep snow to see the Wordsworths at Alfoxden, before he and William returned to the Lime Street cottage and Wordsworth had finally gone back to Alfoxden.

It had been a clear day of perfect quiet, summoning from Dorothy one of her most beautiful entries, as still and cloudless as a vase:

> A deep snow upon the ground ... The sun shone bright and clear. A deep stillness in the thickest part of the wood, undisturbed except by the occasional dropping of the snow from the holly boughs; no other sound but that of the water, and the slender notes of a redbreast, which sang at intervals on the outskirts of the southern side of the wood. There the bright green moss was bare at the roots of the trees, and the little birds were upon it. The whole appearance of the wood was enchanting; and each tree, taken singly, was beautiful. The branches of the hollies pendent with their white burden, but still showing their bright red berries, and their glossy green leaves. The bare branches of the oaks thickened by the snow.

The poem occurs in one of Coleridge's moments of perfect enclosure, down in the valley, away from any wind, protected by the snow and the silence, with Sara and Nanny now asleep upstairs. He is sitting by the fire, and Hartley is contentedly asleep in his cradle beside him. It is a winter twin for the summer's 'Lime Tree Bower', with Coleridge alone and thinking of the significance of this moment, the conceptual opposite of those high and open, starlit mountain tops on which Wordsworth's imagination was even now roaming through memories of his eight-year-old self in ecstasy.

The frost performs it's* secret ministry,
Unhelp'd by any wind. The owlet's cry
Came loud – and hark, again! loud as before.
The inmates of my cottage, all at rest,
Have left me to that solitude, which suits
Abstruser musings, save that at my side
My cradled infant slumbers peacefully.

Rarely can fatherhood have been enshrined in such a moment. And yet it is not quite as innocent as it looks. The memory was still fresh of the Home Office's covert interest in them the previous autumn. Coleridge was still being attacked as a Jacobin in the pro-government press. The general 'caballing' against the Coleridges and the Wordsworths had not ceased, and the lease on Alfoxden would not be renewed by Mrs St Albyn, the ministry-loyal landlady. In that context, the idea of a secret, chilling, stilling and even paralysing frost performing its hidden ministry is the opposite of comforting.

'Tis calm indeed! so calm that it disturbs
And vexes meditation with it's strange
And extreme silentness. Sea, hill, and wood,
This populous village! Sea, and hill, and wood,
With all the numberless goings on of life,
Inaudible as dreams!

These are Quantock conditions. When the water runs down the gutters of Stowey, its noise is never absent. When the wind blows, as Dorothy described, it 'beats furiously' down from the tops; dogs howl; the sea in certain winds can roar far inland. Not in this frost though. And with that snow-muffled silence, all human life in the village is quiet too. Aloneness for Coleridge is not what

---

* Sic for 'it's' and later examples.

it is for Wordsworth. This is a diminution of existence, not the grand elevation of it.

> The thin blue flame
> Lies on my low-burnt fire, and quivers not;
> Only that film which flutter'd on the grate
> Still flutters there, the sole unquiet thing.
> Methinks, it's motion in this hush of nature
> Gives it dim sympathies with me, who live,
> Making it a companionable form
> With which I can hold commune. Idle thought!
> But still the living spirit in our frame,
> That loves not to behold a lifeless thing,
> Transfuses into all it's own delights
> It's own volition, sometimes with deep faith
> And sometimes with fantastic playfulness.

The loneliness of Coleridge makes him long to commune with that piece of soft, sooty membrane that wavers with the fire, as if it too were a living thing. And so, empathising even with that strange dark, inanimate but fluttering half-object – half-process, half-object, the very fading-and-becoming that Coleridge saw at the heart of life – he starts to drop down into the deeper levels of himself, wondering if he too might not be the same kind of wavering soul as the thing he watches. And then, indeed, he wavers, realising first the cosmic significance of the idea that all might be holy and all might be communicative, and then thinking how such an idea might be nothing but the playful fantasy at work.

Pause here for an instant and consider the two poets, separated by four miles of a snowy night, the owls outside, the trees dropping now and then their load of snow, their pens over their notebooks in the candlelight, each considering the strange and potent idea that everything might be animate, but radically diverging in their response to it. Wordsworth in Alfoxden finds a life-resolution in that understanding; Coleridge in Stowey is led by it towards a radical uncertainty about himself and the world.

Coleridge turns away, and starts to think also of his childhood, not of himself as a grand visionary in the mountains of his home, but as an unhappy, lonely, disowned child exiled at school in London.

Ah me! amus'd by no such curious toys
Of the self-watching subtilizing mind,
How often in my early school-boy days,
With most believing superstitious wish,
Presageful have I gaz'd upon the bars,
To watch the *stranger* there! – and oft belike,
With unclos'd lids, already had I dreamt
Of my sweet birthplace, and the old church-tower
Whose bells, the poor man's only music, rang
From morn to evening, all the hot fair-day,
So sweetly, that they stirr'd and haunted me
With a wild pleasure, falling on mine ear
Most like articulate sounds of things to come!
So gaz'd I, till the soothing things, I dreamt
Lull'd me to sleep, and sleep prolong'd my dreams!

He longs for that sweet and soothing dream, as a place to console him for the pains of separation, for some human being who would love him, but who never came. There is nothing here of Wordsworth's 'greatness still revolving', nor of Wordsworth's contempt for 'littleness'. Coleridge's poem is at heart a hymn to the beauty and importance of littleness, to the beautiful and little human being beside him. Everything else might be dead in the still of the frost, but Hartley is not.

Dear babe, that sleepest cradled by my side,
Whose gentle breathings, heard in this dead calm,
Fill up the interspersed vacancies
And momentary pauses of the thought!
My babe so beautiful, it fills my heart
With tender gladness, thus to look at thee,
And think, that thou shalt learn far other lore,
And in far other scenes!

Coleridge has absorbed and borrowed his vision for this baby
from Wordsworth:

For I was rear'd
In the great city, pent mid cloisters dim,
And saw nought lovely but the sky and stars.
But thou, my babe, shalt wander like a breeze
By lakes and sandy shores, beneath the crags
Of ancient mountain, and beneath the clouds
Which image in their bulk both lakes and shores
And mountain crags;

Grandeur has arrived in the Lime Street cottage. It is an unmistakable signal of the standing Wordsworth had achieved in
Coleridge's mind. The mountainous landscape of Wordsworth's
boyhood now seems to Coleridge like a guarantee of his son's
wellbeing.

There are other subterranean currents here. The armies of the
French Republic had invaded Switzerland in January, burning
towns and killing hundreds, a bloody land-grab that scandalised
and horrified those friends of liberty – including Wordsworth
and Coleridge – who until then had believed at least in the
possibility of a good outcome to the revolutionary process. It is
possible that this poem about domesticity is part of Coleridge's
political programme, declaring his love of country, and his love

of family and home as testament to that patriotism. Edmund Burke, in his *Reflections on the Revolution in France*, had established the connection. English liberty, in Burke's mind, was an 'inheritance derived to us from our forefathers'. The constitution of the country was bound up 'with our dearest domestic ties'. For Burke, the state and 'our hearths' – the very spot Coleridge was sitting – were 'inseparable'. For Burke and the Pitt administration, love of family was love of country. For Coleridge to describe so beautifully his beloved child could be taken, by the Home Office and the ministry, as a declaration of loyalty to country.

To see 'Frost at Midnight' exclusively in those terms is to diminish the greatest hymn to fatherly love ever written. He sends Hartley on his way with a prayer for his wellbeing, whatever state the world might be in, whatever the ministry might do or be, whatever freeze or thaw might grip the world, whether the wind blew or frost imposed its silence on creation:

> Therefore all seasons shall be sweet to thee,
> Whether the summer clothe the general earth
> With greenness, or the redbreasts sit and sing
> Betwixt the tufts of snow on the bare branch
> Of mossy apple-tree, while all the thatch
> Smokes in the sun-thaw: whether the eave-drops fall
> Heard only in the trances of the blast,
> Or whether the secret ministery* of cold
> Shall hang them up in silent icicles,
> Quietly shining to the quiet moon.

Finally, he thinks of him the following morning, before the sun has melted away the world of ice, when Hartley will also become a winged and treasured creature who will flutter eagerly at the

---

* Sic.

241

beauty and marvel of existence. Any icicles of the future, the loving father promises, will be

> Like those, my babe!, which ere tomorrow's warmth
> Have capp'd their sharp keen points with pendulous drops,
> Will catch thine eye, and with their novelty
> Suspend thy little soul; then make thee shout,
> And stretch and flutter from thy mother's arms,
> > As thou would'st fly for very eagerness.

12

Emerging

March 1798

I'm on the Quantock heights, the only pupil in the Dorothy Wordsworth School for the Observation of Nature. She is calling the class to attention. Look into the crevices of things, she says. Have you seen the hail grains caught in the groins and angles of the thistles? Have you seen how the March sun is reaching into that wood like a hand into an inner pocket, its fingers feeling for any secrets the wood might contain? How the bellies of the larks are lit beneath them? How that bird drops, wings up and out, as if lowering to the moor on a hidden wire? And how the light of the sun, coming through the wing and tail feathers, is bright in the translucence of the primaries, darkening in the coverts? Look at the wrens dancing inside the prison of the gorse. And do you see where a sheep has been caught there, where the pulled-out tufts are still taut between the thorns and stems of the bramble? Every moment has its history.

And what colour is the sea? Today, now, it is brown and earthy. Yesterday it was ravaged, bruised. But are there not stripes in it? Yes, striped, as if its pelt has been thrashed. Look over to the west. Spring clouds are bubbling up there into towers and cities, over Butterfly Combe and Hodder's Combe, over the saddle at Bicknoller Post. These are our places. The map of these hills is as creased now as a work-worn palm.

243

In the hedges, the fruits of winter: ivy berries, rose hips, an occasional yew and its pink little nipple seeds, hart's tongue ferns, their undersides striped in the dragoon dress of spore-lines. Moss makes cushions on the cut stubs of the ashes. The first flowerless sprigs of cow parsley are up by a tiny bit of butterbur, its leaves furled in cigars. Mud is splashed on them from passing traffic, the ferns clogged in the lowest of their pleats.

I have been looking for firsts: 5 February, the first snowdrop splaying with age; 12 February, the first primrose tucked into the bank of a side-stream in Adscombe; 14 February, in Quantock Combe, the first newly dug rabbit burrow, with stony trash at its entrance; 17 February, sheep found in the oakwood up at Danesborough, sheltering from the wind, as unexpected as a flock of unicorns; 21 February, on the edge of Pardlestone Lane that runs from Alfoxden to the sea, the first periwinkles, the same Wordsworth saw in 1798 'trailing their wreathes ... through primrose-tufts'; 22 February, the hazels in blossom, just up from the path to Kilve, lit from behind and shaken by the wind, the lime-green catkins waggling their tails.

By 1 March the snowdrops were already looking tired and over, winter flowers, their moment done. The first time I felt the sun warm on my cheek was 2 March. The same day, the leaves of the wild garlic were spreading by the church in the green combe at Aisholt, one of the places Coleridge thought he might be happy. Song thrushes in pairs were jumping up in front of me from the beds of bilberries in the oakwoods at Friarn. On the spires of gorse up above Crowcombe on the top of the Quantock ridge, chaffinches were sitting wobbling in the wind, the shifting of the birds' own bodies accommodating the swaying of the stems beneath them. On 3 March, a low tight squadron of migrating golden plovers came up over my shoulder and away to the north, a tawny cape of them, swept and gone.

A pair of early-nesting ravens on 4 March twisted and flicked down over the farm at Adscombe, a gloss-black waterfall, satin ribbons as they fell. Pairs of buzzards displayed over the pine wood in Ramscombe. All winter long the robins had been singing in the hollies at Alfoxden, filling the woods with their brilliance, each note frozen. Now others were joining them, the great tit – 'Teacher, teacher' – the raucous shouting of the rooks above their rookeries and the mimicry of the starlings. Walking with a friend, I heard one on the path Coleridge habitually took from Stowey over to Alfoxden, not far from the road, which sounded like a police-car siren, wee-wawing from the depths of an ashwood.

6 March, walking over the Quantock ridge to Crowcombe in the evening, a blackbird began, in the last of the light, to sing the beginnings of its summer song. Not the starburst of its alarm call, but something warmer, a rounded, fruity, cherry-like song bubbling up above the overgrown beech hedges of Crowcombe Park wall, where the Wordsworths' landlords lived. A few brief fragments of song, golden drops, not the bulbous, lovely anthem of summer, but a cast at it, a first try in the clinging cold.

On 10 March I found a mossy spot welcoming and dry enough actually to lie down in, a Coleridgean dell, hidden away on the upper margin of the oakwoods. (Wordsworth had been able to lie down under the trees in Alfoxden park on the 3rd.) By mid-month, the bluebell leaves had begun to coat the floors of the woods. The skylarks were up above the wet meadows of the Levels, Wurlitzers singing forever the same requested song. The first cherries were in flower. Celandines were coating the edges of the rhynes on the Levels, those on the south-facing banks three or four days ahead of those on the unsunny sides. The first violets I saw and smelled on 14 March, the smell so faint it was like the memory of a smell. In the woods, the blue tits and coal tits were jumping all day from one stance to the next, so quick that every moment looked like a blink for them, their lives lived as birdsong sounds. I have seen them in the mornings skipping around the mossy boughs of the oaks in Holford Combe, pulling off the moss in little tufts here and there, jumping, busy, twirr and schurr, for minutes at a time high up in the crooks of the trees.

By now the children were outside playing in the evening after school. (The children in 1798 were playing outside on the 10th.) It was as if every living thing was responding to the light. The tips of the oak trees, when seen from some way off, had acquired a pink tinge, a whole-tree blush, as the thousands of leaf buds prepared to break. Close-up, the stems of the hawthorns were covered in little pregnant pustules, crab eyes on stalks. In the ponds on the Quantock tops, where little else had yet emerged, the water was clotted with frogspawn, the future frogs as still as pennies. Just one early wriggle-headed sperm.

Spring is a softness, a balm on bones. There is something creamy about it, a yellowness, as if the blue of winter had been sent back into the earth to think again.

At the very end of February and on into the first few days of March 1798, cold bright easterlies blew in for day after day from the continent of Europe and held England in the tail end of winter. Only after 4 March did the regime begin to shift, and mild if damp Atlantic air start to arrive from the south-west, bringing with it the first tendrils of warmth and spring. On one of those mornings, perhaps on 6 March, Wordsworth sat out in the park at Alfoxden and wrote a poem of a kind he had never written before.

Seen in isolation, and knowing nothing of the darkness and trouble of the winter months they were now leaving behind, this poem might seem soft and sentimental, not the great poetry of a great poet, something curiously thin and slight. But in the knowledge of the winter that had just passed, this March poem becomes a kind of sunlight, guileless and dedicated to the simplicity of a shared pleasure in the arrival of spring.

By the hand of little Basil Montagu – who is called Edward in the poem – Wordsworth sent his lines to Dorothy, who was at work, probably by her favourite window in the north-eastern

Frost at Midnight

FOLLOWING PAGE: Blessing in the air

corner of the house, looking out eastwards to the trees on the far side of the park, and northwards down to the sea. She was probably copying out lines from 'The Pedlar' or 'The Ruined Cottage'.

The new poem's title is as naked as the poem itself: 'Lines written at a small distance from my House, and sent by my little Boy to the Person to whom they are addressed'.

It is the first mild day of March:
Each minute sweeter than before,
The red-breast sings from the tall larch
That stands beside our door.

It is as if Dorothy is now writing a poem. Where has the grandeur gone, the giant self-conception, the dark, Romantic winter cloak?

There is a blessing in the air,
Which seems a sense of joy to yield
To the bare trees, and mountains bare,
And grass in the green field.

This is the language of the middle classes conversing among themselves, as ordinary as the grass he was seeing in the pastures dropping away towards Kilve and the sea. No starlight, no heroic solitude, no specialised language, no antiquities, no guilt, no shadows, no sexuality, no metaphysics. One could read it, in that way, as a response to all the elaborations of the poetry Coleridge was also writing this spring. It is after breakfast, and so he talks to Dorothy, his other self.

My sister! ('tis a wish of mine)
Now that our morning meal is done,
Make haste, your morning task resign;
Come forth and feel the sun.

There is an imperiousness in that, but does he remember her reproving tone, when he was sunk in gloom at Racedown, instructing him to pursue his calling as a poet? And is he feeling now that their lives might consist, at least for a moment, in not obeying that calling? Has she mended him?

> Edward will come with you, and pray,
> Put on with speed your woodland dress;
> And bring no book, for this one day
> We'll give to idleness.

The dress is no poeticism: it is the dress she wore when they went out rambling in the combes, collecting sticks or gathering moss. But this is not a workaday outing; it is a new beginning:

> No joyless forms shall regulate
> Our living Calendar:
> We from to-day, my friend, will date
> The opening of the year.

He has been guided to this point by Coleridge, and now repeats to his sister the mantras of universal connectedness he has learned and absorbed from his great friend.

> Love, now an universal birth,
> From heart to heart is stealing,
> From earth to man, from man to earth,
> – It is the hour of feeling.

Coleridge had told them that 'A Poet's *Heart & Intellect* should be combined, *intimately* combined & *unified*, with the great appearances in Nature …' That was now a universal truth for Wordsworth, one which, for the time being, he felt would be the gospel of their lives:

Some silent laws our hearts may make,
Which they shall long obey;
We for the year to come may take
Our temper from to-day.

There is an air of ritual about his invitation, as if he and Dorothy
were both to be initiates in a new understanding of the world.
There is even a suggestion of marriage in it, that their love would
somehow be sealed on this new morning. And it is a return to
childhood, the time in which the two of them had been bonded
as one, before the catastrophes had struck and their family was
broken. The childlike language, delivered in the hands of a five-
year-old boy, is so simple that, as readers would often think about
Wordsworth's poetry in years to come, it hangs on the borders of
the empty. Its means of expression are so flat that one can trip up
over them, as you can stumble on a flagstone where you thought
a step might have been.

This simplicity is radical minimalism. Wordsworth had already
practised great elaboration and complexity as a poet, toying with
all kinds of modes and languages. The moralist, the satirist, the
landscape painter, the gentleman poet, the gothic artist, the
visionary, the agonised soul and the prophet – all of which he had
been over the last few years – have been banished. He has shed
his clothes and is now free of them, free of books, free of learning,
free of pretension and out in the world, as free as a child. As an
aspect of that simplicity, having learned this from the Coleridge
of 'Frost at Midnight', he repeats as his final verse almost word
for word a verse from earlier in the poem. This is no pose, that
repetition says, but life itself, truly, openly and happily led.

Then come, my sister! come, I pray,
With speed put on your woodland dress;
And bring no book; for this one day
We'll give to idleness.

This atmosphere, which takes as gospel all that Coleridge had been telling him in the Quantocks, would not last, but it was a gateway to an astonishing three-month period in which poetry of many different kinds would pour out of Wordsworth. Much of it became his contribution to the volume he shared with Coleridge, to be published in the autumn of this year as *Lyrical Ballads, with A Few Other Poems.*

As Wordsworth was coming into that apparently calm and open light of spring, Coleridge was still embedded in a different imaginative world. In March, he was still finishing the last parts of *The Rime of the Ancyent Marinere.* Alongside it, and as a dark companion to 'Frost at Midnight', he was writing the first part of his most mysterious ballad. 'Christabel' shares the conditions of 'Frost at Midnight', but reflects them into the world of the uncanny, not the homely but the disturbing, the unhomely, daring to engage – as surely Wordsworth was not engaged with the ambivalences of love and desire for his sister – with the unaccommodated lusts that lurk in the psyche.

There was no simplicity in Coleridge. Behind every one of his statements and attitudes lie something like their opposites: the love of home conceals the dread of home; the love of self conceals the contempt for self; the love of others obscures distance from others; the love of his wife conceals a lust for others; the love of love may enshrine a fear of love.

And so 'Christabel' and 'Frost at Midnight', written within the same few days, are each other's Manichean twin. Both begin in midnight, in candlelit rooms, where a fire burns towards its close, and both are entranced by the dark, still world beyond those walls. In both the owls are hooting. But they are the points of a twin-tined fork. 'Frost at Midnight' luxuriates in the beauty of enclosure; 'Christabel' edges out into the terror of uncertainty. The beauty of Hartley's childhood and the sweetly

gathered family under the snowy thatch is displaced in
'Christabel' by the less comfortable world of desire, of abuse
and dominance, of sexual witchery, of threat and the suggestions of madness.

Coleridge does not make it easy. There is a gothic setting, a
castle, a maiden, a moon, but he makes them absurd. The owls
hooting in the middle of the night wake the cock, which half-
asleep begins to crow: 'And hark again! the crowing Cock,/How
drowsily it crew.' The baying hound which for Wordsworth in
'The Discharged Soldier' had been a strange irritant is now ridiculous, barking in time with the ringing clock, shouting out each
hour 'Sixteen short howls' to each of its pealings.

So what is this poem? A gothic tale? A comic tale? A comic
gothic tale? Nothing is sure. 'Is the Night chilly and dark?'
Coleridge asks, because in gothic tales night must be both. 'The
Night is chilly but not dark,' he replies. There is a moon, but it
casts no spectral light. The moon is 'dull'. The spring has come,
but it is a spring without spring; the season is slow and cold.
Uncertainty hangs in every line.

Then the maiden, a virgin, Christabel, purity herself, betrothed
to an absent knight, goes out into the leafless wood because she
has been dreaming lustful dreams of her lover.

> The Sighs she heaved, were soft and low,
> And nought was green upon the Oak,
> But Moss and rarest Mistletoe.

Her own murmuring sighs find answer from something or someone in the wood:

> There she sees a Damsel bright,
> Drest in a silken Robe of White;
> That shadowy in the moonlight shone:

The Neck, that made that white robe wan,
Her stately Neck and Arms were bare;
Her blue-vein'd feet unsandal'd were;
And wildly glitter'd here and there
The gems entangled in her hair.

Sexual excitement and anxiety tremble through Coleridge's lines. This woman is Christabel's doppelgänger, an unmatched beauty called Geraldine, the vowels of her name the reverse of Christabel's, e-a-i for i-a-e. Geraldine tells her tale of lost innocence: she has been kidnapped, taken and raped – 'They chok'd my Cries with Force and Fright' – and then abandoned at the tree where Christabel found her. Together and quietly, guiltily, the two women go up into the castle tower, where Geraldine, drinking Christabel's wildflower wine, falls into a trance and in that trance turns witchlike, powerful, commanding. She tells Christabel to undress, and then undresses herself,

> drawing in her breath aloud,
> Like one that shudder'd, she unbound
> The Cincture from beneath her Breast:
> Her silken Robe, and inner Vest
> Dropt to her feet, and fell in View,
> Behold! her bosom and half her side –
> A Sight to dream of, not to tell!

With the two of them now naked, Geraldine

> lay down by the Maiden's side:
> And in her arms the Maid she took,
> Ah, weladay!
> And with low Voice and doleful Look
> These Words did say:

'In the Touch of this Bosom there worketh a Spell,
Which is Lord of thy Utterance, Christabel!
Thou knowest to night, and wilt know to-morrow,
This Mark of my Shame, this Seal of my Sorrow ...'

That is the voice of desire-not-to-be-denied, of the unconscious, the inner world to which Coleridge had so clear an access that it arrived on the page without explanation, no dress, naked, complex and coloured by guilt. Coleridge could never finish this poem. Christabel's walk out into the midnight wood had taken him into a part of human experience he could know but not accommodate, a place that was both intimate and mysterious, to be felt but not explained, apprehended but not analysed. 'The story', one contemporary reviewer wrote, was 'a dream of lovely forms, mixed with strange and indescribable terrors', in which sex was both the foundation and antithesis of love, both filled with a mysterious hostility and entirely, overwhelmingly, alluring. It would be difficult to think of a poem, even if set among the same 'bare trees' of early springtime, that was further from Wordsworth's fantasy of spring sweetness. The fork in the path had appeared.

13

Polarising

March 1798

The effect of a long mutual exposure was to make each of the poets more fully himself. Knowing what not to be became a source of conviction. Coleridge's supernaturalism was driving Wordsworth towards the poetry of this world, of the human heart, his own and others', and leaving to Coleridge the poetry of the metaphysical, of other worlds into which his imagination and his learning might lead him. For Wordsworth, increasingly, poetry was coming to reside in the potency of memory and self-realisation; for Coleridge, it was the opposite, not the ever-deeper investigations of the self but the integrative power of the imagination and its ability to absorb the widths of the world. ''Tis a strange assertion,' he would write later to Thomas Poole,

> that the Essence of Identity lies in *recollective*
> Consciousness – 'twere scarcely less ridiculous to affirm,
> that the 8 miles from Stowey to Bridgewater consist in the
> 8 mile stones.

There was surely more to life and the universe than recording where and what one had been.

Nevertheless, this mutual polarisation was understood by them and had come to seem like a *modus vivendi*, a way in which their companionship could continue. Wordsworth would later portray himself and Coleridge as 'Twins almost in genius and in mind', 'Predestin'd if two beings ever were,/To seek the same delights', but the new understanding of this early spring 1798 was for them to see each other not as twins but as interlocking opposites. Difference might allow friendship where similarity could inhibit it.

On 9 March, the entire Coleridge family walked over to Alfoxden and stayed there with the Wordsworths for the next nine days. They were a foursome, with the two young boys alongside. Plans came rippling out of their conversations. The St Albyns, owners of Alfoxden, had been adamant since the previous autumn that they would not renew the lease, however much urging was done by Poole, Coleridge and the Wordsworths themselves. The government investigation and the hints of francophile subversion meant that no patriotic Tory family could tolerate such tenants. The Wordsworths were reluctant to go, but now that Coleridge could rely on the Wedgwood money (although it was late coming), and with a steady if intermittent income from Wordsworth's own investments and lendings, they could make ambitious plans. Germany may have been suggested by Coleridge, who was keen to drink at the source of German science and philosophy. For the Wordsworths, the idea appealed of learning German and being able to make a living from translation. The Alfoxden lease would come to an end in June; they would leave soon after.

At the same time, they thought they might be able to make some money from their poetry. For months, and especially after the December failure of the plays, they had been toying with different cash-raising schemes: a volume of Wordsworth's poetry, or two; another edition of Coleridge's own poems; a printing of the two tragedies; or maybe a collaborative venture between the two poets. The patient Bristol bookseller-publisher Joseph Cottle had calmly responded to one suggestion after another, but nothing was settled.

Years later in *Biographia Literaria*, published in 1817, Coleridge made it seem as if he and Wordsworth had devised a division of the poetic world early in their year together and had calmly carried out a programme to fulfil it. That is far from the truth, but perhaps in this March, with Coleridge now heavily engaged both in *The Marinere* and in 'Christabel', and Wordsworth sensing a surge of lyric force within him, they did decide on the outline for a joint book.

'During the first year that Mr. Wordsworth and I were neighbours,' Coleridge wrote in 1817,

> our conversations turned frequently on the two cardinal
> points of poetry, the power of exciting the sympathy of the
> reader by a faithful adherence to the truth of nature, and the
> power of giving the interest of novelty by the modifying
> colours of imagination.

What was poetry? this formulation asks. Was it truth or was it dream? Or both? There was at least one kind of poetry which could cross that boundary, stemming from the walks to which they had both devoted hundreds of hours all year.

> The sudden charm, which accidents of light and shade,
> which moon-light or sun-set diffused over a known and
> familiar landscape, appeared to represent the practicability of
> combining both. These are the poetry of nature.

Beyond that coalescence of dream and reality in the beauty of dusk and moonlight, the attention to the real and the claims of the imagined drove a cleft between them:

> The thought suggested itself (to which of us I do not
> recollect) that a series of poems might be composed of two
> sorts. In the one, the incidents and agents were to be, in part

at least, supernatural; and the excellence aimed at was to consist in the interesting of the affections by the dramatic truth of such emotions, as would naturally accompany such situations, supposing them real ... For the second class, subjects were to be chosen from ordinary life; the characters and incidents were to be such, as will be found in every village and its vicinity, where there is a meditative and feeling mind to seek after them, or to notice them, when they present themselves.

It seems likely that this conversation did not occur at the beginning of the year, in the summer months when Thelwall and Lamb were their visitors, but only in this March, after the revelations of 'Kubla Khan', *The Marinere* and 'Christabel' had taken up residence in Coleridge's mind; and after Wordsworth had begun to sense the excitement and value of poetry emerging from the ordinary, even from his own childhood. If that is true, then this division was not a programme for the reformation of English poetry, merely a recognition of differences between the two of them. It was a retrospective acknowledgement of the change that had occurred in the course of the year.

That is not, famously, how Coleridge portrayed it in *Biographia Literaria*. 'In this idea originated the plan of the "Lyrical Ballads",' he wrote,

in which it was agreed, that my endeavours should be directed to persons and characters supernatural, or at least romantic; yet so as to transfer from our inward nature a human interest and a semblance of truth sufficient to procure for these shadows of imagination that willing suspension of disbelief for the moment, which constitutes poetic faith.

Mr. Wordsworth, on the other hand, was to propose to himself as his object, to give the charm of novelty to things of every day, and to excite a feeling analogous to the supernatural, by awakening the mind's attention from the lethargy of custom, and directing it to the loveliness and the wonders of the world before us; an inexhaustible treasure, but for which in consequence of the film of familiarity and selfish solicitude we have eyes, yet see not, ears that hear not, and hearts that neither feel nor understand.

Few more famous words have been written about the way in which poetry works. Is it possible to practise any sort of archaeology on them? Can one detect beneath the mysteriously polite and gentlemanly surface something of the conversation they might have had in March 1798? The power lies in the expression Coleridge uses to justify his own art: an imaginative embodying of the truth to produce 'that willing suspension of disbelief for the moment, which constitutes poetic faith'. There is a sense of importance in those phrases, the urgency of a man justifying to a sceptic listener the validity of poems such as *The Ancyent Marinere* and 'Christabel', when that listener was having difficulty in seeing the virtue in them. They are the core of Coleridge's case. He does not give the same argumentative weight to the phrases he chooses for Wordsworth. 'The charm of novelty' and 'the loveliness and the wonders of the world' are the oddest of expressions for the lyrics Wordsworth would now produce. Charm and loveliness were scarcely his interests or targets.

There was no stopping Wordsworth this spring. Over the next eight or ten weeks he embarked on one of the great experiments in English, writing the series of poems he came to call 'lyrical ballads', a run of varying, rhyming forms that combined the story-telling and quick rhythms of the ballad with all the close emotional focus and intensity of lyric poetry, so that vivid, inward states of mind could be made to inhabit the lolloping, picaresque sequences by which a ballad makes its way.

That mixing and transmigration of forms allowed Wordsworth to move outside the received way of doing things. The magazines were full of poems about the poor, the abused and the deranged, suffering the battery of life itself, but none had been as linguistically radical as what Wordsworth would now write. Extraordinarily, these March and April poems remain as strange now as when they were written: intractable, uncomfortable, indefinable, unsettling and uncertain, repeatedly motivated by the double negative that lay somewhere near the centre of Wordsworth's own mind. Are the stories they tell true or untrue? Or not untrue? They often seem impossible, but are they not also not *un*impossible? Do they matter? Are they about anything at all? Are the tellers of the tales trustworthy, or maybe simply not untrustworthy? Where are the truths they seem to orbit around? Do the marginal lives of their characters allow them access to a kind of truth which a more ordinary and mainstream narrator could never reach? And what is the relationship between those truths and a sense of ambivalence, of possibility but no certainty, that lies beneath them?

In poem after poem, there is no destination, but a kind of retraction from reliability, in the way a snail's horns pull back when touched. Everywhere the reader is wrong-footed, believing and then not believing what he is being told, trusting in the numinous atmosphere around a place or an incident, only to be held up short by the absurdity of the tale or its telling. So experimental are these poems that they seem less conventionally 'romantic' than modern, as if in one leap Wordsworth had moved beyond the conventions of romanticism, the sweetness and consolations of nature, or the ability of poetry to reach towards some kind of cosmic understanding, into a more alienated and modern frame of mind. This is not the world either of wind-tossed daffodils or of anything resembling Wordsworth's ecstatic boyhood memories. The *Lyrical Ballads*, for all their sophisticated 'ordinariness', remain odd, and, as Hazlitt said, full of 'seeming simplicity and real abstruseness'.

There is no doubt the poems come from the Quantocks, and are filled with the landscapes and the people the Wordsworths had been encountering all year.

The most located of them is 'The Thorn'. On the very top of the ridge, at Bicknoller Post, a mile or two from Alfoxden and beside the track to Crowcombe, are some wind-bitten thorns, with a little archipelago of small, muddy, reed-fringed ponds next to them, and one or two strange grass- and moss-covered mounds.

The Wordsworths had often passed this way 'in calm and bright weather', but this spring, on a day of wind, storm and mist, Wordsworth quite suddenly saw the tree and its surroundings in a different light, ominous and numinous, and decided to use the place as the occasion for a poem which stepped beyond the mere description of place or weather.

The story is told, by an old sea captain, of a pregnant young woman, Martha Ray, who is betrayed by her lover, murders her child and buries it here, in a place which she then haunts for the rest of her life, and where the ghost of the dead child will always be seen by those who are capable of seeing it. Or so the suggestions and rumours go; nothing is quite clear.

The poem is the archetypal Lyrical Ballad, fringing at its edges into the beautiful and the troubling, but also into the ridiculous, repetitive and loquacious, always somehow hinting at a significance beyond what is said, cultivating atmosphere and doubt in the destabilising context of an over-chatty and gullible narrator. Some truth may lurk here, but in a mist.

At all times of day and night, the sea captain says, Martha goes to the mossy mounds beside the pond,

And she is known to every star,
And every wind that blows;
And there beside the thorn she sits
When the blue day-light's in the skies,

And when the whirlwind's on the hill,
Or frosty air is keen and still,
And to herself she cries,
'Oh misery! oh misery!
Oh woe is me! oh misery!'

For all the gothic poignancy of that, Wordsworth's description of the little landscape at Bicknoller Post is one of the most notorious he ever made:

Not five yards from the mountain-path,
This thorn you on your left espy;
And to the left, three yards beyond,
You see a little muddy pond
Of water, never dry;
I've measured it from side to side:
'Tis three feet long, and two feet wide.

These were to become his most infamous lines, declaimed by London and Edinburgh wits to general amusement, publicly criticised by Coleridge for their 'laborious minuteness and fidelity in the representation of objects, and their positions', thought by the diarist Henry Crabb Robinson to be incapable of being repeated 'in company' for fear of laughter, testily defended by Wordsworth – 'they ought to be liked' – and later revised by him to make them seem less crazy.

What can be said in their defence? First, perhaps, that they are a true description of what you find at Bicknoller Post, even today: the track, the wrinkled thorn, the muddied puddle of a pond. As such, the words are part of the poetic experiment on which Wordsworth was now engaged, purifying his language, making poetry into an aspect of the real, laying the foundations against which all else might also be measured. 'There is a thorn', the poem begins in all nakedness, part of a deliberate imprisoning of Wordsworth's poetic gift, a self-restriction from which it is possible, and perhaps even necessary, to wonder what the point of poetry might be, as if, in the plainness of the description, he has opened the skin of poetry and looked inside.

There was certainly courage in publishing those words. And they, together with the equally notorious 'Peter Bell', have generated the funniest and cruellest of Wordsworth parodies, this one by Walter de la Mare:

The Bards

My aged friend, Miss Wilkinson,
Whose mother was a Lambe,
Saw Wordsworth once, and Coleridge, too,
One morning in her p'ram*.

This was a three-wheeled vehicle
Of iron and of wood.
It had a leather apron,
But it hadn't any hood.

Birdlike the bards stooped over her
Like fledgling in a nest:
Wordsworth said, 'Thou harmless babe!'
And Coleridge was impressed.

The pretty thing gazed up and smiled,
And softly murmured 'Coo!'
William was then aged sixty-four
And Samuel, sixty-two.

I have spent so long with Wordsworth that I now think of him as a friend who makes mistakes, and for whom things have a way of coming out wrong, but whom I trust and admire for his other

And she is known to every star

PREVIOUS PAGE: She unbound the cincture from beneath her breast

qualities. I want to maintain that this childlike simplification of his language, for all its ridiculousness, opens a door into the heart of the poem, and perhaps, for all the uncertainty of the tale, allows the reader to take as truth the lonely companionship of the bereft woman with the exhausted tree, the thorn which is 'a mass of knotted joints,/A wretched thing forlorn', the two of them together on the windswept hilltop, crushed by life and all its circumstances.

There had been many eighteenth-century precursors to this grieving and abandoned woman, many with a lonely thorn, but rarely had the uncertainty of dread clung so close:

'But what's the thorn? and what's the pond?
'And what's the hill of moss to her?
'And what's the creeping breeze that comes
'The little pond to stir?'
I cannot tell; but some will say
She hanged her baby on the tree,
Some say she drowned it in the pond,
Which is a little step beyond,
But all and each agree,
The little Babe was buried there,
Beneath that hill of moss so fair.

The simplicity which the measuring of the pond introduced has given access to human meanings that greater sophistication and elaboration would only have obscured.

Ludicrous or tragic, beautiful or absurd, perceptive or superstitious, 'The Thorn' is a transcription of the kind of suffering that was everywhere in the England of the late 1790s, and of the frame of mind that attempts or fails to understand that suffering. The poem is an act of empathy. The people of the villages are muttering about Martha, as they did of Wordsworth and his family. Their gossip is a means of exclusion. Wordsworth has renounced his membership of that gossiping world, dropped all pretence at decorum and left behind the assumptions of privilege. He now inhabits the voice of the woman for whom he is demanding understanding from his readers. That is the act of courage represented by 'The Thorn': the daring to be absurd because the absurd is close to the bereft. And, in that, the poem makes one giant claim: the point of poetry is not beauty but truth, and if truth is awkward and uncertain then poetry should be like that too.

Half-mad people, those in distress and those who had lost everything – the voices of the unheard run through these poems. Some are weak through age, some through feebleness of mind, some are apparently suffering under a curse whose origins are unclear. Simon Lee, the old huntsman whose house was on the green at Holford, just up from the waterfall in Mare's Pool, has aged.

> And he is lean and he is sick;
> His little body's half awry,
> His ancles they are swoln and thick;
> His legs are thin and dry.

He and his wife are the poorest of the poor, and he is on the point of death. Eight verses go by describing his destitution and his memories of running with the hounds. Only then does Wordsworth show his hand:

> My gentle reader, I perceive,
> How patiently you've waited,
> And now I fear that you expect
> Some tale will be related.

This is the Wordsworth of the shrugging shoulders, breaking open the mould into which a poem might expect to be poured. But the denial of expectations is his purpose, and here he can

introduce, at least in a hint, the Coleridgean vision of wholeness
to his own new stripped and naïve style:

O reader! had you in your mind
Such stores as silent thought can bring,
O gentle reader! you would find
A tale in every thing.
What more I have to say is short,
And you must kindly take it:
It is no tale; but should you think,
Perhaps a tale you'll make it.

In three more verses, Wordsworth delivers his point. The old
man had been trying to uproot an old tree in his little patch of
ground, but he was too weak – 'The mattock totter'd in his hand'.
Wordsworth himself offered to help, and with a single blow
severed the difficult root.

The tears into his eyes were brought,
And thanks and praises seemed to run
So fast out of his heart, I thought
They never would have done.
– I've heard of hearts unkind, kind deeds
With coldness still returning.
Alas! the gratitude of men
Hath oftner left me mourning.

The social purpose is obvious, but is there a whiff of sentimen-
tality here? Late in life Wordsworth remembered the old huntsman, who had been employed by the St Albyns of Alfoxden, and
the way he wistfully spoke of the hounds in pursuit of the stags
on the hill: '"I dearly love their voice" was word for word from
his own lips.' But this man was Christopher Trickie, who had
played such a central part in telling the Home Office spies the

previous summer that the Wordsworths and their friends were revolutionary Frenchmen who spent their time investigating the rivers of Quantock while preparing for an enemy invasion.

Trickie was known in the neighbourhood to live up to his name. The Reverend William Holland of Over Stowey hated him:

> On to the top of Quantock. Saw the turf [i.e. peat] man. He showed me the turf cut. In the afternoon the rascal came to ask for the money and a cup of drink. 'What' answered I, 'before I receive the turf; that is not a right mode of proceeding', but he begged hard, said he had not eat a bit of bread since yesterday, and wanted money to procure some. I gave it like a fool as I was, but the moment he turned his back, all cried out, on enquiry, that I should never get the turf now that he had got the money, so that I am laughed at by every one. But I will look sharp after the scoundrel, for I hate to be thus tricked. His name is Tricky. Had I consulted his physiognomy I never would have trusted him.

A late-eighteenth-century class drama is embedded in these relationships. A poor, old working man is suspicious of strangers or of anything resembling a gentleman-intellectual. He takes from the equally conservative vicar of Over Stowey as much as he can get, whether the work to earn it has been done or not. Wordsworth, suspected as much by Holland as by Trickie, aims to dissolve those class antagonisms. The three men occupy the three corners in a triangle of distrust. Working man hates and is hated by old gent, who hates and is hated by romantic poet, who is hated by working man but who claims, at least, to love him for his dignity and gratitude. It is that last element in the triangle which does not ring true. Surely Wordsworth would have been aware of Trickie's informing against him? Why does he not allow that resentment to surface in the poem? Perhaps because it does not conform with his Coleridgean social agenda of universal love? Perhaps because he wants his universal human sympathy to be truer than it is?

In the midst of all this, and using all the same materials of mental disturbance, social isolation, poverty, radically simplified language, and the wooded combes and open tops of the Quantocks, Wordsworth suddenly drops in a comedy.

Thomas Poole had told him a story about an idiot boy who had been out all night under the moon and had come home saying that 'The cocks did crow to-whoo, to-whoo, & the sun did shine so cold.' Using that as his starting point, Wordsworth had composed 'The Idiot Boy', all 463 lines of it, 'in the groves of Alfoxden, almost extempore; not a word, I believe, being corrected, though one stanza was omitted. I mention this in gratitude to those happy moments, for, in truth, I never wrote anything with so much glee.'

All the contents of the Quantock year come bubbling up in the quick gaiety of the ballad. Here are the hooting owls and the sleepy cocks. Here are the sick and lonely women that had been a constant presence in Wordsworth's poetry. Here is the simple love of a mother for her child that has rocked back and forth between Coleridge and Wordsworth all year. Here is the desperate confusion of a person in crisis, as Betty Foy wonders if her Johnny is now lost. Here is the moon reflected in a brook, as it had been in the glittering streams of the Quantocks all summer and winter, but now as a joke, when Johnny thinks he can actually find it there. Through moonlight lanes and moonlight dales Betty Foy goes in search of her child.

> She listens, but she cannot hear
> The foot of horse, the voice of man;
> The streams with softest sound are flowing,
> The grass you almost hear it growing,
> You hear it now, if e'er you can.

The nature of laughter is the hardest of all aspects of the past to recover, but 'The Idiot Boy', playing with the most important and touching elements of the year Wordsworth and Coleridge had shared here, brings one close to that particular fusion of the funny and the serious which was the lifeblood of their friendship. This is Wordsworth in pure delight, dancing and scampering in the precincts of his own holiest places.

> Perhaps he's turned himself about,
> His face unto his horse's tail,
> And still and mute, in wonder lost,
> All silent as a horseman-ghost,
> He travels on along the vale.
>
> And now, perhaps, is hunting sheep,
> A fierce and dreadful hunter he!
> Yon valley, that's so trim and green,
> In five months' time, should he be seen,
> A desert wilderness will be!

Wordsworth even plays with the idea of his own great 'office upon earth' as a poet, giving a tiny glimpse of a comic *Prelude* that dates the beginning of his devotion to poetry to when he was thirteen, the year in which his father died:

> I to the muses have been bound
> These fourteen years, by strong indentures;
> O gentle muses! let me tell
> But half of what to him befel,
> For sure he met with strange adventures.

It is a momentary identification of Wordsworth with the idiot boy, perhaps a momentary insight into himself as a holy, versifying fool.

When Johnny's midnight ramblings at last are over, Betty finds her beloved son:

> She looks again – her arms are up –
> She screams – she cannot move for joy;
> She darts, as with a torrent's force,
> She almost has o'erturned the horse,
> And fast she holds her idiot boy.

'The Idiot Boy' is yet another of the circular forms which this year repeatedly generated, the movement out into strangeness and back into safety, working as some essential pattern of risk and relief, exposure and asylum. Underneath the gaiety there is something of supreme importance, only recognised as the laughter dies away: the power of a love that can almost turn a horse upside down.

14

Delighting

April, May and June 1798

Coleridge was not the simple man, the gardener, husband, father, clusterer, which his ideology would persuade him was the core of virtue. He was, inevitably, with his subtilising mind, aware of the mismatch in himself, of his own inescapable complexity, and early this year had written to Wordsworth bewailing it. He had heard a beautiful and simple ballad sung on the stage, composed by 'Monk' Lewis.

> The simplicity and naturalness is his own, and not imitated;
> for it is made to subsist in congruity with a language
> perfectly modern, the language of his own times ... This, I
> think, a rare merit: at least, I find, I cannot attain this
> innocent nakedness, except by assumption. I resemble the
> Duchess of Kingston, who masqueraded in the character of
> 'Eve before the Fall,' in flesh-coloured Silk.

Coleridge's genius was to throw off revelatory, charming, joco-serious moments like this. Fifty years before, in 1749, Elizabeth Chudleigh, who had bigamously married the Duke of Kingston when her first husband was still alive, had attended the Venetian Masquerade at Ranelagh. She came 'almost in the unadorned simplicity of primitive nature', as Iphigenia, the daughter of

Agamemnon, sacrificed by him so that a fair wind would blow the Greek fleet to Troy. In this tale of masculine and martial wickedness, Iphigenia was the embodiment of innocence, the archetypal girl, purity, beauty, unaffectedness itself.

Amazed onlookers mistook the duchess for Eve in Paradise. In the words of the unreliable and vastly popular *Life and Memoirs of Elizabeth Chudleigh*, published in 1788,

> … this lady appeared in a shape of flesh-coloured silk so nicely and closely fitted to her body as to produce a perfect review of the unadorned mother of mankind.

It is one of the most poignant of all Coleridge's self-descriptions, inescapably funny, summoning images of his own pursy limbs half-squeezed into and half-escaping from a sheath of flesh-coloured silk, pretending nakedness, wanting simplicity but never more himself. All the brilliance and sadness of his life is bound up in that image as it sails across his brain.

Wordsworth, this spring, had no such self-doubt. Down in the park at Alfoxden, he was as happy as he had ever been. The weather in early April was a blessing, and on a morning when the sun shone he was out walking in the park with little Basil Montagu, his charge:

> A day it was when I could bear
> To think, and think, and think again;
> With so much happiness to spare,
> I could not feel a pain.

The two of them strolled together side by side on the dry gravel of Alfoxden's garden paths, away from the dewy grass,

Our quiet house all full in view,
And held such intermitted talk
As we are wont to do.

The shy five-year-old boy, again called Edward in this poem, the tall, intimidating figure of Wordsworth, the air between them pregnant with things that might be said, or might be too much to be said. It is one of the most touching scenes in the whole year. Wordsworth loved Basil, and felt loved in return:

I have a boy of five years old;
His face is fair and fresh to see;
His limbs are cast in beauty's mould,
And dearly he loves me.

Wordsworth thinks, in his silences, of the time they had all been together in Racedown – he calls it Kilve in the poem – a time that felt as if it was 'a long, long year before'. And as he thought of it, he wanted to compare it to Alfoxden where they were now walking, a place in the poem he called Liswyn farm. What did Basil think? Which did he prefer? Wordsworth held him by the arm as he asked the question, as if to compel him.

In careless mood he looked at me,
While still I held him by the arm,
And said, 'At Kilve I'd rather be
'Than here at Liswyn farm.'

Then, according to Wordsworth's own rigorously self-examining account, he pinions the boy with his questioning:

'Now, little Edward, say why so;
'My little Edward, tell me why;'
'I cannot tell, I do not know.'
'Why this is strange,' said I.

'For, here are woods and green-hills warm:
'There surely must some reason be
'Why you would change sweet Liswyn farm
'For Kilve by the green sea.'

At this, my boy, so fair and slim,
Hung down his head, nor made reply;
And five times did I say to him,
'Why? Edward, tell me why?'

His head he raised — there was in sight,
It caught his eye, he saw it plain —
Upon the house-top, glittering bright,
A broad and gilded vane.

Then did the boy his tongue unlock,
And thus to me he made reply:
'At Kilve there was no weather-cock,
'And that's the reason why.'

O dearest, dearest boy! my heart
For better lore would seldom yearn,
Could I but teach the hundredth part
Of what from thee I learn.

This moment of tenderness and humility, in which Wordsworth
comes to acknowledge – again – the inadequacy of adult methods, adult forms of understanding, adult evaluations of worth
and the adult grasp of less distorted minds, is another of the

triumphs of this year. The beauty and dignity of the five-year-old boy instructs the older man in a way page after page of *The Prelude* would attempt in years to come, if with a larger orchestra and grander stage machinery. This is a chamber piece, set in the springtime air, and in the fineness of its music is a gospel for life.

Spring, as the Reverend Holland in Over Stowey would repeatedly and delightedly record in his journal, was the time for 'fine little ducks', 'gleams of sunshine', 'flying clouds', hatching the chickens, sowing kidney beans and 'brocolo seed', 'walking out with my little boy to look for birds' nests', getting busy with the cucumbers and catching the elvers to go in a duck-egg omelette. Every living thing was responding to the urge to life.

> The cow, being furious for a bull, got out of the churchyard and ran towards Mr. Rich's. Robert went after her, and I too marched downstairs in my night cap, took down the lantern and lit the candle in it, and so like another Quixote sallied forth in quest of her. After hollowing some time at last I heard Robert's gruff voice, and soon bounce comes the cow in the narrow lane near the workhouse. I ran before, and at last with difficulty turned her and the yearling into the churchyard, as the most secure place for her, on account of the walls.

Bounce comes the cow. Up in the combes, birdsong fills the woods as much as the fuzz of bugs fills the globe of an oak tree. Those combes are skinned in song, an aural twin for the flush of new leaves, rhapsodic freshness in every molecule, a skin of leaves and a skin of song. Spiders sway down on their ropes from the trees as if trapeze art were their lives. The coal tits and blue tits dance-hop from one branch to another. The birds arrive from Africa and each province of each combe fills with its own cuckoo: one in Willoughby Cleeve, where the Wordsworths used to come for their eggs, and one in Short Combe just up from it; one in Sheppard's Combe and another further down in Lady's Edge; one in Frog Combe and another across the valley at the spring called Lady's Fountain. They overlap in their world-owning song: cuck-cuck-oo-oo, cuck-cuck-oo-oo. The pied flycatchers have come from the Congo, the male in his sharp black-and-white court dress, the female, softened, the same but grey, as if seen in moonlight; with them, the quivering red-tailed redstart, and the little lime-green wood warbler, green above, smoke grey below, as light and perfect as a syllabub, opening his bill again and again to sing his silvery, filigreed staircase of song.

Spring is a party in which the dress code is green. The bilberries are a green carpet on bright green stems, with tiny new green ferns among them; the tops of the oaks green out the sky so that their slim grey trunks become the connections between a green roof and a green floor, enclosing between them a green air, where the birds swim in a green lagoon.

Too much is happening too fast for it to be seen or caught. The world is tumbling on. Skylarks jump up from among the gorse, silent for the first ten or fifteen feet, bouncing up steps as if there were storeys in the air, and only then, when they have reached the upper floors, do they begin their song, bubbled, chaotic, as full of unexpectedness as a dream, strings of scarcely connected notes, a long and lyric account of a life fit to burst, the tale of unstoppability, the incontinent lark singing in and of a filterless world.

Everywhere, life: the bees humming on a goat willow make the noise of a small town; buzzards lift and sink on the air, riding each invisible crest and trough in the ripples of the wind; the kestrels below me this morning in Slaughterhouse Combe had backs the colour of bracken fields in winter. There was just enough breeze to hold them still, geostationary above the oaks. From down there came the manly, big-engine grunt of the stags.

* * *

Early in May 1798 Coleridge wrote the last of his great conversation poems of the year. He sent it by post-boy to Wordsworth at Alfoxden on 10 May with a self-deprecating verse letter,
asking for his opinion and wondering if it started well but
tailed off:

> In stale blank verse a subject stale
> I send per post my Nightingale;
> And like an honest bard, dear Wordsworth,
> You'll tell me what you think, my Bird's worth.

It is his great spring poem, enfolding almost everything the year
had addressed, pregnant with the beauty of what they had known
and felt, neither dark nor troubled in the way of Wordsworth's
winter verses, nor at angles to the world like the poems
Wordsworth was then writing for *Lyrical Ballads*, but, at least in
its beginning, as majestic as the night-time stream.

Coleridge is out in the warmth of a spring night with his
friends, somewhere between Alfoxden and Stowey, perhaps on
the old bridge that crosses the stream at Holford.

> No cloud, no relique of the sunken day
> Distinguishes the West, no long thin slip
> Of sullen Light, no obscure trembling hues.
> Come, we will rest on this old mossy Bridge!
> You see the glimmer of the stream beneath,
> But hear no murmuring: it flows silently,
> O'er its soft bed of verdure. All is still,
> A balmy night! and tho' the stars be dim,
> Yet let us think upon the vernal showers
> That gladden the green earth, and we shall find
> A pleasure in the dimness of the stars.
> And hark! the Nightingale begins its song,
> 'Most musical, most melancholy' Bird!

Coleridge is at his most embracing, as much in love with his friends as with the world, gliding from grandeur to intimacy, from them to nature. He quotes Milton from 'Il Penseroso', but only to deny that the bird is sad, and stays instead with the moment and the place he loves in the darkening woods, with the nightingale's 'capricious passagings,/And murmurs musical and swift jug jug/And one low piping sound more sweet than all –/Stirring the air with such an harmony'.

There are no nightingales in the Quantocks now, but the poem is evidence enough of Coleridge's having heard one. The pauses and passages of a nightingale's song, the silences within it, the different moods and manners, a high then low trilling, the *taca-tacatac*, followed by the marvellous drawn-out weeping as if coming from a bird in pain – all of that is here, in a poem which is the first ever record of a nightingale in Somerset.

He moves on, as they must move on – the Wordsworths back to Alfoxden, he back to Sara and Hartley in Stowey. And he remembers a moment recorded not long before in his notebooks.

Farewell, O Warbler! till to-morrow eve,
And you, my friends! farewell, a short farewell!
We have been loitering long and pleasantly,
And now for our dear homes. – That strain again!
Full fain it would delay me! – My dear Babe,
Who, capable of no articulate sound,
Mars all things with his imitative lisp,
How he would place his hand beside his ear,
His little hand, the small forefinger up,
And bid us listen! And I deem it wise
To make him Nature's play-mate. He knows well
The evening star: and once, when he awoke
In most distressful mood (some inward pain
Had made up that strange thing, an infant's dream)

I hurried with him to our orchard plot,
And he beholds the moon, and hush'd at once
Suspends his sobs, and laughs most silently,
While his fair eyes that swam with undropt tears,
Did glitter in the yellow moon-beam!

The Hartley of 'Frost at Midnight' has come out into the spring-time woods. Just as the bird pours its song into Coleridge's ear, the moonlight floods into Hartley's soul. His beautiful eyes that swam with undropped tears are as open to Nature as Coleridge's mind is to beauty and friendship. The poem is a statement of unadulterated hope, of allowing the dignity and sweetness of the natural word to colour and shape the people we are.

Into all of this, as the Wordsworths continued to worry about money, as Wordsworth and Coleridge together worried about what form of publication they might now arrange with Cottle, as they went on walking in the hills, less often now at night, more regularly in the spring glow of the morning, Sara Coleridge gave birth on 14 May to a little boy, Berkeley. He was 'a fine boy', and as Coleridge wrote to Tom Poole that morning, he was

> already almost as large as Hartley. She had an astonishingly good time, better if possible than her last; and excepting her weakness, is as well as ever. The child is strong and shapely, and has the paternal beauty in his upper lip. God be praised for all things.

This was a joke, as Coleridge knew his mouth was not the most beautiful part of his face. He had been careful and solicitous for Sara in the last stages of her pregnancy, but it is disturbingly symptomatic of the year that two days after Berkeley was born, Coleridge went off on a walking tour with Wordsworth and Dorothy to see the rocks of Cheddar Gorge on the far side of the

All silent as a horseman ghost

FOLLOWING PAGE: Tree Life

Levels. What to make of that choice? How might seeing Cheddar Gorge and its caves, or being with the Wordsworths, matter more to the author of 'The Nightingale' and 'Frost at Midnight' than being with his wife and newborn child?

The only excuse to be given is the distress Coleridge was under from a multiple disagreement with three of his sometime friends – Charles Lamb, Charles Lloyd and Robert Southey – whom he had insulted with his facetious parody-sonnets the previous autumn. Lloyd had now published a novel (with Joseph Cottle in Bristol, which was itself upsetting) in which Coleridge's behaviour as a young man was made to look absurd. Lamb had written a letter, perhaps in cahoots with both Lloyd and Southey, in which he had attacked Coleridge's pretensions to sanctity and greatness, portraying them in a series of mock-scholastic questions as a form of vastly enlarged vanity.

Coleridge was upset. 'I have had many sorrows and some that bite deep,' he wrote to a Unitarian friend in Bristol, 'calumny and ingratitude from men who have been fostered in the bosom of my confidence! I pray God that I may sanctify these events by forgiveness and a peaceful spirit full of love.' To Tom Poole, he said that 'So many unpleasant and shocking circumstances have happened to me in my immediate knowledge within the last fortnight, that I am in a nervous state, and the most trifling thing makes me weep.' The walking tour to Cheddar may, in part, have been designed to soothe Coleridge's troubled mind. Charles Lloyd's novel had been sent to the Wordsworths, and Dorothy had read it. And from Cheddar, it was Wordsworth's intention to go to Bristol to find Lloyd, whose mind was disturbed, and bring him back to Stowey. Coleridge was convinced that Southey, still intent on revenge after the angry ending of their friendship more than a year before, had got to Lloyd, and that Lloyd's 'infirmities have been made the instruments of another man's darker passions'. Lloyd had in fact already gone north to his parents in Birmingham by the time Wordsworth reached Bristol, and so did not return with him when Wordsworth came back to Stowey, driven by Cottle in his gig, on 22 May.

By then, yet another visitor had arrived to drink up the beauties of Somerset in May. The young William Hazlitt, so entranced by Coleridge when he had seen him on his January visit to Shropshire, had set off to find his heroes. Coleridge had repeated the invitation, and now Hazlitt walked all the way, down through Worcester and Gloucester, by Upton and Tewkesbury, reading novels, spending two days at Bridgwater before finally making his way to the Quantocks. His account of the poets' lives there, written only in 1823, is not entirely accurate, but he remembers it with a kind of immediacy no one else matched:

> I arrived, and was well received. The country about Nether Stowey is beautiful, green and hilly, and near the sea-shore. In the afternoon, Coleridge took me over to All-Foxden, a romantic old family mansion of the St Aubins, where Wordsworth lived.
>
> It was then in the possession of a friend of the poet's, who gave him the free use of it. Somehow, that period (the time just after the French Revolution) was not a time when nothing was given for nothing. The mind opened and a softness might be perceived coming over the heart of individuals ...

Alfoxden was not rent-free, but Hazlitt absorbed the more general atmosphere of a deep interconnectedness between things:

> Wordsworth himself was from home, but his sister kept house, and set before us a frugal repast; and we had free access to her brother's poems, the 'Lyrical Ballads,' which were still in manuscript ... I dipped into a few of these with great satisfaction, and with the faith of a novice.

Dorothy put him up for the night – it was easier than in the Lime Street cottage – and he slept 'in an old room with blue hangings, and covered with the round-faced family portraits of the age of George I. and II.' The next morning, at dawn, through the open window of his bedroom he 'could hear the loud stag speak'.

> That morning, as soon as breakfast was over, we strolled out into the park, and seating ourselves on the trunk of an old ash tree that stretched along the ground, Coleridge read aloud, with a sonorous and musical voice the ballad of 'Betty Foy.'

'The Thorn' and other poems soon joined Coleridge's recitation of 'The Idiot Boy',

> and the sense of a new style and a new spirit in poetry came over me. It had to me something of the effect that arises from the turning up of the fresh soil, or of the first welcome breath of Spring.

It is the most life-filled comparison of the year: all tilth and loam, the smell of earth in the nostrils, mixing memory and desire, the worms writhing between the grains of soil, the winds blowing not as winter bullies but as spring companions, and the suggestion that these spades pushed into this earth by these poets were turning the world upside down.

Hazlitt and Coleridge walked back to Stowey that evening, 'through echoing grove, by fairy stream or waterfall, gleaming in the summer moonlight!' Coleridge spoke with admiration of his great friend: 'His philosophic poetry had a grand and comprehensive spirit in it,' he told Hazlitt, 'so that his soul seemed to inhabit the universe like a palace, and to discover truth by intuition, rather than by deduction.'

But all was not perfect in their friendship. Coleridge had been writing some of the greatest metaphysical poetry ever written in English, but Wordsworth had seemed distant from it.

> He lamented that Wordsworth was not prone enough to believe in the traditional superstitions of the place, and that there was a something corporeal, a matter-of-fact-ness, a clinging to the palpable, or often to the petty, in his poetry, in consequence, 'His genius was not a spirit that descended to him through the air; it sprung out of the ground like a flower, or unfolded itself from a green spray, on which the goldfinch sang.'

The next day, Wordsworth arrived back in Stowey from Bristol. Hazlitt watched him in the front room of the Lime Street cottage.

> He answered in some degree to his friend's description of him, but was more gaunt and Don Quixote-like. He was quaintly dressed (according to the costume of that unconstrained period) in a brown fustian jacket and striped pantaloons. There was something of a roll, a lounge in his gait … There was a severe, worn pressure of thought about his temples, a fire in his eye (as if he saw something in objects more than the outward appearance), an intense, high, narrow forehead, a Roman nose, cheeks furrowed by strong purpose and feeling, and a convulsive inclination to laughter about the mouth, a good deal at variance with the solemn, stately expression of the rest of his face.
>
> He sat down and talked very naturally and freely, with a mixture of clear, gushing accents in his voice, a deep guttural intonation, and a strong tincture of the northern burr, like the crust on wine. He instantly began to make havoc of the half of a Cheshire cheese on the table, and said,

triumphantly, that 'his marriage with experience had not
been so productive as Mr. Southey's in teaching him a
knowledge of the good things of this life.'

That is how feelings surface in conversation between friends:
jokey resentment at a rival's better fortune, while scoffing lumps
of cheese. And so there is a sense of funny, warm, clever collec-
tivity in the room, and a feeling of shared superiority to those
who are leading lusher lives. When in Bristol, Wordsworth had
been to see the great hit of the gothic theatre, *Castle Spectre* by
Monk Lewis, which had made Lewis a fortune. He knew
Coleridge had read and despised the play, and now remarked in
this same sardonic tone that 'it fitted the taste of the audience
like a glove'. This was a tease, a joke embedded in the seriousness,
one aspect of Wordsworth's love of what a hostile critic called his
'comico-lugubrious peculiarities'.

Hazlitt, some nine years younger, listened in awe.

Wordsworth, looking out of the low, latticed window, said,
'How beautifully the sun sets on that yellow bank!' I thought
within myself, 'with what eyes these poets see nature!' and
ever after, when I saw the sun-set stream upon the objects
facing it, conceived I had made a discovery, or thanked Mr.
Wordsworth for having made one for me!

Cottle, who strangely and inexplicably neither mentions nor is
mentioned by Hazlitt, also left an account of the day he came to
Stowey. They arrived first in Lime Street, and he was more
amused than starstruck.

We called for Mr. Coleridge, Miss Wordsworth, and the
servant, at Stowey, and they walked, while we rode on to Mr.
W's house at Allfoxden, distant two or three miles, where we

purposed to dine. A London alderman would smile at our prepation, or bill of fare. It consisted of philosophers' viands; namely, a bottle of brandy, a noble loaf, and a stout piece of cheese; and as there were plenty of lettuces in the garden, with all these comforts we calculated on doing very well.

Our fond hopes, however, were somewhat damped, by finding, that our 'stout piece of cheese' had vanished! A sturdy *rat* of a beggar, whom we had relieved [i.e. given him some pennies] on the road, with his olfactories all alive, no doubt, *smelt* our cheese, and while we were gazing at the magnificent clouds, contrived to abstract our treasure! Cruel tramp! An ill return for our pence! We both wished the rind might not choke him! The mournful fact was ascertained a little before we drove into the courtyard of the house. Mr. Coleridge bore the loss with great fortitude, observing, that we should never starve with a loaf of bread, and a bottle of brandy.

Coleridge, while showing off his skills at unhitching the horse from the gig, managed to smash the bottle of brandy on the stone court outside Alfoxden.

We were now summoned to dinner, and a dinner it was, such as every *blind* and starving man in the three kingdoms would have rejoiced to *behold*. At the top of the table stood a superb brown loaf. The centre dish presented a pile of the true coss lettuces, and at the bottom appeared an empty plate, where the 'stout piece of cheese' *ought* to have stood! (cruel mendicant!) and though the brandy was 'clean gone,' yet its place was well, if not *better* supplied by an abundance of fine sparkling Castalian champagne!

The maid had also forgotten to buy any salt.

This was nothing. We had plenty of other good things, and while crunching our succulents, and munching our crusts, we pitied the far worse condition of those, perchance as hungry as ourselves, who were forced to dine, off aether alone.

At Alfoxden the next day, under the trees of the park, Wordsworth read the story of 'Peter Bell' to the assembled company. This enormously long ballad about a potter and his ass, which has one revolving ear, may well be Wordsworth's most experimental poem, pushing to the limits the ability of the most ordinary language to convey emotional truths. When it was eventually published, which was not until 1819, 'Peter Bell' was lampooned up and down the country, but it remained one of Wordsworth's favourites, and this May day at Alfoxden, his face as he read it to Hazlitt and the others 'was as a book where "men might read strange matters"' – Hazlitt was quoting from *Macbeth* – 'and he announced the fate of his hero in prophetic tones'.

The sad ass with the revolving ear, the wild potter Peter, the abandoned woman, the lonely cottage, visions in woody dells, a body in a river, a little boy Robin, stars and the moon, woods and repentance, guilt and forgiveness – it is a comico-lugubrious pasty full of Wordsworth's most treasured ingredients. When Leigh Hunt reviewed it in the *Examiner*, he called it 'another didactic little horror'.

Not for its author. 'There is a chaunt in the recitation both of Coleridge and Wordsworth,' Hazlitt wrote of what he heard at Alfoxden,

which acts as a spell upon the hearer, and disarms the judgment. Coleridge's manner is more full, animated, and varied; Wordsworth's more equable, sustained, and internal. The one might be termed more *dramatic*, the other more *lyrical*. Coleridge has told me that he himself liked to compose in walking over uneven ground, or breaking through the straggling branches of a copse-wood; whereas Wordsworth always wrote (if he could) walking up and down a straight gravel walk, or in some spot where the continuity of his verse met with no collateral interruption.

There was nothing eccentric in their thinking that poetry must be spoken. Schools taught children how to speak poetry aloud. It was normal to read aloud to family and friends. C.P. Moritz, a German travelling in England in 1782, described how his 'land-lady, who is only a tailor's widow, reads her Milton; and tells me, that her late husband first fell in love with her, on this very account; because she read Milton with such proper emphasis'.

Wordsworth composed aloud as he walked, increasingly observed by the shepherds and farmers around him, sunk into a bleak solitude. 'It was a queer thing,' a Westmorland farmer remembered much later, 'but it would like eneuf cause him to be desolate; and I'se often thowt that his brain was that fu' of sic stuff, that he was forced to be always at it whether or no, wet or fair, mumbling to hissel' along t'roads.'

Another saw him on the grass paths at his house, Rydal Mount, near Ambleside:

> He would set his heäd a bit forrad, and put his hands behint his back. And then he would start bumming, and it was bum, bum, bum, bum, stop; then bum, bum, bum reet down till t'other end, and then he'd set down and git a bit o'paper out and write a bit; and then he git up, and bum, bum, bum, and goa on bumming for long enough right down and back agean. I suppose, ya kna, the bumming helped him out a bit.

As Wordsworth 'went bumming and booing about',

Miss Dorothy, kept close behint him, and she picked up the
bits as he let 'em fall, and tak 'em down, and put 'em on
paper for him. And you med be very well sure as how she
didn't understand nor make sense out of 'em.

Poetry was spoken or sung, *bummed* and hummed, mumbled
and murmured, words given rhythmic power in the world as a
bodily act. Poetry was like walking. Walking and poetry were
inseparable parts of one thing, by which the music heard on
the inner ear emerged into the shared reality of the physical
world.

The walking and the talking went on uninterrupted. On the
evening of 23 May, on the path from Alfoxden to Stowey, Hazlitt
tackled Wordsworth over the way he was leading his life, not
sufficiently immersed in books, apparently doing little more than
dreaming as he stared into the distance for half a day or more.
Was it good enough to be like a newborn child? What about the
gifts of civilisation, everything the past has given the present?
Surely life was incomplete without reading?

Wordsworth replied that books were not the answer. Only a
response to the full physical life could lead to wisdom or
understanding.

> The eye it cannot chuse but see,
> We cannot bid the ear be still;
> Our bodies feel, where'er they be,
> Against, or with our will.
>
> Nor less I deem that there are powers
> Which of themselves our minds impress,
> That we can feed this mind of ours
> In a wise passiveness.

If the world were speaking, and the mindbody could hear it, what point was there in actively looking for what its meanings might be? There may have been in here, somewhere, a reproach to Coleridge's ever more anxious addiction to books. It is another facet of the growing difference between them: Wordsworth self-sufficient in his own presence in the world, Coleridge's appetite undimmed for everything that lay beyond him.

A page in Wordsworth's Alfoxden notebook, some rough lines for 'The Pedlar' which were never used, sketches out the thought that Wordsworth clarified and simplified for Hazlitt:

> there is a holy indolence
> Compared to which our best activity
> Is oftimes deadly bane
> They rest upon their oars
> Float down the mighty stream of tendency
> In the ~~deep~~ calm mood of holy indolence
> A most wise passiveness in which the heart
> Lies open and is well content to feel
> As nature feels and to receive her shapes
> As she has made them.

Wordsworth wrote a pendant to this poem, also addressed to Hazlitt, in which he turned the tables and upbraided the brilliant young man as he had been upbraided himself. Hazlitt, like Coleridge, was never without a book in his hand.

> Up! up! my friend, and clear your looks,
> Why all this toil and trouble?
> Up! up! my friend, and quit your books,
> Or surely you'll grow double.

It is Rousseau talking. Civilisation as a distortion of the natural.
The over-read and the over-civilised end up with bodies contorted
and bent over their pages. Wordsworth, teasingly maybe, looks
over to the beautiful yellow evening light, of which his description in the Lime Street cottage had so impressed Hazlitt.

> The sun, above the mountain's head,
> A freshening lustre mellow
> Through all the long green fields has spread,
> His first sweet evening yellow.

Then the lines that would begin to make him famous, a distillation of the process through which Coleridge had led him in the
course of the last nine months.

> Books! 'tis a dull and endless strife,
> Come, hear the woodland linnet,
> How sweet his music; on my life
> There's more of wisdom in it.

> One impulse from a vernal wood
> May teach you more of man;
> Of moral evil and of good,
> Than all the sages can.

> Sweet is the lore which nature brings;
> Our meddling intellect
> Mishapes the beauteous forms of things;
> – We murder to dissect.

> Enough of science and of art;
> Close up these barren leaves;
> Come forth, and bring with you a heart
> That watches and receives.

Few poems are more in need of being read in context. Pulled out, quoted and anthologised as they have been continuously ever since, the lines become pious, a spring posy of sentimental wishfulness – and indifference to the realities of the world. But seen and heard in the light of the year that has passed, in which Wordsworth has been reading carefully and assiduously, repeatedly asking Cottle for books to be sent down to him from Bristol, drawing poetry out of those books, tussling with the complexities of the braided and intellectualised Coleridgean stream pouring over him, this poem represents an intellectual triumph. It is made with care and precision, with a wit and linguistic command that is reminiscent, strangely enough, of the finest of Pope's couplets: 'nature brings/beauteous forms of things' pairs with the sterile cuts of 'meddling intellect/murder to dissect'. 'Close up these barren leaves' means what it does because there are other more beautiful and fertile leaves to be found in the vernal wood. Come out, he instructs the young man, out into the widths and expanses of nature, but in coming out make sure that you bring your inwardness with you, so that it is not you who must come out, but your heart, and your heart is not to be a blinking, stupefied organ as it emerges, but attentive, watching, shaping and receiving.

It is likely that memories of this whole year were coloured by these wonderful days. The winter was over, summer had deepened into June. They were living in the knowledge that the lease on Alfoxden would soon be up. As the poets talked to Cottle about the contents of their joint publication, a sense of an ending gathered around them. This is the atmosphere, with a mournful air of love and loss, that Wordsworth summoned at the very end of the 1805 *Prelude*, as he addressed Coleridge as his heart's companion, wanting to justify his own long poem about himself.

... belovèd friend
When, looking back, thou seest, in clearer view
Than any sweetest sight of yesterday,
That summer, when on Quantock's grassy hills
Far ranging and among her sylvan coombs,
Thou in delicious words, with happy heart,
Didst speak the vision of that ancient man,
The bright-eyed Mariner, and rueful woes
Didst utter of the Lady Christabel;
And I, associate in such labour, walked
Murmuring of him, who – joyous hap – was found,
After the perils of his moonlight ride,
Near the loud waterfall, or her who sate
In misery near the miserable thorn;
When thou dost to that summer turn thy thoughts,
And hast before thee all which then we were,
To thee, in memory of that happiness,
It will be known – by thee at least, my friend,
Felt – that the history of a poet's mind
Is labour not unworthy of regard:
To thee the work shall justify itself.

That was the year when they had 'first/Together wantoned in wild Poesy', when *The Marinere* and 'Christabel', 'The Thorn' and 'The Idiot Boy' – Wordsworth makes no mention of either 'Kubla Khan' or the great conversation poems – had populated their minds and conversations. It is a passage filled with nostalgia and love for 'all which then we were'.

Hazlitt spent three weeks in Somerset,

generally devoting the afternoons to a delightful chat in an arbour made of bark by the poet's friend Tom Poole, sitting under two fine elm trees, and listening to the bees humming round us, while we quaffed our flip.

Walking tours were made down to Lynton, Coleridge in the lead, ever-talking, one with Hazlitt and again with Cottle. Coleridge discussed Shakespeare and Milton, Milton as the great adult of English poetry, Shakespeare the great adolescent. He despised Thomas Gray and was bored by Pope. The whole concept of the rhymed couplet, on which eighteenth-century English poetry had been based, was wrong because it came to a conclusion once every two lines. 'The ears of these couplet writers might be charged with having short memories, that could not retain the harmony of whole passages.' It was another of the reformations these poets were making, providing through poetry not the neat consumable *amuse-gueules* of well-made deliciousness in which their predecessors had specialised, but long, loping excursions out into the wider and wilder country of the imagination. If the heart of the eighteenth-century aesthetic had been the elegant and well-framed view from a window, the new poetry belonged out here, on the long walk, high on the moors, with friends in the sun and wind, and on the clifftops level with the wheeling birds.

Many years later, Hazlitt remembered the golden glory of Coleridge's talk as they swept from height to height and valley to valley:

His genius at that time had angelic wings, and fed on manna. He talked on for ever; and you wished him to talk on for ever. His thoughts did not seem to come with labour and effort; but as if borne on the gusts of genius, and as if the wings of his imagination lifted him from off his feet. His voice rolled on the ear like the pealing organ, and its sound alone was the music of thought. His mind was clothed with wings; and raised on them, he lifted philosophy to heaven. In his descriptions, you then saw the progress of human happiness and liberty in bright and never-ending succession, like the steps of Jacob's ladder, with airy shapes ascending and descending, and with the voice of God at the top of the ladder.

They also discussed the form of the *Lyrical Ballads*. The poems

were an experiment about to be tried by him and
Wordsworth, to see how far the public taste would endure
poetry written in a more natural and simple style than had
hitherto been attempted; totally discarding the artifices of
poetical diction, and making use only of such words as had
probably been common in the most ordinary language since
the days of Henry II.
    We loitered on the 'ribbed sea-sands', in such talk as this a
whole morning ... A fisherman gave Coleridge an account of
a boy that had been drowned the day before, and that they
had tried to save him at the risk of their own lives. He said
'he did not know how it was that they ventured, but, Sir, we
have a nature towards one another.'

That conversation was another binding moment, words in the mouth of a Devon fisherman which in their embrace of others and their simplicity and their assumption of connectedness, with no rationalisation, expressed everything Coleridge and Wordsworth had come jointly to believe. Here, astonishingly, was a mariner who, quite unprompted, out on the ribbed sea sands, could tell them that if he happened to find someone drowning in the sea, he would be able to say that 'A spring of love gusht from my heart,/And I bless'd them unaware.'

I made a long valedictory walk to Lynton at the very end of May, the path deep in the woods or high above the brutal shoreline, with its grey stone desert exposed at low tide, and the rough whaleback slopes of the cliffs withdrawing from that sea in gorse-skinned shambles of red rock. Every morning, the green woods sprinkled sunlight on my path; every evening greeted me with the backlit glamour of the headlands to come, every stream a fountain, every hilltop a prospect.

The seabirds were never far from view, in blazing sunshine or freezing wind, fulmars in the blasting westerlies, never a wing-beat, scarcely a lifted feather, and ravens hanging close, a yard off the cliff, together in their pairs making dives from clifftop to sea-crest, the gloss on their backs so flawless that as they spread their wings in a turn, the feathers flared white in the sun.

What doesn't feel like Coleridge country now? His recognition of the validity of all life has, not before time, taken its place at the centre of what we now think of the world. His idea that he *was* a bird, that the bird's inventiveness and fluency were what he was – that is the template on which modern understandings of our relationship to nature are now based. This is not a form of anthropomorphism – thinking the birds are like us – but the opposite, *zoomorphism*, that we are like the birds, part of one world, and that what we are is visible in what they are. The mariner shoots the albatross, and in doing that shoots himself. Murder is self-murder. The destruction of birds is a destruction of ourselves.

His tiny fragment on the gull, 'The Sea Mew', was in my mind. It may have been written at Clevedon in 1796 before he came to the Quantocks, or perhaps more likely many years later, but, as Richard Holmes has said, it too is auto-description.

> Seaward, white-gleaming thro' the busy Scud
> With arching Wings the Sea-mew o'er my head
> Posts on, as bent on speed; now passaging
> Edges the stiffer Breeze, now yielding *drifts*,
> Now floats upon the Air, and sends from far
> A wildly-wailing Note.

Poet Dreaming

PREVIOUS PAGE: The Coleridge bird

These north Devon cliffs are full of those Coleridge-birds, lifting in the cliffside updraughts as if they were balloons, rising four hundred feet in five seconds, buoyant on the currents of life, but subtle, posting on, messengers on the turnpike, intent on delivery, then making their way on a sea passage between harbours, on a reach, with the wind on the beam, before turning downwind, loosening the sheets, drifting off on the tendencies of existence, and then pausing again, now head to wind, aloft and afloat, before emitting the wild and desperate cry, as if they were wailing on the lonely slopes of Mount Amara. Here in miniature is Coleridge's description of his life, voyaging in the winds of the world, a model of empathy and observation, permeated with every possible dimension of genius and despair.

15

Authoring

June 1798

By the very end of May, almost a year after Coleridge had walked over to Racedown, and just after Cottle had gone back to Bristol, Coleridge wrote to his publisher in his best authorish, charming-imperious style, knowing that Cottle loved him:

> My dear Cottle
> You know what I think of a letter – how impossible it is to *argue* in it. You must therefore take simple statements, & in a week or two I shall see you & endeavor to *reason* with you.

He and Wordsworth had '*maturely weigh'd*' Cottle's proposal, which was to publish each of their collections individually, only to reject it. Neither of them wanted that. Their poems lacked variety, and were not good enough in themselves. But published together they would be mutually supportive, as the stanzas of an ode supported each other. Each would be the other's friend on the page. They would stick with what they had previously suggested: all Wordsworth's spring poems, one or two bits lifted from the failed tragedies, plus *The Rime of the Ancyent Marinere*, all lumped in together, and to be published with no names on the title page. Cottle had objected to that idea, but Coleridge was adamant:

As to anonymous Publications, depend on it, you are
deceived. – Wordsworth's name is nothing – to a large
number of persons mine stinks – However, I waive all
reasoning, & simply state it as an unaltered opinion, that you
should proceed as before, with the ancient Mariner. –

Cottle had arranged for Wordsworth to be painted by William
Shuter, who had come down to Alfoxden for the purpose.
Coleridge promised that 'The picture shall be sent.' Pity poor
Cottle: on the brink of bankruptcy, patronised by the young men
who were only interested in his money, perhaps half-aware that
this was the price of his place in history.

For all the reality of the friendship of the two poets and the
mutual interpenetration of their lives, the distance and the difference between them was now coming seeping out of the corners.
It is not discernible in what they wrote to each other, nor perhaps
in each other's company, but it was increasingly revealed to
others. Coleridge had told Hazlitt, in private, at night in the
woods on the way back to Stowey, that Wordsworth was prosaic
in some of his attitudes, hobbled by 'a clinging to the palpable',
as if his mind lacked a certain receptivity. When Wordsworth
wrote to his friend James Tobin of the Wedgwood annuity that
Coleridge was now receiving, his scepticism fringed into the
margins of contempt:

No doubt you have heard of the munificence of the
Wedgwoods towards Coleridge. I hope the fruit will be good
as the seed is noble.

When Coleridge had written to Josiah Wedgwood himself about
the possibility of going to be a minister in Shropshire, he
explained his reluctance:

It is chilling to go among strangers – & I leave a lovely
country, and one friend so eminently near to my affections
that his society has almost been consolidated with my ideas
of happiness.

That friend was not Wordsworth but Thomas Poole, and the
embrace of friendship was not extended to the other. Coleridge
apparently had no regrets about leaving the Wordsworths behind.
At almost the same moment, Wordsworth made the same
pointed distinction in his account of leaving Alfoxden:

We have no particular reason to be attached to the
neighbourhood of Stowey but the society of Coleridge, &
the friendship of Poole.

There was no doubt that Coleridge admired Wordsworth. He
wrote to Cottle in Bristol to say so, but again the admiration is
chilled:

The Giant Wordsworth – God love him! – even when I speak
in the terms of admiration due to his intellect, I fear lest tho[se]
terms should keep out of sight the amiableness of his manners –
he has written near 1200 lines of a blank verse, superior, I
hesitate not to aver, to any thing in our language which any
way resembles it. Poole (whom I feel so consolidated with
myself that I seem to have no occasion to speak of him out of
myself) thinks of it as likely to benefit mankind much more
than any thing, Wordsworth has yet written.

Are those sentences written in friendship? Or in awe? More in
adulation than affection? 'The amiableness of his manners'?
Could that phrase describe a person you loved?
When Coleridge wrote to his friend and mentor John Prior
Estlin, the Unitarian minister in Bristol, he hesitated and

withdrew as he described Wordsworth. It is a letter in which Coleridge's subtilising mind seems often to be saying what he thinks but concealing what he feels, even from himself:

> I have now known him a year & some months, and my admiration, I might say, my awe of his intellectual powers has increased even to this hour – & (what is of more importance) he is a tried good man.

Perhaps Coleridge cannot bring himself to say what is uppermost in his mind – that his own sense of wellbeing as a poet is being overwhelmed by Wordsworth's giant presence alongside him. They had disagreed about religion:

> On one subject we are habitually silent – we found our data dissimiliar, & never renewed the subject/It is his practice & almost his nature to convey all the truth he knows without any attack on what he supposes falsehood, if that falsehood be interwoven with virtues or happiness – he loves & venerates Christ & Christianity – I wish, he did more – but it were wrong indeed, if an incoincidence with one of our wishes altered our respect & affection to a man, whom we are as it were instructed by our great master to say that not being against us he is for us.

That paragraph takes some unweaving. Coleridge had detected that Wordsworth did not agree with him about the presence and power of God in the world, and yet Wordsworth seemed to understand that Coleridge's sense of virtue and happiness was closely involved with that belief. Wordsworth had refused to engage on this question, perhaps because he did not want to hurt Coleridge, but also perhaps because his natural direction was now inward, not to correct the errors of others but to make his own presence so vast that others came to shrink beside it.

299

Coleridge struggles to forgive him, describing this deepest of all possible disagreements as 'an incoincidence'. And then, intriguingly and characteristically, quotes selectively from the Bible. In Mark's gospel, Christ does indeed say that 'he that is not against us is on our part'. But the better-known passage is in Matthew's gospel, where a ferocious and demanding Christ talks to his disciples about his own power and its effect on those who disagree with him:

> If I cast out devils by the Spirit of God, then the kingdom of God is come unto you. Or else how can one enter into a strong man's house, and spoil his goods, except he first bind the strong man? and then he will spoil his house.
>
> He that is not with me is against me; and he that gathereth not with me scattereth abroad.
>
> Wherefore I say unto you, All manner of sin and blasphemy shall be forgiven unto men: but the blasphemy *against* the *Holy* Ghost shall not be forgiven unto men. And whosoever speaketh a word against the Son of man, it shall be forgiven him: but whosoever speaketh against the Holy Ghost, it shall not be forgiven him, neither in this world, neither in the *world* to come.

That passionate and vengeful speech lurks behind Coleridge's letter to Estlin. Both would have had it by heart. It is possible that Coleridge's description of Wordsworth as the strong man and of his refusal to believe in the governing presence of the Holy Spirit encodes a violent feeling towards him: a desire to bind his power and to spoil his goods. It is perhaps in the light of this that Estlin, who was a father figure to Coleridge, was fiercely against him going to Germany with the Wordsworths.

Coleridge could say none of this openly. Now, and in the years to come, he would abase himself before Wordsworth's power,

changing his poems according to Wordsworth's strictures, labouring over revisions of Wordsworth's own poems, coming to think
that he was no poet and having his own poems included in a
second and enlarged edition of *Lyrical Ballads*, published two
years later, under Wordsworth's name alone.

Over the next few months, in the correspondence that survives,
further hints emerge of an anxiety felt by Coleridge's friends that
his relationship with Wordsworth, even while they were still in
Somerset, had begun to be destructive. After the two of them
had left for Germany and for financial reasons had ended up in
different cities, Poole wrote to Coleridge: 'The Wordsworths
have left you – so there is an end of our fears about amalgama-
tion etc.' They had clearly discussed the possibility when together
in Somerset that Wordsworth was in danger of swamping
Coleridge. Wordsworth's sudden effusion of poetry in the spring,
which meant that their joint publication was dominated by him,
had left Coleridge trailing behind. Josiah Wedgwood also hoped
that in Germany they would 'continue separated. I am persuaded
that Coleridge will derive great benefit from being thrown into
mixed society.' The problem was that Coleridge both loved and
feared the prospect of the Wordsworthian embrace. 'I am sure I
need not say how you are incorporated into the better part of my
being,' he wrote to him, 'how, whenever I spring forward into
the future with noble affections, I always alight by your side ...'

Faced with this tendency, Poole continued with his avuncular
advice. Coleridge was to be careful, to ensure that he did not
damage himself by overvaluing Wordsworth. In response,
Coleridge became ever more certain of Wordsworth's greatness.

You charge me with prostration in regard to Wordsworth.
Have I affirmed anything miraculous of W.? Is it impossible
that a greater poet than any since Milton may appear in our

days? … Would it not be an assurance to you that your admiration of the Paradise Lost was no superstition, no shadow of flesh and bloodless abstraction, but that the Man was even so, that the greatness was incarnate and personal? Wherein blame I you, my best friend? Only in being borne down by other men's rash opinions concerning W. You yourself, for yourself, judged wisely …

One phrase is often repeated in describing the psychological landscape of this year: 'Three people but one soul' is said to have been coined by Coleridge as a description of the relationship he, Wordsworth and Dorothy had enjoyed in Somerset, precisely the melting of boundaries between self and self and self and world that often flowed through their poetry and Dorothy's journal. But, as the American scholar Ruth Aldrich has shown, the phrase is a garbled factoid, the reverse of what Coleridge actually wrote.

The Wordsworthian editor William Knight had first used something like it in 1889: 'Coleridge said of them, "We are three people, but only one soul."' Knight had taken the words from a distorted English version of a partial German translation, misleadingly relocated to 1797, of a letter Coleridge had written to William Godwin in November 1801. Coleridge had in fact been telling Godwin how relieved he was to be in London, surrounded by all kinds of people and away from the suffocating atmosphere of the Wordsworths:

I saw so many People on Monday and walked to & fro so much, that I have been ever since like a Fish in air, who, as you perhaps know, lies panting & dying from excess of Oxygen/– A great change from the society of W. & his sister – for tho' we were three persons, it was but one God – whereas here I have the amazed feelings of a new Polytheist, meeting Lords many, & Gods many …

Through these Chinese whispers, 'Three persons, but one God' in 1801 had been flipped on its back to become 'Three people but one soul' in 1797–98. The 'one God' Coleridge was describing in 1801 can only have been the pantocrator Wordsworth; the 'one soul' of the false 1797 version was a sentimentalised, wish-fulfilment expression of romantic togetherness which the evidence from Somerset and afterwards tends, in large part anyway, to contradict.

The embryo of their unhappy futures was already present: not a meltingly perfect dream-bonding of Romanticism's founding fathers but, in among the sinews of true companionship and true admiration, a thread of reservation and mutual uncertainty, the dark line in the flesh of the lobster's tail, a doubt fuelled for Coleridge by Wordsworth's turn towards potency, and for Wordsworth by a sense of Coleridge's drift into doubt.

16

Arriving

July 1798

On 25 June the Wordsworths left Alfoxden. Dorothy was distraught at leaving 'that Dear and beautiful place'. They had to say a sad goodbye to their maid Peggy, who was now married and expecting a child but 'would have gone to the world's end with us'. And they had to send young Basil Montagu back to the care of his own family; his father could not afford the expenses of his coming to Germany. The weave was unravelling.

For a crowded week they stayed with Sara Coleridge in the Lime Street cottage in Stowey, and with some reluctance stored boxes of their possessions there. The house was too damp for anything valuable to survive for long. Coleridge himself was away in London and Surrey, and early in July, walking at least part of the way, the Wordsworths also left for Bristol. Sara stayed in Stowey with the babies, but they were all due, when the time was right, to join the expedition to Germany. Not that Dorothy was convinced of the arrangements:

> We talk of being on board the vessel in two months but I do
> not think this is very probable as I have no doubt many
> things will delay the Coleridges which they have no idea of
> at present.

I walked the fifty miles to Bristol from Stowey as my own farewell to the year. It took two and a half days, through some of the
poorest country in England. Pushed away down the narrow lanes
that cross the Levels are tiny farm holdings, vulnerable to winter
floods, with stinking, trashed yards where guinea fowls poke
about in piles of junked machinery, the birds shrieking as you
approach; or little pony farms where the grazing has been gnawed
to the bone and only the ragwort now stands above the mud.
From afar, the distant view, all is pretty enough: overgrown
willows on the edge of rhynes glow golden with lichen in the
evening. Starlings glisten in the cherry trees like African exotics
on the banks of the ditches. Where the slow fat rivers of the
Levels pour through the gates of a sluice, the water runs blue-
green and perfect over the weed beneath, a laminar curl, as
smooth as shampoo.

That perfection is not how it is for the rural poor: broken and
fraying asbestos sheets; burning, rotting piles of overheating
manure; the flag of St George tied to a satellite dish; oily-eyed
half-puddles in paths that are muck-strewn in the rubbishy edges
of caravan parks; chickens living in the remains of huge dirty
American cars, coppery-red or cigarette-smoke-blue, the suspension gone; all shops shut down in the villages; stream beds full of
plastic rubbish; and always the unending scorching howl just
behind the trees of the motorway from Bristol to Plymouth.

There are some done-up, middle-class places with willow
hurdles, a patch of cut grass with two fat rams and goalposts for
the children, or occasionally a brutally industrialised dairy where
every growing thing has been weedkilled, but those places, coherent enough in themselves, only serve to exaggerate the poverty
that surrounds them.

As I walked slowly across the Levels towards the city, I
wondered how much this year had been a success. Had these two
poets altered the way in which we understand nature, each other
and ourselves? Had they won? Perhaps they had in relation to

our ideas of the self, as something that is bodily as well as mental, and whose health relies on deep connections to the natural world. That may be the greatest legacy of this year of marvels: the dissolution of the boundaries of the self, so that we all now think, to a greater or lesser extent, that a tide floods and ebbs through us, often unnoticed, usually unrecognised, but in constant rhythmic motion, a dynamic psychic geography that makes us who we are.

And in relation to nature? Perhaps we all now revere nature as a source of wisdom and consolation. But in a thousand other ways we don't, and continue to treat it either as a quarry for our needs and desires, or as something to be revered when convenient, abused when not.

Above all, though, any sense of social justice, of the validity of the voices and requirements of the poor, has failed to make itself felt in a way that Coleridge and Wordsworth both thought necessary in the 1790s. Nothing is more revealing of this aspect of their legacy than walking through places where people on their holiday tours don't usually walk. At the back end of the beautiful, in its hidden corners, is a rotten and broken world. The degraded life of the rural poor in Somerset now, never usually visited or encountered, is as shocking and disturbing as it was two centuries ago. And this is the central failure of the Quantocks year: its hope for integration, for the general understanding that a love of nature needed to be intimate with a love of self and a love of man, remains unfulfilled, and no more likely to be fulfilled now than it was two centuries ago.

Bristol comes at you hard and heavy after the quiet of Somerset. The Wordsworths lodged with the long-suffering Cottle above his shop on the corner of Wine Street and Corn Street, right in the middle of the commercial city, just up from the Corn Exchange, across from the Bush, the great inn where the stage-coaches came and went night and day. Cottle's shop is now Warren's Bakery, with sausage rolls and swirls of meringue in the windows. The rooms above it, where the Wordsworths stayed, are a camera store. In the street outside, artisan cooks sell a hundred variations on the gluten-free organic felafel wrap of modern Bristol life.

The Wordsworths got out as much as they could, visiting Bath and dining with friends for a week or so before the noise of the city made them pine for something else. 'I am writing in a front room in one of the most busy streets of Bristol,' Dorothy told Elizabeth Rawson, the wife of her mother's cousin, who she called her aunt.

> You can scarcely conceive how the jarring contrast between the sounds which are now forever ringing in my ears and the sweet sounds of Allfoxden, makes me long for the country again. After three years residence in retirement a city in feeling, sound, and prospect is hateful.

A radical minister they met in Bath, the Reverend Richard Warner, had described a picturesque *Walk Through Wales in 1797*, published this January. He may have urged them to escape up the valley of the Wye.

Wordsworth knew it already. Five years before, in the summer of 1793, at a time of acute personal and national crisis, he had walked this way, en route to a friend in Wales, riven by guilt and uncertainty, frantic with haste and appetite, on the run from Annette and the ideals of the Revolution in France, ideals which the bloody turn of events in Paris were even then abandoning. The air in 1793 had been thick with betrayal: of the mother of his child, of the child itself, of revolutionary hope and perhaps of Wordsworth's own hopes for himself. The French king had been guillotined. France, the realm of liberty, had declared war on Britain. Since then, five long years had passed. He had changed. A kind of certainty and conviction had entered his life, and the contrast between the loneliness and hopelessness of 1793 and the strength and connectedness of 1798 would colour the great poem he wrote after the four-day walk he and Dorothy now took up the Wye.

On 10 July they set out together, crossing the Severn by ferry from the little settlement of Aust, ninepence each, to Beachley on the far side. The signs of the ferry at Aust are still there: the old passage house, a stone road and the remains of the elm baulks of the jetty. More, of course, than the modern motorway bridge, the small-boat crossing, about a mile, is a threshold to otherness. This is not a river mouth but a tongue of the sea, licking long and deep into the folds of England. The air is thick with iodine. Short-eared owls hunt across the reeds and channels of the salt marshes. Swallows audit every inch above them. A boat, tacking against the wind, is swept inland on the running of the tide. Pools of flat water, ringed with sunlight, spread down from the mudbanks, a moment of calm before the boat is pulled out again into the flow. Inland, the huge hollows of the estuary, labelled on the chart as Whirls End and Slime Road, fill with the encroaching sea. Not long before the boat kicks and turns into the shoreside eddies, the inshore back-flow against the current in the channel, a pull on the oars, and the boat grates its stem on the landing stones of the slipway at Beachley.

It was no gentle stroll for the Wordsworths: twenty-three miles' walking plus the ferry crossing on the first day, at least seventeen miles on the next past Monmouth up to Goodrich Castle, and another twenty-two miles on the third day, retracing their steps downriver, then taking to a boat and coasting five miles back on the tide to spend the night once again at Tintern. On the fourth day, 13 July, they again boarded a boat, down the Wye, across the Severn and up the Avon to Clifton, before finally walking down into the streets of Bristol that evening.

It was the kind of expedition hundreds of tourists had made in the late eighteenth century, guided by any number of printed and written accounts of the beauties to be enjoyed en route, past the many quarries along the banks of the Wye, the charcoal burners' huts in the woods and the clamour of the ironworks that glowed red night and day, where as Richard Warner had written, tourists could watch 'the dingy beings who melt the ore' in a 'scene of bustle amidst smoke and fire ... only interrupted by the intonations of the bar-hammer', which 'produced a most impressive effect on the mind'.

On the last day of their walk, as they were making their way back to Bristol, Wordsworth composed the greatest poem he had yet written. In it, he mentions almost nothing the tourists usually mention: nothing about the great Cistercian abbey at Tintern, nothing about the ironworks with their Virgilian fires and luminous shadows, nothing about the strenuous miles they had walked, and nothing about the many ruined castles 'bosomed high in tufted trees' (as the Reverend Warner had described them, quoting Milton).

The Wye remains huge and yet hidden, its course sewn in and out of the border between England and Wales, running down a wide trug of a valley cut into the country but so entirely clothed, its cliffs and rocks buried in lush, generous and accommodating green, that there is a sense of the deepest possible settlement here. In the riverside villages the fields are cultivated on an almost garden scale, with the grass in the summer hay meadows mown, tedded and rowed up for the baler with such care it looks as if a coiffeur has been at work. Cultivation alternates with wildness in the woods that fill mile after mile of the river's looping, sinuous progress to the sea.

It could not be a more different landscape to the Quantocks. The scale of the river, forty or fifty yards wide, provides a kind of depth to the place, the river's width a measure of the distance it has come. The Quantock streams ran for no more than ten miles from source to sea, but the Wye is twelve or thirteen times as long, and for that reason this is more of a Wordsworthian than a

Coleridgean place, summoning memory more than immediacy, full of ancient meanings from distant sources. That idea of a river carrying hints of its own significance was in Wordsworth's picture of Dorothy as an irrigating brook, and had been with him ever since he was a boy in his father's house beside the Derwent in Cockermouth. Even at Racedown, jotted into a notebook perhaps at the beginning of 1797, he had remembered the river of his childhood:

> and yet once again,
> Standing beneath these elms, I hear thy voice,
> Beloved Derwent, that peculiar voice
> Heard in the stillness of the evening air,
> Half-heard and half-created.

The Wye this summer seems to be some recreation of that whispering and calming river, half the product of the senses, half the product of the mind, speaking to Wordsworth in a way nothing in Somerset had quite spoken to him all year.

Visually, it is a beautiful thing, glimpsed through the trees, the swans chin-deep, leaving wide V-wakes behind them. Every now and then, lit rings break across the slow waters where a fish's lips are nibbling at a fly. 'Sylvan' Wordsworth called it, which carries the hint of the 'silver' in the glitter of the river's passage over the rocks, but above all the Wye in its wanderings through the woods is an aural experience, so that you hear more than see below each of the falls the spirals making their patterns in the stream, and you hear more than see the wild and rippling presence of the birds alive in every corner of the woods.

Walking now along the green paths of the valley, accompanied in the early morning by a necklace of blackcaps singing their diamond-tipped songs from branch to branch, the cataracts and weirs in the river provide, even half a mile downstream, murmured undertones of a distant life. As you walk, the noise of

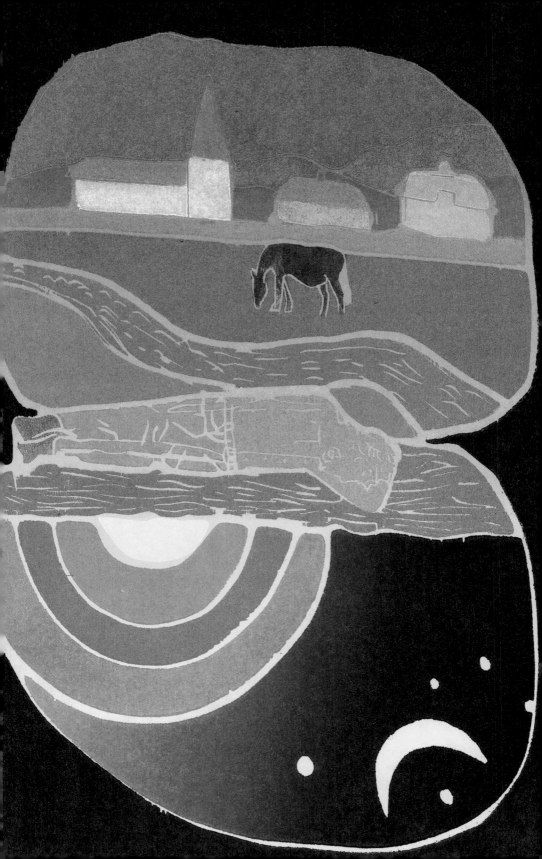

Cuxhaven packet

PREVIOUS PAGE: The vision of completeness

each weir rises to meet you, is vivid and alive in your presence, and then sinks away to the level of the wood-pigeons. The river becomes a model of the Wordsworthian mind, in which vivid, present reality gives way to something less clearly but more richly seen, the known but scarcely remembered as the heart of the significant.

'Lines Composed a Few Miles above Tintern Abbey, On Revisiting the Banks of the Wye during a Tour. July 13, 1798' is more than a tourist poem. It had its roots in standard eighteenth-century loco-descriptive poetry, but everything that had happened in the year fed into it, so that Wordsworth used this new stretch of country to give an account of the evolution he had undergone since 1793, and above all in the course of the last thirteen months. Partly thanks to Dorothy, and in part because of the changes Coleridge had worked in him, he was a different man. 'Tintern Abbey' celebrates that change in a hymn of self-love and self-recognition. It is a rite of passage, marking the moment Wordsworth left his youth behind, and as such is the fruit of this transforming year, the song of adulthood, exchanging fear for love, anxiety for reassurance, the quivering pleasures of the sublime for the firmness and steadiness of the beautiful. It is a poem dedicated to the earth and all other beings in a universal embrace. It is a poem of which in June 1797 he would never have been capable.

The Coleridge of 'Frost at Midnight' and 'The Nightingale' is everywhere in the manner of 'Tintern Abbey': its quiet voice-in-the-ear confiding of deep and private truths and its loose ways with the rhythms of the English pentameter, so that it moves seductively across the realm of the almost-heroic, able now and then to lift its timbre into vast and cosmic statements of the relationship between mind and world, and at others to drop into the whispered intimacy and affection of friend to friend and brother to sister, just as Coleridge had whispered to Hartley in the firelit cradle beside him.

All this Wordsworth had learned from Coleridge, but Coleridge is nowhere in 'Tintern Abbey'. He too has been left behind, much as the Quantocks have been left behind. This valley of the Wye is Wordsworth's country, not Coleridge's. No Coleridgean miasma hangs over it, no network of indispensable friends, none of Coleridge's ghosts or mysterious figures from the ancient past, and nothing conforming to that Coleridgean shape of up and back, out and in. The valley of the Wye and the geography of the poem are more singular than that. It is, unlike every Coleridge poem, not a journey but an arrival, and it begins with Wordsworth taking his position, high above the murmuring waters of the river, speaking with the authority of a man who has come to know where he is in the world and how he stands or rests in it. Coleridge is not there as his companion. Dorothy alone is with him, the other Wordsworth, the mind-sister, a person alongside him who is no challenge and who alone can make the circle complete.

> Five years have passed; five summers, with the length
> Of five long winters! and again I hear
> These waters, rolling from their mountain-springs
> With a sweet inland murmur.

Self and world fuse. The quiet inwardness of those distant mountains and the murmuring of the stream are part of the quiet inwardness of Wordsworth himself. He is above the world of flux, further inland than any turning of the tide. From under the shady tent of a 'dark sycamore' he looks out at a pastoral world in which a sea of unbroken green spreads its mantle over human life:

> These plots of cottage-ground, these orchard-tufts,
> Which at this season, with their unripe fruits,

Are clad in one green hue, and lose themselves
'Mid groves and copses. Once again I see
These hedge-rows, hardly hedge-rows, little lines
Of sportive wood run wild: these pastoral farms,
Green to the very door; and wreathes of smoke
Sent up, in silence, from among the trees.

All kinds of sublime effects might have been available to Wordsworth – the savage cliffs, the abandoned monastery, the booming of the hammers and the Cyclopean night-time glow of the iron foundries – but he drapes them all in something beyond the sublime: the deep consolations of an enveloping nature.

Though absent long,
These forms of beauty have not been to me
As is a landscape to a blind man's eye:
But oft, in lonely rooms, and mid the din
Of towns and cities, I have owed to them,
In hours of weariness, sensations sweet,
Felt in the blood, and felt along the heart;
And passing even into my purer mind
With tranquil restoration: – feelings too
Of unremembered pleasure; such, perhaps,
As have no slight or trivial influence
On that best portion of a good man's life;
His little, nameless, unremembered, acts
Of kindness and of love.

Nature, in its quietness far more penetrative than any sublime horror, has infected him with kindness. Deep in the unconscious and unremembered parts of his mind, nature has made him good. There is nothing intellectual about this; Wordsworth has not decided to be good because he sees goodness in nature. Everything is working at a deeper level than the conscious mind can recognise. Nature has released him from his own tendency towards violence, cruelty and pride, and from the idea that only in those experiences can reality be glimpsed. Now, like the Mariner and like Hartley Coleridge with 'his Brahman love & awe of Life', Wordsworth has also learned to bless man and nature unaware.

Nature is not merely a moral force. It is the gateway to eternity and permanence, to a form of being in which the discordant and broken signals of daily human existence, the Miltonic 'shapes/Of joyless daylight', are swept up into a single harmony, a disembodied lightness in which 'the life of things' becomes clear and present.

> Nor less, I trust,
> To them I may have owed another gift,
> Of aspect more sublime; that blessed mood,
> In which the burthen of the mystery,
> In which the heavy and the weary weight
> Of all this unintelligible world,
> Is lightened: – that serene and blessed mood,
> In which the affections gently lead us on, –
> Until, the breath of this corporeal frame
> And even the motion of our human blood
> Almost suspended, we are laid asleep
> In body, and become a living soul:
> While with an eye made quiet by the power
> Of harmony, and the deep power of joy,
> We see into the life of things.

This may seem like the conclusion of the poem, but it is not. The dialogue continues between mind and world, between the receiving power of the senses and the shaping power of the mind:

Arriving: July 1798

> when the fretful stir
> Unprofitable, and the fever of the world,
> Have hung upon the beatings of my heart,
> How oft, in spirit, have I turned to thee
> O sylvan Wye! thou wanderer through the woods,
> How often has my spirit turned to thee!

Wordsworth and Wye are both wanderers through the woods.
Both have emerged from mountain trouble to this sylvan sliding
through a dream of calm. And Wordsworth can give thanks to
the great river god, for shaping his mind and for allowing his life
to be shaped by it in the future. Five years before, fear had driven
him. He was 'more like a man/Flying from something that he
dreads, than one/Who sought the thing he loved'. He had been
tormented then by the sublime world of immanent horror:

> I cannot paint
> What then I was. The sounding cataract
> Haunted me like a passion: the tall rock,
> The mountain, and the deep and gloomy wood,
> Their colours and their forms, were then to me
> An appetite: a feeling and a love.

That time is past. He has no need of the sublime now to feel that
he is connected to the underlying reality of things. That desire
for the reality-effect of fear and horror feels like an immaturity,
and it has been replaced by something else which nature and this
silver river in its green world have given him:

> For I have learned
> To look on nature, not as in the hour
> Of thoughtless youth; but hearing oftentimes
> The still sad music of humanity,
> Not harsh nor grating, though of ample power

315

To chasten and subdue. And I have felt
A presence that disturbs me with the joy
Of elevated thoughts; a sense sublime
Of something far more deeply interfused,
Whose dwelling is the light of setting suns,
And the round ocean and the living air,
And the blue sky, and in the mind of man:
A motion and a spirit, that impels
All thinking things, all objects of all thought,
And rolls through all things.

Those lines are the triumph of this year, and represent one of the great moments of human consciousness. A love of humanity, in all its quietness and grief, is bonded to the reality of cosmic significance. That significance extends both across the vastness of the universe and deep into the mind of man. All width and all depth are within its grasp. It lives in every dimension of what is. For all that, there is no certainty as to what the 'something' might be. Everything is fluid here, joyful but disturbing, with a vitality that depends upon that uncertainty. It may be that the 'something' is the sense of interfusion itself, the total mutual penetration of the whole of being, the giant self-fertilising of an entirely connected and communicative universe, through which meaning flows with calm and chastening power much as the Wye slides below Wordsworth now in its majestic, glittering progress to the sea.

At one level, 'Tintern Abbey' is an exploration of the relationship of the Sublime and the Beautiful, much as the eighteenth century had known it. Edmund Burke, as a young Irish lawyer in 1756, had first made the distinction. Beauty for Burke was about continuity and connectedness. 'Vegetables,' he says, in one of the great pre-Romantic sentences, 'are not sublime.' Vegetables, in fact, are beautiful because they are constant and continuous, and because beauty is the quality of perfect continuity: 'The sense of being swiftly drawn in an easy coach on a smooth turf with gradual ascents and declivities is a better idea of the beautiful than anything.'

The sublime is the opposite, needing deep distances, withdrawals and chasms, the *Abgrund*, in the resonantly expressive German word for 'an abyss'. And where can you find the *Abgrund*, that hollow of otherness, on an average English day? Burke's answer is in the gaps between the strokes of a single, slowly ringing bell, that chasm of a pause as you wait for the next stroke, each gap a hole opened in the texture of the world, a repeated view into silence, as if it occupied a floor below the one on which we stand.

The sublime, this potent otherness, depends on privations: 'All general privations are great,' Burke wrote: 'Vacuity, Darkness, Solitude and Silence.' These privations are not objects, nor are they great in themselves, but are great because they withdraw stimulus, and, in the gaps they create as they withdraw, a sense of the unaddressably large floods in around them. Burke's sublime requires the world to diminish as you watch, and for that diminution to leave you not with something less, but something immeasurably more.

As Wordsworth stands in his imagination high above the river, under his dark sycamore, in a trance of otherness, he is on the lip of Burke's sublime world. But this poem is revolutionary because it aims beyond those old distinctions, blurring the boundaries of the beautiful and the sublime, replacing them with a third category, outside Burke's dualities, the quality which from this moment on, in July 1798, can be called the Wordsworthian.

Wordsworth's 'something far more deeply interfused' is not part of the ordinary continuities of vegetable life and carriage drives, and yet does not depend on the dis-continuities of the sublime. It occupies the space usually occupied by the sublime – the giant, the ineffable, the partly-not-there, the realm of the great privations – but in that realm Wordsworth's 'something' has all the aspects of the beautiful, of continuousness and full-ness, with the governing characteristics of love, not of fear. It is in other words a new understanding of what truth and beauty might be: beauty occupying the place of the sublime, as a cosmic, universal and profoundly mysterious sense of love and oneness, in which everything is deeply interfused with everything else, where the boundaries are not clear and where substance is uncertain.

In the wake of this magnificent claim on the cosmic, 'Tintern Abbey' turns into a hymn of thanks. Wordsworth is grateful that as a living and embodied person he is embedded in the world of sense, of his half-making, half-receiving eye and ear, leading him towards a modesty and wisdom which effectively bury his heart, mind and self in the enveloping and tender folds of 'this green earth':

> Therefore am I still
> A lover of the meadows and the woods
> And mountains; and of all that we behold
> From this green earth; of all the mighty world
> Of eye, and ear, – both what they half-create,
> And what perceive; well pleased to recognise
> In nature and the language of the sense
> The anchor of my purest thoughts, the nurse,
> The guide, the guardian of my heart, and soul
> Of all my moral being.

Subtle political echoes ripple around these lines. Five years before, Britain had embarked on a long war with revolutionary France. The French king had been guillotined. Rivers of blood were flowing in the streets of Paris. The date of this poem's composition, 13 July, is the day before the anniversary of the storming of the Bastille. That political turmoil might be thought of as 'the mighty world', but 'Tintern Abbey' claims something different: nature – meadows, woods and mountains – is the still mightier world that embodies and enshrines the world of the senses and of love.

From these abstruser musings, Wordsworth turns finally to the woman at his side, 'thou my dearest Friend,/My dear, dear Friend'. He loves her as unequivocally as he loves the universe of which they are both a part. Still, though, he thinks of her as a lesser being, immature, some way back on the path he has already travelled:

> in thy voice I catch
> The language of my former heart, and read
> My former pleasures in the shooting lights
> Of thy wild eyes.

It is the great failing of this great poem, to imagine that the woman who through her care has led him to his present magnificence is somehow still disabled as he had been. He lectures her on the power of nature and its ability to inculcate lovingness:

> this prayer I make,
> Knowing that Nature never did betray
> The heart that loved her; 'tis her privilege,
> Through all the years of this our life, to lead
> From joy to joy: for she can so inform
> The mind that is within us, so impress
> With quietness and beauty, and so feed
> With lofty thoughts, that neither evil tongues,
> Rash judgments, nor the sneers of selfish men,
> Nor greetings where no kindness is, nor all
> The dreary intercourse of daily life,
> Shall e'er prevail against us, or disturb
> Our chearful faith, that all which we behold
> Is full of blessings.

Nature may never betray those that love her, but these lines could be read as a form of betrayal of the sister who loved Wordsworth. The lines record, unconsciously, his central flaw: his own sense of his own greatness was also his greatest weakness.

At least it can be said that he speaks of the two of them together as fellow sufferers, a 'we' who, throughout their youth, had felt betrayed: by the death of one parent and then another; by the treachery of the Lowthers, evicting them and refusing to pay them their inheritance; by their own relations who treated them as lesser beings; by the turn of political events; perhaps by the hypocritical inhabitants of Stowey and Holford, publicly greeting and privately sneering; by the Home Office spy network; and by their own country. It is together that they can now feel the world to be full of blessings. He wants those blessings to pour on her, to

> let the moon
> Shine on thee in thy solitary walk;
> And let the misty mountain winds be free
> To blow against thee: and, in after years,
> When these wild ecstasies shall be matured
> Into a sober pleasure; when thy mind
> Shall be a mansion for all lovely forms,
> Thy memory be as a dwelling-place
> For all sweet sounds and harmonies.

It is as if, at this summit of confidence and self-fulfilment, and in his desire to give his sister all the forms of mental life which seem at the moment to be his alone, he had nevertheless removed himself into a temple of supreme grandeur and isolation, imagining himself dead, watching his younger sister and disciple walking alone through the world.

A tiny glimpse of this Wordsworth can be had from the journal of his friend James Losh, to whose elegant house at

Shirehampton near Bristol (the site now occupied by the Shirehampton Co-op) the Wordsworths now moved. 'Wordsworth pleasant and clear,' Losh wrote of a dinner they had together, 'but too earnest and emphatic in his manner of speaking in conversation.'

It was something Coleridge was also coming to recognise, and would describe to Poole the following year:

> My many weaknesses are of some advantage to me; they
> unite me more with the great mass of my fellow-beings – but
> dear Wordsworth appears to me to have hurtfully segregated
> and isolated his being. Doubtless his delights are more deep
> and sublime; but he has likewise more hours that prey upon
> the flesh and blood.

In Coleridge's generous and loving estimation, Wordsworth was suffering from the isolation he also needed. The irony of that judgement is that none suffered more from Wordsworth's self-separation than Coleridge himself. Nowhere in Wordsworth's concluding paean to love in 'Tintern Abbey' is there any mention or suggestion of gratitude to Coleridge. So much of what Wordsworth was now saying was indebted to Coleridge's example and teaching, to his guidance over the months in the combes and on the Quantock heights, and yet he has been written out of this story. Dorothy is Wordsworth's only 'dearest Friend,/My dear, dear Friend'. Coleridge, whose precise whereabouts at this moment are not even known, is now absent from the story.

17

Leaving

August and September 1798

Wordsworth loved 'Tintern Abbey'. 'Not a line of it was altered,' he told Isabella Fenwick at the end of his life, 'and not any part of it written down till I reached Bristol.' Within a day or two he put the manuscript into the hands of Joseph Cottle, who had undertaken to publish *Lyrical Ballads*.

Coleridge was still away, and in his absence Wordsworth attended with extreme care to the physical form the book of poems would take. By 18 July, when Dorothy could write that 'William's poems are now in the press', he had established with Cottle exactly how the book would appear to the world.

However much the genesis of the poetry was oral, and its reception initially intended for the ear, the physical book – its paper, size and typography – was an integral part of the way it would reach its public. Books were usually sold unbound, or in simple, temporary, paper-covered boards, to be replaced by the buyer with their own choice of binding. There were no dust-jackets until the 1820s, and so it was the eighteenth-century habit to display new books in bookshop windows open either at their title pages or at a sample page within. The pages of the book itself were there to advertise its worth.

Wordsworth and Coleridge had already been insistent to Cottle on what the book should look like: a simple eighteen lines of text to the page, cool, plain and without decoration of any kind. There were to be page numbers but no running heads and no kind of embellishment – none of the little sprigs of printed flowers or curlicues often used to fill the bottom half of a page. A plain and dignified Roman typeface would establish the tone. The paper was to be simple and not 'hot-pressed' to give a smoothed surface, as in the more expensive books of the age. The page size, scarcely bigger than their own notebooks, was also cheap, and suited to a book intended for a wider audience than the leisured reading classes. The initial letters of poems were to be of the same size as the rest, unlike many contemporary books, in which the initial letters are enlarged. Visual restraint, austerity and simplicity would declare to the reader – and to the buyer – that this was no lush pastoral hollow. Something stricter was in play, and both the unflauntingness of the title itself – *LYRICAL BALLADS, WITH A FEW OTHER POEMS* – and the wide open spaces of the layout demonstrate a kind of radical new-born nakedness.

To drive the point home, to be 'earnest and *emphatic*', as Losh recognised, Wordsworth wrote a brief 'Advertisement' for the volume, to be bound in with it and perhaps for potential buyers to read in the bookshop. It is an austere piece of prose. In almost every syllable it reveals Wordsworth's anxious and uncompromising frame of mind. 'It is the honourable characteristic of Poetry that its materials are to be found in every subject which can interest the human mind,' he begins. 'The evidence of this fact is to be sought, not in the writings of Critics, but in those of Poets themselves.' Do not think you can judge. Only a poet can instruct you in the value of what this book contains.

The familiar readers of poetry, he went on, probably wouldn't understand that point of view, and so wouldn't like the kind of poems he had written. They would be wrong, and almost certainly inadequately versed in the full breadth of poetry, ancient and modern. 'An accurate taste in poetry ... is an acquired talent,' he tells his readers. Most of them, he says, will not have made the effort, and so their judgement will be 'erroneous'.

The Wordsworth who glows in the privacy of his notebooks, who shamefacedly shrugs and smiles at Coleridge when he cannot deliver what he has promised, who is in love with the spring, with his sister and the little boy they have been looking after – that figure makes no appearance in what is surely one of the most hostile pieces of marketing material ever published. It is more a pre-emptive defence of a territory than any invitation to enter it. Where, you might ask, is the universal love of 'Tintern Abbey'?

He drives on with his attack. This is no pleasure ground, but a laboratory:

> The majority of the following poems are to be considered as experiments. They were written chiefly with a view to ascertain how far the language of conversation in the middle and lower classes of society is adapted to the purposes of poetic pleasure. Readers accustomed to the gaudiness and inane phraseology of many modern writers, if they persist in reading this book to its conclusion, will perhaps frequently have to struggle with feelings of strangeness and aukwardness.

The expectations delivered by the typography of a calm, rational and careful experience of pleasure for the reader will be denied by these poems, much as the poems offer the prospect of the traditional pleasures of ballad and lyric only to withdraw from and baffle them. Awkwardness is not to be seen as a flaw of this book, the Advertisement warns, but its purpose.

The vision of a deep and loving connection between nature and people that Wordsworth had entertained only a day or two before in 'Tintern Abbey' is now buried in hostile schoolmasterly instructions. He advises his readers that

while they are perusing this book, they should ask
themselves if it contains a natural delineation of human
passions, human characters, and human incidents; and if the
answer be favorable to the author's wishes, that they should
consent to be pleased in spite of that most dreadful enemy to
our pleasures, our own pre-established codes of decision.

The audience is in as much need of reform as the self-serving
aristocrats of France and England. The look of this book may
have led them in, and was intended to lead them in, but in its
pages they would find a place of fierce and complex instruction,
a reformatory in which their stale ideas of man, nature and society, of truth and poetry, and all the connections between them,
would be turned upside down. The book aims to destroy assumptions – political, aesthetic and social. In that way, and in Hazlitt's
words, the poetry of *Lyrical Ballads* 'partakes of, and is carried
along with, the revolutionary movement of our age: the political
changes of the day were the model on which [Wordsworth]
formed and conducted his poetical experiments'. The Quantocks
had become the English Bastille.

By the beginning of August, Coleridge had returned to Bristol.
He wrote to Poole to tell him that he had decided not to take
Sara and the children with him to Germany. To Poole he claimed
this was on financial grounds, but later letters written from
Germany itself hint at stormy and difficult passages in his
marriage, 'moments of fretfulness and imbecility' in which
Coleridge had been 'disposed to anger or reproach'. It is perfectly
likely that Sara did not come to Germany because Coleridge, at
least in part of his mind, wanted to be away from her.

Coleridge and the Wordsworths made another walking tour
for a week for so into Wales, visiting John Thelwall en route,
with no suggestion that Sara might come. While they were in
Wales, Cottle went on with his preparations, and the way was

becoming clear both for the publication of *Lyrical Ballads* and, now that Sara and the babies were to be left behind, for the voyage to Germany.

Cottle had printed a few copies of the book and bound them with his own imprint on the title page. But he was starting to get cold feet, perhaps because of his own looming bankruptcy, perhaps because he had given an advance copy to Robert Southey, another of his authors, who had warned him, perhaps out of spite, perhaps out of a lack of sympathy for the kind of poetry the book contained, that it was likely to fail.

Certainly, by the end of August Southey knew who the authors were, and early in September he wrote at least half-disparagingly to a friend:

Have you seen a volume of Lyrical Ballads, &c? they are by Coleridge and Wordsworth, but their names are not affixd. Coleridges ballad of the Auncient Marinere is I think the clumsiest attempt at German sublimity I ever saw. many of the others are very fine & some I shall re-read, upon the same principle that led me thro Trissino whenever I am afraid of writing like a child or an old woman.

The best that Southey could summon in response to Wordsworth's strange experiments was to use them as an example of how not to write, just as a vastly descriptive Italian Renaissance poet could instruct him in how not to compose an epic.

Cottle decided at some point in August that he could not bear the costs of publication himself. He had previously worked with Thomas Norton Longman, one of the great dynasty of London booksellers and publishers, and now contacted him again, arranging for Longman to publish the book with a new title page proclaiming 'Bristol: Printed by Biggs and Cottle for T.N. Longman, Paternoster Row, London 1798', and using the sheets already printed. At about the same moment, the poets decided to withdraw one of Coleridge's poems, 'Lewti', which had already been published in a newspaper, and replace it with 'The Nightingale', as yet unseen, only because people would guess Coleridge was one of the authors if 'Lewti' were included.

In early September, a publishing shambles unfolded. Five hundred copies had been printed when Longman withdrew from any arrangement he had made with Cottle. Wordsworth himself was by then in London. Cottle had given him a letter of introduction to Longman, but Wordsworth had forgotten it in Bristol and instead arranged with the radical publisher-bookseller Jo Johnson (who had printed his first poems years before) to publish the book. At the same time, unaware of all of this, Cottle sold the whole edition to yet another bookseller, John and Arthur Arch of Gracechurch Street near Leadenhall Market in the City of London. And it is their names, not Cottle's, Longman's, Johnson's, Wordsworth's or Coleridge's that appear on nearly all of the first editions of the book.

The financial arrangements were equally chaotic. Cottle had promised Wordsworth thirty guineas, but by the time the party left for Germany he had paid over no more than £9.11s. The rest would only reach Wordsworth the following year.

On 14 September they were ready: both Wordsworths and Coleridge, plus John Chester, the rich farmer's son from Over Stowey who had taken up with Coleridge as his devoted friend and ally, regularly walking with him to Lynton and back.

The peacetime routes to the Continent via Dover and Calais were closed off by the war, and the only passage available was via Great Yarmouth on the coast of East Anglia, more than 120 miles from London, and from there across the North Sea in a fast government mail packet, two days' sailing with a fair wind, to Cuxhaven at the mouth of the Elbe.

A stage-coach left every day at noon from the White Horse in Fetter Lane off Fleet Street, £1.16s per passenger, travelling via

Ipswich and arriving in Yarmouth by noon the next day, depositing the passengers outside the Star Inn on Hall Quay, next to the tidal lengths of the River Yare.

Arriving in Yarmouth already feels like abroad: hedgeless, Dutch willow flats, long perspectives, isolated villages, dairy and suckler herds out in the big marshland grazings, windmills standing lit against distant grey skies, pantiles, stray cattle on the road, flatness and pools of light falling between the clouds.

A busy port town with more than two thousand yards of quay on the river: timbers from the Baltic stacked on the south side of the harbour, men-of-war at anchor in the Roads, 150 fishing boats in the mackerel, herring and cod trades on and off the beaches, the bowsprits of hundreds of seagoing colliers hanging over the long quayside, half the ships drying their hemp sails from the yards, constant unloading of corn and north-country coal from the seagoing hulls into Norwich wherries. And just away from the business of the quays, a saltwater bath-house, theatre and assembly house, 'much resorted to by the genteelest company from the counties of Suffolk and Norfolk, and even from London'.

That is not why the poets were here. In one of the narrow alleys or Rows next to the elegant brick Custom House on the quay, they bought their tickets for the packet from Richard Warmington, the Post Office agent: 12*s*.6*d* each, one way. Wordsworth was still writing to Cottle, asking him to transfer his rights in the *Lyrical Ballads* to Jo Johnson 'on account of it being likely to be very advantageous to me'. But he had no knowledge of what would happen to the book, nor who its publisher might be.

Until the morning of Saturday the 15th, the wind was in the east and north-east, on the nose for any passage to Cuxhaven. Only in the course of that day did it veer into the south and then on Sunday morning into the south-west, a following wind for the mouth of the Elbe, some 330 miles away.

In 1786 the German novelist Sophie von La Roche had
described the layout of a Cuxhaven packet:

> Two rooms and two cabins hold 26 berths for passengers; it
> is all very attractive. The outer room is panelled with
> mahogany and has a fine mirror and lamp brackets fastened
> to the wall. The berths are arranged along the side walls in
> two rows, like theatre boxes, one above the other; they have
> thoroughly good mattresses, white quilted covers, neat
> curtains, and on a ledge in the corner is a chamber made of
> English china used in case of sickness. In order to lie down,
> the outer board of these boxes is removed and then fitted in
> again by the sailors to prevent people from tumbling out. It
> holds one person quite comfortably and the whole looks
> very neat.

A big brown tide starts to slip out down the Yare. At eleven
o'clock that Sunday morning the Post Office packet the *Carteret*,
Captain William Hammond, warps herself out from the quay on
the anchor, the pilot on board, so that tide and wind can begin to
take her down-channel with the ebb. At the mouth, where the
river sidles out between the sandbanks and the enclosing break-
waters, the sea begins to lift and buckle like a river after a rock in
its bed. The sea itself is a deep tea brown, kicking up into a steep-
walled chop where it meets the outgoing tide, now running at five
knots or so, and sweeping the packet away from the shore. To the
east, the North Sea horizon is earth-brown as far as you can see.
The pilot is dropped, and then all canvas is hauled up and tight,
as the hull of the packet starts to lift and surge in the swell and
she gathers way. With the wind on the quarter, the *Carteret* will
drive for the Elbe all day and night at not far short of seven knots.

Among the fourteen passengers who had bought tickets from
the agent, there are Frenchmen, Danes, Germans and Swedes on
board, along with their servants, conducting war business or spy

business through Yarmouth, the naval depot for the southern North Sea, and in London. Everybody starts the voyage on deck. As, for the first time in his life, Coleridge watches his 'native land retiring from me', its houses and fields dropping below the horizon, he has a vision:

> My dear dear Babies ... when the land quite disappeared, they came upon my eye as distinctly as if they had that moment died and were crossing me in their road to Heaven!

None of the party was used to the sea.

> Chester began to look Frog-coloured and doleful – Miss Wordsworth retired in confusion to the Cabin – Wordsworth soon followed – I was giddy, but not sick, and in about half an hour the giddiness went away, & left only a feverish Inappetence of Food, arising I believe, from the accursed stink of the Bilge water, & certainly not decreased by the Sight of the Basons from the Cabin containing green and yellow specimens of the inner Man & brought up by the Cabin-boy every three minutes – I talked and laughed with the Passengers – then went to sleep on the deck.

Little more is heard of the Wordsworths, grieving in the privacy of their boarded coffins down below: 'Chester was ill the Whole time – Wordsworth shockingly ill! – Miss Wordsworth worst of all – vomiting & groaning & crying the whole time!'

Coleridge was on a voyage. He fell asleep on deck, but by mid-afternoon was down below in the mahogany-lined cabin next to the sleeping quarters, engaged in a riotous drinking session with the other passengers. He was dressed 'all in black with large shoes and black worsted stockings', so that the Danes and Swedes took him for a pastor. He reassured them he was '*un Philosophe*', and would be more than happy to give them wisdom for their drink.

– Well, I drank some excellent wine & devoured Grapes &
part of a pine-apple – And in a short time became their Idol
– Every now and then I entered into the feelings of my poor
Friends, who in all the agonies of sea-sickness heard us most
distinctly, spouting, singing, laughing, fencing, dancing
country dances – in a word being Bacchanals.

Coleridge rolled on into the evening, ever drunker, ever more
wonderful:

(Dane) Vat imagination! vat language! vat fast science! vat
    eyes! – vat a milk vite forehead! – O my Heafen! You are a
    God! – Oh me! if you should tink I flatters you – no, no,
    no – I hafe ten tousand a year – yes – ten tousand a year –
    ten tousand pound a year! – vell, vat's that? a mere trifle! –
    I 'ouldn't give my sincere heart for ten times the money.
    – Yes! you are a God! – I a mere Man! – But my dear
    Friend! tink of me as a Man. Is I not speak English very
    fine? Is I not very eloquent?
(STC) Admirably, Sir! most admirably! – Believe me, Sir! I
    never heard even a Native talk so fluently.
(Dane squeezing my hand most vehemently) My dear
    Friend! vat an affection & fidelity we hafe for each other!
    – But tell me, do tell me – Is I not now & den speak some
    fault? Is I not in some wrong? –
(STC) Why, Sir! perhaps it might be observed by nice Critics
    in the English Language that you occasionally use the
    word 'is' instead of 'am' – In our best Companies We
    generally say 'am I' not 'Is I' – Excuse me Sir! – It is so
    mere a Trifle
(Dane) O! o! o! – Is – is – is – Am – am – am – ah – hah –
    yes – yes – I know – I knows –

The packet thrashed on through the night, hurrying the mails to the commercial and government agents in Europe. All around Coleridge and his Dane the other passengers were suffering, but the conversation that had rolled through the year and through the whole of Coleridge's life in an unstoppable tide rolled on between them.

At last the Dane was exhausted and retired to his bunk. The cabin stank, but Coleridge had equipped himself in London with a magnificent coat, twenty-eight shillings' worth – 'a weighty, long, high caped, respectable rug – The Collar will serve for a night Cap, turning over my head' – and with that around, up and over him, he went on deck, lay in the ship's boat 'and looked at the water, the foam of which, that beat against the Ship & coursed along by it's sides, & darted off over the Sea, was full of stars of flame'. 'The Ocean is a noble Thing by night,' he wrote to Sara, remembering this moment, alone in his coat on the deck of the North Sea packet, seeing how

> a beautiful white cloud of foam at momently intervals roars
> & rushes by the side of the Vessel, and Stars of Flame dance
> & sparkle & go out in it – & every now and then light
> Detachments of Foam dart away from the Vessel's side with
> their galaxies of stars, & scour out of sight, like a Tartar
> Troop over a Wilderness!

That is surely where to leave them: the Wordsworths alone in their white linen bunks below, tight up against the mahogany boards, filled with memories and ideas of what they had been and might yet be; while no more than a foot or two above their heads, also alone but wrapped in his magnificence, gazing at the stars as the packet plunged and drove to the east, the other poet, alert to the marvels of the world, no longer giddy, but seeing in the phosphorescent surge of the zooplankton around him a vision of Asiatic cavalrymen-cum-galaxies – the Coleridgean self! – ever alive to the dancing and sparkling of the universe.

ACKNOWLEDGEMENTS

One of the ideas bequeathed to us by the Romantics is that books are written by people on their own. As this story of the Quantocks shows, it isn't true, and so these acknowledgements are a continuation of what this book has to say: my thanks to the people who are the sea in which I swim.

First, to the scholars and writers who have thought about Coleridge and the Wordsworths over the last two centuries, none more than James Butler, Karen Green, Stephen Parrish and the other editors of the great Cornell editions of Wordsworth's poems and notebooks, on which this book has deeply and gratefully relied. Pamela Woof's edition of Dorothy Wordsworth's journal takes its place alongside them.

As I have written in the first pages of this book, Richard Holmes has for decades been a model for me of how to write about writers as people in the world. I am immensely grateful to him for the humane and civilised path he has forged and for the footsteps I have followed.

Many thanks to the staff of the National Archives at Kew for access to the Home Office records for the 1790s and to David Worthy of Friarn, the local historian who has done more than anyone to recover the history of the Quantocks, and who with enormous generosity gave me access to the transcription of William Holland's journal held in the Somerset Heritage Centre, supervised and edited by him. For more details of his and other books, please see the Bibliography.

In Somerset, Ben Bartlett housed me with warmth and comfort for many months at Adscombe Farm. I would like to thank Justin Shepherd for the great care he took in reading an earlier version of the book and steering it in simpler, truer and better directions.

More particularly the staff of both Combe House Hotel in Holford and Musgrave Park Hospital in Taunton looked after me one November morning when the bank of Holford Glen collapsed beneath me and I fell twenty-five or thirty feet, knocking myself out on the way down, and lay for some time unconscious in the stream at the bottom.

A man whose name I don't know found me later as I wandered through the park, dazed and half-present, sodden, the blood running down from the wounds in my head.

He walked beside me, talking gently about the rain, the weather. Not a word of his do I remember. Only his gentle presence. Love as the guarantee of meaning. No touch of the hand but an embrace simply in his being there. It was in its way a Coleridgean blessing of comfort and connection, understanding that acts of kindness are puffs of wind in which those in need can only nod to and fro.

Then an ambulance, the hospital, a brain scan, a full-body scan, ultrasound, talk of brain surgery, stitches in my scalp. Two of the processes, the protruding fins of my vertebrae, had been broken. Then pain relief, the embrace of certainty, the wonders of the NHS.

For all of this, deep thanks.

The National Trust staff at Coleridge's Cottage in Nether Stowey were, later, the source of many fascinating conversations, and Mark Drysdale of Quantock Mariner Ltd gave me and Tom Hammick full access to Alfoxden and its park.

'FRIEND is a sacred appellation,' Coleridge wrote, and I

would love to thank these friends for everything they have given me during the years this book has been in the making: Marcia Blakenham, Charlie Boxer, Kate Boxer, Charlie Burrell, Aurea Carpenter, Alexandra Chaldecott, William Dalrymple, Tim Dee, David Dimbleby, Montagu and Sarah Don, Belinda Eade, Louise Farman, Hugh Fearnley-Whittingstall, Maggie Fergusson, Lucinda Fraser, Simon Fraser, Belinda Giles, Martha Hammick, Alexandra Harris, Richard Holmes, Kate Hubbard, Nigel Leask, Sam Leith, Robert Macfarlane, Patrick Mackaskie, Deborah Needleman, Andrew Palmer, Vassilis Papadimitriou, Katrina Porteous, Alex Preston, Stephen Romer, Ivan Samarine, Claire Spottiswoode, Isabella Tree, Jacob Weisberg and Sofka Zinovieff.

Above all, I want to thank Tom Hammick for the wonderful collaboration we have been embarked on, for his encouragements and the effort and skill he has put into making the woodcuts for this book. I have dedicated it to him first because he is a truly good friend, but more than that because his images recognise that everything the Wordsworths and Coleridge were reaching for two hundred years ago remains valid, inspiring and important today.

The team at HarperCollins have bent over backwards to make this book as good as can be, and my heartfelt thanks to them all: Arabella Pike, Robert Lacey, Julian Humphries, Helen Ellis, Martin Wells and Jo Thompson.

In New York, Jack Macrae, Paula Cooper and Jonathan Galassi have been the spirit of welcome and encouragement itself.

My agents Georgina Capel and Zoe Pagnamenta remain treasured lifelong companions.

To my family, my sisters Rebecca and Juliet, my children Tom, Will, Ben, Rosie and Molly; and to their partners Becca, Klara, Karina and Liam, all love and thanks. And Sarah: Wordsworth said that poetry was 'the first and last of all knowledge'. That is what she is to me.

A NOTE ON TOM
HAMMICK'S PICTURES

Many of the woodcuts in this book are made with fallen timber taken from Alfoxden in the Quantocks. The eighteenth-century house and park where the Wordsworths lived for a year is not what it was. The ancient oaks, chestnuts, ash, beech and cherries have all dropped limbs, and that broken timber now lies beneath the trees like the fragments of cast skeletons.

In August 2018, with the permission of Mark Drysdale of Quantock Mariner Ltd, the development company that now owns the house and park, Tom Hammick and Adam Nicolson spent a day there cutting sections from the fallen logs. The timber was planked and pieces butted together for Hammick to make the woodcuts. The grain and growth of the trees remains visible in the finished images, all of which draw their inspiration from what the poets wrote in the Quantocks and from the story of their lives there.

The troubled nature of our connections to each other and to the natural world have long been the artist's concern. Here in the visions of the poets, in the luminous shadowed trees, in Coleridge's dream worlds and Wordsworth's sense of winter loneliness and springtime gaiety, Hammick summons a visual vocabulary that reconnects the present to those foundations of modern sensibility. Fusion of scale and intimacy is his subject as much as it was the Romantic poets'. Connectedness was all for them, and these woodcuts, made from the trees under which Wordsworth and Coleridge, their friends and families, sat, talked and read, embody some of that understanding.

NOTES

Abbreviations Used in the Notes

CL I: E.L. Griggs, *Collected Letters of Samuel Taylor Coleridge*, Vol. I, 1795–1800, Clarendon Press, Oxford, 1956, 1966

CN I: Kathleen Coburn, *The Notebooks of Samuel Taylor Coleridge, Vol. I, 1794–1804*, Routledge, London, 1957

EY: E. de Selincourt, *The Letters of William and Dorothy Wordsworth*, 2nd edn, rev. C.L. Shaver, Vol. I, *The Early Years 1787–1805*, Clarendon Press, Oxford, 1967

Butler & Green: James Butler & Karen Green, *Lyrical Ballads and Other Poems 1797–1800 by William Wordsworth*, Cornell UP, Ithaca, 1992

Butler, *RC & Pedlar*: James Butler, ed., *The Ruined Cottage and The Pedlar*, Cornell UP, Ithaca, 1979

Keach: William Keach, ed., *Samuel Taylor Coleridge: The Complete Poems*, Penguin, Harmondsworth, 1997

Sandford: Mrs Henry Sandford, *Thomas Poole and His Friends*, Macmillan, 1888, 2 vols

Holland, MS Journal: The journals of William Holland, vicar of Over Stowey, the originals held at Somerset Heritage Centre, ref A/BTL/2, transcribed by Peter Stone and Stella Mathias and edited by David Worthy

Chapter 1: *Following*

2 the sense of difficulty: Butler & Green, Appendix III (LB 1800 Preface), p.757

2 historical crisis: Seamus Heaney, 'Crediting Poetry', his address on receiving the Nobel Prize, included in *Opened Ground: Poems 1966–1996*, London, 1998, p.464

2 It was not about: Butler & Green, Appendix III (LB 1800 Preface), p.756

2 I wish to keep: Ibid., p.747

3 corporeal: CL I, Letter 74, to Robert Southey, 11 Dec 1794, p.137

3 'neuropathology' and 'psychosomatic': See Frederick

Burwick, *The Oxford Handbook of Samuel Taylor Coleridge*, 2012, 476

3 touching territory: Speaking to Patrick Garland on *Poets on Poetry*, BBC 1, Oct 1973

4 close behint him: For these and following records, see H.D. Rawnsley, 'Reminiscences of Wordsworth among the Peasantry of Westmoreland', in William Knight (ed.), *Wordsworthiana*, London, 1889, pp.81–119, reprinted Dillon's, London, 1968

4 enduring and creative: 1805 *Prelude*, XIII, 311–12

5 Of all the men: Kathleen Coburn, ed., *Inquiring Spirit: A New Presentation of Coleridge and Unpublished Prose Writings*, Pantheon, New York, 1951, p.296; Thomas McFarland, 'The Symbiosis of Coleridge and Wordsworth', *Studies in Romanticism*, Vol. XI, No. 4, Samuel Taylor Coleridge (Fall 1972), 271

5 time of unrememberable being: DCMS 19 Zr; Stephen Parrish, *The Prelude 1798–99*, Cornell, 1977, pp.114–15

5 the first and last: Butler & Green, Appendix III (1802 addition to *Lyrical Ballads* Preface), p.753

Chapter 2: *Meeting*

6 the quick-set hedge: CL I, Letter 105, to Joseph Cottle, p.185

7 my spirit courses: CL II, Letter 484, to Tom Wedgwood, 14 Jan 1803, p.916

7 pursy: William Hazlitt, in 'My First Acquaintance with Poets', *The Liberal*, Apr 1823; now online at ourcivilisation.com

7 almost shillingless: CL I, Letter 192, to J.P. Estlin, 10 Jun 1797, p.327

7 *The scatter'd cots*: Cottle's *Malvern Hills* quoted in *Analytical Review: Or History of Literature, Domestic and Foreign, on an Enlarged Plan*, Vol. XXVIII, J. Johnson, London, 1799, pp.77–8

8 that in the course of: CL I, Letter 190, to J. Cottle, 8 Jun 1797, p.325

8 most of the better people: Sandford, Vol. I, p.231

8 the more I see: CL I, Letter 191, to J.P. Estlin, 9 Jun 1797, p.326

8 endeavoured to awaken: Ibid.

8 like a comet: L. Patton & P. Mann, eds, STC, *Lectures 1795: On Politics and Religion*, Princeton UP, 1971, p.xxviii; *Monthly Magazine*, Vol. XLVIII (1819), p.203

8 against his better interests: Ibid.; CL II, Letter 1000, to Sir George and Lady Beaumont, 1 Oct 1803

8 the best poet: CL I, Letter 127, to John Thelwall, 13 May 1796, p.215

9 broth made of flour: Sir Frederic Morton Eden, *The State of the Poor*, 3 vols, London, 1797, Vol. II, 146–51

9 drink and some victuals: William Holland, MS Journal, 7 Jun 1800

9 Gifts were made: Barry Williamson, ed., *The Account*

Books and Papers of Everard and Ann Arundel of Ashcombe and Salisbury 1745–1798, Wiltshire Record Society Vol. LXX, 2017, xl–xli

10 Bad teeth: Ibid., xlvi

10 slovenly: CL I, Letter 66, to Robert Southey, 23 Oct 1794, p.120

10 spend their little wages: Sir Frederic Morton Eden, *The State of the Poor*, 3 vols, London, 1797, Vol. II, pp.146–51

11 Fences were often stolen: 'Goody Blake and Harry Gill', one of Wordsworth's poems in *Lyrical Ballads*, hinges on the theft of a fence in a frosty winter by a poor old woman and the vengeance she wreaks on the farmer who catches her.

11 to have been milked: Holland, MS Journal, Thursday, 26 Jun 1800

11 plucked: Ibid., Saturday, 24 Jan 1801

11 swarming with the workhouse children: Ibid., Monday, 6 Jul 1807

11 Carrion Beef: Joseph Gill's journal, 7 Jan 1797, in Bergen Evans & Hester Pinney, 'Racedown and the Wordsworths', *The Review of English Studies*, Vol. VIII, No. 29 (Jan 1932), p.14

11 walked as far as: Holland, MS Journal, Saturday, 27 Jul 1805

12 an air that whizzed: 'Aria Spontanea', 10 Sept 1823. Wednesday Morning, 10 o'clock, in Richard Holmes, ed., *Coleridge Selected Poems*, HarperCollins, London, 1996, 257

15 dim: For the repeated significance of dimness for Coleridge see e.g. 'Frost at Midnight': 'I was reared/In the great city, pent mid cloisters dim/And saw nought lovely but the sky and stars.'; 'Christabel', 'The moon shines dim in the open air'; *Ancient Mariner*, 'The stars were dim, and thick the night', etc.

15 I hate the word *but*: CL I, Letter 241, to Josiah Wade, 21 Mar 1798, p.401

16 He could get lost: See R.W. Armour & R.F. Howes, *Coleridge the Talker*, Cornell, 1940, p.16: 'In order fully to comprehend and develop any one subject, it was necessary I should make myself master of some other'; p.20, Coleridge asks himself in the midst of a giant, multi-claused disquisition, 'Now how shall I get out of this sentence? the tail is too big to be taken up into the coiler's mouth.'

16 schemes for everything: CN I 161, 174

17 For I am now busy: CL II, Letter 876, to Tom Wedgwood, 20 Oct 1802

17 My heart seraglios: CN I, 133

17 a smack of Hamlet: *Table Talk*, 24 Jun 1827

17 and the images: *Notes and Lectures on Shakespeare* (1818), New York, 1868, Vol. IV, p.144

17 All actual objects: Edith J. Morley, ed., *Blake, Coleridge, Wordsworth, Lamb, etc., being Selections from the Remains of*

Henry Crabb Robinson, Manchester UP, 1922, p.35

17 the dim awakening: CN II, entry 2546

18 supported by the images: CN I, entry 1648, 6.45 p.m., 9 Nov 1803

18 a thought-bewilder'd man: 'To the Rev W.L. Bowles', first version, line 7, Keach, p.72

18 a man of *perpendicular Virtue*: CL I, Letter 81, to George Dyer, Feb 1795, pp.152–3

18 a coxcomb: EY, Letter 60, WW to William Mathews, 21 Mar 1796, p.169

18 You are *lost* to *me*: CL I, Letter 93, to Robert Southey, 13 Nov 1795, p.163

18 the power of saying one thing: In a letter transcribed by Henry Crabb Robinson, *Diary, Reminiscences, and Correspondence*, Fields, Osgood & Co., 1870, II, 632. See also STC's question in CN II, 2370: 'Who ever *felt* a *single* sensation?'

18 a Surinam toad: CN 4, entry 4518 (and other places)

19 *Every step an arrival*: Denise Levertov, quoting Rilke in 'Overland to the Islands'. See Levertov's essay 'The Sense of Pilgrimage' in *The Poet in the World*, New Directions, New York, 1973, 69

19 Southey once said: Coburn, *Inquiring Spirit*, p.114

20 An excellent house: EY, Letter 54, to Francis Wrangham, 20 Nov 1795, p.159

20 a very good house: EY, Letter 50, to Jane Pollard, 2 & 3 Sept 1795, p.148

20 the mansion of our friend: CL I, Letter 190, to Joseph Cottle, 8 Jun 1797, p.325

20 A tight parapeted formality: For life at and contents of Racedown see Bergen Evans & Hester Pinney, 'Racedown and the Wordsworths', *The Review of English Studies*, Vol. VIII, No. 29 (Jan 1932), pp.1–18

22 I have lately been: EY, Letter 63, to Francis Wrangham, 25 Feb 1797, p.178

22 Gill carefully records: Bergen Evans & Hester Pinney, 'Racedown and the Wordsworths', *The Review of English Studies*, Vol. VIII, No. 29 (Jan 1932), 1–18

23 The Wordsworths' father: See John Worthen, *A Life of William Wordsworth*, John Wiley, Chichester, 2014, pp.21–2; Wallace W. Douglas, 'Wordsworth as Business Man', *PMLA*, Vol. LXIII, No. 2 (Jun 1948), pp.625–41; Joanne Dann, 'Some Notes on the Relationship Between the Wordsworth and the Lowther Families', *The Wordsworth Circle*, Vol. XI, No. 2 (Spring 1980), pp.80–2

23 How we are squandered: She was quoting *The Merchant of Venice*, I, iii, 22. EY, Letter 5, to Jane Pollard, 27 Jan 1788, p.16

23 an idler among: 1850 *Prelude*, VIII, 503

23 standing on the top: 1805 *Prelude*, VI, 354–5

24 my life became: 1805 *Prelude*, III, 339–41

24 A general amendment: Richard Price, *Discourse on the Love of Our Country*, 1789

25 Injuries/Made *him*: 1805 *Prelude*, IX, 301–5, 309–24

26 And when we chanced: 1805 *Prelude*, IX, 511–34

27 spent six weeks in Paris: For a review of Wordsworth's time in France and his affair with Annette Vallon, see Stephen Gill, *William Wordsworth: A Life*, Oxford, 1989, pp.56–67, and K.R. Johnston, *The Hidden Wordsworth*, Norton, 1998, pp.209–38

28 his present mind: 1805 *Prelude*, IX, 581–6, 591–5

28 Come, my friend: For Annette's story see G.M. Harper, *Wordsworth's French Daughter*, OUP, 1931, online at archive.org/stream/wordsworthsfrenc00harp/wordsworthsfrenc00harp_djvu.txt; Émile Legouis, *William Wordsworth and Annette Vallon*, J.M. Dent, London, 1922, online at archive.org/details/williamwordswort027658mbp; Guy Trouillard, ed., *Mémoires de Madame Vallon: souvenirs de la Révolution dans le département de Loir-et-Cher.* Émile-Paul, Paris, 1913

29 dead to deeper hope: 1805 *Prelude*, XI, 24–5

29 borrow the very arms: W.J.B. Owen & J.W. Smyser, *The Prose Works of William Wordsworth*, Vol. I, letter to the Bishop of Llandaff, p.52

30 We are taught: Ibid., p.55

31 I scarcely had: 1805 *Prelude*, X, 371–8

31 a man in the moon: EY, Letter 63, to Francis Wrangham, 25 Feb 1797, p.177

31 *unseeking* manners: CL I, Letter 270, to Sara Coleridge, 14 Jan 1799, p.459

31 We plant cabbages: EY, Letter 60, to William Mathews, 21 Mar 1796, p.169

32 We are now at Racedown: EY, Letter 52, WW to William Mathews, 20 Oct 1794, p.154

32 a weary labyrinth: 1805 *Prelude*, X, 922

32 probe/The living body: 1805 *Prelude*, X, 872, 874–6

32 A baker from Clapton: Joseph Gill's diary, 20 Jun 1796, Mary Moorman, *William Wordsworth: A Biography. The Early Years*, 1957, p.314

33 I have seen the Baker's horse: Butler, *RC & Pedlar*, pp.463–5

34 lecherous, animal & devouring: Quoted in R. White, *John Keats: A Literary Life*, Springer, 2010, 63

34 I tremble with sensations: Wordsworth to Mary, 3–4 Jun 1812, A.G. Hill, ed., *The Letters of William and Dorothy Wordsworth*: Vol. VIII, *A Supplement of New Letters*, Clarendon Press, 1967, pp.109–10

34 he, with his Basin: D. Wordsworth, Grasmere journal, 14 Mar 1802

35 to shew that men: EY, Letter 152, WW to Charles James Fox, 14 Jan 1801, p.315

36 walking by moonlight: EY, Letter 105, WW & DW to STC, 14/21 Dec 1798, p.242

36 lined throughout: EY, Letter 106, DW to Christopher Wordsworth, 3 Feb 1799, p.245

36 a blue spencer: EY, Feb 1802, p.343n

36 The Poet binds together: Butler & Green, Appendix III (1802 addition to LB Preface), p.753

37 Wordsworth & his exquisite Sister: Letter from STC, c. 3 Jul 1797, to Joseph Cottle, quoted in J. Cottle, *Early Recollections*, I, p.252

37 watchful in minutest observation: Ibid.

37 I have the brow: Sandford, Vol. I, p.224n, where the phrase is described as 'A Stowey tradition'

37 He is a *wonderful* man: EY, Letter 70, DW to Mary Hutchinson, Jun 1797, pp.188–9

38 that trembling delicate: R. Gittings, ed., *Letters of John Keats*, OUP, 1970, letter to Benjamin Robert Haydon, 8 Apr 1818, p.83

38 We have been endeared: EY, Letter 28, DW to Jane Pollard, 16 Feb 1793, p.88

39 I too exclusively esteemed: 1805 *Prelude*, XIII, 224–36

39 Neither absence nor Distance: EY, Letter 28, DW to Jane Pollard, 16 Feb 1793, p.88

39 was a kind of gentler: 1805 *Prelude*, XIII, 245–6

40 A quiet shower: DW, Alfoxden journal, 21 Mar 1798

40 simultaneously both hovering: Pamela Woof, 'Dorothy Wordsworth as a Young Woman', *The Wordsworth*

Circle, Vol. XXXVIII, No. 3, The Wordsworth-Coleridge Association Meeting: 2006 (Summer 2007), pp.130–8

40 the moonshine like herrings: DW, Grasmere journal, 31 Nov 1800

40 The Fern of the mountain: DW, Grasmere journal, 12 Sept 1800

40 almost like butterflies: DW, Grasmere journal, 16 Mar 1802

40 unseen birds singing: DW, Alfoxden journal, 1 Mar 1798

40 the strength with which: EY, Letter 30, DW to Mrs Christopher Crackanthorpe, her aunt, 21 Apr 1794, p.117

41 the belovèd woman: 1805 *Prelude*, X, 909–20

42 *She whispered still*: 1850 *Prelude*, XI, 344

42 sexual connection: OED quoting Thomas Malthus, *An essay on the principle of population etc*, 1798

43 Your Br. John: CL I, Letter 299, to DW, 10 Nov 1799, p.543

Chapter 3: *Searching*

45 You see the: For the following passages see Butler, *RC & Pedlar*, pp.84–7, 460, 468–75

46 *spectator ab extra: Specimens of the Table Talk of S. T. Coleridge*, John Murray, London, 1837, Vol. I, pp.61–2 (21 Jul 1832)

47 the grandeur in the beatings: S. Parrish, ed. *The Prelude 1798–1799*, Cornell, 1977, p.46

50 In 'The Ruined Cottage': For the fullest possible exploration of this poem see Butler, *RC & Pedlar*

52 something new in Wordsworth's life: Never more richly explored than in Jonathan Wordsworth's magisterial *The Music of Humanity*, J. & J. Harper Editions, New York, 1969

52 without the application: Butler & Green, Appendix III (LB 1800 Preface), p.746

52 several passages describing: Butler, *RC & Pedlar*, as part of a note dictated by W in 1843 to his friend Isabella Fenwick.

Chapter 4: *Settling*

54 always ... very cautious: CL I, Letter 197, to Robert Southey, c.17 Jul 1797, p.336

55 Jubb along: Holland, MS Journal, Thursday, 30 Jan 1800

56 asked him to remind them: Ibid., Monday, 6 Jan 1817

56 I had an umbrella: Ibid., Sunday, 10 Jan 1802

56 Holland liked to 'church': Over twenty times in the journal, usually at the same time the child was christened.

56 was a shocking place: Holland, MS Journal, Friday, 18 Jul 1800

57 Davies is one of: Ibid.

57 raise vegetables & corn: CL I, Letter 164, 17 Dec 1796 to John Thelwall, p.277

58 crooked earth-ward: STC, 'To the Rev. George Coleridge', ll 58–9, Keach, p.136

58 little Hovel is almost: CL I, Letter 294 to Robert Southey, 30 Sept 1799, p.533

58 an impassable Hog-stye: CL I, Letter 259 to Sara Coleridge, p.436

58 a *Social Colony*: J. Cottle, *Early Recollections, chiefly relating to the late Samuel Taylor Coleridge*, London, 1837, 1.2–4

59 a smartish way: Molly Lefebure, *The Bondage of Love*, new edn, Victor Gollancz, London, 1988, p.23

59 *Toujours gai*: Ibid., p.31

59 polished, calculated light style: Ibid., p.30

59 brown as a berry: Ibid., p.41

59 very neat, gay: Ibid.

60 o'ergrown/With white-flower'd: 'Effusion XXXV', Keach, pp.85–6, lines 3–4, 7–8

61 How exquisite: Lines 9–12

61 And that simplest Lute: Lines12–17

62 And now, its strings: Lines 17–25

62 I feel strongly: CL I, Letter 164, to John Thelwall, 17 Dec 1796, p.279

62 And what if all of: Lines 36–40

63 wishing & praying: CL I, Letter 294, to Robert Southey, 30 Sept 1799, p.534

64 more sinful: Holland, MS Journal, Friday, 29 Dec 1809

65 composing poetry: Sandford, Vol. I, p.239

65 a most amiable: Thomas Poole's verdict on 10 Jun 1792. Ibid., p.25

65 an absent-minded: Cornelia A.H. Crosse, *Red Letter Days of My Life*, R. Bentley & Son, London, 1892, p.99

66 Saw that Democratic hoyden: Holland, MS Journal, Wednesday, 23 Oct 1799

66 Sally Pally: e.g. in CL I, Letter 470, to Sara, 25 Nov 1802, p.886

66 heart-chilling sentiments: CL I, Letter 93, to Southey, 13 Nov 1795 p.172

67 not of a yielding: Sandford, Vol. I, p.24

67 the very top: Holland, MS Journal, Monday, 4 Dec 1809

67 Tom Poole has imbibed: Charlotte Poole's journal for 18 Dec 1792, quoted in Sandford, Vol. I, p.35

67 tore it from his hand: Ibid., pp.36–7

67 Many thousands: Ibid., p.41

68 a declining country: Ibid., p.43

68 to load the higher class: Charlotte Poole's journal for 15 Mar 1796, quoted in ibid., p.136

68 considered by Government: Letter from Poole to Samuel Purkis, 23 Aug 1794, ibid., p.92

68 Now an absolute controul: Ibid., p.93

68 Met the patron: Holland, MS Journal, Wednesday, 23 Oct 1799 (Satan); Thursday, 2 Jan 1806 (shabby); Monday, 17 Jan 1814 (vain)

69 For these opinions: Sandford, Vol. I, p.94n

69 he would rather hear: Ibid., p.101

69 stout of heart: Butler & Green, p.254

70 Where am I to find: CL I, Letter 163, to Thomas Poole, 13 Dec 1796, p.271

70 I adhere to Stowey: Ibid., p.273

70 a small company: Barbara E. Rooke, *The Collected Works of Samuel Taylor Coleridge*, Vol. IV (Part I): *The Friend*,

Princeton University Press, 2016, p.224

71 The thermometer stood: 'Meteorological Journal, Kept at the Apartments of the Royal Society, By Order of the President and Council', *Philosophical Transactions of the Royal Society of London*, Vol. LXXXVIII (1798), pp.1–26

71 walk from place to place: Holland, MS Journal, Tuesday, 19 Nov 1799

72 after supper: Ibid., Wednesday, 2 May 1804

72 to the jogging of: Ibid., Wednesday, 17 Aug 1804

72 After dinner: Ibid., Thursday, 9 Jan 1806

72 the women wore pattens: Ibid.

72 There is everything: EY, Letter 71, DW to an unknown correspondent, probably Mary Hutchinson, 4 Jul 1797, p.189

73 The house is: EY, Letter 72, DW to ?Mary Hutchinson, 14 Aug 1797, pp.190–1

74 covered with the round-faced: William Hazlitt, 'My First Acquaintance With Poets' (first published in *The Liberal*, No. 3, 1823)

76 mild creative breeze: 1805 *Prelude*, I, 43, 48

Chapter 5: *Walking*

80 the ever-present sound '… brooks clear and pebbly as in Cumberland': EY, Letter 71, DW to an unknown correspondent, probably Mary Hutchinson, 4 Jul 1797, p.189

81 so overshadow'd: CN I 213 G. 209, p.217

82 If, looking round: MS Verse 42: PW ii 479–80; also J. Wordsworth, *The Music of Humanity*, J. & J. Harper Editions, New York, 1969, pp.87–8

83 in many a walk: From 'There is creation in the eye', lines 8, 9–16, composed Grasmere Oct–Dec 1800, in *Christabel* notebook DCMS 15 90 v; Butler & Green, p.324

84 Consciousness is given up: Coburn, *Inquiring Spirit*, p.31

84 How warm this woodland: 'Recollections of Love', lines 1–10 in Keach, pp.342–3; another version is in a notebook from 1807, where instead of 'here and there, like things astray' in line 9, Coleridge writes 'upward on the fav'ring wind', which doesn't work with his rhyme scheme but is an acute sensuous memory, ten years later, of listening to the Quantock streams when high above them, their sound brought up in snatches on the changing breeze.

85 always slightly behind: EY, Letter 105, DW to STC, 14 or 21 Dec 1799, p.241: 'I would once more follow at your heels, and hear your dear voices again.'

85 He runs up and down: Virginia Woolf, Monk's House Papers, University of Sussex, notebook 18, 1940

86 The images of the weeds: Coburn, *Inquiring Spirit*, p.37

86 solacing himself: 1850 *Prelude*, IV, 258–67

87 Incumbent o'er the surface: 1850 *Prelude*, IV, 272

87 that *in understanding*: Mary Warnock, *Imagination*, University of California Press, 1978, p.102

87 as *his* world: Ibid., p.105

88 we should remove: CL I, Letter 93, to Robert Southey, 13 Nov 1795, p.163

88 in that nice little: Charles Lamb to Coleridge 1 Dec 1796 in Edwin Marrs, *The Letters of Charles and Mary Anne Lamb*, Vol. I, *Letters of Charles Lamb 1796–1801*, Cornell, 1975, p.65

88 You first kindled: In Lamb's Dedication of his 1818 *Poems* to Coleridge

88 almost immaterial legs: E.V. Lucas, *The Life of Charles Lamb*, Methuen, 1834, p.91, quoting the artist Thomas Hood

88 a light frame: Sir Thomas Noon Talfourd, *The Works of Charles Lamb: Complete in One Volume. With a Sketch of His Life*, Henry Carey Baird, 1857, p.108

89 must have books: C. Lamb, 'Imperfect Sympathies', in *Selected Prose*, Penguin, 2013, p.110; first published in the *London Magazine* in Aug, 1821; see also David Duff, 'Charles Lamb's Art of Intimation', *The Wordsworth Circle*, Vol. XLIII, No. 3 (Summer 2012), pp.127–34

89 content with fragments: C. Lamb, 'Imperfect Sympathies', p.105

89 better far than this: 1805 *Prelude*, I, 250–2

90 The bird a nest: W. Blake, 'Proverbs of Hell', in Sir G. Keynes, *The Marriage of Heaven and Hell* (1790–93) OUP, 1975, p.xviii

90 FRIEND: CL I, Letter 93, to Robert Southey, 13 Nov 1795, p.166

90 friable, incohesive: CL V, 3 Jan 1823, pp.266–7

90 Friendship is sympathy: *Specimens of the Table Talk of the Late Samuel Taylor Coleridge*, Harper & Brothers, 1836, 27 Sept 1830, p.110

91 The Heart, thoroughly: CL I, Letter 141, to Thomas Poole, 24 Sept 1796, p.235

91 Philanthropy (and indeed: CL I, Letter 51, to R. Southey 13 Jul 1794, p.86

91 instinctive Sense of: CN 4, 4730

91 I cannot love: Coburn, *Inquiring Spirit*, p.34

94 in a menacing manner: Sir Thomas Noon Talfourd, *The Works of Charles Lamb: Complete in One Volume. With a Sketch of His Life*, Henry Carey Baird, 1857, p.216

95 May I, can I: E.V. Lucas, *Works of Charles and Mary Lamb*, Vol. VI, *Letters*, Charles Lamb to Coleridge, no date, ?29 Jun 1797, Methuen, 1905, p.107

95 a calm not unlike: Ibid., Charles Lamb to Coleridge, 24 Jun 1797, p.106

95 only by the silence: Ibid., Charles Lamb to Coleridge, 19 or 26 Jul 1797, p.108

96 here he loved to sit: Butler & Green, p.49

97 pride,/Howe'er disguised: Ibid., pp.49–50

98 These half-tortured lines: The dating of different parts of this poem can only be tentative. Butler & Green assumes most of it was written in Dorset in early 1797 and finished before July that year (p.47). Jonathan Wordsworth in *The Music of Humanity*, J. & J. Harper Editions, New York, 1969 (pp.206–7n) suggests that the last part of the poem, which turns towards a Coleridgean sense of a beneficence, is unlikely to have been composed before the Alfoxden period, and may be as late as the early summer of 1798.

98 Well, they are gone: 'This Lime-Tree Bower My Prison', Keach, p.138, lines 1–2

99 The roaring dell: Lines 10–16, p.138

100 for thou hast pined: Lines 28–32, p.139

100 So my Friend: Lines 37–43, p.139

100 A delight/Comes sudden: Lines 43–5, p.139

101 still the solitary: Lines 58–61, pp.139–40

101 when the last rook: Lines 68–9, p.140

101 Flew creeking o'er: Lines 74–6, p.140

102 Mr. Coleridge welcomed me: Joseph Cottle, *Reminiscences of Samuel Taylor Coleridge and Robert Southey*, Houlston and Stoneman, 1847, p.150

102 After the grand circuit: Ibid.

102 While the dappled: Ibid., pp.150–1

Chapter 6: *Informing*

105 an invaluable friend: John Thelwall, 'A Pedestrian Excursion through Several Parts of England and Wales during the Summer of 1797', *Monthly Magazine*, Aug 1799, p.532

105 fraternal band: John Thelwall, 'Lines Written at Bridgewater', in *The Fairy of the Lake: a dramatic romance; Effusions of relative and social feeling: and specimens of The hope of Albion; or, Edwin of Northumbria, an epic poem. With a prefatory memoir of the life of the author*', Printed by W.H. Parker, Sold by West and Hughes, R. Phillips [&c., &c.], 1801, p.129

106 You talk loudly: Coleridge's essay on 'Modern Patriotism' in *The Watchman*, Mar 1796, in *Collected Works*, Vol. II, Princeton, 1970, p.98

106 So should all tyrants: Tim Fulford, *Coleridge's Spiritual Language*, Springer, 1991, p.9

107 his notes and letters: His correspondence and others' can be found in HO 42/41 (Domestic Correspondence George III Jun–Dec 1797), National Archives, Kew

108 of riotous disposition: In HO 43 Domestic Correspondence Aug 1796 to Mar 1797

108 Coastes and Bays: Dundas memorandum in HO 43 Domestic Correspondence Aug 1796 to Mar 1797

109 for treasonable practices: Narrative of the Proceedings of the Messenger, &c. on the Seizure of J. Thelwall's papers; with his Examination before the PRIVY COUNCIL; Treatment at the Messengers, &c. in *The Tribune*, No. IV, Saturday, 4 Apr 1795

110 Jacobin fox: Thelwall's own imagery in the *Champion*, 6 Jun 1819. See E.P. Thompson, 'Hunting the Jacobin Fox', *Past & Present*, No. 142 (Feb 1994), p.102

110 by writing quarto volumes: Thelwall's accusation thrown at William Godwin in *Tribune*, ii (1796), preface, p.xvi

110 He was possessed: *The Complete Works of William Hazlitt*, ed. P.P. Howe, 21 vols (London, 1930–4), xii, *The Plain Speaker*, 'On the Difference between Writing and Speaking', p.264

110 about ninety sailors: For a full account see E.P. Thompson, 'Hunting the Jacobin Fox', *Past & Present*, No. 142 (Feb 1994), pp.98–100

111 mobs attacked him: See E.P. Thompson, p.102

111 Among the subscribers: Ibid., p.99

112 the volume of nature: John Thelwall, *The Peripatetic …* Vol. I, London, 1793, p.10

112 I have been rambling: John Thelwall, *The Tribune, A Periodical Publication, consisting chiefly of the Political Lectures of J. Thelwall*, Taken in Shorthand by W. Ramsey and revised by the Lecturer, London, Vol. II, No. 16 (1796), 'The PRESENT WAR a principal cause of the

STARVING CONDITION of the PEOPLE. The first Lecture "On the causes of the Dearness and Scarcity of Provisions;" delivered by J. Thelwall, Wednesday, 29 Apr 1795, pp.16–17

113 Every question was: *Monthly Magazine*, Sept 1799, p.619

113 inquisitive, shrewd: Ibid.

114 ascendency which people: William Hazlitt, 'My First Acquaintance With Poets' (first published in *The Liberal*, No. 3, 1823)

114 I love a public road: 1805 *Prelude*, XII, 145–52

115 When I began: 1805 *Prelude*, XII, 161–8, 178–83

116 already warm by seven o'clock: Royal Society meteorological journal for Jul 1797

116 Everything but my Stella: Letter, 18 Jul 1797, quoted in Sandford, Vol. I, pp.232–3

117 deficient in that patience: CL I, Letter 200, to Josiah Wade, 1 Aug 1797, p.339

117 During the whole: Thelwall to his wife, 18 Jul 1797, quoted by Kenneth R. Johnston, *Unusual Suspects: Pitt's Reign of Alarm and the Lost Generation of the 1790s*, OUP, 2013, p.238

117 how opposite even then: STC, *Biographia Literaria*, 2 vols, London, 1817. Thelwall's copy is in Fales Library, New York University. See Judith Thompson, *John Thelwall in the Wordsworth Circle*, Palgrave, 2012, for a full analysis of his many annotations. Quoted in John Cornwell, *Coleridge: Poet*

and Revolutionary, 1772–1804: A Critical Biography, Allen Lane, 1973, p.170

118 being carried away: CL, Vol. II, 1000–1, to Sir George and Lady Beaumont, 1 Oct 1803, quoted in Lewis Patton & Peter Mann, eds, STC, *Lectures 1795: On Politics and Religion*, xxviii

118 squeaking baby-trumpet: CL I, Letter 238, to Rev. George Coleridge, 10 Mar 1798, p.397

118 Thought followed thought: J. Thelwall, *The Daughter of Adoption*, 1801, Vol. I, p.283

119 the truth of nature: STC, *Biographia Literaria*, 1817, II, 5

121 lived in a little house: Holland, MS Journal, 21 Mar 1800

121 I thought it unfair: *Specimens of the Table Talk of the Late Samuel Taylor Coleridge*, Harper & Brothers, 1836, 27 Jul 1830

122 a stream, traced: STC, *Biographia Literaria*, 1817, pp.189–90

122 Almost daily: Ibid.

122 Discontent mild as: CN I, note 202

122 Love transforms: STC, *Biographia Literaria*, 1817, p.189

122 the neighing wild-colt: Ibid., p.213

122 the prophetic soul: Ibid., p.214

122 a long deep Lane: Ibid., p.213

122 and affright them: Ibid., p.187

122 from the/Miller's: Ibid., p.213

123 Broad-breasted Pollards: Ibid.

123 Dim specks: Ibid., p.192

123 The swallows interweaving: Ibid., p.213

123 Never to see or describe: CL II, Letter 459, to William Sotheby, 10 Sept 1802

123 The needle trembles: CL IV, to Rest Fenner, Letter 677, 22 Sept 1816

124 incorporating the Reason: Coleridge, *The Statesman's Manual*, London, 1816, p.35

124 his darling hobby-horse: Thelwall to Dr. Crompton, Eton House, Nr. Liverpool, 3 Mar, 1798.

125 a gentry party: See the Rev. Holland's account of a dinner at Alfoxden (with the St Albyns) Tuesday, 13 Aug 1805: 'The day passed off very well: a glorious haunch of venison, a good dinner and everyone in good humour. All the silver and grandeur made their appearance this day, the equipage quite brilliant and the china uncommonly handsome.'

125 particularly unpopular: CL I, Letter 203, to John Chubb, 20 Aug 1797, p.342

125 not already taken: Ibid.

126 the whole Malignity: CL I, Letter 204, to John Thelwall, 21 Aug 1797, p.343

126 You cannot conceive: Ibid.

126 We are shocked: Charlotte Poole's journal, 23 Jul 1797, quoted in Sandford, Vol. I, 235

127 contrived to get possession: The manuscript sources for all letters surrounding the spying affair are in HO 42/41 (Domestic Correspondence George III, Jun–Dec 1797), in National Archives, Kew, from which this and the following letters are transcribed; STC in

Biographia Literaria, Chapter 10, played with the incident; the Home Office correspondence described here was first discovered and published by A.J. Eaglestone in 'Wordsworth, Coleridge, and the Spy' in E. Blunden & E.L. Griggs, eds, *Coleridge: Studies by Several Hands* (London, 1934), pp.73–87. See also Mary Moorman, *William Wordsworth: A Biography. The Early Years*, 1957, pp.329–32; E.P. Thompson, 'Disenchantment or Default? A Lay Sermon', in *Power and Consciousness*, eds C.C. O'Brien & D. Vanech (1969), p.150; Nicholas Roe, 'Who Was Spy Nozy?', *The Wordsworth Circle*, Vol. XV, No. 2 (Spring 1984), pp.46–50 and the section in N. Roe, *Wordsworth and Coleridge: The Radical Years*, Oxford, 1988, pp.248–62, are the best modern studies.

129 Was this the poet?: See Kenneth R. Johnston, *The Hidden Wordsworth: Poet, Lover, Rebel, Spy*, New York: Norton, 1998, for the initial suggestion that the 'Mr Wordsworth' who appeared in Portland's paybook (Grasmere Item 1994.125) was the poet. K.R. Johnston, 'Wordsworth's Mission to Germany: A Hidden Bicentenary?', *The Wordsworth Circle*, Vol. XXX, No. 1 (Winter 1999), pp.15–22, brings more evidence to bear on the theory. By the time of the second edition, now called *The Hidden Wordsworth*,

2000, p.xiii, Professor Johnston had abandoned the idea, a decision he explained in 'A Tale of Two Titles', *Romantic Biography*, ed. Arthur Bradley & Alan Rawes, Aldershot, 2003, p.54

131 and, passing himself off: STC, *Biographia Literaria*, CUP Archive, 1983, p.164

131 Mr Tucker: Holland often identifies Tucker as landlord at the Globe, e.g. Friday, 16 Dec 1799

132 large and tall: Holland, MS Journal: Wednesday, 8 Jan 1806 (fat); Monday, 10 Mar 1800 (insolence)

133 surely a desperd: Joseph Cottle, *Reminiscences of Samuel Taylor Coleridge and Robert Southey*, Houlston & Stoneman, 1848, p.181

134 sick of public turmoil: John Thelwall, 'Lines Written at Bridgewater' in *The Fairy of the Lake: a dramatic romance; Effusions of relative and social feeling: and specimens of The hope of Albion; or, Edwin of Northumbria, an epic poem. With a prefatory memoir of the life of the author*', Printed by W.H. Parker, Sold by West and Hughes, R. Phillips [&c., &c.], 1801, p.129

134 it would be sweet: Ibid., pp.129–30

134 Thy Sara: Ibid., pp.130–1

134 Arcadian Pool: Ibid., p.131

Chapter 7: *Dreaming*

136 He travels on: For this and the following lines and revisions, see Butler & Green, p.273, for a reading text, pp.482–7 for facsimiles of and transcriptions from the notebook

138 with a vast quantity: M.L. Reed, *Wordsworth: The Chronology of the Early Years 1770–1799*, 1967, p.210

139 The barley for malting: Holland, MS Journal: plums 17 Sept 1805; wheat and barley gathered into ricks 3 Sept 1813; threshed 14 Sept 1812; partridges 1 Sept 1818, 22 Sept 1803; dung spread 14 Oct 1804, 15 Oct 1803; honey in the comb for tea 7 Sept 1800; nectarines 9 Sept 1805; hedge shorn 2 Sept 1804; asparagus cut 24 Oct 1804, 16 Oct 1809; strawberries tidied 20 Oct 1800; cabbages hoed 6 Sept 1818; planting winter wheat 23 Oct 1800; first frost 31 Oct 1805; greatcoats 6 Oct 1805; mushrooming 15 Oct 1800

139 The Pooles and their: Holland, MS Journal, 11 Sept 1802

140 frequently *all things* appear: CL I, Letter 209, to John Thelwall, 14 Oct 1797, p.349

140 It is better: Ibid.

140 The hanging Woods: Ibid., quoting *Osorio*, V, i, 8–9

141 in some small skiff: Ibid., p.350

141 At a Farm House: This note and the subsequent quotations are all from the 'Crewe manuscript' of the poem, its earliest surviving state, pre-dating the version published in 1816. Now in the British Library, Add MS 50847. Online in facsimile at

www.bl.uk/collection-items/
manuscript-of-s-t-coleridges-
kubla-khan#

143 the calm oblivious: 'Ruined
Cottage', lines 504–6, Butler,
RC & Pedlar, p.73

144 he summoned Mr Lyng:
Holland, MS Journal, 18 Sept
1804

144 As Victoria Berridge has
described: Victoria Berridge,
'Victorian Opium Eating:
Responses to Opiate Use in
Nineteenth-Century England',
Victorian Studies, 21(4) 1978,
437–61

145 sumptuous house: Facsimile of
the relevant page 418, Chapter
13 of *Purchas his Pilgrimage*,
London, 1626, online at www.
bl.uk/collection-items/purchas-
his-pilgrimage-or-relations-of-
the-world-and-the-religions.
See also *Purchas's Pilgrimes*,
1625, p.80, quoted on the
British Library site, for a longer
description of Xanadu, which
also has verbal echoes of
Coleridge's poem.

145 In Xannadù: 'Crewe
manuscript', lines 1–11

147 But o! that deep: Lines 12–16

147 ~~And from~~ From forth: Lines
17–27

148 the orgasm: *Collected Letters of
Robert Southey, Part 2*, Letter
477, Southey to Coleridge, 16
Jan 1800, www.rc.umd.edu/
editions/southey_letters/Part_
Two/HTML/letterEEd.26.477.
html

148 A damsel with: Lines 37–41

149 Could I revive: Lines 42–7

150 And all, who heard: Lines
48–54

150 be a light sleeper: Jean-Jacques
Rousseau, *Discourse on the
Origin of Inequality* (1755), ed.
and tr. Donald A. Cress,
Hackett, Indianapolis, 1992,
p.24

Chapter 8: *Voyaging*

153 Trees in winter: CN Vol. III,
4468; S. Perry, *Coleridge's
Notebooks: A Selection*, Oxford,
2002, p.132, entry 549.
Difficult to date: ?1818.

154 the robins singing: DW,
Alfoxden journal, 23 Jan
1798

155 afloat and mingling in his
mind: John Livingston Lowes,
*The Road to Xanadu: A Study in
the Ways of the Imagination*,
Houghton Mifflin, 1927

155 To make anything: 'A
Philosophical Enquiry into the
Origin of our Ideas of the
Sublime and the Beautiful',
(1757) in *The Works of the
Right Honourable Edmund
Burke*, Vol. I, J. Dodsley,
London, 1792, Part II, Section
III: Obscurity, p.121

156 seems better to have: Ibid.,
p.122

156 shape,/If shape it might:
Paradise Lost II, 666–9

156 a significant and expressive: 'A
Philosophical Enquiry into the
Origin of our Ideas of the
Sublime and the Beautiful',
(1757) in *The Works of the
Right Honourable Edmund
Burke*, Vol. I, J. Dodsley,
London, 1792, Part II, Section
III: Obscurity, p.122

156 Like one, that on: Coleridge,
The Rime of the Ancyent

Marinere, lines 451–6; Keach, p.161

156 Millions of spiritual creatures: *Paradise Lost* IV, 677–8

157 as a fugitive: King James Bible, 1611, Genesis 4:12

158 pursueth my soul: 'The Wanderings of Cain', online, edited by N. Santilli, at http://www.rc.umd.edu/editions/cain/readingtext.html

158 Thus as he stood: Ibid.

158 Me-thinks I see: Prefatory note to 'The Wanderings of Cain', online, edited by N. Santilli, at http://www.rc.umd.edu/editions/cain/preface.html

159 The evening was dark: EY, Letter 77, DW to ?Mary Hutchinson, 20 Nov 1797, p.194

159 in the autumn of 1797: Jared Curtis, ed., *The Fenwick Notes of William Wordsworth*, London: Bristol Classical Press, 1993, p.2; Keach, p.499

160 As we endeavoured: Ibid., p.3

161 for a mind so eminently: Prefatory note to 'The Wanderings of Cain', online at http://www.rc.umd.edu/editions/cain/preface.html

161 ten thousand times: Quoted in David Vallins, Kaz Oishi, Seamus Perry, *Coleridge, Romanticism and the Orient: Cultural Negotiations*, A&C Black, 2013, p.74

162 like Chaff: Line 48

162 wond'rous cauld: Lines 50–2

162 thro' fog-smoke: Lines 75–6

162 The bloody sun: Lines 107–10

162 The day-light dawn'd: Lines 339–55

163 Wordsworth would, soon enough: Butler & Green, Appendix IV (Wordsworth's Note to *Ancient Mariner* in *Lyrical Ballads* 1800), p.791

164 like a three year's child: Lines 17, 19

164 I fear thee: Lines 216–19

165 The breezes blew: Lines 99–102

166 If the will: *Specimens of the Table Talk of the Late Samuel Taylor Coleridge*, Vol. I, John Murray, 1835, 28 Sept 1830, pp.213–14

166 roused a throng: 'To William Wordsworth', lines 64, 69–70, Keach, p.340. Date uncertain, 1807–15

167 The very deeps: Lines 119–26

167 Beyond the shadow: Lines 264–8

167 Within the shadow: Lines 269–83

168 He prayeth best: Lines 647–50

168 The spirit who 'bideth: Lines 407–14

169 The Marinere, whose eye: Lines 651–8

Chapter 9: *Diverging*

170 A play by 'Monk' Lewis: The play was *The Castle Spectre*, which went through forty-seven performances at Drury Lane between late 1797 and the first half of 1798. Nigel Leask, 'Lewis, Matthew Gregory', *Oxford Dictionary of National Biography* (online edn), Oxford University Press; EY, Letter 84, WW to J.W. Tobin, 6 Mar 1798, p.211n

171 an inward feeling: CL II, Letter 509, to R. Southey, 1 Aug 1803, p.959

171 A sense of weakness: Ibid.

172 When I got there: William Hazlitt's famous essay 'My First Acquaintance with Poets' was first published in *The Liberal*, Apr 1823; now online at ourcivilisation.com, from which this and subsequent quotations are taken

174 To have a genius: Kathleen Coburn, ed., *The Philosophical Lectures of Samuel Taylor Coleridge*, New York, 1949, p.179

175 His thoughts had wings: Hazlitt, 'First Acquaintance'

175 Possessions have I: Wordsworth, 'Home at Grasmere', 1800–1806, Cornell, 1977, ed. Beth Darlington, lines 897–902

177 excitement without the application: Butler & Green, Appendix III, p.746

177 Embodied in the mystery: 1805 *Prelude*, V, 619–21

177 objects recognised: 1805 *Prelude*, V, 628–9

177 proceed from the depth: 1850 *Prelude*, XIII, 311–12

180 I should have written: EY, Letter 105, WW and DW to STC, 14/21 Dec 1798, p.236

181 the obstinate pains: Stephen Parrish, *The Prelude 1798–99*, Cornell, 1977, 164–5

181 a prey to anxiety: CL I, Letter 217, to Josiah Wedgwood, 5 Jan 1798, Vol. I, p.367

181 seas of pain: 'Pain' or 'Sonnet: Composed in Sickness', maybe 1790, line 7, Keach, p.20

181 The hiding places: 1805 *Prelude*, XI, 340–1

182 be considered as: Butler & Green, Appendix III (LB 1802 addition to Preface), p.752

183 Do you not see: R. Gittings, *Letters of John Keats*, OUP, 1970, to George & Georgiana Keats, Apr 1819, p.250

183 had hardly known: A. de Vere, 'Recollections of Wordsworth', *Essays Chiefly on Poetry*, Macmillan, 1887, Vol. II, pp.267–8

185 Why is it we feel: DCMS 14 20v; Butler, *RC & Pedlar*, pp.120–1

185 In all forms: DCMS 14 23v; Butler & Green, pp.530–1

186 Transfigured by: DCMS 14 21r; Butler, *RC & Pedlar*, pp.122–3

187 And thought of that poor woman: DCMS 14 15r; Butler, *RC & Pedlar*, pp.110–11

187 And thought of that poor woman as of one: In the Alfoxden notebook the added phrase 'as of one' is in a slightly lighter ink than the words of the lines as they first stood, and are fitted awkwardly into the margins of the page.

187 Of unknown modes: DCMS 14 21r; Butler, *RC & Pedlar*, pp.122–3

187 ~~There would he~~ wander: DCMS 14 15v and a revised version on 20r; Butler, *RC & Pedlar*, 112–13 and 118–19

188 The winds watched over: Wallace Stevens, 'The World as Meditation', *Selected Poems*, ed. J.N. Serio, Knopf, 2009, p.292, line 12

188 He lov'd to contemplate: DCMS 14 16r; Butler, *RC & Pedlar*, pp.114–15

188 Oh listen listen: DCMS 14 15v; Butler, *RC & Pedlar*, pp.112–13

189 I lived without: DCMS 14 21v; Butler, *RC & Pedlar*, pp.124–5

189 ~~In~~ To every natural: *Ruined Cottage* MS B 16r; Butler, *RC & Pedlar*, pp.180–1

189 Are there no: Butler & Green, p.284; DCMS 14 21v; facsimile in Butler, *RC & Pedlar*, p.124

190 Away away: Butler & Green, pp.530–1; DCMS 14 23v

191 and beneath the star: Butler & Green, p.286; DCMS 14 23v, facsimile and transcription pp.530–1

191 Many a time: Butler, *RC & Pedlar*, pp.170–1; *Ruined Cottage* MS B 13 v

191 I love upon: DCMS 16 89v–90 r; see *Peter Bell*, ed. J.E. Jordan, Cornell, 1975, pp.629–31

191 Sensation, soul and form: *Ruined Cottage* MS B 9r; Butler, *RC & Pedlar*, pp.156–7

193 The green paths: DW, Alfoxden journal, 20 Jan 1798, in P. Woof, ed., *The Grasmere and Alfoxden Journals*, Oxford, 2002, p.141

193 to rectify men's feelings: EY, Letter 170 to John Wilson, 7 Jun 1802, p.355

193 Those oaks fanned by: DW, Alfoxden journal, 21–23 Jan 1798, Woof, p.141

194 We attribute this: DW, Alfoxden journal, 23 Jan 1798, Woof, pp.141–2

194 I have often tried: *Letters of William and Dorothy Wordsworth*, Vol. II, pp.24–5,

quoted Nicola Healey, *Dorothy Wordsworth and Hartley Coleridge: The Poetics of Relationship*, Macmillan, 2012, p.216

194 The manufacturer's dog: DW, Alfoxden journal, 27 Jan 1798, Woof, pp.142–3

195 The trees almost: DW, Alfoxden journal, 1 Feb 1798, Woof, pp.143–4

196 more literal Fricker: As quoted by her daughter Sara in Earl Leslie Griggs, *Coleridge Fille: A Biography of Sara Coleridge*, Oxford, 1940, pp.105–6

196 his privileged role: Lefebure, p.87

197 She was all fire: Thomas De Quincey, *Recollections of the Lakes and the Lake Poets*, Cambridge, 2013, pp.190–1

197 greater enthusiasm: Griggs, *Coleridge Fille*, p.106

197 Often it would: De Quincey, *Recollections of the Lakes and the Lake Poets*, p.64

198 Mrs. Coleridge viewed: Ibid., pp.64–5

199 The sky spread over: DW, Alfoxden journal, 25 Jan 1798, Woof, p.142

199 spread out/a broad: Butler & Green, pp.276–7; DCMS 14 inside front cover, Butler & Green, pp.498–9 for photo and transcription

200 A Fragment: Butler & Green, DCMS 15 2r, pp.500–1 for photo and transcription

Chapter 10: *Mooning*

202 When shape was: Stephen Parrish, *The Prelude 1798–99*, Cornell, 1977, pp.74–5

203 Without a touch: Butler &
Green, DCMS 14 2r,
pp.502–3 for photo and
transcription
204 Howeer disguised: Ibid.,
DCMS 11 17v, pp.478–9
204 the gaudiness and inane: Ibid.,
Appendix III, pp.738–9
207 the hawthorn hedges: DW,
Alfoxden journal, 31 Jan 1798,
Woof, p.143
207 She would sit: Ibid., 1 Feb
1798, Woof, p.144
207 a silvery line: Ibid., 18 Feb
1798, Woof, p.146
207 the moon, a many-coloured:
Ibid., 27 Apr 1798, Woof, p.152
207 While the twilight: Ibid., 26
Feb 1798, Woof, p.148
208 young lasses: Ibid., 4 Feb 1798,
Woof, p.144
209 Met a soldier: Holland, MS
Journal, 28 Jul 1813
209 Wm. and I walked: DW,
Alfoxden journal, 22 Feb 1798,
Woof, p.147
209 'The Discharged Soldier': For
the many drafts and early
versions of 'The Discharged
Soldier' from which these pages
are taken see Butler & Green,
pp.277–82; for DCMSS 14,
15 and 16, see photographs
and transcriptions pp.502–23
212 strange and uncouth: Butler,
RC & Pedlar, p.165; DCMS
17 12 r, 3–6

Chapter 11: *Remembering*
216 Basil is a charming boy: EY,
Letter 55, DW to Jane
Marshall, 30 Nov 1795, p.160
217 When I told him: CL I, Letter
294 to Southey, 30 Sept 1799,
p.536

217 a very Seraph: CL I, Letter 182
to Josiah Wade, 16 Mar 1797,
p.181; Letter 342, to
Humphry Davy, 25 Jul 1800,
p.612
217 Splother! splother! splother!:
HNC *Table Talk* Workbook,
14 Aug 1833; STC, *Poetical
Works* Vol. I, Part 2, ed. J.C.C.
Mays, Princeton UP, 2001,
p.638
217 Babies touch *by taste*: CN I,
924
217 Hartley fell down: CN I,
2192
218 Hartley, just able: CN I, 918
218 Hartley's intense wish: CN I,
959
218 I hear his voice: CL, Letter
343, to James Webbe Tobin, 25
Jul 1800, p.614
218 all the *Cake* was eat up: CN I,
1643
220 We obtained a temporary
image: *Mechanics' Magazine*
(London), Saturday, 9 Feb
1839, Vol. XXX (No. 809),
pp.327–8
220 The copy of a painting: Sold at
the house of the Institution,
Albemarle Street; by Cadell &
Davies, Strand; Johnson, St.
Paul's Churchyard; Longman
& Rees, & H.D. Symonds,
Paternoster Row, 1802
221 that which is about to be:
S.T. Coleridge, *Aids to
Reflection*, George Bell, 1884,
p.166
221 an ever industrious Penelope:
CN II, 2351
222 a host of half-formed: T.
Wedgwood to William
Godwin, Jul 1797, quoted in
Reggie Watters, "'A limber

elf": Coleridge and the Child',
The Coleridge Bulletin, New
Series No 9, Spring 1997,
pp.2–24

222 one, or two, superintendents:
David Erdman, 'Coleridge,
Wordsworth, and the
Wedgwood Fund', *Bulletin of
New York Public Library*, Vol.
LX (1956)

223 My aim is high: Ibid.

224 must have the ear: CL II,
Letter 810, to William
Sotheby, 13 Jul 1802

224 Let us not therefore: R.
Gittings, *Letters of John Keats*,
OUP, 1970, letter to J.H.
Reynolds, 19 Feb 1818,
pp.66–7

224 Till a child is four years old:
EY, Letter 93, DW to Mrs
William Rawson, p.222

225 a stout fellow: Ibid., p.221

225 one tale of which: CL I, Letter
208, to Thomas Poole, 9 Oct
1797, p.347

226 I read every book: CL I, Letter
210, to Thomas Poole, 16 Oct
1797, p.354

226 For from my early reading:
Ibid.

227 And so the babe: 'The Foster-
Mother's Tale', Keach, pp.140–
2, lines 28–32

228 Till his brain turned: Lines
43–4

228 He went on shipboard: Lines
72–4, 75–81

229 saw the hills: *Ruined Cottage*
MS B 4v; Butler, *RC & Pedlar*,
p.145

229 time of unrememberable being:
DCMS 19 Zr; Stephen Parrish,
The Prelude 1798–99, Cornell,
1977, pp.114–15

229 So the foundations: *Ruined
Cottage* MS B 4v; Butler, *RC &
Pedlar*, p.145

230 he had felt the power: *Ruined
Cottage* MS B 8r; Butler, *RC &
Pedlar*, pp.154–5

230 Oh! then what soul: *Ruined
Cottage* MS B 9r; Butler, *RC &
Pedlar*, pp.154–7

231 Sensation, soul and form: Ibid.,
pp.156–7

231 He did not feel: Ibid.

231 His mind was: Ibid.

231 But in the mountains: *Ruined
Cottage* MS B 10r; Butler, *RC
& Pedlar*, pp.158–9

232 I should not think of: CL I,
Letter 184, to J. Cottle, early
Apr 1797, pp.320–1

233 I have written 1300 lines: EY,
Letter 84, WW to J.W. Tobin,
6 Mar 1798, p.212

233 tolerably industrious: EY,
Letter 85, WW to J. Losh, 11
Mar 1798, p.214

233 that mighty Orb: *Ruined
Cottage* MS B 10v; Butler, *RC
& Pedlar*, pp.160–1; *The
Excursion*, Book I, line 249

233 Not useless do I deem: *Ruined
Cottage* MS B 46r; Butler, *RC
& Pedlar*, pp.260–1

234 All things shall live: *Ruined
Cottage* MS B 50r; Butler, *RC
& Pedlar*, pp.268–9

234 The old man ceased: *Ruined
Cottage* MS B 52r; Butler, *RC
& Pedlar*, pp.274–5

235 his thoughts now flowing:
Ruined Cottage MS B 46r;
Butler, *RC & Pedlar*,
pp.260–1

235 with bliss ineffable: *Ruined
Cottage* MS B 14r; Butler, *RC
& Pedlar*, pp.172–3

235 six or seven degrees below freezing: 'Meteorological Journal, Kept at the Apartments of the Royal Society, By Order of the President and Council', *Philosophical Transactions of the Royal Society of London*, Vol. LXXXIX (1799), p.4

236 A deep snow upon the ground: DW, Alfoxden journal, 17 Feb 1798, Woof, p.146

237 The frost performs it's: Keach, pp.231–3, lines 1–7; text from facsimile of 1798 edition of *Fears in Solitude*, Jo Johnson, London, Woodstock Books, Oxford, 1989, pp.19–23

237 'Tis calm indeed!: Lines 8–13

238 The thin blue flame: Lines 13–25

239 Ah me! amus'd by: Lines 26–40

240 Dear babe, that sleepest: Lines 49–56

240 For I was rear'd: Lines 56–63

241 inheritance derived to us: *The Works of Edmund Burke*, Vol. I, Harper & Brothers, 1847, p.469

241 our hearths: Ibid., p.470

241 Therefore all seasons: Lines 470–9

242 Like those, my babe!: Lines 480–5

Chapter 12: *Emerging*

244 trailing their wreathes: 'Lines Written in Early Spring', lines 9–10, Butler & Green, p.76

245 had been able to lie down: DW, Alfoxden journal, 3 Mar 1798

246 playing outside on the 10th: Ibid., 10 Mar 1798

246 mild if damp Atlantic air: 'Meteorological Journal, Kept at the Apartments of the Royal Society, By Order of the President and Council', Source: *Philosophical Transactions of the Royal Society of London*, Vol. LXXXIX (1799), pp.1–26, published by Royal Society

247 It is the first mild day: 'Lines written at a small distance from my House', lines 1–4, Butler & Green, p.63

247 There is a blessing: Lines 5–8

247 My sister!: Lines 9–12

248 Edward will come: Lines 13–16

248 No joyless forms: Lines 17–20

248 Love, now an universal birth: Lines 21–24

248 A Poet's *Heart*: CL II, Letter 459, to William Sotheby, 10 Sept 1802, p.863

249 Some silent laws: Lines 29–32

249 Then come, my sister!: Lines 36–40

250 writing the first part: Keach, 'Christabel', Part I, pp.188–96

251 And hark again!: Lines 2–5, 12

251 Is the Night: Lines 14–22

251 The Sighs she heaved: Lines 32–4

251 There she sees: Lines 58–65

252 They chok'd my Cries: Line 83

252 drawing in her breath: Lines 247–53

252 lay down by: Lines 262–70

253 know but not accommodate: See Mary Jacobus, *Tradition and Experiment in Wordsworth's Lyrical Ballads* (1798), Oxford, 1976, p.37

253 The story: An anonymous review in *The Times*, London, 20 May 1816, p.3. See David

V. Erdman, 'A New Discovery: The First Review of "Christabel"', *Texas Studies in English*, Vol. XXXVII (1958), pp.53–60. Probably by Henry Crabb Robinson. See also Jonas Spatz, 'The Mystery of Eros: Sexual Initiation in Coleridge's "Christabel"', *PMLA*, Vol. XC, No. 1 (Jan 1975), pp.107–16

Chapter 13: *Polarising*

254 towards the poetry of this world: See Mary Jacobus, *Tradition and Experiment in Wordsworth's Lyrical Ballads* (1798), p.7

254 'Tis a strange assertion: CL I, Letter 274, to Thomas Poole, 6 Apr 1799, p.479

255 Twins almost in genius: *Prelude*, VI, 263, 267–8

256 During the first year: STC, *Biographia Literaria*, 1817, Vol. II, p.1

256 The sudden charm: Ibid.

256 The thought suggested: Ibid., pp.1–2

257 In this idea: Ibid., pp.2–3

259 as linguistically radical: See Robert Mayo, 'The Contemporaneity of the Lyrical Ballads', *PMLA*, Vol. LXIX, No. 3 (Jun 1954), pp.486–522 for the precursors of the *Lyrical Ballads* in contemporary magazines.

259 seeming simplicity: William Hazlitt, *Lectures on the English Poets* and *The Spirit of the Age*, Oxford, 1970, p.253

260 On the very top of the ridge: Scholars in the past (see Butler & Green, p.350) have identified other places as the location of the thorn, but Bicknoller Post seems the most likely location to me. The four necessary ingredients – thorns, muddy pool, mossy mounds and a path – are found nowhere else in the Quantocks in this combination. Nor are the mounds new: on the Ordnance Survey's nineteenth-century twenty-five-inch maps they are labelled with the abbreviation 'Und.' – undulations. None of the present thorns will be the tree Wordsworth saw, but they could well be its descendants. The clinching piece of evidence is that in her journal on 20 Apr 1798 DW records passing the thorn and the 'little muddy pond' on the way back to Alfoxden, taking 'the Crookham way'. Bicknoller Post lies on the way to Alfoxden from Crowcombe. None of the other suggested places does.

260 And she is known: Lines 69–77, Butler & Green, p.79

261 Not five yards: Lines 27–33, Butler & Green, p.78

261 publicly criticised: STC, *Biographia Literaria*, 1817, Vol. II, p.139 for 'laborious minuteness'; E.J. Morley, *Henry Crabb Robinson on Books and their Writers*, London, 1938, I, 166 for absurdity; 'ought to be liked' in Helen Darbishire, *The Poet Wordsworth*, Oxford, 1950, p.49; Wordsworth in 1820 changed the lines describing

the size of the pond to 'Though but of compass small, and bare/To thirsty suns, and parching air.' Both less interesting and less memorable.

262 The Bards: Henry Charles Duffin, *Walter de la Mare: A Study of His Poetry*, Ardent Media, 1969, p.160

263 a mass of knotted joints: Lines 210–20, Butler & Green, pp.83–4

264 And he is lean: 'Simon Lee', lines 33–6, Butler & Green, p.66

264 My gentle reader: Lines 69–72

265 O reader!: Lines 73–80

265 The mattock totter'd: Lines 97–104

266 On to the top: Holland, MS Journal, 10 Jul 1800

267 in the groves of Alfoxden: Note dictated to Isabella Fenwick, Butler & Green, p.354

267 She listens: 'The Idiot Boy', lines 292–6, Butler & Green, p.99

268 Perhaps he's turned: Lines 332–41, p.100

268 I to the muses: Lines 347–51, p.101

269 She looks again: Lines 382–6, p.102

Chapter 14: *Delighting*

270 The simplicity and naturalness: CL I, Letter 225, to Wordsworth, 23 Jan 1798, p.379

271 this lady appeared: R. Randall, *The Life and Memoirs of Elizabeth Chudleigh: Afterwards Mrs. Hervey and Countess of Bristol, Commonly Called Duchess of Kingston. Written*

from Authentic Information and Original Documents, London, 1788, p.10

271 A day it was: 'Anecdote for Fathers', lines 13–16, Butler & Green, p.71

272 Our quiet house: Lines 6–8

272 I have a boy: Lines 1–4

272 Liswyn farm: The name of the farm in the valley of the Wye to which John Thelwall had retreated

272 In careless mood: Lines 32–5

273 Now, little Edward: Lines 36–60

274 fine little ducks: Holland, MS Journal: 4 May 1800 for ducks; 17 May 1800 for gleams; 21 May 1800 for flying clouds; 7 May 1803 for broccoli seed; 13 May 1803 for birds' nests; 7 May 1803 for cucumbers; 3 May 1804 for kidney beans

274 The cow, being furious: Holland, MS Journal, 26 May 1800

276 In stale blank verse: CL I, Letter 244, to WW, 10 May 1798, p.406

277 capricious passagings: Keach, pp.244–7, lines 1–13; 59–62

277 There are no nightingales: David K. Ballance, *A History of the Birds of Somerset*, Isabelline Books, Penryn, 2006, p.256; E.M. Palmer & D.K. Ballance, *The Birds of Somerset*, Longmans, London, 1968, p.156, quoting Anon, *Lyrical Ballads*, London, 1798

277 Farewell, O Warbler!: Lines 87–105

278 already almost as large: CL I, Letter 246, to T. Poole, 14 May 1798, p.408

279 I have had many sorrows: CL I, Letter 245, to J.P. Estlin, 14 May 1798, p.407

279 So many unpleasant: CL I, Letter 249, to T. Poole, 20 May 1798, p.411

279 infirmities have been: CL I, Letter 248, to John Prior Estlin, 18 May 1798, p.410

280 I arrived, and was: Hazlitt, 'First Acquaintance'

280 Wordsworth himself was: Ibid.

281 could hear the loud stag: Ibid.

281 and the sense of: Ibid.

281 His philosophic poetry: Ibid.

282 He lamented that: Ibid.

282 He answered in some degree: Ibid.

283 comico-lugubrious peculiarities: *The Edinburgh Monthly*, 2, 1819, pp.654–6; quoted in John E. Jordan, 'Wordsworth's Most Wonderful as Well as Admirable Poem', *The Wordsworth Circle*, Vol. XXXVII, No. 3 (Summer 2006), pp.116–22

283 Wordsworth, looking out: 'First Acquaintance'

283 We called for: J. Cottle, *Reminiscences of Samuel Taylor Coleridge and Robert Southey*, London, 1847, pp.182–3

284 We were now summoned: Ibid., pp.184–5

285 There is a chaunt: Hazlitt, 'First Acquaintance'

286 landlady, who is only: Karl Philipp Moritz, *Travels, Chiefly on Foot, Through Several Parts of England, in 1782: Described in Letters to a Friend*, London, 1797, p.38

286 It was a queer thing: For these and following records, see H.

D. Rawnsley, 'Reminiscences of Wordsworth among the Peasantry of Westmoreland', in William Knight (ed.), *Wordsworthiana* (London, 1889), pp.81–119, reprinted Dillon's, London, 1968

287 The eye it cannot chuse: 'Expostulation and Reply', lines 17–24, Butler & Green, p.108

288 there is a holy indolence: DCMS 14 16r; Butler, *RC & Pedlar*, pp.114–15

288 Up! up! my friend: 'The Tables Turned', lines 1–4, Butler & Green, pp.108–9

289 The sun, above: Ibid., lines 5–8, p.109

289 Books!: Ibid., lines 9–12, 21–33, p.109

291 belovèd friend: 1805 *Prelude*, XIII, 390–410

291 first/Together wantoned: 1850 *Prelude*, XIV, 420–1

292 The ears of: Hazlitt, 'First Acquaintance'

292 His genius at that time: William Hazlitt, *Lectures on the English Poets: Delivered at the Surrey Institution*, Taylor & Hessey, Fleet Street, 1818, p.330

293 We loitered on: 'First Acquaintance'

293 the 'ribbed sea-sands': Hazlitt by 1823 had of course read *The Ancient Mariner*.

294 Seaward, white-gleaming: Keach, p.356, tentatively dated to May 1814; Richard Holmes, equally tentatively, dates it twenty years earlier. CN, Vol. III, entry 4194

Chapter 15: *Authoring*

296 My dear Cottle: CL I, Letter 250, to J. Cottle, 28 May 1798, p.411

297 As to anonymous: Ibid., p.412

297 No doubt you have heard: EY, Letter 84, to J.W. Tobin, 6 Mar 1798, p.211

298 It is chilling: CL I, Letter 217, to Josiah Wedgwood, 5 Jan 1798, p.367

298 We have no particular: EY, Letter 84, to J.W. Tobin, 6 Mar 1798, p.211

298 The Giant Wordsworth: CL I, Letter 235, to Joseph Cottle, 7 Mar 1798, p.391

299 I have now known him: CL I, Letter 248, to John Prior Estlin, 18 May 1798, p.410

299 On one subject: Ibid.

300 he that is not against us: Mark 9:40

300 If I cast out devils: Matthew 12: 28–32

301 The Wordsworths have: CL I, Poole to STC, 8 Oct 1798, p.419n

301 continue separated: Ibid.

301 I am sure: CL I, Letter 268, STC to WW, Dec 1798, p.453

301 You charge me with: CL I, Letter 330, to Thomas Poole, 31 Mar 1800, p.584

302 a garbled factoid: Ruth I. Aldrich, 'The Wordsworths and Coleridge: "Three Persons", but Not "One Soul"', *Studies in Romanticism*, Vol. II, No. 1 (Autumn 1962), pp.61–3

302 I saw so many People: CL, Vol. II Letter 775, to William Godwin, 19 Nov 1801; quoted by Aldrich, pp.61–2

Chapter 16: *Arriving*

304 that Dear and beautiful: EY, Letter 93, DW to Mrs William Rawson, 3 Jul 1798, p.223

304 The house was too damp: EY, Letter 100, WW to Poole, 3 Oct 1798, p.231

304 We talk of being: EY, Letter 93, DW to Mrs William Rawson, 3 Jul 1798, p.223

307 I am writing: Ibid.

308 boarded a boat: For the geography of the poem see David S. Miall, 'Locating Wordsworth: "Tintern Abbey" and the Community with Nature', *Romanticism on the Net*, 20, Nov 2000; John Bard McNulty, 'Wordsworth's Tour of the Wye: 1798', *Modern Language Notes*, 60 (1945), pp.291–5; and Donald E. Hayden, *Wordsworth's Travels in Wales and Ireland*, University of Tulsa Press, Tulsa OK, 1985

309 the dingy beings: Richard Warner, *A Walk Through Wales, in August 1797*, C. Dilly, London, 1798, p.232

309 bosomed high: Ibid., p.222, quoting Milton's *L'Allegro*

310 and yet once again: Butler & Green, p.274

312 Five years have passed: 'Lines written a few Miles above Tintern Abbey', lines 1–4, in Butler & Green, pp.739, 116–20

312 These plots of: Lines 11–19

313 Though absent long: Lines 23–36

314 shapes/Of joyless daylight: Lines 36–50

315 when the fretful stir: Lines 53–8

315 more like a man: Lines 76–81
315 For I have learned: Lines 89–103
316 Vegetables are not sublime: 'A Philosophical Enquiry into the Origin of our Ideas of the Sublime and the Beautiful' (1757) in *The Works of the Right Honourable Edmund Burke*, Vol. I, J. Dodsley, London, 1792, Section XV: 'Gradual VARIATION', pp.99–100
317 All general privations: Section VI, 'PRIVATION', p.50
318 this green earth: Lines 103–12
319 thou my dearest Friend: Lines 117–20
319 this prayer I make: Lines 122–35
320 let the moon: Lines 135–43
321 Wordsworth pleasant: James Losh, journal, 10 Jun 1798
321 My many weaknesses: CL I, Letter 277, to Thomas Poole, 6 May 1799, p.491

Chapter 17: *Leaving*
322 Not a line of it: Jared Curtis, ed., *The Fenwick Notes of William Wordsworth*, Bristol Classical Press, London, 1993, p.4
322 William's poems are now: EY, Letter 95, DW to unknown correspondent, p.226
322 the physical book: For an outstanding discussion of this physical book see Alan D. Boehm, 'The "1798 Lyrical Ballads" and the Poetics of Late Eighteenth-Century Book Production', *English Literary History*, Vol. LXIII, No. 2 (Summer 1996), pp.453–87

322 a simple eighteen lines: CL I, Letter 250, to J. Cottle, 28 May 1798, p.412
323 It is the honourable: Butler & Green, p.739
323 An accurate taste: Ibid.
324 The majority of: Ibid., p.738
325 while they are perusing: Ibid., p.739
325 partakes of: William Hazlitt, 'Mr Wordsworth', in *The Spirit of the Age* (1825), Oxford, 1970, Essay 9, online at http://www.blupete.com/Literature/Essays/WorksHaz.htm
325 moments of fretfulness: CL I, Letter 275, 8 Apr 1799, p.483
326 Have you seen: Robert Southey to William Taylor, 5 Sept 1798, in *The Collected Letters of Robert Southey*, Part II, 1798–1803, Letter 347, online at https://www.rc.umd.edu/editions/southey_letters/Part_Two/HTML/letterEEd.26.347.html
327 And it is their names: Robert W. Daniel, 'The Publication of the "Lyrical Ballads"', *The Modern Language Review*, Vol. XXXIII, No. 3 (Jul 1938), pp.406–10; James A. Butler, 'Wordsworth, Cottle, and the "Lyrical Ballads": Five Letters, 1797–1800', *The Journal of English and Germanic Philology*, Vol. LXXV, No. 1/2 (Jan–Apr 1976), pp.139–53
328 on account of it: See Robert W. Daniel, 'The Publication of the "Lyrical Ballads"', *The Modern Language Review*, Vol. XXXIII, No. 3 (Jul 1938), pp.406–10
329 Two rooms: Clare Williams, *Sophie in London, 1786: Being*

the Diary of Sophie v. la Roche, with a foreword by G.M. Trevelyan, Cape, 1933, pp.75–6

329 the Post Office packet: See POST 4/25–29 and POST 4/1–15 in the Royal Mail Archive, Postal Museum Archives, Phoenix Place, London WC1X 0DA for details of the Cuxhaven packets

329 there are Frenchmen, Danes: Coleridge's listing of the fifteen passengers and two servants nearly matches the Post Office's own account book, in which fourteen whole tickets and three halves were sold for this packet by Richard Warmington, their Yarmouth agent. Coleridge had mistaken

one servant for a full-fare-paying gentleman. POST 4/25 Harwich and Yarmouth Packet Stations, Passenger, Freight and Agents' Accounts 1793–1800

330 My dear dear Babies: CL I, Letter 256, to Sara Coleridge, 3 Oct 1798, p.420

330 Chester began to look: Ibid., pp.420–1

330 Chester was ill: CN Vol. I, entry 335

331 Well, I drank: Ibid., p.421

331 (Dane) Vat imagination!: Ibid., pp.421–2

332 a weighty, long: Ibid., p.425

332 The Ocean is: CL I, Letter 254, to Sara Coleridge, 18 Sept 1798, p.416; CN Vol. I, entry 335

BIBLIOGRAPHY

Manuscript Sources
National Archives, Kew
HO 42/41 Home Office Domestic Correspondence George III Jun–Dec
  1797
HO 43 Home Office Domestic Correspondence Aug 1796 to Mar 1797

Postal Museum Archives
POST 4/25–29 Harwich and Great Yarmouth: passenger, freight
  (including bullion) and Agents' accounts
POST 4/1–15 Agents' accounts, packet stations and ports in the United
  Kingdom, Europe, West Indies and Canada

Somerset Heritage Centre
William Holland's Journal A/BTL/2, The journals of William Holland,
  vicar of Over Stowey, transcribed by Peter Stone and Stella Mathias and
  edited by David Worthy

University of Sussex
Virginia Woolf, Monk's House Papers, University of Sussex, Notebook
  18, 1940

Maps
OS Explorer 1:25,000:
140: Quantock Hills & Bridgwater
141: Cheddar Gorge & Mendip Hills West
153: Weston-Super-Mare & Bleadon Hill
154: Bristol West & Portishead
OL 9: Exmoor: Barnstaple, Lynton, Minehead & Dulverton
OL 14: Wye Valley & Forest of Dean/Dyffryn Gwy a Forest y Ddena

PRIMARY TEXTS

Wordsworths

James Butler, ed., *The Ruined Cottage and The Pedlar*, Cornell, 1979

James Butler & Karen Green, *Lyrical Ballads and Other Poems 1797–1800 by William Wordsworth*, Cornell, 1992

Jared Curtis, ed., *The Fenwick Notes of William Wordsworth*, Bristol Classical Press, 1993

Beth Darlington, ed., *Wordsworth, 'Home at Grasmere', 1800–1806*, Cornell, 1977

E. de Selincourt, *The Letters of William and Dorothy Wordsworth*, 2nd edn, rev. C.L. Shaver, Vol. I, *The Early Years 1787–1805*, Oxford, 1967

A.G. Hill, ed., *The Letters of William and Dorothy Wordsworth*, Vol. VIII, *A Supplement of New Letters*, Clarendon Press, 1967

J.E. Jordan, *William Wordsworth: Peter Bell*, Cornell, 1975

Robert Osborn, *The Borderers by William Wordsworth*, Cornell, 1982

W.J.B. Owen & J.W. Smyser, *The Prose Works of William Wordsworth*, Humanites-Ebooks, 2013

S. Parrish, *The Prelude 1798–1799*, Cornell, 1977

P. Woof, ed., *Dorothy Wordsworth: The Grasmere and Alfoxden Journals*, Oxford, 2002

J. Wordsworth, M.H. Abrams & S. Gill, *The Prelude 1799, 1805, 1850*, Norton, London, 1979

Coleridges

Kathleen Coburn, ed., *The Philosophical Lectures of Samuel Taylor Coleridge*, New York, 1949

Kathleen Coburn, ed., *Inquiring Spirit: A New Presentation of Coleridge and Unpublished Prose Writings*, New York, Pantheon, 1951

Kathleen Coburn, *The Notebooks of Samuel Taylor Coleridge, Vol. I, 1794–1804*, Routledge, London, 1957

Kathleen Coburn, *The Notebooks of Samuel Taylor Coleridge, Vol. I, 1794–1804, Notes*, Routledge, London (1957), 2002

S.T. Coleridge, *Fears in Solitude*, Jo Johnson, London (1798), facsimile from Woodstock Books, Oxford, 1989

S.T. Coleridge, *Poems*, selected by James Fenton, Faber, London, 2006

S.T. Coleridge, *The Complete Poems*, ed. William Keach, Penguin, Harmondsworth, 1997

S.T. Coleridge, *Selected Poems*, ed. Richard Holmes, HarperCollins, London, 1996, p.257

S.T. Coleridge, *Poetical Works*, ed. J.C.C. Mays, Princeton, 2001

S.T. Coleridge, *Aids to Reflection*, George Bell, London, 1884

S.T. Coleridge, *Biographia Literaria*, 2 vols, London, 1817

S.T. Coleridge, 'Modern Patriotism' in *The Watchman*, Mar 1796, in *Collected Works*, Vol. II, Princeton, 1970

Bibliography

S.T. Coleridge, *Notes and Lectures on Shakespeare* (1818), New York, 1868

S.T. Coleridge, *Specimens of the Table Talk of S.T.Coleridge*, London, John Murray, 1837

E.L. Griggs, *Collected Letters of Samuel Taylor Coleridge*, Vol. I, 1795–1800, Clarendon Press, Oxford, 1956 (1966)

Lewis Patton, ed., *The Watchman*, Princeton, 1970

L. Patton & P. Mann, eds, STC, *Lectures 1795: On Politics and Religion*, Princeton UP, 1971

S. Perry, ed., *Coleridge's Notebooks: A Selection*, Oxford, 2002

Stephen Potter, *Minnow Among Tritons: Mrs S.T. Coleridge's Letters to Thomas Poole 1799–1834*, Nonesuch, London, 1934

Barbara E. Rooke, ed., *Collected Works of Samuel Taylor Coleridge*, Vol. IV (Part I): *The Friend*, Princeton University Press, 2016

Contemporaries in Somerset

Alfred Ainger, *The Letters of Charles Lamb*, London, 1904

Gregory Claeys, ed., *The Politics of English Jacobinism: Writings of John Thelwall*, Pennsylvania State University Press, 1995

J. Cottle, *Early Recollections, chiefly relating to the late Samuel Taylor Coleridge*, London, 1837

J. Cottle, *Reminiscences of Samuel Taylor Coleridge and Robert Southey*, London, 1847

Cornelia A.H. Crosse, *Red Letter Days of My Life*, R. Bentley & Son, London, 1892

Thomas De Quincey, *Recollections of the Lakes and the Lake Poets*, Cambridge, 2013

William Hazlitt, *Lectures on the English Poets: Delivered at the Surrey Institution*, Taylor & Hessey, Fleet Street, 1818

William Hazlitt, 'My First Acquaintance With Poets' (first published in *The Liberal*, No. 3, 1823

William Hazlitt, *The Spirit of the Age* (1825), Oxford, 1970

P.P. Howe, ed., *The Complete Works of William Hazlitt*, 21 vols, London, 1930–34

C. Lamb, 'Imperfect Sympathies', in *Selected Prose*, Penguin, 2013, p.110; first published in the *London Magazine*, Aug 1821

E.V. Lucas, *Works of Charles and Mary Lamb*, Vol. VI, *Letters*, Methuen, 1905

Edwin Marrs, *The Letters of Charles and Mary Anne Lamb*, Vol. I, *Letters of Charles Lamb 1796–1801*, Cornell, 1975

Robert Southey, *Collected Letters*, Part II, *1798–1803*, online at https://www.rc.umd.edu/editions/southey_letters/Part_Two/HTML/letterEEd.26.347.html

Sir Thomas Noon Talfourd, *The Works of Charles Lamb: Complete in One Volume. With a Sketch of His Life*, Henry Carey Baird, 1857

John Thelwall, *The Peripatetic* ... Vol. I, London, 1793

John Thelwall, *The Tribune, A Periodical Publication, consisting chiefly of the Political Lectures of J. Thelwall*, Taken in Short-hand by W. Ramsey and revised by the Lecturer, Vol. II, No. 16, London, 1796

John Thelwall, 'A Pedestrian Excursion through Several Parts of England and Wales during the Summer of 1797', *Monthly Magazine*, Aug 1799

John Thelwall, *Daughter of Adoption*, 4 vols, London, 1801

John Thelwall, 'Lines Written at Bridgewater', in *The Fairy of the Lake: a dramatic romance; Effusions of relative and social feeling: and specimens of The hope of Albion; or, Edwin of Northumbria, an epic poem. With a prefatory memoir of the life of the author*, Printed by W.H. Parker, Sold by West and Hughes, R. Phillips [&c., &c.], 1801

Richard Warner, *A Walk Through Wales, in Aug 1797*, C. Dilly, London, 1798, p.232

Other Contemporaries

Edmund Burke, 'A Philosophical Enquiry into the Origin of our Ideas of the Sublime and the Beautiful' (1757), in *The Works of the Right Honourable Edmund Burke*, Vol. I, London, 1792

Donald A. Cress, ed. and tr., *Jean-Jacques Rousseau, Discourse on the Origin of Inequality* (1755), Hackett, Indianapolis, 1992, p.24

Sir Frederic Morton Eden, *The State of the Poor*, 3 vols, London, 1797

Sir G. Keynes, ed., *William Blake: The Marriage of Heaven and Hell* (1790–93), OUP, 1975

Karl Philipp Moritz, *Travels, Chiefly on Foot, Through Several Parts of England, in 1782: Described in Letters to a Friend*, London, 1797

Edith J. Morley, ed., *Blake, Coleridge, Wordsworth, Lamb, etc., being Selections from the Remains of Henry Crabb Robinson*, Manchester UP, 1922

Thomas Paine, *Rights of Man*, Oxford, 1995

R. Randall, *The Life and Memoirs of Elizabeth Chudleigh: Afterwards Mrs. Hervey and Countess of Bristol, Commonly Called Duchess of Kingston. Written from Authentic Information and Original Documents*, London, 1788

Henry Crabb Robinson, *Diary, Reminiscences, and Correspondence*, Fields, Osgood, & Co., 1870, 2 vols

OTHER BOOKS CONSULTED
Chronology

Valerie Purton, *A Coleridge Chronology*, Macmillan, Basingstoke, 1993

M.L. Reed, *Wordsworth: The Chronology of the Early Years 1770–1799*, Harvard, 1967

Biography

R.W. Armour & R.F. Howes, *Coleridge the Talker*, Cornell, 1940

Maurice Cranston, *The Solitary Self: Jean-Jacques Rousseau in Exile and Adversity*, Allen Lane, 1997

Helen Darbishire, *The Poet Wordsworth*, Oxford, 1950

A. de Vere, 'Recollections of Wordsworth', *Essays Chiefly on Poetry*, Macmillan, 1887

Henry Charles Duffin, *Walter de la Mare: A Study of his Poetry*, Ardent Media, 1969

Stephen Gill, *William Wordsworth: A Life*, Oxford, 1989, pp.56–67

Earl Leslie Griggs, *Coleridge Fille: A Biography of Sara Coleridge*, Oxford, 1940

William Haller, *The Early Life of Robert Southey*, Columbia UP, New York, 1917

G.M. Harper, *Wordsworth's French Daughter*, OUP, 1931

Donald E. Hayden, *Wordsworth's Travels in Wales and Ireland*, University of Tulsa Press, 1985

Richard Holmes, *Coleridge: Early Visions*, Hodder & Stoughton, London, 1989

Richard Holmes, *Footsteps: Adventures of a Romantic Biographer* (2005), Harper Press, 2012

Kenneth R. Johnston, *The Hidden Wordsworth: Poet, Lover, Rebel, Spy*, Norton, New York, 1998; 2nd edn, *The Hidden Wordsworth*, 2000

Kenneth R. Johnston, *Unusual Suspects: Pitt's Reign of Alarm and the Lost Generation of the 1790s*, OUP, 2013

Berta Lawrence, *Coleridge and Wordsworth in Somerset*, David & Charles, Newton Abbot, 1970

Molly Lefebure, *The Bondage of Love*, new edn, Victor Gollancz, London, 1988

Émile Legouis, *William Wordsworth and Annette Vallon*, J.M. Dent, London, 1922

R.B. Litchfield, *Tom Wedgwood: The First Photographer*, Duckworth, London, 1903

E.V. Lucas, *The Life of Charles Lamb*, Methuen, 1834

Mary Moorman, *William Wordsworth: A Biography. The Early Years*, 1957

Lucy Newlyn, *William & Dorothy Wordsworth: All in Each Other*, Oxford, 2013

Steve Poole, ed., *John Thelwall: Radical Romantic and Acquitted Felon*, Pickering & Chatto, London, 2009

Nicholas Roe, *Wordsworth and Coleridge: The Radical Years*, Oxford, 1988

Mrs Henry Sandford, *Thomas Poole and His Friends*, 2 vols, Macmillan, 1888

Adam Sisman, *Wordsworth and Coleridge: The Friendship*, Harper Press, 2006

Guy Trouillard, ed., *Mémoires de Madame Vallon: souvenirs de la Révolution dans le département de Loir-et-Cher*, Émile-Paul, Paris, 1913

R. White, *John Keats: A Literary Life*, Springer, 2010

Clare Williams, *Sophie in London, 1786: being the diary of Sophie v. la Roche*, with a foreword by G.M. Trevelyan, Jonathan Cape, 1933, pp.75–6

Pamela Woof, *Dorothy Wordsworth: Wonders of the Everyday*, Wordsworth Trust, Grasmere, 2013

John Worthen, *The Gang: Coleridge, the Hutchinsons and the Wordsworths in 1802*, Yale, 2001

John Worthen, *A Life of William Wordsworth*, John Wiley, Chichester, 2014

Criticism

Jonathan Bate, *Romantic Ecology: Wordsworth and the Environmental Tradition*, Routledge (1991), 2013

Harold Bloom, *The Anxiety of Influence*, 2nd edn, Oxford, 1997

Frederick Burwick, *The Oxford Handbook of Samuel Taylor Coleridge*, 2012

Marian Butler, *Romantics, Rebels and Reactionaries*, Oxford, 1981

Tim Fulford, *Coleridge's Spiritual Language*, Springer, 1991

Stephen Gill, ed., *The Cambridge Companion to Wordsworth*, Cambridge, 2003

Nicola Healey, *Dorothy Wordsworth and Hartley Coleridge: The Poetics of Relationship*, Macmillan, 2012

Mary Jacobus, *Tradition and Experiment in Wordsworth's Lyrical Ballads* (1798), Oxford, 1976

Felicity James, *Charles Lamb, Coleridge and Wordsworth: Reading Friendship in the 1790s*, Macmillan, Basingstoke, 2008

K.R. Johnston, *Wordsworth and The Recluse*, Yale UP, 1984

John Livingston Lowes, *The Road to Xanadu: A Study in the Ways of the Imagination*, Houghton Mifflin, 1927

Thomas McFarland, *Romanticism and the Forms of Ruin*, Princeton, 1981

Paul Magnuson, *Coleridge and Wordsworth: A Lyrical Dialogue*, Princeton, 1988

J.C.C. Mays, *Coleridge's Experimental Poetics*, Macmillan, Basingstoke, 2013

Lucy Newlyn, *Wordsworth and the Language of Allusion*, Oxford, 1986

Lucy Newlyn, ed., *The Cambridge Companion to Coleridge*, Cambridge, 2002

George S. Rousseau, *Nervous Acts: Essays on Literature, Culture and Sensibility*, Macmillan, Basingstoke, 2004

Fiona Stafford, *W. Wordsworth and S.T. Coleridge, Lyrical Ballads 1798 and 1802*, Oxford, 2013

Fiona Stafford, *Local Attachments: The Province of Poetry*, Oxford, 2010

Lionel Trilling, *Sincerity and Authenticity*, Oxford, 1972

Bibliography

David Vallins, Kaz Oishi & Seamus Perry, *Coleridge, Romanticism and the Orient: Cultural Negotiations*, A&C Black, 2013

Mary Warnock, *Imagination*, University of California Press, 1978

Jonathan Wordsworth, *The Music of Humanity*, J. & J. Harper Editions, New York, 1969

Jonathan Wordsworth, *William Wordsworth: The Borders of Vision*, Oxford, 1982

History

Quentin Bailey, *Wordsworth's Vagrants: Police, Prisons, and Poetry in the 1790s*, Ashgate, Farnham, 2011

Geoffrey Batchen, *Burning with Desire: The Conception of Photography*, MIT, Cambridge, 1999

Alexandra Harris, *Weatherland: Writers and Artists Under English Skies*, Thames & Hudson, London, 2015

Pamela Horn, *The Rural World 1780–1850: Social Change in the English Countryside*, Hutchinson, London, 1980

Roy Porter, *English Society in the 18th Century*, Penguin (1982), 1991

E.P. Thompson, *The Making of the English Working Class*, new edn, Pelican, 1980

Roger Wells, *Wretched Faces: Famine in Wartime England 1793–1801*, Breviary Stuff Publications, London, 2011

Roger Wells, *Insurrection: The British Experience 1795–1803*, Alan Sutton, Gloucester, 1986

Barry Williamson, ed., *The Account Books and Papers of Everard and Ann Arundel of Ashcombe and Salisbury 1745–1798*, Wiltshire Record Society, Vol. LXX, 2017

Poetry

Seamus Heaney, *Opened Ground: Poems 1966–1996*, Faber, London, 1998

Denise Levertov, *The Poet in the World*, New Directions, New York, 1973

John Milton, *The Major Works*, ed. S. Orgel & J. Goldberg, Oxford (1991), 2003

Wallace Stevens, *Selected Poems*, ed. J.N. Serio, Knopf, 2009

Somerset

David K. Ballance, *A History of the Birds of Somerset*, Isabelline Books, Penryn, 2006

E.A. Edmonds & B.J. Williams, *Geology of the Country Around Taunton and the Quantock Hills*, British Geological Survey, 1985

Peter Haggett, *The Quantocks: Biography of an English Region*, Point Walter Press, Chew Magna, 2012

Hans Martin Jahns, *Collins Guide to Ferns, Mosses and Lichens of Britain*, Collins, 1983

Berta Lawrence, *Quantock Country*, Westaway, London, 1952

Tom Mayberry, *Coleridge and Wordsworth: The Crucible of Friendship*, rev. edn, Alan Sutton, Stroud, 2000

Adam Nicolson & Patrick Sutherland, *Wetland: Life in the Somerset Levels*, Michael Joseph, London, 1986

E.M. Palmer & D.K. Ballance, *The Birds of Somerset*, Longmans, London, 1968

Hazel Riley, *The Historic Landscape of the Quantock Hills*, English Heritage, 2006

David Worthy, *The Old Quantocks: People and Places*, The Friarn Press, 2010

David Worthy & Audrey Mead, *The Quantocks and Their Villages*, Friends of Quantock, 2001

David Worthy & Audrey Mead, *Quantock Miscellany*, The Friarn Press, 2006

Articles

Ruth I. Aldrich, 'The Wordsworths and Coleridge: "Three Persons", but Not "One Soul"', *Studies in Romanticism*, Vol. II, No. 1 (Autumn 1962), pp.61–3

Anon., 'Meteorological Journal, Kept at the Apartments of the Royal Society, By Order of the President and Council', *Philosophical Transactions of the Royal Society of London*, Vol. LXXXVIII (1798), pp.1–26

Anon., 'Laudanum Drinking', *British Medical Journal*, Vol. I, No. 1567 (10 Jan 1891), pp.82–3

Anon., 'Laudanum: Its Varieties and Etymology', *British Medical Journal*, Vol. I, No. 1940 (5 Mar 1898), p.647

Anon., 'Admiral Lord Nelson', *The Dublin Penny Journal*, Vol. III, No. 155 (20 Jun 1835), pp.404–5

J. Robert Barth, 'Coleridge's Ideal of Love', *Studies in Romanticism*, Vol. XXIV, No. 1, Samuel Taylor Coleridge (Spring 1985), pp.113–39

N. Stephen Bauer, 'Early Burlesques and Parodies of Wordsworth', *The Journal of English and Germanic Philology*, Vol. LXXIV, No. 4 (Oct 1975), pp.553–69

Toby R. Benis, 'Martha Ray's Face: Life during Wartime in "Lyrical Ballads"', *Criticism*, Vol. XXXIX, No. 2 (Spring 1997), pp.205–27

Victoria Berridge, 'Victorian Opium Eating: Responses to Opiate Use in Nineteenth-Century England', *Victorian Studies*, 21(4), 1978, pp.437–61

Victoria Berridge, 'Opium Over the Counter in Nineteenth Century England', *Pharmacy in History*, Vol. XX, No. 3 (1978), pp.91–100

Alan J. Bewell, 'Wordsworth's Primal Scene: Retrospective Tales of Idiots, Wild Children, and Savages', *ELH*, Vol. L, No. 2 (Summer 1983), pp.321–46

Bibliography

Ian D. Boehm, 'The "1798 Lyrical Ballads" and the Poetics of Late Eighteenth-Century Book Production', *English Literary History*, Vol. LXIII, No. 2 (Summer 1996), pp.453–87

James A. Butler, 'Wordsworth, Cottle, and the "Lyrical Ballads": Five Letters, 1797–1800', *The Journal of English and Germanic Philology*, Vol. LXXV, No. 1/2 (Jan–Apr 1976), pp.139–53

Robert W. Daniel, 'The Publication of the "Lyrical Ballads"', *The Modern Language Review*, Vol. XXXIII, No. 3 (Jul 1938), pp.406–10

Joanne Dann, 'Some Notes on the Relationship Between the Wordsworth and the Lowther Families', *The Wordsworth Circle*, Vol. XI, No. 2 (Spring 1980), pp.80–2

Wallace W. Douglas, 'Wordsworth as Business Man', *PMLA*, Vol. LXIII, No. 2 (Jun 1948), pp.625–41

David Duff, 'Charles Lamb's Art of Intimation', *The Wordsworth Circle*, Vol. XLIII, No. 3 (Summer 2012), pp.127–34

A.J. Eaglestone, 'Wordsworth, Coleridge, and the Spy' in E. Blunden & E.L. Griggs, eds, *Coleridge: Studies by Several Hands*, London, 1934

Timothy P. Enright, 'Sing, Mariner: Identity and Temporality in Coleridge's "The Nightingale"', *Studies in Romanticism*, Vol. XXXIII, No. 3 (Fall 1994), pp.481–501

David Erdman, 'Coleridge, Wordsworth, and the Wedgwood Fund', *Bulletin of New York Public Library*, Vol. LX, 1956

David Erdman, 'A New Discovery: The First Review of "Christabel"', *Texas Studies in English*, Vol. XXXVII (1958), pp.53–60

Bergen Evans & Hester Pinney, 'Racedown and the Wordsworths', *The Review of English Studies*, Vol. VIII, No. 29 (Jan 1932)

Thomas Peter Garrett, 'The Wonderful Development of Photography', *The Art World*, Vol. II, No. 5 (Aug 1917), pp.489–91

Earl Leslie Griggs, 'Coleridge and the Wedgwood Annuity', *The Review of English Studies*, Vol. VI, No. 21 (Jan 1930), pp.63–72

Earl Leslie Griggs, 'Robert Southey's Estimate of Samuel Taylor Coleridge: A Study in Human Relations', *Huntington Library Quarterly*, Vol. IX, No. 1 (Nov 1945), pp.61–94

Iain Hampsher-Monk, 'John Thelwall and the Eighteenth-Century Radical Response to Political Economy', *The Historical Journal*, Vol. XXXIV, No. 1 (Mar 1991), pp.1–20

T.V. Jackson, 'British Incomes Circa 1800', *The Economic History Review*, New Series, Vol. LII, No. 2 (May 1999), pp.257–83

Michael C. Jaye, 'William Wordsworth's Alfoxden Notebook: 1798', in D.H. Reiman et al., *The Evidence of the Imagination: Studies of Interactions between Life and Art in English Romantic Literature*, New York, 1978

K.R. Johnston, 'Philanthropy or Treason? Wordsworth as "Active Partisan!"', *Studies in Romanticism*, Vol. XXV, No. 3, Homage to Carl Woodring (Fall 1986), pp.371–409

Bibliography

K.R. Johnston, 'Wordsworth's Mission to Germany: A Hidden Bicentenary?', *The Wordsworth Circle*, Vol. XXX, No. 1 (Winter 1999), pp.15–22

K.R. Johnston, 'A Tale of Two Titles', *Romantic Biography*, ed. Arthur Bradley & Alan Rawes, Aldershot, 2003, p.54

John E. Jordan, 'Wordsworth's Most Wonderful as well as Admirable Poem', *The Wordsworth Circle*, Vol. XXXVII, No. 3 (Summer 2006), pp.116–22

Judson S. Lyon, 'Romantic Psychology and the Inner Senses', *PMLA*, Vol. LXXXI, No. 3 (Jun 1966), pp.246–60

Scott McEathron, 'Wordsworth, Lyrical Ballads, and the Problem of Peasant Poetry', *Nineteenth-Century Literature*, Vol. LIV, No. 1 (Jun 1999), pp.1–26

John Bard McNulty, 'Wordsworth's Tour of the Wye: 1798', *Modern Language Notes*, LX (1945), pp.291–5

Robert Mayo, 'The Contemporaneity of the Lyrical Ballads', *PMLA*, Vol. LXIX, No. 3 (Jun 1954), pp.486–522

David S. Miall, 'Locating Wordsworth: "Tintern Abbey" and the Community with Nature', *Romanticism on the Net* 20, Nov 2000

Alexandra Neel, '"A Something-Nothing out of its Very Contrary": The Photography of Coleridge', *Victorian Studies*, Vol. XLIX, No. 2, Papers and Responses from the Fourth Annual Conference of the North American Victorian Studies Association, Held Jointly with the North American Society for the Study of Romanticism Annual Meeting (Winter 2007), pp.208–17

W.J.B. Owen, 'The Sublime and the Beautiful in *The Prelude*', *The Wordsworth Circle*, Vol. IV, No. 2 (Spring 1973), pp.67–86

John A. Phillips, 'The Social Calculus: Deference and Defiance in Later Georgian England', *Albion: A Quarterly Journal Concerned with British Studies*, Vol. XXI, No. 3 (Autumn 1989), pp.426–49

H.D. Rawnsley, 'Reminiscences of Wordsworth among the Peasantry of Westmoreland', in William Knight, ed., *Wordsworthiana*, London, 1889, pp.81–119, reprinted Dillon's, London, 1968

William Richey, 'The Politicized Landscape of "Tintern Abbey"', *Studies in Philology*, Vol. XCV, No. 2 (Spring 1998), pp.197–219

Nicholas Roe, 'Who Was Spy Nozy?', *The Wordsworth Circle*, Vol. XV, No. 2 (Spring 1984), pp.46–50

Robert Sayre, 'The Young Coleridge: Romantic Utopianism and the French Revolution', *Studies in Romanticism*, Vol. XXVIII, No. 3, English Romanticism and the French Revolution (Fall 1989), pp.397–415

Ronald A. Sharp, 'Romanticism and the Zone of Friendship', *New England Review* (1990–), Vol. XXVIII, No. 4 (2007), pp.165–73

Jonas Spatz, 'The Mystery of Eros: Sexual Initiation in Coleridge's "Christabel"', *PMLA*, Vol. XC, No. 1 (Jan 1975), pp.107–16

Bibliography

E.P. Thompson, 'Hunting the Jacobin Fox', *Past & Present*, No. 142 (Feb 1994), p.102

E.P. Thompson, 'Disenchantment or Default? A Lay Sermon', in *Power and Consciousness*, eds C.C. O'Brien & D. Vanech (1969), p.150

Judith Thompson, 'An Autumnal Blast, a Killing Frost: Coleridge's Poetic Conversation with John Thelwall', *Studies in Romanticism*, Vol. XXXVI, No. 3 (Fall 1997), pp.427–56

Alannah Tomkins, 'The Decline of Life. Old Age in Eighteenth-Century England by Susannah R. Ottaway, a Review', *Social History*, Vol. XXX, No. 4 (Nov 2005), pp.530–2

David Travis, 'Photography as a Print-Making Medium: The Early Successes', *Bulletin of the Art Institute of Chicago* (1973–1982), Vol. LXIX, No. 3 (May–Jun 1975), pp.15–19

William A. Ulmer, 'Wordsworth, the One Life, and "The Ruined Cottage"', *Studies in Philology*, Vol. XCIII, No. 3 (Summer 1996), pp.304–31

Ralph M. Wardle, 'Basil and Anna Montagu: Touchstones for the Romantics', *Keats-Shelley Journal*, Vol. XXXIV (1985), pp.131–71

Reggie Watters, '"A limber elf": Coleridge and the Child', *The Coleridge Bulletin*, New Series, No. 9 (Spring 1997), pp.2–24

George Whalley, 'Coleridge and Southey in Bristol, 1795', *The Review of English Studies*, New Series, Vol. I, No. 4 (Oct 1950), pp.324–40

Pamela Woof, 'Dorothy Wordsworth as a Young Woman', *The Wordsworth Circle*, Vol. XXXVIII, No. 3, The Wordsworth–Coleridge Association Meeting: 2006 (Summer 2007), pp.130–8

David Worthy, 'On Life in Late Georgian Somerset', *The Coleridge Bulletin*, New Series, No. 25 (Summer 2005)

WOODCUTS

Woodcuts

Between pp.214 and 215
The discharged soldier
Grow like good boys!

Between pp.230 and 231
And, all alone, set sail by silent
    moonlight
In the high mountains the boy
    beheld the sun

Between pp.246 and 247
Frost at Midnight
Blessing in the air

Between pp.262 and 263
She unbound the cincture from
    beneath her breast
And she is known to every star

Between pp.278 and 279
All silent as a horseman ghost
Tree Life

Between pp.294 and 295
The Coleridge bird
Poet Dreaming

Between pp.310 and 311
The vision of completeness
Cuxhaven packet

All woodcuts photographed by Leigh Simpson

INDEX

Adscombe, 64, 103, 179–82, 204, 205
Aldrich, Ruth, 302
Alfoxden: celebratory dinner at, 124–5; Coleridge family stay at (March 1798), 255; Cottle at, 284–5; DW's journal, 192–5, 198–200, 207–8, 211, 235–6; government spying on, 127–9, 130–3, 265–6, 320; Hazlitt at, 280–1, 285–6; landscape, 72–4, 76–7, 146, 152, 190–1, 195, 245, 271–4; lease on not renewed, 237, 255, 290; in present day, 75–7; WW's departure from, 298, 304; WW's discovery of, 72–4; WW move in, 116; WW's composition at, 136–8, 184–92, 199–201, 209–15, 231, 246–50, 267–9, 271–4
The Arabian Nights, 225
Arch, John and Arthur, 327

Bartlett, Ben, 179, 208
Bath, 307
Beaupuy, Michel, 24–7, 28, 29, 60
Berridge, Victoria, 144
Blake, William, 90
Bridgwater, Unitarian chapel in, 8

Bristol, 133, 176, 279–80, 283; and Fricker family, 58, 59, 60, 66; the Pinneys of, 21, 22, 30, 32, 71, 131, 219; walk from Stowey to, 304–6; WW stays at, 306–9; WW and STC meet in, 8, 32
British government: *agents provocateurs*, 109; coastal defences, 108–9; and French Revolutionary Wars, 10–11, 30, 68; invasion scares, 107–8; Lord Lieutenants, 108; reactionary mobs, 105–6, 110, 111; spy networks, 11, 68, 70, 106–11, 126–33, 138, 237, 255, 265–6, 320; suspends Habeas Corpus (May 1794), 30, 109; Treason Trials (autumn 1794), 70, 109–10
Burke, Edmund, 155–6, 207, 316–17; *Reflections on the Revolution in France*, 241

Cain and Abel story, 157–9
Cambridge University, 23–4, 92
Cat and Salutation, 88, 92, 99
Cheddar Gorge, 278–80
Chester, John, 65, 327, 330
childhood, 5, 216–19, 221–32, 236–7, 239–42, 268, 271–4

381